GANDHI

ADVANCE PRAISE FOR THE BOOK

'Manash Firaq Bhattacharjee's outstanding counter-history of contemporary India walks with Gandhi into the catastrophic vortex of the violence of Partition. Against a rush of events that seem retrospectively to unfold a terrible destiny, the book sustains a measured narrative that in its very pace rubs history against the grain and permits fugitive glimpses of other possible futures and directions of struggle. Bhattacharjee's Gandhi keeps his mind in hell without permitting himself the luxury of despair, continuing to struggle even as he is stripped of his voice and his non-violent power. This book is a profound philosophical and historical meditation on non-violence, and the politics of truth and friendship that it makes possible. By challenging our assumptions about Gandhi's last days, it teaches a hard but ultimately inspiring lesson in the power of non-violent resistance under even the most adverse of circumstances.

'*Gandhi: The End of Non-Violence* makes an essential contribution to the theory and practice of non-violent resistance that for many remains a last hope in the face of global war and growing ecological catastrophe'—**Howard Caygill, professor of modern European philosophy, Centre for Research in Modern European Philosophy, Kingston University London**

'*Gandhi: The End of Non-Violence* is a valuable account of the complex twists and turns in the road to the partition of British India into two independent states: Pakistan and India. Manash Firaq Bhattacharjee traces the arguments and fantasies that drove the leading figures in this story, and weaves Gandhi's important distinction between "senseless" and "sensible" violence into it. The partition was not only an unfortunate form of independence from British rule; it led to ruthless violence by Hindu and Muslim gangs despite Gandhi's efforts to prevent it. The eventual political outcome that led to the emergence of two states was based, on the one side, on the hope of making independent India "governable", and on the other side on the fanciful claim that the Indian Muslims were a separate nation and so had the right to their own state. This book is an illuminating contribution to our understanding of Gandhi's political and ethical thought—as well as of the end of British rule in India'—**Talal Asad, distinguished professor of anthropology, City University of New York**

'A robust and refreshing defence of Gandhi's moral and political career. It is a remarkable achievement to weave together a strong historical narrative with considerable philosophical nuance. *Gandhi: The End of Non-Violence* is a riveting account of India's struggle for freedom understood as a battle of ideas. Rather than being confined to the past, this book tells us how such a battle continues to be fought in India and around the world'—**Faisal Devji, professor of Indian history, St Antony's College, University of Oxford**

'*Gandhi: The End of Non-Violence* is a detailed and fascinating examination of Gandhi's final months of life and his attempt to pit his own moral, non-violent strength against the explosive outbreaks of violence that accompanied the partition of the subcontinent. Bhattacharjee uses, among much other evidence, the diary of Gandhi's young female relative, Manu, with whom he conducted a novel experiment to prove his own chastity. It was misunderstood and caused much disapproval even among those close to him. It seemed a distraction from the serious business of politics, but for Gandhi, it lay at the heart of his "moral" politics of non-violence. This book raises important, pertinent questions about the role of non-violence in public life, and also the nature of mass violence and its organization'—**Judith M. Brown, former Beit Professor of Commonwealth History and former Fellow of Balliol College, University of Oxford**

'The experiments of collective non-violence and fearlessness—*Ahimsa* and *Abahya*, respectively,—were central to Gandhi's quest for India and himself. Gandhi's ethical resistance lies in this possibility that as collectivities, we are capable of forging a politics of non-violence and that we are free from fear. Gandhi hoped for a violent death as an object-lesson in this. He had hoped that we would find our *Swaraj*, while he his *Svadharma*.

'Manash Firaq Bhattacharjee brings his literary sensibility and philosophical inclination to this historically grounded study to illuminate Gandhi's final years, not as biography but as meditations upon the limits of both violence and non-violence and gives us a book of lasting value'—**Tridip Suhrud, Gandhi scholar, writer and translator**

'*Gandhi: The End of Non-Violence* is part of the rediscovery of Gandhi by a new generation. This new Gandhi has become salient in some of the Gandhian studies over the last forty to fifty years. First, this involves an awareness of Gandhi as an ecologist who was alert to the global issues we have been facing in the last two decades. Second, these new studies on Gandhi are aware that though Gandhi had mobilized rural India into mainstream politics, there is a new transactional style in politics that dominates India, which keeps Gandhi out. Third, in this new Gandhi, you hear for the first time Gandhi's name figuring in international relations and global conflict, defying professional foreign policy experts who consider him an outcast. The overall ethical norms and technologies of human survival projected in Gandhi's work are now having an impact on a large number of civil rights movements. Future generations will find new Gandhis according to their needs. Manash Firaq Bhattacharjee's Gandhi is a marvellous exploration on these lines'—**Ashis Nandy, political psychologist, social theorist, futurist and critic**

GANDHI

The End *of* Non-Violence

Manash Firaq Bhattacharjee

VINTAGE
An imprint of Penguin Random House

VINTAGE

Vintage is an imprint of the Penguin Random House group of companies whose addresses can be found at global.penguinrandomhouse.com

Published by Penguin Random House India Pvt. Ltd
4th Floor, Capital Tower 1, MG Road,
Gurugram 122 002, Haryana, India

First published in Vintage by Penguin Random House India 2025

10 9 8 7 6 5 4 3 2 1

ISBN 9780143471707

Typeset in EB Garamond by MAP Systems, Bengaluru, India
Printed at Replika Press Pvt. Ltd, India

www.penguin.co.in

To
the dog watching over its caregivers' skeletons
in Noakhali

'Now that the British were voluntarily quitting India, apparent non-violence had gone to pieces in a moment.'

—Gandhi, talk with Stuart Nelson,
Calcutta, August 1947

Contents

Preface

This book is a combination of intellectual history and political history. It deals with the last phase of Gandhi's life, beginning with the winter of 1946 to 30 January 1948, the day of his assassination. I was not interested in writing yet another book discussing Gandhi's thinking alone, often without context, to frame a general and atemporal perspective on his key concepts of *satya*/truth, ahimsa/non-violence, and *satyagraha*/passive resistance.

Gandhi was a thinker-practitioner. He was a thinker on the move. He was as much a writer as a leader of political movements. He was the thinker-architect behind a few historic events during the anti-colonial movement, such as the Champaran Satyagraha in 1917, the Non-cooperation Movement of 1920, the Civil Disobedience Movement of 1930 and the Quit India Movement of 1942. Gandhi's contribution is not just central to India's freedom movement against British rule but also key to the twentieth century's imagination of non-violent politics.

Gandhi was un/doing politics, and un/making history. The study of his ideas through a specific political moment is more productive, as it offers both empirical and intellectual details of how his ideas translated into speech and action. Gandhi is not just the name of an idea. His political practices define the nature of his ideas and give a more comprehensive picture of the man. It is worth noting and analysing how Gandhi's key ideas frame his encounters with political opponents, friends and associates, and with people. This framing may involve deviations and departures from the general understanding of Gandhi's views, as much as they may offer reconfirmations.

Gandhi interrupts the history of twentieth-century violence as an epic force. He thought and practised politics in their immediacies. In a suggestive statement, he made in *Harijan* on 28 September 1934, Gandhi wrote:

> I have never made a fetish of consistency. I am a votary of truth, and I must say what I feel and think at a given moment on the question, without regard to what I may have said before on it . . . It is for the reader to find out how far my present views coincide with those formerly expressed. Wherever he finds that what I have said or written before runs contrary to what I am writing now, he should without hesitation reject the former . . . I claim to be a votary of truth and to follow to the best of my ability what seems to be the truth at a given time. As my vision gets clearer, my views must grow clearer with daily practice.[1]

Truth does not have a priori (Kantian) status for Gandhi. He seems closer to David Hume's idea of knowledge in *An Enquiry Concerning Human Understanding* (1760) as coming from experience. The idea of truth can be altered by time; hence it is changeable. Experience is prone to variations in our understanding of life, the world and truth. For Gandhi, truth is always in the present tense. It belongs to the moment of consideration. The experience of time and practice together bring clarity.

India's modern political thinkers, unlike political thinkers from the modern West, are not professional and systematic thinkers. Their thinking is often expressed *otherwise*, through their acts in the real field of politics. Speech and writing are part of their political acts, and form part of their discourse. The gaps and contradictions between thinking and action are often at the mercy of superficial (and rational) expectations of congruence.

This book is about Gandhi's peace mission in Noakhali, Calcutta, Bihar and Delhi. Jinnah sounded the horn of Partition in the middle of August 1946, and it turned out to be the declaration of an uncivil war. The relationship between the Congress and the Muslim League had precipitated towards a rift. Gandhi was politically sidelined. He had also grown quite old and fragile. Yet, he managed to gather his strength and will and make a last and epic gesture. His heroic efforts managed to recover a semblance of sanity between Hindus and Muslims after their gory violence against each other left nothing to the imagination.

The long introduction offers an assessment of significant episodes and debates related to the Hindu–Muslim question. Gandhi's involvement in the cause of Hindu–Muslim relations from the Khilafat Movement of 1919 to Partition in 1947 forms an arc across time. I also offer a critical reading of notable political and religious figures (some of whom have been political activists) such as Ambedkar, Vivekananda, Aurobindo, Mohamad Ali, Iqbal, the Arya Samajists and Savarkar, who had a stake in the Hindu–Muslim question.

The first chapter on Gandhi's four-month sojourn in Noakhali is the central story. It occupies a prominent place and finds extensive attention in the book. Vinay Lal put it in his email of 15 December 2024: 'Noakhali alone is deserving of a book: it is the epic within an epic life, one of the most extraordinary dialectical journeys through non-violence and violence in history.'

Giving Noakhali its due, I found it compelling to stay with Gandhi in his epic 'last phase' till the end and complete the arc.

The remaining chapters dealing with Gandhi's trip to Bihar, his return to Calcutta and his time in Delhi are of varying length depending on the duration of Gandhi's stay in each place and the significant details of his activities.

This book is not on the larger story of Partition. It focuses on Gandhi's peace mission. Excessive details on political intrigues (public and behind the scenes) and negotiations are not my concern. The point is not to lose the thread, and the mood, of the central story.

The historical narrative is foundational. The story is enriched by the texture of the witness accounts of Gandhi's associates. The details they offer are part of their experience of the peace mission. These layered historical accounts inform the theoretical analysis, critical discussions and philosophical meditations in the book. Sometimes, the narrative speaks for itself and does not need too much explanation.

An important aspect of engagement in the book is my metahistorical assessment of the politics of historiography. My contention is that sincere scholarship on genocidal violence needs to go deeper than ideological analysis to do intellectual justice to a phenomenon that marks a tragic limit case in history. Ideological manoeuvres serve motivated preoccupations that do not match up to truth.

The style of writing does not follow a strict academic protocol. Scholarly writing must be free to cut across genres and transgress disciplinary boundaries. Truth is not the monopoly of a single discipline. I prefer the hybrid form of writing where I can summon literature, philosophy, political theory and history and reflect *through* them, and sometimes, reflect *on* them.

In this book, I think on Gandhi, Partition, non-violence, violence, genocide, ethics and truth. I follow the essay form, which allows me to *think* on the subject as much as theorize. It is necessary to think before theorizing. Often, our thinking is guided by theoretical grids, or frameworks, that enforce ideological techniques of interpretation and certainty. You must be able to reflect on a subject like experiencing a fresh encounter. It creates an opening for thought.

New Delhi
26 January 2025

Introduction: 'Rift in the Lute'

Senseless/Sensible Violence

At Sevagram, Mohandas Karamchand Gandhi made a public statement on 19 August 1946 for the first time on hearing the news of explosive mass violence pouring out from Calcutta (Kolkata since 2001) after the Muslim League declared 'Direct Action Day' on 16 August.

> 'Calcutta has given an ocular demonstration of what direct action is and how it is to be done . . . Violence may have its place in life but not that which we have witnessed in Calcutta, assuming of course that newspaper accounts are to be trusted. Pakistan of whatever he does not lie through senseless violence. When I write of senseless violence, I naturally assume the possibility of sensible violence, whatever the latter may be. The Calcutta demonstration was not an illustration of sensible violence. What senseless violence does is to prolong the lease of the life of British or foreign rule . . . Let us not ride that horse to death.'[1]

The political motive behind Mohammad Ali Jinnah's call for 'Direct Action' was spectacularly carried out in the streets of Calcutta. Mass violence has a spectral element that is performed with vengeance to drive home the intended message. Jinnah and the Muslim League had laid the ground for this violence by conspiring to stake their claim for the formation of Pakistan and undermine the move for the independence of an unbroken India.

Gandhi was clear that news of the carnage pouring in from Calcutta was directly related to the call for direct action by the Muslim League. He admitted that human life is prone to its share of violence. Gandhi made an interesting distinction between 'sensible' and 'senseless' violence. The difference is of a measure or proportion that would be in turn predicated upon a sense, or lack, of reason. Gandhi tried to explain the distinction between sensible and senseless violence through an event. The mass violence that ran wild in the streets and neighbourhoods of Calcutta did not appear to be a sensible act. It was out of proportion (not just in degree, but also in sheer numbers) and lacked *the order of reason*. The political consequence—and danger—of such an immeasurable degree of violence, according to Gandhi, will ensure the further legitimation of British rule. Sensible and senseless violence can also be differentiated in terms of what we call structural violence (which is more long-term, ubiquitous, even camouflaged, but in all conditions controlled by power and hierarchy), and war/civil war or genocide (which is sudden, temporally short-lived and whose effects and consequences run of control). However, 'senseless' violence is also a feature of power (racist, colonial, totalitarian, fascist, communal) of a particularly brutal design that seeks to establish a new regime, or a new order of structural violence. The order of reason can only be broken by a rival dis/order of reason. In this sense, senseless and sensible violence have a deep connection.

Senseless violence, Gandhi knew, is not beneficial for colonized subjects. By going overboard, they ruin their real, political interests. The political distinction between sensible and senseless violence under imperial rule is determined by imperial power. The presence and nature of that power adds a politico–juridical condition of order where colonized subjects need to be mindful of the methods they use to resolve political conflicts *within*. If the nationalist struggle commits violence that threatens to overwhelm public order, it jeopardizes the claim to freedom. The transfer of power is the transfer of order. If India's social order is in disarray, it creates a volatile condition and a perfect excuse for British rule to overstay and meddle with our plans to rule ourselves. In other words, colonial power has the absolute authority to judge and decide under what conditions it will transfer power to its colonized subjects. What about the founding, law-preserving violence of the colonial state? How to understand the lawbreaking mass violence in Calcutta in relation to the order of law established by colonial power?

In July 1908, focusing on the question, 'What is Just?' in his long series on 'Sarvodaya', Gandhi wrote in *Indian Opinion* from Johannesburg what he would repeat and expand in *Hind Swaraj* (1909):

> 'It is wrong normally for one nation to rule over another. British rule in India is an evil but we need not believe that any very great advantage would accrue to the Indians if the British were to leave India. The reason why they rule over us is to be found in ourselves; that reason is our disunity, our immorality and our ignorance.'[2]

Gandhi was clear that we must earn the right to replace the colonial order of law by putting our own house in order. To argue freedom from colonial rule, colonized Indians must prove that they can found a new political order. What may be construed as lawbreaking is in fact law-enhancing. Violence between Hindus and Muslims must be avoided as it would unsettle not the British but India's own claim to wrest power and declare itself free from colonial rule.

That was not to be.

'Direct Action Day' interrupted the vexed negotiations of Transfer of Power by unleashing an irreparable saga of hate-filled brutality.

Even though the violence that engulfed Calcutta—and spread to Noakhali, Bihar, Delhi and the Punjab—could be characterized as 'senseless', the political thinking that manufactured it had a chilling rationale. Lethal political calculations and motives often lurk beneath apparently senseless violence.

Jinnah's Muslim Making

The story that precedes the announcement of 'Direct Action Day' is a complex one. The intention and scope of this book is not to cram the reader's mind with a surfeit of historical details. The purpose here is to seek a measure of contextual clarity by tracing the political thinking that led to the declaration of Partition and contrast it with the thinking and efforts that tried to prevent it.

Jinnah, as the leader of the Muslim League that announced 'Direct Action' after the rejection of the Cabinet Mission Plan, is a central figure to this debate. His idea of Pakistan as antipodal to the idea of India needs to be understood.

The Mission Plan was the last imperial effort to put in place a single constituent assembly and an interim government. The Mission Plan (announced on 16 May 1946) was primarily a response to tackle the demand for Pakistan and find a viable way to avoid partition. It rejected the idea of Pakistan, citing the fact that the proposed idea of both western and eastern Pakistan would have a high percentage of non-Muslim minorities, and that neither Bengal nor Punjab could be divided owing to their 'common language and a long history and traditions.'[3] The Mission Plan suggested that the provinces be divided into three sections: 'Group A should include the Hindu-majority provinces of Madras, Bombay, the United Provinces, Bihar, the Central Provinces and Orissa. Group B should include the Muslim-majority provinces of the north-west: the Punjab, the North-West Frontier Province and Sind. Group C should include the Muslim-majority provinces of the northeast: Bengal and Assam.'[4] Group B and C were Muslim-majority areas, aimed to 'satisfy the League and give it a substance of Pakistan'.[5]

Pyarelal Nayyar, commentator, eyewitness and Gandhi's personal secretary, used strong words against the Plan. He found it a desperate bid to assuage the 'Frankenstein of communalism whom the British power had . . . cradled into being'.[6] He felt that the Plan was 'the doubtful expedient of the ambiguous middle,' caught between the reluctance to divide India and 'the Muslim League's inflexible demand for a sovereign Pakistan'.[7]

Drawing a literary analogy, Pyarelal felt that the Plan was 'fashioned somewhat after the heroine in one of Goethe's classics in whose lineaments everybody saw the image of his own beloved. There was in it something for everybody.'[8]

Lampooning the Mission Plan, Jinnah's biographer, Ayesha Jalal, called it a 'three-tier wedding cake'.[9]

Jinnah was upset about having been offered anything short of his demand for a sovereign state of Pakistan. The Congress, Jalal writes, was initially opposed to 'giving the Muslim provinces too much autonomy and also of giving Jinnah and the League too much weight at the centre', as they thought it would result in 'a weak federal centre'.[10] The Congress Resolution of 24 May 1946 reiterated the party's wish for a strong centre, and was not agreeable to the proposed plan allowing the three provinces to make policy decisions on their own (apart from foreign affairs, defence and finances that shall rest with the centre).[11]

Matters came to a standstill when the Congress did not accept Lord Wavell's proposal of 6 June 1946 on the composition of the interim government. Problems arose when Gandhi first wanted Zakir Husain, a non-League and non-Congress Muslim member to be part of the fourteen member team[12]. Jinnah rejected it outright saying, both 'Muslim India' and the Muslim League won't accept the nomination of any Muslim member who wasn't part of the League.[13] Gandhi insisted that Congress had the right to nominate a Muslim candidate in the interim government as a matter of his 'lifelong principle that the Congress is a non-communal organization',[14] while Jinnah was opposed to the idea.

In the meeting on the Transfer of Power with the Cabinet Mission on 10 June, Nehru, in the company of Abul Kalam Azad, made it clear that the Congress preferred to work towards a 'strong centre' and would like 'to break the group system'.[15] He added that the Congress 'did not think that Mr Jinnah had any real place in the country.'[16] On 5 July

1946, the *National Herald* published Nehru's speech at Jhansi the previous day, where he had announced that the Congress was willing to take part in the deliberations of the Constituent Assembly 'with its own interpretation of the Cabinet Mission's long-range proposals'.[17] Nehru added the firm rejoinder that 'we will not touch anything, even with the tips of our fingers, if it is incompatible with the dignity of our organisation and its principles.'[18] Even more momentous and decisive was Nehru's interview to the press in Bombay on 10 July, where he made it clear that apart from agreeing to the electoral procedure of candidates joining the constituent assembly, nothing else was agreed upon. Nehru said that they would honour the treaty only if the British treated them like equals. The 'slightest attempt at imposition'[19] wouldn't work. Regarding minorities, Nehru emphasized that 'the minorities question has to be settled satisfactorily', but he considered it 'our problem' and wouldn't accept 'outsiders' interference'.[20] He also said that everyone except the Muslim League was 'opposed'[21] to the grouping of provinces. Azad called Nehru's statements of 10 July 'astonishing,' 'one of those unfortunate events that change the course of history'.[22] Azad wrote further that Nehru's remark came as a 'bombshell'[23] for Jinnah.

Gandhi wrote to Nehru on 17 July: 'Your statement as published in the papers does not sound good. If it is correctly reported, some explanation is needed.'[24] Gandhi agreed with Azad that the Congress had to work within the limits of the 'State Paper' and said that if there was a difference in the interpretation of the proposals with the 'Federal Court', the Congress must 'be firm', or else, 'Jinnah Saheb's accusation will prove true.'[25] On principle, Gandhi agreed with Nehru's concerns. In his letter to Stafford Cripps on 8 May 1946, Gandhi told him:

> 'The Muslim majority Provinces represent over nine crores of the population as against over 19 crores of the Hindu majority Provinces. This is really worse than Pakistan.'[26]

Even reactions from sympathetic scholars later were critical. A.G. Noorani called Nehru's statement 'fatuous',[27] and Ishtiaq Ahmed called it 'ill-considered'.[28] In hindsight, more than the merits of Nehru's position, it was Jinnah's reaction to it that swayed judgements. Nehru wanted to bargain without contradicting his principles, which was not simply based on the desire for a strong centre. Nehru was sincere about solving the minority question but not from the territorial perspective that was forwarded by Jinnah and the League. The Muslim League politically invented a communal divide in consonance with the British policy of divide-and-rule and they wanted Congress to not just endorse it but to claim it as well. As if it was incumbent on the Congress to honour Jinnah's communal image of the party rather than its own principles. In other words, the Congress was asked to fit into the mirror image of the League. Politics inspires crooked expectations.

Nehru, however, makes a strange but serious error of judgement in considering Jinnah a weak political figure. The delegates of the Mission Plan 'obliquely warned'[29] Jinnah that if he did not have a convincing argument for Pakistan, the delegate would invite Congress to form the interim government. Jinnah's response is well articulated by Ishtiaq Ahmed:

> 'Jinnah maintained a defiant and uncompromising façade, sticking to his demand for Partition to create

> Pakistan until 5 June. His diametrically opposite advice on 6 June to the Muslim League Council to accept the Cabinet Mission Plan shows that he understood that his ability to bargain to get a deal on his terms had been severely limited.'[30]

Behind Jinnah's façade of dilly-dallying with the Mission Plan was a real crisis of imagination. The truth slips out despite Jalal's rhetorical apologia:

> 'Since 1940, Jinnah had maintained an immaculate silence on the inner meaning of the Pakistan demand. But once the Cabinet Mission began its enquiries and made its proposals, he allowed its members, and hence the historian, to get a tantalising hint of his real aims and a glimpse of the goal towards which he had been tacking and turning. Upon this flash of candour, so fleetingly revealed in the intentional obfuscations of Jinnah's tactics, the historian of Pakistan must pounce.'[31]

Once the brainchild named Pakistan was immaculately born in Jinnah's head, he clearly didn't seem to have any material clarity on its raison d'être or feasibility. Jalal's phrase 'inner meaning' suggests that she thinks the idea of Pakistan held some deep or profound explanation that Jinnah found difficult to articulate. The 'tantalising' truth or meaning meanwhile was wrapped like a hollow enigma within the 'tactics' or the game of manoeuvres and postures with the political opponent and the British Empire. It was all 'demand and counter-demand, of tactical side steps, and strategic retreats, of propaganda'[32] that Jinnah indulged in to persist with his case. But what was ultimately Jinnah's idea of Pakistan?

It is best to read Jinnah's thoughts *after* the creation of Pakistan, when his need to defend its coming into being was no longer necessary.

On 19 February 1948, explaining Pakistan in a broadcast to the people of Australia, Jinnah said,

> 'Pakistan is made up of two blocks of territory, one in the North-East and one in the North-West of the sub-continent of India . . . The people are mostly simple folk, poor, not very well educated and with few interests beyond the cultivation of their fields . . . They make good soldiers, and have won renown in many battles.'[33]

The description, 'two blocks of territory' to mark the regions on two sides of India is a physical description of location. But we shall see that it also betrays a psychological anxiety to prove something. Jinnah identifies the nation with its subaltern class, fusing the identity of the 'Kisan' and the 'Jawan', the peasant who can also play the role of an able soldier. Jinnah takes pride in telling his Australian audience that these soldiers fought 'by your side in the two world wars.'[34] It is pathetic to read about a colonized compulsion being sold to a white audience as a matter of pride. When your less privileged countrymen suffer the hardships of war, all you are left with is pride. Elite pride is the pathological surplus of other people's labour. Jinnah's statement is also a reminder of how the Muslim League propaganda instigated the Muslim peasantry to turn against Hindus in Noakhali.

Jinnah returns to the territorial question to offer a communal fantasy:

> 'West Pakistan is separated from East Pakistan by about a thousand miles of the territory of India. The first question

> a student from abroad should ask himself is—how can this be? How can there be unity of government between areas so widely separated? I can answer this question in one word. It is "faith": faith in Almighty God, in ourselves and in our destiny.'[35]

Jinnah clarified that his idea of Pakistan's sovereignty was not based on any profound 'inner meaning' that historians had to discover. It was the crude logic of territory and (religious) identity all along. Jawaharlal Nehru's imagination of India as 'some ancient palimpsest on which layer upon layer of thought and reverie had been inscribed'[36] in contrast echoes Homi Bhabha's critical observation about nationalist historiography being prone to narratives of mythically constructed origins (what Bhabha calls 'impossibly romantic and excessively metaphorical').[37] Nevertheless, it has a deep, speculative element that is the opposite of Jinnah's reductionist imagination of a nation being purely based on ethnocentric or religious terms. Nehru's idea of unity is located in a mysterious, cultural unconscious that exists within a certain geocultural space:

> 'Some kind of a dream of unity has occupied the mind of India since the dawn of civilization. That unity was not conceived as something imposed from outside, a standardization of externals or even of beliefs. It was something deeper and, within its fold, the widest tolerance of belief and custom was practised and every variety acknowledged and even encouraged.'[38]

What may be initially construed as a woolly description to cushion a hard, political reality as the nation turns out to be a principle of unity based on the supportive spirit between diverse religions. Even if Nehru is exaggerating the history of tolerance, he is at least holding tolerance of belief as a historical and civilizational value rather than pure belief itself.

Jinnah's idea of territorial unity based on faith betrays his anxiety to bridge the cultural differences between East and West Pakistan. The supreme faith on faith was betrayed by history with the creation of Bangladesh in 1972. The language of culture, of the material expressions of life and selfhood was the real text that turned out to be equally, if not more, fundamental than the homogenous idea of religion.

In a speech at a public meeting at Dacca (Dhaka, since 1982) on 21 March 1948, Jinnah said,

> 'What we want is not to talk about Bengali, Punjabi, Sindhi, Baluchi, Pathan and so on. They are of course units. But I ask you: have you forgotten the lesson that was taught to us thirteen hundred years ago? If I may point out, you are all outsiders here. Who were the original inhabitants of Bengal—not those who are now living. So what is the use of saying "We are Bengalis, or Sindhis, or Pathans, or Punjabis". No we are Muslims.'[39]

The secular godfather of religious faith came to Dacca to remind the Bengalis of East Pakistan about their pan-Islamic identity after he heard that 'people financed by foreign agencies' were 'intent on creating disruption' and 'to disrupt and sabotage Pakistan.'[40] Jinnah's usage, 'You are all outsiders,' is interesting. He reminded the Muslim Bengalis that their religious ancestors were from elsewhere. Those who converted to Islam belonged to a new, historical ancestry. It meant an erasure of local, pre-Islamic pasts. Local culture and language were 'units' in relation to the 'original' identity of the people who had ruled Bengal during the establishment of the Bengal Sultanate in the fourteenth century. The singular religious identity that Islam bestowed on Muslim Bengalis was a transnational one. Language and locality are taken as a lesser and weaker marker of identity. Jinnah did not live to see the complete overturning of his surgical idea of identity. It took a war for Muslim Bengalis to wrest their freedom from the Muslim Punjabis of Pakistan in 1971.

The complex relationship between Islam and the markers of cultural locality in the Indian subcontinent had yet another contentious aspect to it.

In his letter to Jinnah on 14 September 1944, Gandhi began by showing his willingness to open room for discussion:

> '[In] view of your dislike of the Rajaji formula, I have, at any rate for the moment, put it out of my mind and I am now concentrating on the Lahore resolution in the hope of finding a ground for mutual agreement.'[41]

Jinnah, in his letter of 14 September 1944 sought clarifications from Gandhi on the provincial interim government as envisaged in the Rajaji formula. He particularly wanted to know if the cooperation of the Muslim League was being sought 'on the basis of a united India'[42]. This formula, Jinnah famously said, offered 'a shadow and a husk, maimed and mutilated, and moth-eaten Pakistan.'[43]

It did not occur to Jinnah that the moth-eaten nature of his desperate demand for Pakistan would regionally mutilate India on communal lines. Ultimately, the Gandhi–Jinnah talks failed. With amused disdain, Wavell wrote in his journal entry on 30 September 1944:

> 'Anything so barren as their exchange of letters is a deplorable exposure of Indian leadership. The two great mountains have met and not even a ridiculous mouse has emerged.'[44]

Wavell did not have a great opinion of Gandhi.[45] He was partial to Jinnah, unthinkingly borrowing his conclusions about the Rajaji formula from what Jinnah thought about it: 'Gandhi offered Jinnah the maimed, mutilated Pakistan of the Rajagopalachari formula, but without real sincerity or conviction.'[46]

From a statement made by Jinnah that Pakistan was bound to be a reality even if it was the size of his handkerchief, Devji observed that the League leader 'imagined Pakistan as a piece of cloth rather than of land'[47]. The act of imagining the nation he demanded as being made of pliant material that was torn and foldable and could fit into his pocket betrays both intense insecurity and an infantile sense of possession. Jinnah feared that Pakistan wasn't going to be tailor-made for his dreams.

Gandhi, in response to Jinnah's letter, began by reiterating he was putting his mind 'very seriously' to the Lahore resolution.[48] Immediately afterwards, he raised two issues against Jinnah's demand of Pakistan:

> 'I find no parallel in history for a body of converts and their descendants claiming to be a nation apart from the parent stock. If India was one nation before the advent of Islam, it must remain one in spite of the change of faith of a very large body of her children.'[49]

Gandhi had had long-standing and contentious debates on the issue of conversion, particularly with Christian missionaries, since the early 1930s. His *religious* aversion to conversion came from the argument that religion was a matter of personal identity and needs 'reform' rather than renunciation.[50] Gandhi's *political* anxiety was based on 'the impact conversions could have on communal electorates, a right granted by the India Bill of 1935'.[51]

Gandhi's claim that India was a single 'nation' even before Muslims arrived on the scene requires explanation. Anthony Parel explains the word used for nation in the original *Hind Swaraj* is '*praja*', which acquires new meanings over time: Before the advent of Islam, 'the ancient *acharyas* (teachers of Indian philosophy) contributed immensely towards the consolidation of the idea of *praja*' and the pilgrimages they established across the land were '*praja*-building centres'[52]. 'Indian philosophy' is a euphemism for various strands of Vedic, non-Vedic, Buddhist and Jain philosophies. In modernity, *praja* takes on a dual meaning: the word 'refers to the Indian people as a whole composed of Hindus, Muslims, Christians, Sikhs, Parsees, Buddhists and others' and also stands for 'the modern educated elite – the lawyers, the doctors, the wealthy, etc.'[53] If the earliest, or ancient, idea of *praja* maps a purely spiritual and cultural geography based on the influence of religious schools (ignoring political rule), the modern idea has a twofold conception, a cultural collectivity of people from various religions, and a professional collectivity. The word *praja* has however undergone a political transformation in modernity from being the subject (*praja*) of the King (*raja*) and the colonial master, to being the citizen of a democracy (*prajatantra*). The premodern connotation of a cultural collective can't be superimposed on a modern collective whose meaning is clearly derived from the birth of the modern state and the idea of territoriality. India was not a nation at the time when Islam arrived in the twelfth century. The idea of national sovereignty is a modern political concept that arrived with the British. Gandhi's point that converts and their descendants claiming a nation against the ancestral community were unprecedented marks of the recognition of a new historical problem.

Gandhi follows it up with a provocative question that strikes at the heart of Jinnah's internally conflicted and ill-founded project of Muslim making:

> 'You do not claim to be a separate nation by right of conquest but by reason of acceptance of Islam. Will the two nations become one if the whole of India accepted Islam? Will Bengalis, Oriyas, Andhras, Tamilians, Maharashtrians, Gujaratis, etc., cease to have their special characteristics if all of them become converts to Islam?'[54]

Gandhi's questions exposed Jinnah's mindset on his abstract Islamist notion of the nation, and brought to the fore a sociological point about converts: even if they change their religion, people's cultural modes of expression and practice don't get washed away overnight.

Gandhi could not compete with Muhammad Iqbal's influence on Jinnah. After all, Iqbal was the poet and thinker who came to be regarded as 'Pakistan's spiritual father'.[55] Jinnah partly echoed Iqbal's political idea idea of Islam, but partly contradicted him.

Iqbal, Faisal Devji explained in *Muslim Zion*, saw race, geography and matter itself, as forms of 'idolatry'.[56] He clarifies that territoriality meant a hindrance for the Muslim political thinker: 'Iqbal maintained that territorial belonging, in the populist form it assumed with the nation state, destroyed or at the very least enfeebled all ethical or idealistic imperatives in political life'.[57] In a section titled 'Muslim Solidarity' from his highly aphoristic *Stray Reflections*, Iqbal emphasized 'our solidarity as a community rests on our hold on the religious principle. The moment this hold is loosened we are nowhere.'[58]

This betrays a deep paranoia about community in the face of modernity, but also displays historical escapism. To hold on to the 'religious principle' becomes a matter of survival and negotiation, and marks off the Muslim community within (the possibility of) a secular nation.

Iqbal defined Islamism as something 'which constructs nationality out of a purely abstract idea, i.e., religion'.[59] This establishes the idea that the Muslim community's fundamental (political) ties (and allegiance) lies with religion. It extends to the argument that the idea of nationality, or national status, of the Muslim community is paradoxically derived from a sense of solidarity whose roots lie *outside* the nation.

For Iqbal, Devji writes, 'India's Muslims represented the Islamic principle of solidarity'.[60] This led Muslims in the subcontinent to believe and invest in what Devji identifies as a Zionist utopia, where an abstract (de-territorialized) idea of identity becomes the basis of nationality and nationalism. Devji takes the idea of Urdu as Pakistan's national language as akin to 'the adoption of Hebrew as Israel's national language [as] an attempt to create a nationality by reaching for a unity that necessarily broke with the past of those who had to be made into the citizens of either state.'[61] To be sure, this abstract idea is also modern with its roots in what Devji calls 'Enlightenment's myth of political consent, when a people is converted to nationhood by the force of its idea alone.'[62]

It appears to be an idea of religion and religious identity that desperately competes against the challenge of modern universalism but gets trapped in trying to adjust it with national sovereignty.

Jinnah was happy to propagate an abstract idea of Islamism as glue for national identity and as a source of belonging for Muslims in Pakistan. But he did not share Iqbal's view (being the pragmatist nation-builder) on territoriality. Pakistan was a new, political territory of faith that Jinnah had managed to successfully bargain for and wrest away from the Congress. It was a nation with a historical project of Muslim making.

Rajagopalachari made the sweeping claim that certain Muslim rulers (he names Akbar, Aurangzeb, Hyder Ali and Tipu Sultan) imagined India as 'one' in times when 'differences seemed more deep-rooted' (not offering any criteria for clubbing these kings with very disparate histories of religious in/tolerance together) which prompted Jinnah in the Lahore Resolution of 1940 to dismiss these kings as 'conquerors and parental rulers'.[63]

Devji has persuasively argued that Jinnah's two-nation theory sought to escape the paradoxical grip of a common past and 'uncouple these communities that had become too intertwined in history.'[64]

But Jinnah, like a clinical surgeon of history, clearly used the past of Muslim rulers as a point of origin (and departure) to draw a religious connection to the present. This approach to history also separates Muslims from the histories of other religious communities living in India. It paved the way for the abysmal status of official, nationalist history writing in Pakistan, the history that became part of the curriculum.[65]

Devji's reading that Jinnah 'reviled the achievements of Muslim rulers in the past by describing them as imperialists no different from the British'[66] is partly true as Jinnah also drew a sense of religious ancestry from these rulers for his political project. So the disdain is modernist and partial.

Jinnah had a modern, secular optimism when it came to the future of religious communities. In his presidential address to the Constituent Assembly of Pakistan at Karachi on 11 August 1947, Jinnah said:

> 'We are starting with this fundamental principle that we are all citizens and equal citizens of one State . . . Today, you might say with justice that Roman Catholics and Protestants do not exist: what exists now is that every man is a citizen, an equal citizen of Great Britain and they are all members of the Nation. I think we should keep that in front of us as our ideal and you will find that in course of time Hindus would cease to be Hindus and Muslims would cease to be Muslims, not in the religious sense because that is the personal faith of each individual, but in the political sense as citizens of the State.'[67]

Jinnah's wish of Pakistani Hindus and Muslims seeing themselves as citizens first leaves space for religion in the private sphere. It suits the definition of the ideal citizen in an avowedly liberal, secular state, despite its abstract nature. In Jinnah's case, there is a further problem. Muslim and Hindu citizens were shorn of their historical relationship (of both antagonism and admiration) and thrown together into a nationalist project based on the idea of an exclusivist Islamic idea. Jinnah made mutually exclusive demands on his people. Salman Rushdie, in his novel *Shame*, aptly called Pakistan 'a failure of the imagination . . . *insufficiently imagined*'.[68] Islamic Pakistan, as a product of Jinnah's moth-eaten imagination, couldn't match the demands of secularity.

Sometimes, Jinnah resorted to eyebrow-raising sophistry. In a speech broadcast from Radio Pakistan, Lahore on 30 October 1947, he said:

> 'We have, undoubtedly, achieved Pakistan and that too without bloody war and practically peacefully by moral and intellectual force and with the power of [the] pen which is no less mighty than the sword and so our righteous cause has triumphed.'[69]

This is an outrageous lie. Genocide and civil war went hand in hand with the demand for Pakistan, with glaring circumstantial evidence of Muslim League members playing an active part in manufacturing it. Partition was neither peaceful nor its horror defensible by any sober stretch of the imagination or argument.

Self-denial dies hard. It dies harder in politics.

Direct Action

A month before the announcement of 'Direct Action', a flurry of statements from the Congress and the Muslim League appeared in public after the British failed to implement the Cabinet Mission Plan as a last effort to avoid Partition.

Jinnah made a statement on 13 July 1946 published in the *Dawn* (that Ishtiaq Ahmed calls 'arbitrary'[70]) where he accused Nehru and the Congress of honouring neither the Mission Plan's proposals on the division of provinces, nor Wavell's plan on the composition of the interim government. Jinnah dropped his secular, and even constitutional, pretensions as he issued a crude public statement on 29 July, declaring 'Direct Action':

> 'Throughout the fateful negotiations with the Cabinet Delegation and the Viceroy, the other two parties, the British and the Congress, held a pistol in their hand, the one of authority and the other of mass struggle and non-co-operation. *Today, we have forged a pistol and are in a position to use it.* The decision to reject the proposals and to launch direct action had not been taken in haste, but it was taken with full sense of responsibility and all deliberations that [are] humanly possible.'[71] [Emphasis mine]

Ayesha Jalal plays down the import of Jinnah's language. She writes that the remark about the pistol made by her Qaid-i-Azam was meant more 'as a metaphor not proposed as a fact.'[72] Real threats of violence are often expressed through metaphor. The aftermath of Jinnah's statement is history. It must be mentioned that the Bengal Governor Fredrick Burrows played his sly colonial part behind Jinnah's declaration by allowing the Bengal Chief Minister Huseyn Shaheed Suhrawardy to declare 16 August a holiday[73].

Blaming everything on the Congress, calling it names, Jinnah finally declared his intentions. He was ready to kill for Pakistan. No land-of-the-pure was possible in history without pure violence. When he felt cramped and cornered, Jinnah did not hesitate to give vent to his frustration in a crude manner. When an ambitious man in politics is frustrated, he can turn dangerous. Partition was Jinnah's last temptation, the ace he carried close to his chest.

When Jinnah was asked if the call to direct action would be non-violent, or involve violence, he said,

> 'I am not going to discuss ethics.'[74]

Ethics was not on the cards for Jinnah since he took a communal position on the minority question. It is important to briefly trace that shift in Jinnah's politics.

There are definitive reasons (skirted by Jinnah apologists)[75] behind Jinnah's leaving the Congress. To be precise, Gandhi's influence on the Congress and his emphasis on mass politics did not cut ice with Jinnah's ego, political ambitions and his class background, as 'a privileged scion of the gentry'[76]. In 1916, as the new leader of the Muslim League, Jinnah facilitated the Lucknow Pact with the Congress, securing special representation for Muslims in the legislative councils based on a separate electorate. Despite denouncing separate electorates earlier as a British ploy to divide the two communities, 'the Congress Party was willing to go the extra mile to accommodate the demands of the Muslim League', a fact that Ishtiaq Ahmed thinks 'deserves to be acknowledged'.[77] The Congress was willing to accommodate the League's demands in order to boost Gandhi's attempts to bring Hindu–Muslim unity by supporting the Khilafat Movement and also for the sake of larger Muslim participation in the non-cooperation movement.

Ahmed understands Jinnah's discomfort with Gandhi's role in the Khilafat Movement as one where Gandhi is taking 'the matter to the streets' while Jinnah preferred a 'constitutional protest and opposition'.[78]

The novelty of the Nehru Report of 1928 was its call to discard the idea of 'permanent communal majorities and minorities'[79] and replace it with communal majorities and minorities 'through inclusive political parties open to all citizens'[80] as a means to avoid majority rule. It also proposed a federation with an 'effective centre'.[81] Jinnah came up with 'Fourteen Points' in the December 1928 Muslim Conference held in Delhi, asking for a more 'loose federation' with powers vested in the provinces, and a 'one-third share for the Muslims in the central and all provincial cabinets.'[82] Once these proposals were rejected, Jinnah got the communal monster out of his bag.

When Gandhi heard that Jinnah met Ambedkar and E.V. Naicker (also called Periyar) in January 1940 to create a political front against the Congress, he dashed off a letter to him on 16 January 1940, assuring him that he wasn't opposed to Jinnah's 'opposition to the Congress', and that a joint nature of the opposition gave it a 'national character'.[83] Gandhi added that he found it a perfect move against the 'communal incubus'.[84] Jinnah found his moment to say:

> 'India is not a nation. It is a subcontinent composed of nationalities.'[85]

This division between nation and nationality needs a brief explanation. In another statement that Jinnah made to *The Daily Mail* in 1940, he targeted his bête noire, Gandhi, for proposing a 'representative assembly of Indians . . . to evolve a constitution'.[86] Jinnah countered that proposal raising the 'legitimate minorities' question' where any political settlement must honour 'the social contract' on which an 'agreed constitution' must be based.[87] Jinnah, Devji points out, uses the concept of nationality as a 'purely constitutional category, one crucial to the making of a social contract'.[88] This is how Jinnah fuses the nation, a political concept, with nationality as a 'juridical conception'.[89] By doing so, however, Jinnah communalizes the concept of nationality. A minority can claim a distinct (and divisive) nationality for itself based on its own idea of a nation. In fact, Jinnah communalizes the idea of citizenship itself: Muslim citizens comprise a Muslim nation. With a lawyer's cunning, Jinnah invents an incongruous but effective grid of terminologies with a singular purpose: to deny the possibility of Hindus and Muslims as two religious communities to form a united nation.

In a message sent to the Bombay Presidency Provincial Muslim League Conference held on 26–27 May 1940, Jinnah countered the accusation of communalism with his own rhetoric:

> 'We are told that our demand is the quintessence of communalism. Why? Because we propose that the Hindus and Mussalmans should be provided with their homelands which will enable them to live side by side as two honourable nations, and as good neighbours and not Hindus as superior and Mussalmans as inferior nations, tied artificially together with the Hindu religious majority to dominate and rule over Muslim India.'[90]

Jinnah legitimizes the idea of a Hindu nation in order to claim a Muslim one. It is left unexplained in this twisted statement that if Hindus and Muslims, as majority and minority, are artificially tied to the idea of India, what about the inevitable minorities within the territorial idea of a Muslim Pakistan? Doesn't that fact make Pakistan an artificial construct too? Jinnah is a master at making false arguments in his singularly motivated bid to create a foggy concept called 'two-nation theory'.

Devji explains the political contradiction in Jinnah's position as a 'kind of politics detached from any language of history that, after 1937 allowed Jinnah to reject the category of minority . . . The people he sought to lead, therefore, were now suddenly to be called a nation . . . in order to extricate Muslims from an untenable constitutional position, one that actively prevented the negotiation of a social contract by making the minority forever dependent upon a majority's goodwill.'[91]

It is amply clear that Jinnah's idea of a social contract between the minority and the majority is a destruction of the idea of social contract. He makes the promise of social agreement between two communities impossible. The contract is negated by creating rhetorical hindrances to the Congress and the Muslim League coming to agree on the nature of sovereignty and polity. Jinnah rejects the moral possibility of the social contract. He creates this impasse determinedly to showcase a doomed idea of a united India that would automatically justify his logic for the necessity of Pakistan.

Jinnah holds a unique distinction in modern political history for demanding a nation in the name of the minority by destroying the idea of the minority.

From 1940 onwards, Jinnah sailed single-mindedly on his divisive boat.

The political, for Jinnah, became the communal. He ended up arguing that by default, if any communal minority turns political, it can make a nationalist claim on purely communal lines, and demand territory in its name. In doing so, Jinnah created an argumentative marvel. The minority claim to nationhood presents a critique of a hegemonic majority and wants to annul the majority–minority relationship. But it simultaneously seeks to reproduce that relationship in a different form within its desired territorial and political configuration where they enjoy the status of a majority. The majority–minority relationship is destroyed, but not its framework. The relationship is re-established elsewhere to one's advantage. Religion is central to this scheme of argumentation. The problem of social and political relations between communities is seen through a religious lens. The concept of territory, nation, religion, community and even constitution, circulate in a compressed manner around a central argument that is predominantly communal.

In the territorial divisions that Jinnah and his Muslim League sought to secure for Pakistan through a series of resolutions and statements, the focus shifted from 'the Muslim-minority provinces to the Muslim-majority provinces.'[92] The ironic paradox and political sleight of hand is this: Jinnah and his team argued for Pakistan in the name of India's largest minority, to safeguard its rights and secure its political future, by transforming the minority into a territorial majority. This majority in turn was defined in terms of religion alone.

This play of categories by Jinnah became a template for communal separatists.

Ishtiaq Ahmed writes that beginning with his speech of 22 March 1940 where he forwarded the two-nation agenda, Jinnah showed his 'special contempt for Gandhi'[93] and made up his mind to take 'a negative stand to whatever Gandhi and the Congress leaders proposed.'[94]

In the same conference held on 26–27 May 1940, Jinnah responded to a statement that Gandhi made on 13 May from Sevagram (published in *Harijan* on 15 May).

This is the relevant portion of Gandhi's statement:

> 'The demand for partition puts an end to all effort for unity for the time being. I hold that communal understanding is not a prerequisite to the British doing justice on their part. When they feel that they want to recognize India's right of self-determination, all the difficulties that they put forth as obstacles in their path will melt away like ice before the sun's rays. The right of self-determination means the right of determination by every group and ultimately every individual. The demand for a Constituent Assembly presumes that the determinations of the groups and individuals will coincide. Should it happen otherwise and partition becomes (sic) the fashion, either we shall have partition or partitions rather than foreign rule, or we shall continue to wrangle among ourselves and submit to foreign rule, or else have a proper civil war.'[95]

Gandhi felt that India might be faced with three eventualities if its right to self-determination were to be intercepted by partition. There might be multiple divisions of the country, an endless political quarrel over sovereignty that will help extend colonial rule or a full-fledged civil war. Jinnah retorted by saying,

> 'It is quite clear from this that Mr Gandhi understands or ought to understand that to wrangle over the imaginary one and united India can only result in our submission to foreign rule. I pray that Mr Gandhi's prophecy of "proper civil war" will not come'.[96]

By August 1947, Jinnah would have realized that Gandhi's warnings were prescient. He made a tragic blunder by not heeding Gandhi's prophetic insight. However, Gandhi did not only warn the Muslims.

A reader of *Harijan* reminded Gandhi on 19 May about the statement that he made on 29 April in Sevagram in response to the Lahore resolution of the Muslim League on 23 March, that if Muslims desire partition, 'no power on earth can prevent it'.[97] The reader asked if he was 'underrating' the desire of Hindus by putting a 'premium'[98] on Muslims. Gandhi replied, 'If the majority of Hindus or Christians or Sikhs or even Parsis, small though their number is, stubbornly resist the express wish of the duly-elected representatives of eight crores of Muslims, they will do so at the peril of a civil war. This is not a question of majority or minority. If we are to solve our problems non-violently, there is no other way.'[99]

Gandhi's plea to non-Muslims to non-violently accept the Muslim demand aside, he had anticipated the possibility of civil war resulting from the refusal by Hindus and non-Muslim minorities to accept the demand for Pakistan. The accuracy of Gandhi's prophecy of organized mass violence and the breakdown of social relations is in stark contrast to Jinnah's obliviousness about the nature of the beast he was unleashing upon his own community, as much as on others.

A Poorly Imagined Pakistan

Ambedkar's meeting with Jinnah in January 1940, along with Periyar, to forge an anti-Congress coalition had a history. At the Round Table Conference in 1931, Muslims, the Depressed Classes (later Dalits), Indian Christians and Anglo-Indians came together in what came to be known as the Minorities Pact. Gandhi, representing the Congress, endorsed the Muslim demand but refused to grant Ambedkar the status of a representative for Dalit rights. It led to the Poona Pact where Ambedkar had to reluctantly relinquish his demand for separate electorates and accept the granting of reserved seats for Scheduled Caste candidates after Gandhi exerted his infamous moral coercion by a fast-unto-death. Devji wonders if it was moral compulsion alone that led Ambedkar to relent to Gandhi's demand, or was there also a political reason behind it, fearing 'the possibility that the Mahatma would be able to demonstrate his own command over the Depressed Classes, unjust or coerced though it may have been'.[100]

Despite putting his weight behind a joint minority politics, Ambedkar realized the ambivalence in Jinnah's politics. In an interview to the *Bombay Chronicle* on 20 October 1938, Ambedkar aired his puzzle:

> 'Mr Jinnah is on one side fighting with Congress; while on the other side he intends to come to a pact with the Congress.'[101]

The hypocritical contradiction between principle and politics caused Ambedkar to distrust Jinnah. It led him to fight a lonelier battle in his competitive bid to secure special representation and rights for Dalits vis-à-vis Muslims.

In 1941, soon after the Lahore resolution, Ambedkar presented his stand on the Muslim question in his book *Thoughts on Pakistan* where he put forth his arguments regarding the demand for Pakistan. He republished his thoughts under a new title *Pakistan or the Partition of India* in 1945, where he 'reversed his position', as Ishtiaq Ahmed writes, and 'argued that the division of India was unnecessary'.[102] In the preface to the second edition of the book in 1945, Ambedkar begins with a negative acknowledgement of the demand for Pakistan as an irritable phenomenon that turned out to be a 'headache'[103] for him and others. He is however pleased to mention that both Gandhi and Jinnah considered the book 'an authority on the subject'.[104]

Presenting the case for and against Pakistan from the Hindu and Muslim sides, Ambedkar claimed in the introduction his non-partisanship in the matter. His fundamental intention, in his words, was 'to expound the scheme of Pakistan in all its aspects and not advocate it'.[105] Praising Ambedkar's 'superb skills as a political analyst', Partha Chatterjee observed that the 1941 book was 'almost Socratic in its dialogical structure', where the writer presented the Hindu and Muslim sides of the case from a position of 'perfect neutrality'.[106] However, Chatterjee is quick to remind us that this neutrality is more of a 'narrative strategy', as Ambedkar 'had a great stake'[107] in the Pakistan question vis-à-vis the fate of the untouchables. In other words, Ambedkar had a political strategy beneath the façade of neutrality. Reading the book, it becomes clear that Ambedkar's claim to be non-partisan is misleading. His central arguments in the debate makes the ominous political move for Pakistan appear logical and inevitable.

Ambedkar begins his probe on whether India is a nation by referring to Anglo-Indians (a community that came into being during the colonial era from the mixed parentage of Indian women and European men), and goes on to refute the claim. He quotes an anonymous Anglo-Indian for this purpose: '[To] know India was to forget that there is such a thing as India.'[108] This statement is an acknowledgement of India's overwhelming heterogeneity, which may not lend itself to the standard European idea of the nation. Referring to Rabindranath Tagore's lectures on nationalism (delivered in Japan in 1916, and published in 1917), Ambedkar finds Tagore concurring with the Anglo-Indians that India could not be defined as a nation. Hindus refused to accept that they were not a nation, until, Ambedkar writes, the Muslim League made its demand for Pakistan and caused a 'rift in the lute'.[109]

Ambedkar accepts that along with racial and linguistic similarity, there exist common social customs and cultural practices between Hindus and Muslims. Even in the sphere of religious life, Ambedkar writes: 'Muslim *pirs* had Hindu disciples; and similarly some Hindu *Yogis* have had Muslim *chelas*.'[110] But Ambedkar blames the persistence of common features between Hindus and Muslims on a negative phenomenon, underplaying its importance: 'incomplete conversions'.[111] The reasons behind incomplete conversions offered by Ambedkar are limits imposed on 'the method of persuasion' and 'insufficiency of preaching'.[112] He does not consider a more fundamental sociological point: that such conversions indicate the fractured nature of converted selves that navigate in their everyday lives between the grand narrative of religion and local narratives of culture.

Ambedkar next quotes the French scholar Ernest Renan at length to argue that the uniformity of language and race isn't enough as a binding force for a nation. Ambedkar quotes Renan who defines the nation as 'a living soul, a spiritual principle', where two elements are crucial: 'a rich heritage of memories' and 'the desire to live together'.[113] There is an echo of Hegelian fabrications on the nation, especially Hegel's 'General Introduction to the Philosophy of History', where abstract notions like 'Spirit', combine with the concrete, or actual idea of individuals.[114]

Ambedkar quotes from a pamphlet titled 'The Hindu Nationalist Movement' by Bhai Parmanand, a Hindu missionary from the Arya Samaj movement, where Parmanand writes on figures from India's medieval history that created a wedge in historical memory between Hindus and Muslims. Ambedkar quotes Parmanand: 'In history the Hindus revere the memory of Prithvi Raj, Partap, Shivaji and, Be-ragi Bir, who fought for the honour and freedom of this land (against the Muslims), while the Mahomedans look upon the invaders of India, like Muhammad bin Qasim and rulers like Aurangzeb as their national heroes.'[115]

This observation leads Ambedkar to make the evaluative claim that all 'common features' highlighted between Hindus and Muslims are 'accidental and superficial', whereas the history of 'political and religious antagonism' between the two communities is 'essential and fundamental'.[116]

This polemical point adopts the binaries of communal politics. Parmanand's construction of 'memory' as 'history' is part of how communities were being politically constructed across religious lines. The idea of religion and nation underwent a radical change in nineteenth century Europe confronted by the challenge posed by two new universalisms: Enlightenment reason and the idea of revolution. Nations are accidental products of time and history (despite the complex range of factors that legitimize their coming into being).

Nehru's *The Discovery of India* would have offered Ambedkar a more nuanced perspective than the reductive polemics of communal and right-wing texts on the historicity of Hindu–Muslim relations. But Ambedkar was a fierce and brilliant polemicist who passionately analysed—in his bid to intensify—the nature of social and historical antagonisms in society. In this case, however, a counterargument can be made that the reverse of Ambedkar's contention is the real story. The *longue durée* view of Hindu–Muslim relations in India must take into account the everyday life and cultural practices of the communities that are not overdetermined by religion.

Ambedkar's own views on the birth of communal politics contradict his terms. He contends that the 'decline and fall' of Muslims in India began since 'British occupation' and that the executive, administrative and juridical changes introduced by the British 'inflicted a series of blows among the Muslim Community'.[117] The fact that Muslims (via the League) moved from initially demanding rights and representation as a community to demanding a nation has to be understood, according to Ambedkar, in terms of 'the mysterious working of the psychology of national feeling.'[118] If a fall from medieval glory and the machinations of British rule form the basis of an aggrieved Muslim community demanding a nation, it means that the nature of its relationship with the Hindu community is immaterial.

Evoking colonial historians Arnold Toynbee and Ernest Barker, Ambedkar argues that it takes centuries of 'unreflective silence'[119] to transform into national consciousness. The viability of the demand for a nation comes from 'favourable conditions'[120] like collective will and desire on the one hand, and territory on the other. Collective will and territory can be considered objective factors that facilitate the demand of a nation. But the political reasons behind that demand can be superficially constructed.

The point is not whether it was possible for the Muslim League to make a viable, or credible, argument for a separate Muslim nation. The point is how that argument was constructed as a basis for the demand of a nation. If the argument, as we have already seen, brushes aside a complex historical situation to formulate a narrowly communal demand, it lacks the conditions that Ambedkar is thrusting upon it.

It is not fruitful to judge whether a nationalist imagination is authentic or not from a certain prism of historical objectivity. Political ideas can invent new realities. It is enough to critically read the manner in which the Muslim community was defined by the Muslim League.

Pakistan was not illegitimately but poorly imagined.

Ambedkar quotes the writings of V.D. Savarkar at length to bring in the Hindu view to the question of Pakistan. He finds it strange that Savarkar and Jinnah both agree on the two-nation theory. The only difference between them, however, is that Savarkar, despite agreeing that Hindus and Muslims are separate nations, believed that both need to live under one constitution and be part of a single country.[121] For Savarkar, political domination was the only way to solve the conflict between two communities. Ambedkar harps on Savarkar's logical inconsistency, but just as in Jinnah's case, he does not locate the problem in the internally conflicted nature of the communal, right-wing imagination of the nation. Savarkar creates a 'minor nation' by forcing a 'major nation' to submit its sovereignty to the former.[122] It is a perverse idea of domination. If the Muslim nationalist position makes a monolithic claim of its own identity, the Hindu nationalist position splits the idea of nationhood *from within*. Ambedkar finds Savarkar's scheme 'dangerous'[123] for India's security. Both positions are deeply invested in creating majoritarian homelands and hell-bent on inventing any sort of political artifice to make it possible.

Ambedkar leaves a significant warning for liberal nationalists:

> 'Mr Savarkar's scheme has at least the merit of telling the Muslims, thus far and no further. The Muslims know where they are with regard to the Hindu Maha Sabha. On the other hand, with the Congress the Musalmans find themselves nowhere because the Congress has been treating the Muslims and the minority question as a game in diplomacy, if not in duplicity.'[124]

Liberals cannot hope to settle a politically divisive issue by making strategic, juridical moves alone. A matter of politics can't be totally sorted by making adjustments in the law. There is a foundational law of the nation that must address the question of power when it involves a powerful minority. It is, however, surprising that Ambedkar finds any 'merit' in majoritarian forthrightness.

Considering the Muslim League demand, Ambedkar argues that the assumption of some post-war European states that 'constitutional safeguards for minorities should suffice for their protection'[125] turned out to be misplaced. Ambedkar mentions Turkey, Greece and Bulgaria as countries that 'found that the only effective way of solving the minorities problem lay in exchange of population.'[126]

This is the problem with logical blueprints and exposes the limits of comparative politics. Ambedkar didn't anticipate the mass behaviour of a people instigated by communal hatred to carve out fresh boundaries with blood. Venkat Dhulipala also drives home this point on Ambedkar making a case for the transfer of populations:

> 'What he did not perhaps expect was the complete breakdown of the law and order machinery that would occur and the large scale violence and ethnic cleansing that would totally alter the demography of whole regions.'[127]

Levinas and the Ethics of Risk

In *Pakistan or the Partition of India*, Ambedkar writes how, soon after Gandhi joined the national movement, he proclaimed that he could 'perform the miracle' of swaraj in six months if 'certain conditions were fulfilled' that included the 'achievement of Hindu–Muslim unity'.[128] Gandhi laid emphasis on the Hindu–Muslim question as central to his quest for swaraj on numerous occasions. On 11 November 1920, Gandhi wrote in *Young India*: 'Swaraj is as inconceivable without full reparation to the "depressed" classes as it is impossible without real Hindu–Muslim unity.'[129] On 23 February 1921, Gandhi laid down six conditions for swaraj in *Young India* that included the spirit of non-violence, manufacturing cloth through the spinning wheel, the promotion of Hindu–Muslim unity and ridding

Hinduism of untouchability. Gandhi claimed that if these conditions were fulfilled, 'Swaraj will be established in India before next October'.[130]

Ambedkar was sharply critical of Gandhi's overtures towards Muslims. He felt that Gandhi was so keen to please and pacify Muslims to gain their support in the national movement that he often overlooked what was at stake.

Ambedkar writes, '[The Khilafat Movement] was taken up by Mr Gandhi with a tenacity and faith which must have surprised many Mahomedans themselves. There were many people who doubted the ethical basis of the Khilafat movement and tried to dissuade Mr Gandhi from taking any part in a movement the ethical basis of which was so questionable.'[131]

The question about Gandhi disregarding ethical issues concerning Khilafat will be taken up shortly.

Ambedkar did leave a word of praise for Gandhi on this issue:

> 'Mr Gandhi not only agreed with the Muslims in the Khilafat cause but acted as their guide and their friend.'[132]

At a time when Hindus were reluctant to be part of the Muslim cause, Ambedkar writes, 'Mr Gandhi was the only Hindu who joined the Muslims. Not only did he show courage to join them, but also he kept step with them, nay, led them.'[133]

There is an acknowledgement of sincerity and a brave leap of faith on Gandhi's part to join hands with the Muslims in their cause. Ambedkar does not miss the political side of Gandhi's gesture:

> 'In taking up the cause of Khilafat Mr Gandhi achieved a double purpose. He carried the Congress Plan of winning over the Muslims to its culmination. Secondly, he made the Congress a power in the country, which it would not have been, if the Muslims had not joined it.'[134]

This is not a critique, but a political observation on Gandhi's purpose behind wooing the Muslims. Even if Gandhi was seeking political advantage for a nationalist cause, he took a genuine risk of friendship. The language of that risk must be understood, as the element of risk enables the crucial link between ethics and politics.

The Australian theologian Damien Casey finds Gandhi's sensibility closer to that of the French ethical thinker Emanuel Levinas than to that of Martin Buber (though most scholars[135] mention Buber due to his open letter to Gandhi in 1939). Buber's admiration for Gandhi reached its critical limit on the question of politics. The crux of Buber's problem can be found in this passage:

> 'So far as Gandhi acts politically, so far as he takes part in passing parliamentary resolutions, he does not introduce religion into politics, but allies his religion with the politics of others. He cannot wrestle uninterruptedly with the serpent; he must at times get along with it because he is directed to work in the kingdom of the serpent he set out to destroy. He refuses to exploit human passions, but he is chained as political actor to the "political," to *untransformed* men.'[136]

Buber refused to accept Gandhi's central predicament and challenge that he imposed on himself as much as to the world.

It is in 'the politics of others', the realm of politics *where you face others,* that Gandhi seeks god and truth. Politics means nothing if it doesn't involve the transformation of the untransformed. Gandhi believed in the transformative power of Satyagraha.

'What I want to achieve—" Gandhi wrote in the introduction to his *Autobiography* (1929), "what I have been striving and pining to achieve these thirty years—is self-realization, to see God face to face, to attain *Moksha*'.[137] If this was a spiritual quest with an ethical dimension, he takes it closer to politics later:

> 'To see the universal and all-pervading Spirit of Truth face to face one must be able to love *the meanest* of creation as oneself. And a man who aspires after that cannot afford to keep out of any field of life. That is why my devotion to Truth has drawn me into the field of politics; and I can say without the slightest hesitation and yet in all humility, that those who say that religion has nothing to do with politics do not know what religion means.'[138]

It is clear where Buber and Gandhi part ways. For Gandhi, God, or the Truth represented by God, is mirrored in the 'face to face' encounter with others, and that encounter includes politics. 'Gandhi seemed to consider', Casey writes, 'that it was in the act of facing the other *in political conflict*, that the possibility for genuine transcendence arose.'[139] [Emphasis mine] If for Buber, politics was not the place for truth, for Gandhi, politics was the 'field' of truth. This is the point where Levinas and Gandhi's concerns meet, described accurately by Casey:

> 'Levinas echoes Gandhi when he suggests that "communication with the other can be transcendent only as a dangerous life, a fine risk to be run". Genuine openness to the other involves the risk of death. To practice Satyagraha is also to be responsible for the other, a responsibility that mere opposition denies . . . The Satyagrahi could be considered to hold himself as hostage for another.'[140]

French philosopher Étienne Balibar, taking from historian David Hardiman, understands the 'dialogism' of Gandhi's Satyagraha as the idea that 'political struggle must involve *a moment of opening to the adversary* that conditions the transformation of his point of view.'[141] This observation supports the understanding of Gandhi extending Levinas's ethics of risk-taking into the sphere of the political encounter. However, though the Gandhian idea and gesture of otherly love is close to Levinas's notion of risk, there is another aspect to Gandhi's approach to the question of harbouring (and encouraging) a non-violent relationship which is different from Levinas.

On 27 January 1962, Levinas presented a paper, 'Transcendance et hauteur' at the *Société Française de Philosophie* where he summarized a few initial arguments from his major work *Totality and Infinity* (1961). The discussion following the presentation included the French philosopher Jean Wahl and M. Jean Filliozat, the French writer who taught at the Collège de France from 1952 to 1978, and wrote on Indian medicine, and India's religious and historical traditions. When Wahl invited him to speak, Filliozat brought up Gandhi:

> 'Gandhi treats the question of violence as the primary problem. On the one hand, he supposes—with the whole

> of Indian civilization—that the enemy of violence is not another violence; violence opposed is not the opposite of violence. On the other hand, the putting into question of the I in the presence of the Other is justified from the general Indian point of view, in any case from the point of view which Gandhi inherits, without being a philosopher himself, in a completely different way to the one that you (Levinas) spoke about.'[142]

Filliozat goes on to say more about how the I and the other are posited in Indian philosophy, which cannot be compared with Levinas, because in Levinas the Judeo–Christian components of ethics are argued through categories of modern western thought. For instance, Filliozat suggests that in general Indian philosophy, 'The I is not justified in imposing its liberty on the Other because it is not itself a valuable entity, any more than is the Other.'[143] This reading is off the mark at least in Gandhi's case. Gandhi affirmed the idea of a civilizational, anti-modern self and other as positive entities.

In *Hind Swaraj*, Gandhi defines civilization as the 'mode of conduct which points out to man the path of duty.'[144] That duty, apart from the perpetual task of elevating morality, also had an immediate historical and political context: the attainment of swaraj to be 'experienced by each one for himself.'[145] It did not simply mean 'the expulsion of the English'[146] but of modern, western civilization. Gandhi also defined swaraj (or home rule) as 'self-rule or self-control'.[147] The idea of self-control is central to Gandhi's idea of both individual and mass expression of non-violence. It was Gandhi's political ethic. The other Gandhian ethic that was personal was Brahmacharya or practising sexual abstinence. 'Brahmacharya means,' Gandhi wrote in his autobiography, 'control the senses in thought, word and deed.'[148] Gandhi's 'experiments with truth' included synchronic (or parallel) practices of self-control in both public and private spaces.

In addition to the idea of love there exists a paradoxical vocabulary of strict regimentation of the self in Gandhi. The curbing of violence in the encounter with the world has to undergo a process of rigorous self-control, without which it isn't possible to launch a non-violent struggle. In Gandhi, unlike in Levinas, there is a huge emphasis on the preparatory mode of the self in trying to achieve a hospitable relationship with the other.

Towards a Politics of Friendship

The Khilafat question where Gandhi put his stakes behind the Muslims of India was an early act of risk-taking in politics by Gandhi. In a speech delivered in Calcutta in December 1920, Gandhi said:

> 'I have never forgotten Hume's frank confession that the British Government was sustained by the policy of "Divide and Rule". Therefore it is that I have laid stress upon Hindu Moslem Unity as one of the most important essentials for the success of Non-co-operation. But it should be no lip unity, nor bania unity, it should be a unity broad based on a recognition of the heart. If we want to save Hinduism I say for God's sake, do not seek to bargain with the Musalman—I have been going about with Maulana Shaukat Ali all these months, but I have not so much as whispered anything about protection of the cow. My alliance with the Ali Brothers is one of honour . . . Any bargaining would be degrading to us.'[149]

Gandhi found the perfect cause in the Khilafat to counter the British policy of divide-and-rule with his grand gesture towards the Muslims. Gandhi emphasizes here that the principal motive behind his support to the Ali Brothers in the Khilafat Movement is based on sentiment rather than politics. He did not think of extracting concessions for Hindus while offering his support to a Muslim cause. The preservation of religious sentiments is certainly one of Gandhi's concerns. But he realizes that politics is not a good (and reliable) way to secure protection. Sentiments alone can guarantee interreligious bonds.

Writing in *Young India* on 4 October 1919, Gandhi marks the acknowledgement of sentiments as an ethical duty:

> 'It goes without saying that it is the bounden duty of the Hindus and other religious denominations to associate themselves with their Mohammedan brethren. It is the surest and simplest method of bringing about the Hindu–Mohammedan unity. It is the privilege of friendship to extend the hand of fellowship, and adversity is the crucible in which friendship is tested. Let millions of Hindus show to the Mohammedans that they are one with them in sorrow.'[150]

If Hindus and Muslims, Gandhi reiterated on 25 February 1920 in *Young India*, could come together in 'common sorrow,' the 'common goal'[151] of a united nationalism could be achieved. It was a unique moment for Gandhi to pick up an issue dear to Indian Muslims and lecture the colonial state (that never lost an opportunity to arbitrate between Hindus and Muslims) on its duty to recognize the Muslim cause.

On 6 December 1919, Gandhi wrote in *The Bombay Chronicle*:

> 'They [Muslims] are struggling in respect to the Khilafat question on just grounds, and all Hindus and Parsis should share their sorrow. It is our duty to demonstrate to the British people, the King and responsible Ministers that we regard the sentiments of Mussulmans with respect and consider their cause just.'[152]

The politics of sentiment that registers the sorrow of a fellow-community requires public demonstration. In this, the question of justice becomes important.

Even two decades later, Gandhi airs the same views on this subject. Responding to a visitor's queries in Segaon (Sevagram), Gandhi writes in *Harijan* on 27 January 1940:

> 'My belief is unshaken that without communal unity, Swaraj cannot be attained without non-violence. But unity cannot be reached without justice between communities. Muslim or any other friendship cannot be bought with bribery. Bribery would itself mean cowardice, and therefore violence . . . I can disarm suspicion only by being generous. Justice without generosity may easily be Shylock's justice. I must, however, take care that the generosity is not done at the expense of the very cause for which it is sought to be done.
>
> I cannot, therefore, drop the idea of unity or the effort for it. But what is wanted is not so much justice as right action.'[153]

Gandhi re-emphasizes his commitment to Hindu–Muslim unity, but this time introduces the idea of justice after being provoked by the visitor. Justice is understood as a precondition to unity and has to be understood in political terms, as political justice.

Political justice is however a strange term. It is politics that postpones and prevents justice. How to achieve justice in politics *despite politics*? Justice is the desired culmination, or fulfilment, of politics, as much as it is the elimination of politics. To the idea of justice, Gandhi adds the word 'friendship'.

What is the relationship between friendship and justice? In *The Politics of Friendship*, Jacques Derrida asks with eloquent earnestness where the ground of friendship can be found:

> 'The friendship of a justice that transcends right [le droit], the law [la loi] of friendship above laws—is this acceptable? Acceptable in the name of what, precisely? In the name of politics? Ethics? Law? Or in the name of a sacred friendship which would no longer answer to any other agency than itself?'[154]

This echoes the underlying principle behind Gandhi's commitment to Hindu–Muslim friendship: The law of that friendship is above the law of politics. The holy grail of friendship, its objective, is friendship itself. In any realm, including politics, friendship is prone to temptations that may threaten to alter, degrade or snap it. The value of generosity and the idea of justice become guidelines on such occasions. The establishment of swaraj rests on the promise—the 'miracle'—of friendship.

Taking from his reading of Michel de Montaigne's famous essay, 'Of Experience', Derrida writes on the fundamental difference between law and justice: 'Law is not justice. Law is the element of calculation, and it is just that there be law, but justice is incalculable, it demands that one calculate with the incalculable'.[155] Derrida's 'law' can be read in any context, including Gandhi's, as the calculable law of politics. Gandhi is seeking a friendship with Muslims based on the possibility of justice which demands of him a generosity where bargaining and bribery have no place. The desire for unity cannot bypass justice, as much as the compass of justice must not turn away from the desire that inspires it. Gandhi is alert to add that justice in this case is an *act*, hence it involves, 'right action'.

In the case of the Khilafat, Ambedkar saw the movement as trying to side with the Amir. Ambedkar was tilted in favour of the republican movement by Atatürk (who ultimately abolished the caliphate in 1924):

> 'The Khilafat could not be saved simply because the Turks, in whose interest this agitation was carried on, did not want the Sultan. They wanted a republic and it was quite unjustifiable to compel the Turks to keep Turkey a monarchy when they wanted to convert it into a republic.'[156]

It is true that the Khilafat symbolized a conservative pan-Islamic movement out to salvage the Ottoman Caliphate after its power was undermined by Italy and Turkey's defeat in the First World War. Gandhi's terms of evaluation of a political context were always posed outside the dominant values of western modernity and Enlightenment thought. For him, the matter was not about the nature of government or rule. This was due to Gandhi's firm stand and suspicion against everything that the colonial West stood for.

Writing in *Navajivan* on 29 February 1920, Gandhi considers the political problems that have been raised in this matter:

> 'How are we concerned with Turkey? There is no limit to the injustices perpetrated by that country. What good will it do to the world to restore its tyrannical rule? A number of similar questions are raised.'[157]

Gandhi smartly shifts the question from the caliphate to the West and poses the problem differently:

> 'The Allies had accepted, and so had President Wilson, the principle that the boundaries of the different countries as they existed when the War started should remain intact, and that no country should be made to suffer by way of punishment. The Muslims want them to abide by this principle. They demand that the territories held by Turkey in August 1914 be restored to her, that Arabia and the holy places of Islam remain under the control of the Khalifa, and they say that they would not mind the Sultan being asked to furnish reasonable guarantees for the protection of his Christian and Jewish subjects, consistent with his dignity.'[158]

Gandhi didn't waste the opportunity to remind the West of its liberal principles. The caliphate was the papacy of the Muslims. The western powers wanted to dismantle the Ottoman Empire and divide it amongst them. Gandhi knew the cunning ways of the West, and sided with Muslim sentiments. If the monarchy could abide by the modern, democratic expectation of safeguarding the lives and rights of the minorities, it was a better option than allowing Turkey to fall into the hands of western imperialism. For Gandhi, the choice between a religious and a republican order of the modern state was superseded by the more immediate question of anti-colonial friendship.

Faisal Devji finds that Gandhi's idea of Hindu–Muslim friendship bases itself on a 'politics of prejudice'.[159] Devji defines it as a politics that 'constitutes a relationship that is not rationalized into interest through the state and its freedom of ownership or contract.'[160] Prejudice, as the prejudicial order of social relations, demands respect of mutual sentiments. It is not that Gandhi made a virtue out of prejudice, but he felt that it was better to keep it out of the political contract where mutual interests were involved and needed support. Speaking of Maulana Mohamad Ali in the context of the Khilafat, Gandhi said,

> 'He would evidently have us inter-marry and inter-dine if only by way of a beginning. If that is the radical transformation desired by him and if it is a condition precedent to the attainment of swaraj I very much fear that we would have to wait at least for a century. It is tantamount to asking Hindus to give up their religion. I do not say that it is wrong to do so, but I do suggest that *it is reformation outside practical politics*. And when that transformation comes, if it is ever to come, it will not be Hindu–Muslim unity. And what the present movement is aiming at is to achieve unity even whilst a devout Mussulman retains his faith intact and a devout Hindu his.'[161] [Emphasis mine]

The Gandhian recipe for the politics of friendship is to keep matters that need reform *within* the community *outside* the sphere of mutual cooperation. The persistence of prejudice can only be solved at a future time, be it interdining, intermarriage or even cow slaughter. But reform must be an internal process that a community must be allowed to undergo within its own time. It must not be confused with the time of politics. Anti-colonial politics is immediate and in the current time. It involves mutual peace and a combined effort to drive out imperial rule.

Devji sees in Gandhi's politics of friendship a sensibility of neighbourliness 'whose particularistic contiguity overrides all the implicitly universal rights of liberal recognition'.[162] This, I would argue, goes into the heart of Gandhi's ethical understanding of the political.

In *Hind Swaraj*, Gandhi marks the physical limits of an ethical community:

> 'I am so constructed that I can only serve my *immediate neighbours*, but in my conceit, I pretend to have discovered that I must with my body serve every individual in the Universe.'[163] [Emphasis mine]

In a speech at the missionary conference in Madras on 14 February 1916, Gandhi extends this perspective in the context of swaraj:

> 'Swadeshi is that spirit in us to the use and service of our *immediate* surroundings to the exclusion of the more remote.'[164] [Emphasis mine]

Gandhi's political ethics are based on a spatial and relational asymmetry. What is nearest to us deserves primary responsibility and efforts of friendship. The neighbourhood is the first site of concern. If universal principles serve the logic of imperialism, then Gandhi is not interested, irrespective of the political principles involved. This approach, Devji explains, leaves out the third party, in this case, the state as a 'neutral arbiter'[165] of any contractual relationship. What you have, Devji says, is 'a fraternity of subjects'[166] instead of institutional intervention based on liberal universalism. This fraternity may also expand concentrically across space, with Hindus throwing in their support for the Muslim cause of the Khilafat, which is geographically located elsewhere, in Turkey.

Again, Gandhi outlined his approach in *Hind Swaraj*, maintaining that Hindu–Muslim quarrels have 'been often due to the intervention of lawyers'.[167] He questioned the political motive of the British courts: 'Do you think that it would be possible for the English to carry on their government without law courts? It is wrong to consider that courts are established for the benefit of the people . . . If people were to settle their own quarrels, a third party would not be able to exercise any authority over them.'[168] Gandhi, writes Ajay Skaria, 'attacks the third party by questioning Pax Britannica' that meant 'the cornerstone of British rule'[169] for the colonizers. Gandhi also construes it as a general principal.

In politics, however, a non-violent risk is never without consequences. Gandhi had to withdraw the Khilafat movement when Muslims resorted to violence. In *Pakistan or the Partition of India*, Ambedkar not only registers Gandhi's failure, but also passes his judgement on Muslim action:

> 'The Musalmans were not in a mood to listen to the advice of Mr Gandhi. They refused to worship the principle of

> non-violence. They were not prepared to wait for Swaraj. They were in a hurry to find the most expeditious means of helping Turkey and saving the Khilafat. And the Muslims in their impatience did exactly what the Hindus feared they would do, namely, invite the Afghans to invade India.'[170]

Responding to queries on the Khilafat in *Young India* on 3 April 1924, Gandhi was a little on the back foot, conceding:

> 'It were impertinence for me, an outsider, to thrust my views on my Muslim brethren. It is a question which the Mussalmans must settle for themselves.'[171]

The Khilafat movement got complicated when a community of Muslims called the Moplahs perpetrated violence against Hindus in the Moplah uprising of 1921 along the Malabar Coast. The Moplah uprising (also called the Malabar or Mapplla Rebellion) involved the working class and peasant Muslims of Malabar.

The Moplahs or Mappllas were descendants of Arab traders who had settled there since the eighth century. During the reign of Hyder Ali and Tipu Sultan in eighteenth century Mysore, their successive invasions had weakened the social and political position of the caste Hindus (primarily the Namboodiris and the Nairs) and the Moplahs exploited the new-found dominance over their old masters, often indulging in violence against them.[172] This was also the period when large-scale conversions to Islam took place to break away from the exploitative nature of the caste hierarchy and to counter caste hegemony. After Tipu's defeat at the hands of the British, the caste Hindus (whom the British favoured) were back in power. The land settlement policies in Malabar put the Moplahs at a disadvantage. New tenancy laws contributed to uncertainties and material grievances in the socio-economic life of the Moplahs. T.L. Strange, heading a special commission in 1852, rejected reasons of agrarian discontent as the primary reason behind the Moplah revolt, and blamed it on the religious fanaticism stirred by the Ulema. Later, William Logan, the District Collector who was appointed Special Commissioner in 1881, made the observation that class discontent arising from economic disparities was exploited by the politics of religious fervour. E. Ismail sums up the 'cumulative factors' behind the upheaval:

> '[Agrarian] grievances, frustration among the Mappilas in general, suppression by the British raj, religious tension possibly generated by the incoming Islamic revivalist puritanic tendencies, the decline of Muslim primacy in trade and commerce and other economic activities in the region, and the deliberate negligence and marginalisation of Muslims in the sphere of governance and all political dealings.'[173]

The Khilafat Movement intercepted the Moplah upheaval. The Congress supported the grievances of the Moplahs, and a section of them in turn showed enthusiasm for the Khilafat-Non-Co-operation Movement. Gandhi and Shaukat Ali visited Calicut on 18 August 1920, where Gandhi spoke of Hindu–Muslim unity. But a few Moplah religious leaders dismissed Hindu–Muslim unity and swaraj as Hindu propaganda and turned the Moplahs away from the movement. By then, there were already incidents of violent confrontation between Moplah agitators and the police with the military finally being called in. Despite facing reverses with many deaths and arrests (with reports of excesses and state atrocities against prisoners), the Moplah rebels attacked government officials, police posts and Hindus (mostly landlords), and also indulged in acts of forced conversions. Hindus who were part of the rebellion turned against the Moplahs and sided with the military. Bipan Chandra understands the Moplah rebellion as communal politics intercepting class antagonism:

> 'The Mappila peasant uprising of 1921 against landlords and colonial authorities could be given a terrible communal twist by the mullas primarily because the class cleavage and antagonism in Malabar ran along religious lines—the rebellious (Muslim) Mappilas were tenants and their landlords and money-lenders Hindu.'[174]

The movement was clearly ideologically diffused and complicated, being anti-imperialist, anti-landlord and, at a certain stage, turning anti-Hindu. It is difficult to offer (and accept) neat, singular ideological defences or critiques against the Moplah rebellion. It is however possible to conclude from the details that the element of religious supremacism inserted by the Ulema into the minds of the Moplahs caused anti-Hindu feelings to override economic issues and derailed the movement by making it excessively divisive and violent.

Writing an impassioned witness account of the rebellion in *New India* on 29 November 1921, Annie Besant wrote about how 'bitter hatred has arisen there, as fighting men from the dragon's teeth of Theseus.'[175] She blamed 'the preaching of Gandhism'[176] for the gruesome violence.

Ambedkar made a hurried and narrow reading of the Moplah rebellion, highlighting the religious angle alone to vindicate his thesis on Pakistan.[177] He also made the charge that Gandhi 'never called the Muslims to account even when they have been guilty of gross crimes against Hindus.'[178] Ambedkar indicted Gandhi for not reacting adequately against the 'blood-curdling atrocities'[179] of the Moplahs. He said Gandhi was 'obsessed by the necessity of buying Hindu–Muslim unity' and was 'prepared to make light of the doings of the Moplahs and the Khilafatists'.[180] To prove his point, Ambedkar quoted the prominent Hindu religious figure of the 1920s, Swami Shraddhanand (real name, Lala Munshi Ram, till 1917). In his weekly journal, *Liberator*, Shraddhanand wrote in July 1926 that he had accompanied Gandhi to the Khilafat session in Nagpur where the Quran was read with references to jihad and kafir. Shradhanand warned Gandhi that this went against the non-violent ethos and might turn against Hindus, but Gandhi brushed it off jokingly, 'They are alluding to the British Bureaucracy'.[181]

Contrary to the impression that Ambedkar draws from one-sided sources, Gandhi's response to the Moplah violence was sharp but measured. In *Young India*, 8 September 1921, Gandhi made an emphatic statement against Moplah violence:

> 'We must not betray any mental or secret approval of the Moplahs. We must see clearly, that it would be dishonourable for us to show any approval of the violence. We must search for no extenuating circumstance. We have chosen a rigid standard for ourselves and by that we must

abide. We have undertaken to do no violence even under the most provoking circumstances. Indeed we anticipate the gravest provocation as our final test. The misguided Moplahs have therefore rendered a distinct disservice to the sacred cause of Islam and swaraj.'[182]

Gandhi spelt out the Moplah atrocities in the language of his sentiments:

'My heart bleeds to think that our Moplah brethren have gone mad. I am grieved to find that they have killed officers. I am grieved to think that they have looted Hindu houses leaving many hundreds of men and women homeless and foodless. I am grieved to think that they have endeavoured forcibly to convert Hindus to Islam'.[183]

During the incidents of forced conversions, political aims and religious designs converged in a devious manner. Gandhi was not reluctant to name the problem. He addressed the issue, we shall see later, in Noakhali as well.

In an interview to the *Daily Express* (Madras) on 15 September 1921, Gandhi acknowledged 'Moplah lawlessness is a thing which takes one back, but I do not think that it seriously interferes with the Hindu–Muslim unity.'[184] He said, 'Future historians will have to note'[185] the intentional reluctance of the British administration to stop the Moplahs from gathering arms and indulging in violence, and instead using the Moplahs for their own 'base ends'.[186] To the journalist's question, if apart from the British administration's failure to keep the Moplahs from being violent, Gandhi's own movement had equally failed to make peace with the Moplahs, Gandhi replied:

> 'I cannot say that it has failed owing to my movement. My movement started not twelve months ago and against heavy odds, Government laughing, my own people laughing. It was most difficult for me to make them understand the word "non-co-operators". No reformer has been so hampered as I am. I know that the difficulties are all of my own making, but I had no choice.'[187]

This is a telling remark by Gandhi. It explains the extraordinary arrival of the idea of non-violent non-cooperation in India's political context. Both British imperialists in power and Indian nationalists probably found the idea of a non-violent movement a joke, a comic relief amidst the serious business of the anti-colonial struggle. It was against political common sense. You win or lose in history by going through the trial of violence. The suggestion that you could aim for victory by non-violently forcing power to take you seriously was a historical novelty no one was willing to take seriously.

For Gandhi, the idea mattered more than its reception. 'To believe what has not occurred in history,' Gandhi wrote in *Hind Swaraj*, 'will not occur at all is to argue disbelief in the dignity of man.'[188] There is a history of war and power, and a history of 'soul-force or passive resistance'.[189] The trace of the latter kind of history can't be found in the former, just as one can't 'expect silver-ore in a tin-mine.'[190]

It was too early to write it off due to an initial setback. The idea of non-violence was Gandhi's attempt against the established idea of history. However, such a politics has to first contend with the laughter of historical disbelief that greets it.

The *Daily Express* reporter asked Gandhi another question: 'Don't you think that the whole of the Moplahs are under the control of the religious leaders and not of the political?'[191] The reply to this question is significant:

> 'True; that is why I have brought religion into politics. I have endeavoured and endeavoured very successfully to make these religious pandits understand that they cannot exist without the political life of the country affecting them; otherwise the largest part of theirs goes out of their control.'[192]

Gandhi reveals what lies behind the famous proclamation in his autobiography that those who think religion and politics have nothing to do with each other miss the point about the task of religion in modern times. Religion-makers, or those who invent, guide and control the public life of religion, must be made to understand that religion cannot exist without, or outside, politics any longer. If religion-makers fail or refuse to accept the political question at stake, it will come back to haunt them. Gandhi is trying to drive home the point that in order to serve religion, you must serve politics.

This is not a perspective seeking to religionize politics, but to politicalize religion. To religionize politics is to place it under the influence of religion or let religion dictate its course. Unlike what many unthinking opinions have suggested, Gandhi is *not* doing that. To politicalise religion the Gandhian way is to engage with religion politically, and preventing religion from being used for the harmful objectives of modern politics. Gandhi was political about religion in the sense that he acknowledged a new ethic must be produced to address modern sensibilities and newer challenges to the neighbourly and overall political life of the community. But the ideological motivations of politics using religion to suit its deceptively secular ends must be resisted and critiqued by invoking ethical resources from within our spiritual traditions.

By inciting the Moplahs to violence against the Hindus, the Ulema succumbed to petty religious rivalries and derailed the movement for economic rights. They failed to understand two contrary things: the political motive of the colonial government in destabilizing the movement, and the genuine nationalist attempt to forge Hindu–Muslim unity. Mindless violence turns a movement on political demands into a law-and-order issue and fails to empower the community. The second half of Gandhi's reply clarifies his point further:

> 'Here is a disturbance going on. I could have taken one of the Ali Brothers and quelled it in no time if the Government system had been honestly administered. If we had failed it would have cost us our lives. We would have been killed. It would have been nice for the Government and for us; but when we died, out of our ashes the spirit of non-violence would have risen.'[193]

It was in the interests of the colonial government to allow violence to spill over and ensure the defeat of the Khilafat Movement. Religious communities, Gandhi believes, need to understand that non-violence serves the articulation of their political interest. In order to realize it, however, Gandhi proposes what Faisal Devji has convincingly argued as *the politics of disinterest*.

Any politics of friendship between Hindus and Muslims needs to be based on an uncompetitive, or 'disinterested relationship'.[194] Against the politics instituted by the colonial regime that demanded contractual relations based on rational interests (promoting constitutional arrangements like separate electorates), Gandhi wanted Hindus and Muslims to make a concerted move towards building sentimental ties where their political and social needs and ambitions don't get jeopardized by religious rivalries. The 'liberal regime of contending interests',[195] Devji understands, can contribute to a mature political relationship. This, I would argue, is a theoretical contention. The real nature of this colonially tinged liberal framework binds Hindus and Muslims into a competitive politics that keeps their relationship embittered. *The limits of liberalism lie in its management of politics through representation.*

A constitutional framework of power-sharing, maintained by a rational, juridical order, doesn't obliterate the problems of history. It leaves intact social acrimony, religious prejudice and the violence they produce. Gandhi's proposal for disinterested sentiments as a means to forge a politics of friendship is meant to bridge what liberalism fails to address.

Mexican poet–critic and essayist Octavio Paz's insight on Gandhi's politics of religion is strikingly similar to Devji's:

> 'In an impious century such as ours, the figure of Gandhi is almost a miracle. Within him, opposites merged: action and passivity, politics—the most naked form of the appetite for power—at the service of a religion of disinterest.'[196]

Paz locates the crux of Gandhi's politics of resistance as a non-violent confrontation against power where the binary modes of action (as active and passive) are dissolved to produce a new act of resistance. This is Gandhi's unique contribution to the history of resistance in the twentieth century. The other unique aspect of the Gandhian movement that Paz draws our attention to is how he brings politics and religion together by making the desire for power non-competitive (by assuring a politics of friendship).

The Arya Samajists

Swami Shraddhanand came into the political limelight for leading the protests in Delhi against the anti-Rowlatt Act of 1919 when the British government made acts of civil liberties punishable by law. It earned him the rare privilege of addressing a huge crowd at Delhi's Jama Masjid in March 1919. Writing on Shraddhanand's assassination in his *Autobiography*, Nehru recollected impassionedly:

> 'Nearly eight years earlier, he, an Arya Samajist leader, had stood in the pulpit of the great Jama Musjid of Delhi and preached to a mighty gathering of Muslims and Hindus of unity and India's freedom. And that great multitude had greeted him with loud cries of *Hindu–Musalman-ki-jai*, and outside in the streets they had jointly sealed that cry with their blood.'[197]

Nehru endorsed that euphoric moment, and praised Shraddhanand's character without any critical remark on the controversial nature of his political life:

> 'Always I have admired sheer physical courage, the courage to face physical suffering *in a good cause*, even unto death .

> . . His tall and sturdy figure, wrapped in a sanyasin's robe, perfectly erect in spine and advanced years, eyes flashing, sometimes a shadow of irritation or anger at the weakness of others passing over his face—how I remember that vivid picture'.[198] [Emphasis mine]

Even though Shraddhanand left politics in 1917, he took part in Gandhi's non-cooperation movement. Belonging to the Arya Samaj, he was also part of the Hindu Sangathan, and played a major role in the *shuddhi* movement. Shuddhi involved the reconversion of underprivileged caste Hindus and untouchables into the Arya Samaj, which was started in the late nineteenth century by Swami Dayanand Saraswati. The movement was a response by Hindu reformists to Christian missionary activities of proselytization, soon after the famine that swept across the United and Central Provinces between 1897 and 1900.[199] Shraddhanand also took up the issue of untouchability reform, but wanted it to remain outside the political domain, and not be part of Congress activity. Ambedkar showered high praise on Shraddhanand's involvement in the reform programme. Referring to Shraddhanand in his long series of essays published in 1945, *What Congress and Gandhi did to the Untouchables*, Ambedkar wrote: 'The Swami was the greatest and the most sincere champion of the Untouchables.'[200]

Shraddhanand's role in the shuddhi movement eventually curtailed his initial interest in Hindu–Muslim unity. The publication of *Dai-i Islam* (*The Missionary of Islam*) in 1923 by Khwaja Hasan Nizami (who belonged to the Chisti Islamic Order) spurred Shraddhanand to write *Muhammadi sazish ka inkishaf* (*Exposing the Muslim Conspiracy*) in 1924, and *Alarm bell arthat Khatre ka Ghanta* (*Alarm Bell or the Hour of Danger*) in 1925, published by the Hindu Sabha.

Nizami was one of the custodians of the Nizamuddin Dargah in Delhi. In his autobiography, Nizami talks about his pilgrimage to Hindu religious sites, including Ayodhya, Benares, Bodhgaya and Rishikesh among others.[201] He wrote a biography of Krishna, *Krishan biti* (later editions, *Krishan katha*), where Nizami, Mercia Hermansen explains, tries 'establishing parallels to Muslim religious and theological symbolism'[202] to help build associations for his Muslim audience. For instance, Krishna is 'a guide [hadi] and avatar'[203] and is compared to Moses, while Yashodha is compared to Asiya, the wife of Pharoah. Krishna and Radha are treated as symbols of love ('ishq') which Hermansen reads as Nizami's 'strategy' to turn divine Hindu figures into universal principles in a rather similar mode to what his opponents among the Arya Samajists were doing.[204]

Despite these gestures to foster cultural affinities, Nizami took on the responsibilities of the Tablighi Jama'at (society of preachers) in response to the shuddhi movement by Shraddhanand and the Arya Samajists that included attempts to reconvert 'recently converted Muslim castes in India to the Hindu fold.'[205] The alleged large-scale conversion of Hindus during the 1921 Moplah/Mapilla rebellion provoked an immediate response from Arya Samajists who intensified shuddhi activities in the Malabar region.[206]

Nizami rallied against what he considered, in Hermansen's words, a 'threat of assimilation and the loss of Muslim identity'[207] posed by the reconversion movement by the Samajists. The question of re/conversion led to the drawing of battle lines between Shraddhanand and Nizami, two important figures who were earlier involved in concrete efforts to forge sociocultural ties between Hindus and Muslims. The idealism towards Hindu–Muslim unity was short-circuited by concerns of numerical power. Communal politics under the colonial regime became a politics of numbers. Conversions further complicated it.

Conversions were not just a religious, but a political matter. Colonial modernity had an impact on Hindu reformers and Muslim religious leaders alike. For the Hindu reformists in particular, it was a unique predicament as the Hindu faith had no concept of, or allowance for, conversion. The concept of shuddhi, a ritual of purification that Arya Samajists like Shraddhanand propagated, was resented by the Sanatanis, the orthodox Hindus who did not favour reform. Christophe Jaffrelot has emphasized how the Arya Samajists deployed a paradoxical strategy of 'emulation' and 'stigmatisation' towards the Christian West in particular, and attributed a 'mimetic dimension' to their reform of Hinduism by applying 'the values of its Western opponents.'[208] The dual response of emulation and stigmatization explains the logical nature of this encounter.

In Dayanand Saraswati's book written in 1875, *Satyarth Prakash* (*The Light of Truth*),[209] he raises logical questions (and offers logical contradictions) against his own as well as other religious traditions. He upholds the Vedas and rejects parts of the Puranas and Shastras. The values and claims in these ancient Hindu texts are accepted and rejected by offering analogies from science and medicine. Saraswati rejects caste through rational arguments, as a system that hindered the flowering of human (and individual) aptitude.

Modern knowledge systems were welcomed as sources that helped a wholesome development of life. Saraswati counters and even ridicules the claims in the Bible (both Old and New Testaments) on the idea of God, Moses and Christ. The logical strain doesn't always live up to the metaphoric and symbolic language of the text he quotes from.

What Jaffrelot suggests is probably not the most historical in Saraswati's line of argumentation. The advent of the Protestant Reformation through Calvinism in sixteenth-century Europe that led to what Max Weber called the 'rationalization of the world'.[210] It had a particularly huge impact in the religious sphere in the West and, via colonialism, led to reformist movements in colonies like India. The Brahmo Samaj emerged in early nineteenth-century Bengal, repudiating Hindu customs that were regarded superstitious. Peter van der Veer writes that Rammohan Roy (1722–1833) ultimately 'replaced Christian universalism with Hindu universalism'.[211] The Arya Samaj rejected 'image worship' as part of its reformist zeal, which Veer describes as 'an apologetic response to Protestant criticism of primitive idolatry'.[212] Veer also makes the important correlation between the West and colonies in the East that in both cases 'the emergence of a public sphere is crucial for the problematic of nation and religion.'[213]

Apart from the time lag between western and Indian modernity, their societies faced two different sorts of political predicaments. The British colonial machinery in India went hand in hand with the Christianizing mission. This double infringement on political and social life produced a unique situation and form of antagonism. Since what constituted ideas of life and society in the early colonial period were mostly centred on traditional beliefs, the political zone of reception and response was also obviously produced from within this sphere. It was not just a challenge of ideas and beliefs but also one that took place under a new sociopolitical space of urbanity. The birth of the city coincided with the coming of new (secular) institutionalized structures (for instance, modern courts of law) that began to govern life and social relations. These were clear impositions on earlier forms of collective life. A new meaning of tradition emerged within an atmosphere of loss and contestation with cultural modernity. The public sphere emerged as a new site for fierce debates and clashes that initiated the re/formation of faith. Western modernity did a historical dis/favour to Hindus by turning a faith consisting of diverse traditions and belief-systems into a single institutionalized religion. Modern Hinduism was born of a conflict between Christian missionaries and Hindu reformists (with Muslim religious figures playing a middle role in the game). In fact, the denial of a religious status to Hinduism by European Indologists, British colonialists and missionaries alike dictated the very form of reform by Hindu revivalists. All this contributed to what Gauri Viswanathan calls 'the systematization of disparate traditions'[214] in India, marked by diverse tendencies. The Christian missions, Jaffrelot points out, 'shared an aversion to Hinduism, with its idolatrous polytheism and caste system—the very antithesis of individualist values.'[215] Individualism was a newfound value in the West, post Calvinism and the coming of the Protestant ethic. Idolatry and polytheism were more likely a problem for monotheistic rationality, while caste was a system of prejudicial hierarchy that harmed groups as much as individuals. Even though matters are religious, the encounter is political. The larger point is that the double challenge of colonial and missionary power is the reason why modern Hinduism in its diverse forms was bound to be political in one way or the other.

Not all trends, however, took a distinct nationalist form. Jaffrelot contends that the Arya Samaj did *not* become 'a proponent of Hindu nationalism', though he adds that 'its ideological characteristics . . . became one of the first crucibles of Hindu nationalism.'[216] This is a complex and contested issue I shall address shortly.

An ideological shift and precipitation in the thinking of the Arya Samaj may be traced to Shraddhanand's 1926 book, *Hindu Sangathan*: *Saviour of the Dying Race*. In this book, Shraddhanand's earlier concerns regarding Hindu–Muslim relations (and unity) were replaced by the pamphleteering of history that accentuates the religious divide. Extensively using a text on medieval India, written from a purely communal perspective by Chintaman Vinayak Vaidya (1861–1938), a Marathi-language critic and writer, Shraddhanand focuses solely on narratives of religious antagonism: plunder, forced conversions of Hindus and demolition of idols and temples (apart from enforcing economic and other hardships) by Muslim rulers of different ethnicities as strategies of Islamic dominance, and mass conversions by Christian rulers assisted by missionaries from Portugal and England. Even though Shraddhanand identifies cruelty and deceit against Hindus as the norm during these regimes, he concedes that the practice of untouchability and the caste system also weakened Hindu society.

India's medieval history has been a matter of contestation and debate among historians. The following passage by

Raziuddin Aquil sums up the nature of the ideological divide:

> 'Most influential, pluralist and left-oriented scholars deny the existence of any religious struggles between Hindus and Muslims prior to British rule. For them, Hindu–Muslim identities are modern constructions that did not exist in pre-colonial or early-modern India. However, alongside, there has existed a "separatist" Muslim scholarship with its rigid assumption that Hindus and Muslims are two different "nations", and that their separate histories may be traced back to Muhammad bin Qasim's conquest of Sindh. Not surprisingly, there also exists another stream of scholarship with an overt pro-Hindu tinge. The basic premise in the literature produced by this group is that medieval India under Islamic rule, characterized by the large-scale destruction of temples and the constant humiliation of Hindus, was a dark phase in the otherwise glorious history of Hindu civilization. Dubious as the above propositions are, it goes on to conclude that many of the "evils" facing Hindu society today are a legacy of Muslim rule.'[217]

These ideological distortions of community history and their relations are either evasions based on ideological denials or colonially manipulated legacies of communal confrontations. If historical scholarship becomes motivated and indulges in omissions and exaggerations, historical literature will fall short of truth and its reception will be mired in shallow squabbles. Raziuddin Aquil refers to the 'sanitized version'[218] of medieval Indian history by secularists. He mentions how, for instance, the 'defensive, secular scholarship ignores' authoritative texts (by Amir Khwurd, Abdul Haqq Muhaddis Dehlawi, Abdur Rahman Chishti and Ghulam Sarwar) that underline the role that Sufis played in 'conversion and Islamization' and 'declare that the Sufis were never interested in the propagation of Islam.'[219] Aquil also talks about the secular brigade of historians refusing to register 'ulama sodality taking part in shaping the character of political Islam'.[220]

Aquil directs our attention to the responsibility that secular historians have in their treatment of Islam in pre-colonial history. Historical antagonisms can't be sorted out by ignoring or hiding them. Fear of communalism and majoritarianism can't dictate silences. If historical truths have to be skirted to ensure peace, it is clearly false peace. History has no responsibility for hiding them.

Hindus and Muslims competed politically as communities under the colonial regime and got nationalized since the late nineteenth century. This does not mean that they did not exist earlier as distinct communities of faith. It was only after the advent of the British that these distinct communities got homogenized into a singular identity.

Bipan Chandra, however, makes one distinction clear between the pre-colonial and the modern: 'Communal antagonism was not a problem inherited from the past . . . Communalism is not only *in* the present; it is *of* the present. It did not serve, nor does it now serve, the past or decaying social groups and formations.'[221] There might have been Hindu–Muslim quarrels before the British arrived, but that can't be equated with the modern form of antagonism we call communalism. Communal politics is a modern ideology fostered by the competitive logic ushered in by the colonial regime.

Deepening of Conflict

In a long article published in *Young India* on 29 May 1924 ('Hindu–Muslim Tension: Its Cause and Cure'), Gandhi wrote that he found Dayanand's views on Hinduism 'narrow', and *Satyarth Prakash* a 'disappointing' book from a 'great reformer'.[222] He wrote that Dayanand 'unconsciously misrepresented Jainism, Islam, Christianity and Hinduism itself.'[223] Gandhi felt that Dayanand 'succeeded in enthroning idolatry'[224] by trying to prove that all scientific discoveries were already contained in the Vedas. Despite being dismissive of his thoughts, Gandhi thought that Dayanand was a man of 'grand and lofty character'.[225] In a similar vein, Gandhi found Shraddhanand's speeches 'often irritating' and his manner 'hasty and easily ruffled'.[226] Though he believed that Shraddhanand was 'intrepid and brave' and genuinely wanted Hindu–Muslim unity.[227] Gandhi was however categorical about the shuddhi movement as well as the tabligh. In a section titled 'Shuddhi and Tabligh', Gandhi first takes up the Arya Samajists:

> 'In my opinion, there is no such thing as proselytism in Hinduism as it is understood in Christianity or to a lesser extent in Islam. The Arya Samaj has, I think, copied the Christians in planning its propaganda. The modern method does not appeal to me. It has done more harm than good. Though regarded as a matter of the heart purely and one between the Maker and oneself, it has degenerated into

> an appeal to the selfish instinct. The Arya Samaj preacher is never so happy as when he is reviling other religions.'[228]

In contrast to the practice started by the Arya Samajists he considered un-Hindu propaganda, Gandhi finds the idea of conversion permissible only as a deep test of moral enhancement:

> 'The real shuddhi movement should consist in each one trying to arrive at perfection in his or her own faith. In such a plan character would be the only test. What is the use of crossing from one compartment to another, if it does not mean a moral rise?'[229]

Referring to the shuddhi movement launched in early 1923 (and which continued until 1927) among the Malkana Muslims by the Arya Samajists[230] led by Pandit Madan Mohan Malaviya, Gandhi said:

> 'If the Malkanas wanted to return to the Hindu fold, they had a perfect right to do so whenever they liked. But no propaganda can be allowed which reviles other religions. For that would be negation of toleration. The best way of dealing with such propaganda is to publicly condemn it. Every movement attempts to put on the cloak of respectability. As soon as the public tear that cloak down, it dies for want of respectability. I am told that both Arya Samajists and Mussalmans virtually kidnap women and try to convert them.'[231]

Next, Gandhi turned his attention to Nizami's *Dai-i Islam*:

> 'I have read his pamphlet from cover to cover. It gives detailed instructions to preachers how to carry on propaganda. It starts with a lofty proposition that Islam is merely preaching of the unity of God. This grand truth is to be preached, according to the writer, by every Mussalman irrespective of character. A secret department of spies is advocated whose one business is to be to pry into the privacy of non-Muslim households. Prostitutes, professional singers, mendicants, Government servants, lawyers, doctors, artisans are pressed into the service. If this kind of propaganda becomes popular, no Hindu household would be safe from the secret attention of disguised misinterpreters (I cannot call them missionaries) of the great message of the Prophet of Islam. I am told by respectable Hindus that this pamphlet is widely read in the Nizam's dominions and that the methods advocated in it are extensively practised in the Nizam's dominions. As a Hindu I feel sorry that methods of such doubtful morality should have been seriously advocated by a gentleman who is a wellknown Urdu author and has a large circle of readers. My Mussalman friends tell me that no respectable Mussalman approves of the methods advocated. The point, however, is not what the respectable Mussalmans think. The point is whether a considerable number of Mussalman masses accept and follow them.'[232]

It will be interesting to compare Gandhi's views with those of Maulana Mohamed Ali who presided over the 38th annual session of the Congress at Kakinada in 1923. Ali spoke about the shuddhi movement by referring to German Indologist Professor Max Muller's idea that it is the spirit of truth behind conversion that raises it to the 'rank of a sacred duty.'[233] He said that if there were 'evidences of a missionary zeal in the activities of my Hindu brethren'[234] he was not against their conversion programme. Mentioning the Malkana case, he put the onus of sacred duty on the Muslims with a gentle caveat meant for the Hindus:

> '[If] the Malkana Rajputs are in reality so unfamiliar with Islam as to be taken for Hindus, Musalmans must thank Hindu missionaries for so forcibly reminding them of their own duty to look to the conditions of millions of Musalmans whose knowledge of Islam is as defective as their practice of its rites is slack.'[235]

Ali acknowledged the reality of a new era of 'competing types of culture in the world', each with its 'spirit of propagandaism'.[236] He hoped that the world was past the days of the Spanish Inquisition, and no one thought of 'abolishing heresy by wiping out the heretic'.[237] Ali saw conversion as a progressive option, and held that people were free to choose their faith by exercising their 'power of rational choice'.[238] He condemned the 'fanatical Moplahs' for 'forcibly depriving some Nairs of their tufts of hair indicating their Hindu faith'.[239]

Friendship and Propaganda

Gandhi received the news of Shraddhanand's murder in Guwahati. In his speech at the AICC meeting on 24 December 1926, he informed his audience that in response to his telegram asking about Shraddhanand's health, his son had assured Gandhi that 'Dr Ansari was looking after him with solicitude.'[240] Probably provoked by what he read or heard, Gandhi remarked, 'if a Mussalman thinks that Abdul Rashid did well he will be disgracing his religion.'[241]

Speaking two days later, Gandhi narrated how Shraddhanand's male servant had initially refused to admit Abdul Rashid (who came on the pretext of discussing religion with his intended victim) into Shraddhanand's chamber as he had orders from his physician, Dr Ansari, 'to allow no interviews so long as Swamiji was seriously ailing.'[242]

The relationship between Shraddhanand and his Muslim doctor was part of the everyday, fraternal history that Gandhi formulated in *Hind Swaraj*. It also meant that communal sentiments did not disturb intimate relations and personal trust. The communal mindset in India lives by this pathological distinction between private and public, individual and group, when it comes to people from other communities.

Everyday history lies buried in the pages of history without becoming history. Rashid interrupts that buried detail of everyday life with a murderous act that provides the lens—becomes the norm—for judging the strife-ridden relations between Hindus and Muslims.

In *Pakistan*, Ambedkar took up the murders of prominent Hindu leaders like Swami Shradhanand, Lala Nanakchand, Nathuramal Sharma and Mahashay Rajpal. He focused his criticism on Gandhi, with the accusation that he 'never protested against such murders', and instead of not condemning 'these outrages' and calling upon 'leading

Muslims to condemn them', he 'kept silent'[243] on Muslim atrocities on Hindus. Ambedkar alleged that in order 'to preserve Hindu–Muslim unity' Gandhi 'did not mind the murders of a few Hindus'.[244]

These are nasty allegations, but they are grossly untrue. Savarkar also alleged that Gandhi 'rationalised' the crime against Shraddhanand and remained 'ambivalent', remaining kinder to Muslims than Hindus.[245] Ambedkar's thinking and motives were different from Savarkar's. He wanted to stress upon the failure of the Gandhian project to bring unity among Hindus and Muslims to establish his logical belief that political realism alone can determine the fate of the Hindu–Muslim relationship.

Mahashay Rajpal was murdered on 6 April 1929, for his satirical pamphlet *Rangila Rasool* on Prophet Muhammad. Muslims found the pamphlet derogatory. So did Gandhi. Writing in *Young India* on 19 June 1924, Gandhi described the title, 'highly offensive'.[246] He further wrote: 'Abuse and caricature of the Prophet cannot wean a Mussalman from his faith and it can do no good to a Hindu who may have doubts about his own belief . . . I am aware of similar abuse by Mussalman sheets. But that is no answer to or justification for the Hindu or the Arya Samaj abuse.'[247]

Gandhi was forthright in his message to the Muslim community on Shraddhanand's murder. On 30 December 1926, he wrote in *Young India*:

> 'Mussalmans have an ordeal to pass through. There can be no doubt that they are too free with the knife and the pistol. The sword is no emblem of Islam. But Islam was born in an environment where the sword was and still

> remains the supreme law. The message of Jesus has proved ineffective because the environment was unready to receive it. So with the message of the Prophet. The sword is yet too much in evidence among Mussalmans. It must be sheathed if Islam is to be what it means—peace. There is danger of Mussalmans secretly endorsing the mad deed. It will be a calamity for them and the world. There should be, on their part, unequivocal mass condemnation of the atrocity.'[248]

This is an unequivocal demand made on the Muslims. The shadow of political violence pursues the advent of Islam, as much as the birth of Christianity. But Gandhi distinguishes the spirit of Islam and Christianity from the violence surrounding their birth, and asks followers to recover it by their actions.

Gandhi's generalization that Muslims are 'too free' when it comes to violence disturbed some Muslims. Mazharul Haq, an advocate of Hindu–Muslim unity, felt that Gandhi's statement that Muslims were 'too free with the knife and pistol' promoted an unfair stereotype about Muslims in the midst of a communally charged atmosphere.[249]

Gandhi also made no bones about the social apparatus that promotes and provokes the ideology of religious hatred:

> 'Leaders . . . have not known to put a curb upon their tongues or pens. Secret and insidious propaganda has done its dark and horrible work, unchecked and unabashed. It is, therefore, we the educated and the semi-educated class that are responsible for the hot fever which possessed Abdul Rashid.'[250]

Gandhi is unwittingly making the point that freedom of speech and writing can also mean the freedom to express one's prejudice, and act violently through these mediums. Slavoj Žižek made the point in the form of a question: 'What if, however, humans exceed animals in their capacity for violence precisely because they *speak*?'[251] Human violence takes symbolic forms and as Gandhi rightly made the point, it is pedagogical violence, furnished by the educated class.

Apart from making misplaced allegations on Gandhi's silence on Muslim atrocities, Ambedkar also charged Indian Muslims for not speaking up against the murder of Hindu figures by Muslims in the name of religion:

> '[Whether] the number of prominent Hindus killed by fanatic Muslims is large or small matters little. What matters is the attitude of those who count, towards these murderers. The murderers paid the penalty of law where law is enforced. The leading Moslems, however, never condemned these criminals. On the contrary, they were hailed as religious martyrs and agitation was carried on for clemency being shown to them. As an illustration of this attitude, one may refer to Mr Barkat Ali, a Barrister of Lahore, who argued the appeal of Abdul Qayum. He went to the length of saying that Qayum was not guilty of murder of Nathuramal because his act was justifiable by the law of the Koran.'[252]

The point that Ambedkar is raising is an important one. Public condemnation of acts of religious violence is proof of a community's moral spine. The legal punishment of the crime doesn't solve the ethical issue that corrodes intercommunal relations. Acts of indifference contribute to the legitimacy of communal record-books that are used to whip up collective hatred for political gain. The reluctance, or refusal, to seek common grounds of solidarity with the other community damages the possibility of a shared life. In the long run, people also become immune to the tragedy of communal violence. In epic events of mass violence, the idea of reconciliation presupposes and pre-empts the idea of truth and justice. There is no truth and justice *outside* the gesture of reconciliation.

Ambedkar's argument aimed at Muslims is, however, exaggerated. Muslims in positions of power did raise their voices against violence committed by religious fanatics. At the Delhi session of the Muslim League in 1926, the chairperson of the reception committee, Muhammad Hussain, expressing his 'grief' on Shraddhanand's death said that he had lost a 'very old friend'.[253] He further said, 'The dastardly manner in which he was assassinated by a maniac must excite feelings of abhorrence.'[254] The League's president, Sheikh Abdul Qadir, ended his speech with an emphatic statement that Shraddhanand's killing 'deserves to be denounced in the most unmistakable terms', and that his murderer 'could not render a greater disservice to Islam or lend a stronger impetus to the Shuddhi propaganda than he has done by this foul deed.'[255] Qadir also requested Hindus to keep '*the general question of relations between the communities separate from this cowardly deed of a misguided individual*.'[256] [Emphasis mine] It was an important secular appeal to dissociate instances of communal violence from communitarian friendship.

Lala Lajpat Rai acknowledged the condemnation of Shraddhanand's murder by prominent Muslims and said, 'I have no reason to doubt their sincerity.'[257]

Savarkar's Hindutva

The proper origins of Hindu nationalism can be traced to the early 1920s. V.D. Savarkar's book *Hindutva*, written in an Andaman jail in 1917, was published in Nagpur in 1923, the same year as Nizami's *Dai-i-Islam*, and three years before the publication of Shraddhanand's *Hindu Sangathan*.

Ideas of a Hindu nation were solidified in the pages of Savarkar. *Hindutva* is obsessed with names and naming as a means to recover/recapture a pure historical identity and turn it into a political agenda. In the whole book, Savarkar invents a fantastic history of the Hindus. He constructs the origins of the Hindu–Aryan identity in an undated time that precedes even mythology, when Sindhu (the river) and Hindu (a people) become one in phonetic play. The historical origin of Hindu identity is strictly identified in Sanskrit and the Vedas. Savarkar, in a grand leap of historical imagination, dates the origin of the Hindu nation to the coronation of Ramchandra after he returned victorious from Ceylon, defeating Ravana in the epic battle described in the Ramayana. Savarkar considers Buddhism the first religion from India to aim for universality. This universal project of Buddhism brought other people into its sway and created a problem for Hindustan, according to Savarkar. The universal also entails dangerous encounters with foreigners who are a threat to the nation's sacred sovereignty. Buddhism's defeat in history was understood by Savarkar as a misplaced zeal that was undermined by two 'opiates':[258] universalism and non-violence. The defeat meant a blessing for India because Buddhism was trying to smuggle in foreign powers to rule India. The medieval period was quickly passed through (elaborated later in *Six Glorious Epochs of Indian History*, 1971). All Muslim rulers ('Arabs, Persians, Pathans, Baluchis, Tartars, Turks and Moguls') were part of a political force where religion was 'goaded on by rapine'.[259] Apart from delineating a history of condemnation, Savarkar is busy constructing a purist genealogy of identity by describing, 'What is a Hindu' and 'Who is a Hindu'. He tackles both questions by *positively* tracing back Hindu identity to the concepts of race (Aryan), religion (Hindu) and language (Sanskrit), and *negatively* against people they confronted—namely Muslims, Christians and the like. Savarkar's language is however not that of a historian, dispassionate and matter-of-fact. In a classic display of pathetic history, he tries to arouse the Hindu reader with a sense of ideological commitment to the idea of Hindutva that he propagates.

The words 'Hindu' and 'nation' (or 'nationalism') can't be taken separately to mean you can be Hindu, yet your idea of India (and your sentiments for it) can be inclusive, and not sectarian. If someone is a 'Hindu nationalist', the idea of India itself becomes Hindu, concentric to religion. Hindu India can't be India, though there can very well be people who are politically and religiously Hindus, belonging to—and propagating—their faith. These Hindus must acknowledge an India that also belongs to non-Hindus.

Just as Jinnah and his Muslim League associates used Islam as a political tool to make a separatist argument and demand Pakistan, the founding ideologues of the Hindu Mahasabha and the Rashtriya Swayamsevak Sangh (RSS) used the modern idea of Hindu religion[260] to define the nation in religious terms. There are sleight of hand arguments and shallow adjustments made to make one thing appear like an image of the other. Each thing loses its distinct property to become something else. Religious nationalism is a mass-injected alchemical phenomenon (that produces a fearful mass-spectacle). Identity no longer remains a fluid thing to explore, but a hard thing to protect and flaunt. There is nothing left to *think* about one's identity. It is hard to find a religious nationalist who explores the depth, contradiction and uncertainty of being someone in the world.

Jinnah's attempt at Muslim making and Savarkar's attempt at defining the Hindu, despite religious overtones, are fundamentally about religious *identity* and not religion. This identity in the name of religion is a modern cultural construction, where internal differences are erased in an effort to homogenize identity. The term 'culture' in the context of communal nationalism is not used in the anthropological sense but in the ideological sense. It is conceived and produced in communal factories abstractly as a basket of values, beliefs, mores and practices where things can be put in or left out arbitrarily, to suit the immediate, contemporary self-image of a community. This selective picture of culture is painted with a *political* motive: to unify people into a political identity that can claim a nation for itself.

In *Hindutva*, Savarkar repeats the most important formulation that separates him from the many other Hindu reformers who are wrongly associated with the Hindu nationalist project. In a section titled 'Common laws and rites', Savarkar writes: 'We Hindus are not only a Rashtra, a Jati, but as a consequence of being both, own a common Sanskriti'.[261] Peter Van der Veer writes exactly what this means: 'The argument for the term stresses that Hindus form the majority community in the country and that, accordingly, India should be ruled by them as a Hindu state (rashtra).'[262]

This is a crucial distinction between Shraddhanand's communal attitude towards Muslims and Savarkar's. Shraddhanand made noises, raised alarms and forwarded arguments that were communal in nature. It was a response to a communally charged atmosphere. Shraddhanand was in a competitive mode, complaining about Muslim communalism and situating its problem in Islam, but he did not extend it to furnish a political idea of a majoritarian nation–state. He did not offer a blueprint for an exclusivist Hindu nation. This *political* distinction is crucial to define figures like Shraddhanand who were Indian nationalists coming from a communal sensibility that did not preach exclusion of minorities. Shraddhanand can't be described as a precursor to the idea of Hindutva from his views. But Shraddhanand's imagining of the Hindu Sangathan as a communal body working for the fortification of communal identity can be a problem in itself. The history of his political and organizational activities must also be considered. The idea of communal self-preservation is the lowest denominator when it comes to imagining social relations. Communal organizations (belonging to majority or minority communities) that are political in nature are prone to propagating supremacist fantasies and that introduces a surreptitious presence of passive violence in the everyday mode of communal life.

It may not be enough to judge Shraddhanand guilty even if he was later eulogized by proponents of Hindutva who used his ideas as part of their own. The politics of appropriation in the case of the Hindu right works by the simple logic that any proof of communal sentiment is enough for someone to be part of the Hindu nationalist pantheon. This approach helps Hindu right-wing politics to invent its—unconvincing, often dubious—genealogy. Secular critics can't afford to play into the hands of the same logic.

It is necessary at this juncture to briefly mention two other important Hindu religious figures often misconstrued by secularist scholars as precursors to Hindu nationalism, Sri Aurobindo and Swami Vivekananda.

Aurobindo's Shift

Let me first discuss Sri Aurobindo (1872–50), whose views on Muslims and Hindu–Muslim unity underwent a certain shift between the early 1900s and 1920s. In June 1909, in 'Towards Hindu–Muslim Unity', Aurobindo writes 'political adjustments or Congress flatteries'[263] can't bring unity. 'It must be sought deeper down, in the heart and the mind, for where the causes of disunity are, there the remedies must be sought.'[264] Aurobindo held that 'mutual misunderstanding is the most fruitful cause' of Hindu–Muslim differences, and suggested 'better mutual knowledge and sympathy' to overcome it. Aurobindo also proposed that Hindus spread 'juster views'[265] on Muslims and Islamic civilization and equated 'national development' with 'harmonising'[266] communal life. In another piece written in November 1909, he welcomed the birth of the Hindu Sabha but criticized its 'lower and less powerful motive—rivalry with Mohammedan pretensions'.[267] Notice that Aurobindo poses the ethical approach to sort out communal differences in purely communal terms: It is only *through* the communal, *within* the communal sphere of things that the communal problem needed to be addressed and sorted.

If the meaning of secular transformation involves the negating and overcoming of the communal, what is Aurobindo proposing? Can it be considered secular?

We will shortly return to this question.

Referring to the Hindu reaction against the Morley–Minto Reforms (also called the Indian Councils Act) of 1909 when Muslims were granted separate electorate as demanded by the Muslim League, Aurobindo was emphatic about what he saw as a wrong priority:

> 'It is not by rivalry for Anglo-Indian favour, it is not by quarrelling for the loaves and fishes of British administration that Hinduism can rise into a unified and effective force.'[268]

Despite Aurobindo's abiding criticism of Gandhi and his methods, it is interesting how similar his words are to Gandhi's in *Hind Swaraj* on the same issue:

> 'There is mutual distrust between the two communities. The Mahomedans, therefore, ask for certain concessions from Lord Morley. Why should the Hindus oppose this? If the Hindus desisted, the English would notice it, the Mahomedans would gradually begin to trust the Hindus, and brotherliness would be the outcome. We should be ashamed to take our quarrels to the English.'[269]

On 18 April 1923, when Aurobindo was asked about Madan Mohan Malaviya and C. Rajagopalachari's response to the Multan riots, he said, in the future, 'the Hindus may have to fight the Muslims and they must prepare for it' and added that 'Hindu–Muslim unity should not mean the subjection of the Hindus.'[270] On 23 July 1923, Aurobindo dismissed Gandhi's ideal of Satyagraha by calling it a 'one-sided principle' that can't 'transform the spirit of violence' (which, for Aurobindo, was meant to 'spiritualize'[271] violence), something the old figure of the Kshatriya alone was capable of. When a disciple asked him next if non-violence was an effective method to ensure Hindu–Muslim unity, Aurobindo reacted sharply,

> 'But how is it possible to live peacefully with a religion whose principle is "I will not tolerate you"? How are you going to have unity with these people? Certainly, Hindu–Muslim unity cannot be arrived at on the basis that the Muslims will go on converting Hindus while the Hindus shall not convert any Mahomedan. You can't build unity on such a basis. Perhaps the only way of making the Mahomedans harmless is to make them lose their fanatic faith in their religion . . .'[272]

On 7 March 1924, in reply to a question, Aurobindo suggested that some new religious movement like Bahaism could alone help Muslims to 'remodel their religion and change the stamp of their temperament'.[273]

The shift in tone and attitude in Aurobindo on Muslims from 1909 to 1923 can be traced to the series of Hindu–Muslim riots that had been taking place since 1921. Aurobindo was surely aware of these episodes of violence in his Pondicherry ashram. On 18 May 1926, he commented:

> 'Look at Indian politicians: all ideas, ideas—they are busy with ideas. Take the Hindu–Muslim problem: I don't

> know why our politicians accepted Gandhi's Khilafat agitation. With the mentality of the ordinary Mahomedan it was bound to produce the reaction it has produced: you fed the force, it gathered power and began to make demands.'[274]

In Aurobindo's analysis of the Malabar Rebellion, the Khilafat Movement facilitated the political ambitions of Muslims by making them organize themselves as a power-group in the name of religion. They lacked a principle of tolerance. The 'ordinary' Muslim is prone to violence. There was a fanatical streak among Muslims that was detrimental to the cause of Hindu–Muslim unity. Conversion, Aurobindo thought, had to be allowed both ways to secure peace. He was clearly on the side of the Arya Samajists on the conversion issue. These views convey Aurobindo's communal streak, yet he did not propagate communal politics. He was not a votary of Hindu nationalism, or Hindutva.[275]

Vivekananda's Islam

The other Hindu figure often wrongly associated with Hindu nationalism by left ideologues is Vivekananda.[276] It is quite obvious that Vivekananda was a spokesperson of the Hindu religion. He had strains of communal superiority in his manner of seeing the world (of other religions) from a Hindu perspective, both admirably and critically. But this does not make him a proponent of Hindu nationalism or even a precursor to its ideology. Nehru mentioned him admiringly in long passages of *The Discovery of India*.

Vivekananda, as a modern religious reformer and thinker, did not shy away from the questions or challenges that his religion faced in the new world. Even though he pursued a certain philosophical approach (and a clear preference for Vedanta), there were eclectic strains in Vivekananda. He was not a systematic thinker. Indian thinkers, religious or political, weren't formally trained into a school of thought. They must be interpreted differently. In Vivekananda's case, one usually finds an animated tone of language. Whenever he made broad remarks on religions (his own and those of others), he often indulges in a rhetorical dialectic of praise and condemnation. He was a master of hyperbole. It is well known, and often quoted, that Vivekananda praised Hindus as a tolerant race and saw India as a land that provided home to people fleeing persecution. While the former is understood as a stereotype, the latter comment has a measure of truth if you consider the Zoroastrian Parsis fleeing to India from Iran in the seventh century after the Arab conquest of Persia. In the famous 11 September 1893 Parliament of Religions speech in Chicago, Vivekananda said that he was 'proud' to belong to a country 'that has sheltered the persecuted and the refugees of all religions and all nations'.[277] Contrast this with the irony when in the World Hindu Conference held in Chicago in September 2018, to commemorate the 125th anniversary of Vivekananda's speech, the RSS chief Mohan Bhagwat said that Hindus were tolerant enough to 'recognise even the rights of pests to live', but warned of the risk of the unprotected lion 'if he is alone' being devoured by 'wild dogs'.[278] Vivekananda's source of pride was Bhagwat's reason for consternation. Bhagwat's use of the zoological metaphor takes him close to Golwalkar who describes the race spirit in *We or Our Nationhood Defined* (1939):

> 'Surely the Hindu Nation is not conquered. It is fighting on. Ever since that evil day, when Moslems first landed in Hindusthan, right up to the present moment the Hindu Nation has been gallantly fighting on to shake off the despoilers. It is the fortune of war, the tide turns now to this side, now to that, but the war goes on and has not been decided yet . . . The Race Spirit has been awakening. The lion was not dead, only sleeping. He is rousing himself up again and the world has to see the might of the regenerated Hindu Nation strike down the enemy's hosts with its mighty arm.'[279]

Golwalkar, who led the RSS from 1940 to 1973, went a step further than Savarkar's *Hindutva* to dream of an impending race war.[280] Like Savarkar, Golwalkar too admired the Italian nationalist, Mazzini, and 'German race pride'.[281] He used a zoological metaphor for defining the race spirit, and combined it with the idea of a Hindu nation. In order to eliminate Muslims, the race spirit must wake up from sleep. Golwalkar's lion reappeared in Mohan Bhagwat's Chicago speech reiterating the old political fable.

Vivekananda praised the principle of equality and brotherhood in Islam, while he condemned the cult of Islamic violence and forced conversions. There is a first-hand account by Vivekananda's German-born American disciple, Christine Greenfield (quoted by Govind Krishnan V.):

> 'Moguls seemed to have cast a spell over Swami Vivekananda. He depicted this period of Indian history with such dramatic intensity, that the idea often came to us that he was telling the story of his own past . . . We saw Babur, the twelve-year-old king of Ferghana, influenced

> by his Mongol grandmother, and living a hard rough life with his mother . . . Akbar was the undisputed master of India . . . Mohammaden though he was, he listened to teachers of all religions—listened and questioned . . . In later years he conceived the idea of establishing a new religion of which he was to be the head—a Divine Religion, to include Hindus, Christians, and Parsees as well as Mohammedans.'[282]

This is a crucial testimony to Vivekananda's attitude towards Muslim history in India. There seems to be an endearing sense of attachment with the personal history of the Mughal kings which is extraordinary. By describing filial and intimate details from the lives of those Muslim kings, Vivekananda attests a sense of continuity whose historical imagination seems similar to Nehru's.

His remarks on Islam and violence, in contrast, sound generalized and exaggerated without any context. In a speech delivered on the prophets of the world in California, on 3 February 1900, he said, 'Now, *some* Mohammedans are the crudest . . . and the most sectarian. Their watchword is: "There is one God, and Mohammed is His Prophet." Everything beyond that not only is bad, but must be destroyed forthwith . . . From the Pacific to the Atlantic, for five hundred years blood ran all over the world. That is Mohammedanism (Islam)!'[283] [Emphasis mine] In this oft quoted passage, the crucial word 'some' in the beginning is ignored by critics. Vivekananda's point is clearly against Islamic fanatics who believe in a ruthless and uncompromising monotheism. What Vivekananda says right after is left out in the politics of selective quoting:

> 'Nevertheless, among these Mohammedans, wherever there was a philosophic man, he was sure to protest against these cruelties. In that he showed the touch of the Divine and realised a fragment of the truth; he was not playing with his religion'.[284]

This makes it clear that *Vivekananda does not equate Islam with the violence of Islamic history.*[285]

In the same speech, Vivekananda also made the interesting remark: 'So, not any one of these Prophets is born to rule the world for ever. None has yet succeeded and none is going to be the ruler for ever.'[286] This is thinking beyond religions. Vivekananda adds: 'Will other and greater Prophets come? Certainly they will come in this world. But do not look forward to that. I should better like that each one of you became a Prophet of this real New Testament, which is made up of all the Old Testaments.'[287] Vivekananda's radically futuristic imagination foresees a time of religion *after* religion, after the prophets and their testaments have had their day and followers, and a prophetic individuality and radical freedom has emerged.

To conclude, I must go back to the distinction I am making between what can be construed as communal (communally Hindu, in this context) and Hindu nationalism, or Hindutva. There is a spectrum of communal thinking where all hues cannot be strictly identified with Hindu nationalism.

Negotiating Prejudice and Deceptions

The three figures I discussed above, Shraddhanand, Aurobindo and Vivekananda, despite being communal-centric in varying degrees, did not share or propagate views that can be identified with the fundamental tenets or motives of Hindutva. They were responding to the nature of the Hindu–Muslim conflict in social, religious and political zones *as Hindus*. If that made them appear communal-centric at times, it was because they looked at the political relationship between Hindus and Muslim through the frame of their religious identity.

To be communal-minded (or community-centric) is not to necessarily practise communal*ism,* which is a term for communal politics. Being communal does not logically translate into hatred for other communities. There can be communal love and friendship, as much as communal animosity or hatred. Communal critics can be considerate, or prejudiced. To adapt the popular saying, communal is that communal does.

Complaints regarding other communities, or an occasional negative portrayal, are ways of negotiating differences, which can often be political in nature. There is nothing necessarily—by design—sinister about them, unless they galvanize people into a politics of hate. People of all communities who grapple with their association with the nation have concerns they often see through an identitarian lens (or simply, the lens of identity). People can be community-centric yet desire social and religious harmony, and show (critical) respect for other communities and religions. Even those who are non-secular can seek harmony and show respect.

There is an interesting difference between those who are community-centric and those who consider themselves secular, distanced from any feeling of belonging or responsibility vis-à-vis their community is. Community-centric people may hold their own community and faith above—or more important than—that of others, and can yet be open to—and accept—difference. In fact, community-centric people evaluate difference by taking the prejudices of other communities seriously. They however often confront prejudice with counter-prejudice.

Secular members of a community tend to ignore the problem of prejudice altogether as they concentrate on what is *secularly* common in the social and political life and concerns of people from other communities. Prejudice remains unattended, hence unresolved, in the secular case. Secularists believe that secular education and the inculcation of secular principles is a verified antidote to the life and thinking of prejudice. This is a rationalist fantasy of the privileged left and liberal intelligentsia.

Being community-centric is not necessarily detrimental, or antithetical, to the wider ideals of a secular society, unless it works against the aspirations of a secular society and polity. In fact, some political leaders who were nonbelievers and had secular lifestyles viciously propagated communal politics.

Communalism, or communal nationalism, implies an ideological manoeuvre and commitment towards an ethnocentric politics. It involves a political expression that indicates an aggressive posture of a community against others, an othering in political and social terms, a rationalization of group interests and sentiments used for making political demands, and in its most desperate form, used as a lethal tool for political violence. In other words, communal politics is a shortcut to fascism. The demand for political submission and exclusion of minorities is fascist. It will be wise to have a clear and precise criterion to ascertain whether someone who's communal or community-centric has a fascist sensibility or tendency.

My criterion is this: Fascists understand sentiment as argument. Or, they don't understand an argument that is bereft of sentiment. This sentiment is of course group-sentiment. Sentiment is a special type of emotional attachment to a figure of love, or reverence, or both, which serves as a moral ideal. When political constructs like community and nation become imbued with sentiment alone, history itself becomes a sentimental issue. Modern sentiments rigidify feelings and emotions by leaving no scope for being critical, or satirical. If religion and ancestor/parental-worship were the first objects of sentiment, in modernity both individual and group sentiments fused into nation-worship. The extreme political form of this worship fuels majoritarianism, and leads to fascism. Fascism is deceptively secular in the sense that it is this-worldly, but instead of being critical of religion, fascism is sentimental about it. Fascism is also deceptively religious, in the sense that it uses symbols of religion to instrumentally serve the political idea of a (majoritarian) nation. The modernization of religion in a secular state has not simply led to religion being pushed to the private sphere. It has also created a rupture between the genuinely secular and the deceptively secular world. Religious reform movements (in India, for instance, the Brahmo Samaj, the Arya Samaj, the Aligarh Movement) were caught between the two tendencies.

Jesus said in the Gospels, 'You cannot serve God and mammon'. To fuse religion and nation is to invent a dangerous artifice. The evocation of religion is not about religion but religious nationalism, where a single religious identity seeks to dominate against others.

The Pathetic and the Factual

In a series of aphorisms written in 1981 under the title 'A time of eternal peace', the Finnish poet and aphorist, Paavo Haavikko, mentioned two kinds of historiography mediating on the relationship between war, power and history:

> 'Histories are of two kinds, the pathetic and the factual, and the function of the pathetic kind is to bring tears to the eyes so that the reader is blinded. When pathetic writers tell you such and such a horde destroyed such and such a village and such and such town, and such and such a little girl, or bear . . . the list goes on so long, that you begin to weep.
>
> And they harness these waters, harness you to pull the great waggon of history which is already on the road, and which will move on when you—yes, you whom history now summons—, take your place and begin to pull on the great rope, which is fitted over the branch of a tree in such a way that if the waggon does not move, it is stone,
>
> the harder you pull, the tighter the rope begins to twist, angled over the tree-branch it tightens around your neck, which is not yours, and you are told that the only way to stop stop stop it twisting around your neck is to pull harder and make the waggon move.
>
> That was a subclause. With every sentence, they say less than they leave unsaid. With every word, they leave more unsaid, listing villages, because that leads away from the facts, brings tears to the eyes. They know it. Otherwise they wouldn't. Soon they will write more, more, soon they will be speaking all the time, silent about everything.'[288]

Haavikko's description of pathetic history is reminiscent of victim-histories or histories of strife where one side plays the absolute victim against another.

The genocide of Armenians and Assyrians in 1915 by the Ottoman Empire, with thousands of Christian women and children converted to Islam by force, is an appropriate example with which to open the horror book of the twentieth century. It is followed by Nazi crimes against the Polish people in 1939 and again in 1941–42, and of course the mass extermination of Jews in Germany from 1939 to 1945. The Soviet Union's state murder of its own people in the Gulag from the 1920s to the early 1950s (till Stalin's death in 1953) was one of the most long-standing cases of killing millions sent to the detention camps and prisons in Siberia to undergo harsh labour and die as a method of Stalinist punishment. The bombing of Hiroshima and Nagasaki by America in 1945, to signal the end of World War II, was followed by the genocide of India's Partition in 1947, the genocides in Zanzibar (1964) and Guatemala (early 1980s), in the creation of Bangladesh in 1971, the Bosnian and Rwandan genocides in the early 1990s, and that of Rohingyas in 2016.

Is Haavikko a cynic, telling us one shouldn't indulge in writing on these horrors? No, Haavikko is telling us something else. These horrors have been addressed in journalism, literature and history. The critical point is about *recreating horror* through the writing of what Haavikko calls pathetic history. It is a kind of narrative history that is peppered with excessive sentimentality. Pathetic history does double damage. It manipulates the experience of pain by exacerbating it and extracts the most exasperating and limiting aspects of that pain. It also does not allow us to address the everyday history of structural violence and how it can be manipulated sometimes to feed a sinister logic of genocidal violence. The mass character of political violence is rooted in historical and sociocultural narratives of animosity and prejudice. These matters need us to think harder.

The communal history written in modern India by communally-inclined nationalist historians, who can also be untrained non-historians, indulge in pathetic history. These writings tend to excite ethnic and religious emotions in the reader and demand alliance and complacency. They seek to extract emotional bias, make reading an act of commitment to communal sentiments. Other factors related to reading history: objectivity, weighing facts judiciously, wider social and political vision, an ethical sense, critical consideration and judgement regarding aspects of belonging and affectivity, become irrelevant, and meant to be set aside.

Pathetic history has a paradoxical intention: to numb and excite. Numb the reader of any higher ethical and moral sense, and excite the senses at a primordial, animal level. Such an experience, if successfully manipulated by the writing, can have devastating effects. Pathetic history treats readers like wet cloth and squeezes them dry.

Haavikko writes on the other—factual—history in less eloquent and a more matter-of-fact manner:

> 'Scientific history-writing involves a choice of facts and the ability to recognize them. It is produced industrially, because there is a requirement for it—a requirement, because this is war. And he who believes in scientific thought has already ceased, once and for all, to be a thinking person.'[289]

This history is written by professionals. Haavikko does not praise it, or hold it on a higher pedestal vis-à-vis the pathetic kind. Rather, he notes the stakes involved in this history: an ideological necessity against political opponents. The irony is that—and Haavikko's piece is a masterstroke of ironies—the scientific view of history is also at war with other viewpoints. The scientific standpoint in history—from Auguste Comte to Marx—is not neutralist, detached. It is political as it involves, or serves, the ideological project of modern historiography. Scientific ideas challenged religion as new ideas of human beings and human freedom were emerging.

Isaiah Berlin reminded us in his essay 'On the Concept of Scientific History' that since the scientific father of modern philosophy, Descartes, did not take history seriously, historical studies 'laboured under the stigma of Cartesian condemnation'.[290]

Marxism responded to the challenge by discovering 'laws' of history based on universal stages of class struggle, developing political and economic theories that offered a blueprint of a socialist or communist society, even arguing the establishment of what French socialist Pierre-Joseph Proudhon in his famous 1840 work (in the original French), *What is Property?*, called 'scientific government'.[291] We know there is a non-scientific side of Marxism too, which combines both humanist and anti-humanist traditions of thought, explaining the historical nature of class exploitation and class power and how it illuminates our perspective on human labour.

There is a fierce and ethically credible argument for the justice of equality. Social morality remains a mere rhetoric (and justification) of power without equality.

The knowledge of universal humanity propounded by the Enlightenment was found wanting by the discourse of class society. This is precisely Marxism's anti-humanist critique of humanism. It is however significant that this critique introduced a reductive element of defining and explaining societies in scientific terms. The rational side of human beings was alone held valid and valuable, and the 'irrational' side (prejudicial, religious, spiritual, given to passions) was condemned as backward, reactionary and an impediment to progress. This approach that treated the human being as a progressive tool based on rational/scientific knowledge made an ass of itself by inventing a rational fiction. The most decisive violence this did to the understanding of human beings and human societies has been the refusal to accept contradictions, and treat all deviations to the rationalist norm, ruthlessly. Capitalist rationality based on free-market profit and exploitation was one side of the coin.

Nicanor Parra poetically summed up the symbolic lie (the deceiving sign) of American capitalist imperialism in these words: 'United States: the country where / liberty is a statue'.[292] The other side was communist rationality that hinged on dictatorial cruelties to ensure ideological deference. Tagore's *Letters from Russia* (written during the poet's visit to Russia in 1930) described the Soviet state's overshadowing of culture in the name of collective life as the 'shadow side of the moon'.[293] Poets have the uncanny precision to sum up in a few words what would take pages for philosophers and political theorists to prove.

The credible power of rationality and objectivity in the name of modern, progressivist history used as ammunition to critique, tamper or discredit historical voices and events that are away from the line is no longer credible. Contradictions persist with an increasingly legitimate claim that the suppression of contradictions to superficially overcome the structural violence of societies is equally brutal. Slavery was barbaric, and all forms of civilized life in history, Walter Benjamin wrote, are 'a document of barbarism.'[294] To add to this grim picture, political regimes across ideologies—imperialist liberal-democracies, communist regimes, Islamic theocracies—have indulged in war. Carl Schmitt's argument in *The Concept of the Political* (1932) that constitutional democracy does not clearly identify the enemy like fascist and communist politics is ideologically true. But in *actual* history, this distinction did not prevent democracies from going to war. You can't avoid war—in the name of territory, other people, sheer 'interests' —and the necessity to win it. Even the victims of history are caught in the power game. And why not, the victor and the (once) loser, both want to win the war. All wars are fought in the present, often in the name of the past, to re/conquer, secure the future.[295]

In a small series of aphorisms written in 1972, Haåvikko wrote:

> 'When history lectures, fools still make notes. Though there's the street outside. Events, not trends.
>
> The big moment is when the oppressed becomes the oppressor. That's when history takes a deep breath and starts lecturing.'[296]

Haavikko is telling us that it is about time history stops showing off its authority. The claim of knowing the past better is no longer a guarantee of knowing the present better. The past tense of history is no longer reliable. Things are happening at a rapid pace. The world is changing incomprehensibly. We need to pay attention to the immediate changes around us, rather than keep harping (and depending) on historical trends. The street outside is full of meaning, and there is no meaning outside it. The present alone has the power to alter everything, turn history upside down.

The modern communist Greek poet Yannis Ritsos (an active member of the Greek Resistance during World War II, who suffered detention in prison camps by the military junta in power after a coup in 1968) writes in 'The End of Dodona I' (6 October 1968):

> 'Now,
> They've turned everything upside down—altars,
> churches, graveyards. The bones
> thrown out in the alley. They've even chopped down the
> sacred oak—our counselor.
> We no longer have anyone to ask for advice, to confide
> in. Arces
> circulates in the marketplace with his bloodied axe belted
> to his waist'[297]

Ritsos imaginatively juxtaposes the dark time in modern Athens with Dodona's in ancient Greece.[298] It describes images of a lawless destruction of meaning. This happens when madness take over history.

When history is taking place, you don't need history. History is meant for the time of relative peace, when you have time to reflect and make connections, theorize trends. When the oppressed becomes the oppressor, history has been turned upside down. It is time to learn what time is telling us of the oppressor, the oppressed, and their changing roles in history. It is time to follow Gandhi to Noakhali, Calcutta, Bihar and Delhi. We are about to embark on that difficult journey.

The map of Noakhali District in East Bengal, showing Gandhiji's walking tour is reproduced from *Harijan*, 23-2-1947. The map shows the first part of the tour completed on February 4, at Sadhurkhil and the second part ending with February 25 at Haim Char. The dates on which Gandhiji stayed in each village are given below:

Srinagar	5th February	Kafilatali	12th	Char Dukhia	19th
Dharampur	6th	East Keroa	13th	Char Larua	20th
Prasadpur	7th	West Keroa	14th	Kamalapur	21st
Nandigram	8th	Raipur	15th and 16th	Char Krishnapur	22nd
Vijoynagar	9th and 10th	Debipur	17th	Char Soladi	23rd
Hamchadi	11th	Alunia	18th	Haim Char	24th and 25th

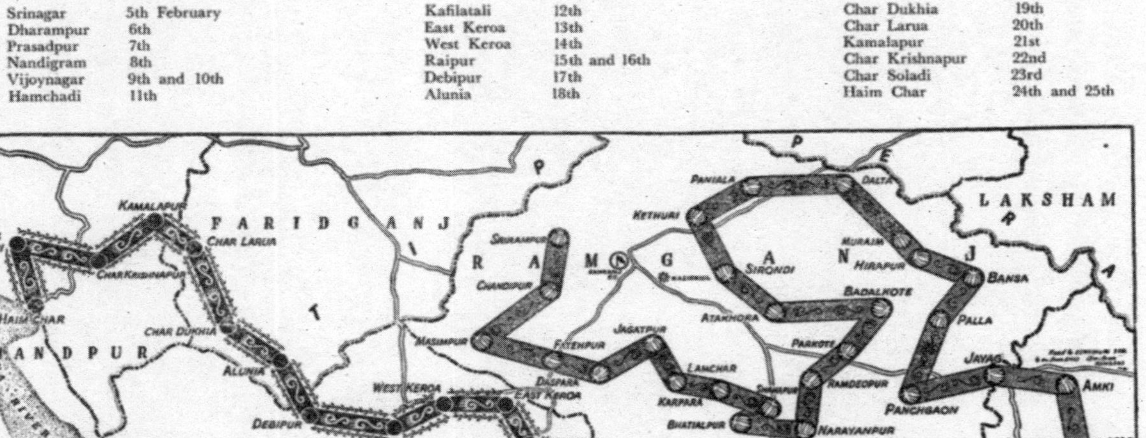

Courtesy : *The Hindustan Standard*

Source: *CWMG*, Volume 87, 1983, opposite page 32, Navajivan Trust

1

'To Die a Beautiful Death'

Gandhi wrote in a letter from Delhi to Chimanlal N. Shah on 21 October 1946:

> 'Bengal is calling.'[1]

In another letter on the same day to Harihar Sharma, Gandhi wrote:

> 'I have your letter. There is art in dying also. As it is, all die, but one has to learn by practice how to die a beautiful death. The matter will not be settled even if everybody went to Noakhali and got killed.'[2]

Gandhi's aesthetic of death involves an idea of praxis. In order to die beautifully, one has to perfect a certain mode of living. The mere event of people dying in Noakhali won't do justice to the cause, Gandhi seems to suggest, if a particular form of dying isn't achieved. Gandhi makes a demand, premised on a certain idea of practice, on those who are risking death in Noakhali.

That Bengal was calling was not just a piece of news that Gandhi shared with Shah. He was telling Shah of his own calling. It was about Gandhi's inner voice.

In a discussion on 13 January 1933, with George Joseph,[3] a Syrian Christian activist from Kerala who raised the question to Gandhi of what he meant by 'Inner Voice', Gandhi explained the 'Inner Voice . . . is a voice *other than our own* . . . Inner Voice is a power beyond us but it is not an outer force.'[4] [Emphasis mine] In May (8–29) and July (16–23) 1933, Gandhi undertook two fasts to draw attention to the condition of the untouchables and to obtain privileges from the British government. Explaining the 'voice' behind the former fast, Gandhi wrote in July 1933 in the *Harijan*:

> 'For me the voice of God, of Conscience, of Truth or the Inner Voice or "the still small Voice" mean one and the same thing. I saw no form. I have never tried, for I have always believed God to be without form . . . The night I got the inspiration, I had a terrible inner struggle. My mind was restless. I could see no way. The burden of my responsibility was crushing me. But what I did hear was like a Voice from afar and yet quite near. It was as unmistakable as some human voice definitely speaking to me, and irresistible. I was not dreaming at the time I heard the Voice. The hearing of the Voice was preceded by a terrific struggle within me. Suddenly the Voice came upon me. I listened, made certain that it was the Voice, and the struggle ceased. I was calm.'[5]

This is a heteronomous force at work. For Immanuel Kant, autonomy (of the will) is 'the ground of the dignity of human nature and of every rational nature.'[6] (Notice how human and rational is treated as synonymous, rationalizing the meaning of human) Autonomy, Kant writes, is the only permissible force that establishes the moral law, and any action not in accordance with it is '*forbidden*'[7]. To submit to heteronomy is owing allegiance to a power that works to the detriment of the self's moral and political agency and freedom. Autonomy is regarded as the legitimate and universally applicable source of a rational subject. The rational cult of autonomy treats the idea of heteronomy as a danger, a dangerous lure for the rational will. In Kantian terms, the act of listening to (and acting upon) a force outside yourself is succumbing to unfree laws and temptations that compromise sovereignty.

If rationality is supposed to singularly define the freedom of the self and enable it to make choices, these choices are conditioned and limited not by the law of freedom but rationality, which isn't the same thing. Freedom is not a predominantly rational gift or a gift of rationality alone. Reason is not a dependable guide to relationality, to how we make, unmake and understand relations in the world. Reason comes into play regarding self-centric concerns, which are an important part of the self's well-being. But it is not the source for affectivity and relations (that include both thought and feeling).

Heteronomy, in the Levinasian sense, is a force born from the other direction, from the direction of the other which calls for an asymmetrical relationship of reciprocity with a real person, and not merely an idea or a thing[8]. It involves a risk that is unknown to reason. The *forbidden* act in Kant imagines what is forbidden both within and outside, in other words, the forbidden other. If the philosophy of reason forbids acting towards—or being under the influence of—other people, ethics on the other hand is the promise of alterity, this real and risky encounter.

The act of listening to a voice is not a rational act. *The voice has no resemblance to the voice of reason.* If reason demands justifications for an act, hearing is its own justification. Gandhi invites us to imagine another origin that is more speculative, and less categorical. Gandhi listening to his 'small, still voice' is able to open his ears to the peasants of Kheda, to the needs of the untouchables, to the victims of intercommunal genocide in 1946–47. It is surrender to a commandment. The authorial voice from within appears from a source that comes from an intense state of 'hearing'.

In the letter to Sharma, Gandhi dramatically phrases what is at stake for him in Noakhali: to die beautifully. The 'art in dying' is a matter of cultivation, an aesthetic practice. It involves, in Gandhi's context, an intimate association with the politics of non-violence: to face death at the hands of others by resisting without violence. This unique predicament, in Levinas's words, is 'the resistance of what has no resistance—the ethical resistance.'[9]

The final act of Satyagraha is risking death. Gandhi describes this act as 'love-force, soul-force', which he clarifies, is 'more popularly but less accurately, passive resistance.'[10]

Resistance is not wholly understood as pure negativity, or pure positivity. Gandhi was aware of the philosophical paradox of this non-violent act, negotiating political violence: Satyagraha was in its negativity a non-doing, or an undoing of a certain kind of politics, a refusal to act violently under provocation. While it was by its very act of doing so—a positivity, an expression of one's presence in the world, of confronting violence with concrete acts of non-violence. One can understand this paradox of negativity and positivity further, through Gandhi's assertion of self-control and love. Self-control was a negation of activity while love was its positive side, its desire and appeal, the positivity that propelled it. Gandhi's sense of ethics lies within this double pull of withdrawal and expression. To withdraw in order to express, to express by withdrawing, is the paradoxical mode of Gandhi's ethical politics.

To recollect Paz's insight, Gandhi's act of resistance dissolves the active/passive binary. It confronts a situation of 'securing rights by personal suffering' which, Gandhi added, 'involves sacrifice of self'.[11] It is an act of securing by sacrifice. Crucial in this Gandhian economy of sacrifice is what lies *between* securing and sacrificing: a method of political action. There is no choice between violence and death, one must choose the latter. Resistance is faced with the promise of leaping across multiple hurdles: you resist one thing to gain another, even if that mode of resistance fails to achieve what is sought. Failure is a triumph of method. Failure is the infinite possibility of non-violent sacrifice. Gandhian ethics is means-to-an-infinite-end.

Playing at Civil War

Gandhi invokes the possibility of death because Noakhali had recently seen genocidal violence. There is gloomy pessimism in Gandhi's anticipation that it won't be enough sacrifice and the end of violence *even if everybody went to Noakhali and got killed.* Violence and the sacrifice of violence are both endless possibilities in the world.

Gandhi pointed out on 23 October that Sheikh Saheb Hisam-ud-Din, former President of the All India Majlis-e-Ahrar, issued two separate public statements condemning the murder and forced conversions in Noakhali. Gandhi reiterated the importance of Sheikh Saheb's statements,

> 'The value of these statements lies not so much in the numbers of Muslims supporting it, but in the fact that these Muslims of undoubted repute in Islam have no hesitation in condemning in unmeasured terms the nefarious deeds of the Muslims in East Bengal.'[12]

In a prayer meeting in Delhi on 24 October, Gandhi admonished the men for creating a scene that made the women in the audience leave. He remarked that it was an ironic demonstration, considering their empathy for outraged women in East Bengal. Gandhi said that his statement that women would have done better to commit suicide than experience dishonour was misunderstood. He clarified that he was not against them carrying weapons for self-defence, but that it wouldn't work if the odds were overwhelming. In that case, he had suggested, taking recourse to poison was better than submitting to dishonour. Gandhi made the argument (paraphrased in Pyarelal's 'Weekly Letter'): 'Their very preparedness should make them brave. No one could dishonour a woman who was fearless of death. They had two ways of self-defence —to kill and be killed or to die without killing. He could teach them the latter, not the former. Above all he wanted them to be fearless. There was no sin like cowardice.'[13]

At first glance, Gandhi's clarification doesn't seem to improve or change the perception that he preferred suicide for women facing the horror of rape. On closer reading, he seems to be saying two things that are connected but can be taken separately. On the one hand, Gandhi seems to be emphasizing that in situations where you face radical violence, you must be *prepared* for death. To be prepared to die is a state of bravery where you become fearless. To fear is to lose the battle in advance, and proof of cowardice. This can be an ethic of courage not restricted to a premodern culture, but can be meaningful for people with modern sensibilities facing violence in our times.

There is, however, another side to Gandhi's argument. His use of the word 'honour' comes uncomfortably close to an ethic of chivalry that connects it to medieval ideas of honour and ownership. It provokes certain questions: Why—and for whom—is sexual dis/honour of a woman a matter of life and death? Is sexual humiliation a permanent state of dishonour? The harping on dis/honour adds a patriarchal burden to the ordeal of humiliation. If a woman is sexually humiliated, does she lose moral resources to live? Does her voluntary death become a mark of bravery that purifies the humiliation?

There is a slippage between the personal and the communal. A woman's humiliation affects the community, so it is a matter of affective ownership. Modern sensibility based on autonomy and freedom does not subscribe or aspire to this gendered law of belonging to a community. It is true that self-defence doesn't work when confronted by brutal power. Life's options against such power are limited. To act out of vulnerability and confusion, trying to protect oneself with the means at hand is not a sign of cowardice. The strength of vulnerability lies in the ability to survive humiliation and heal its scars. Gandhi's discourse of honour does not leave women with the right to live with their humiliation freely, from within the depths of their horrifying experience.

A month earlier, at the prayer meeting on 2 September after reaching Delhi from Sevagram, Gandhi was still making the lost argument on the Muslim League not abiding by the principles of Islam in its non-cooperation with Hindus. Taking the violent events in Calcutta into account, Gandhi added:

> 'I have said a good deal about communal unity. Unlike the abolition of salt tax this cannot be achieved by a stroke of the pen. The Ministers will have to stake their lives for it. If I had my way I would not let them seek military or police help. Well, if Hindus and Muslims must fight each other it is better they bravely do their fighting themselves. So long as we depend on the British for protecting us, true freedom will not be ours.'[14]

Gandhi invokes the figure of the idealist politician, or government representative as the best arbitrator or negotiator of peace in a communal conflict, rather than men in uniform. He is not innocent about the politician's role (as we will see), but is airing his democratic expectations. Military peace is not a genuine, long-lasting option.

On 9 September, in response to a question Gandhi said,

> 'We are not yet in the midst of civil war. But we are nearing it. At present we are playing at it. War is a respectable term for goondaism practised on a mass or national scale.'[15]

Gandhi could see where the Calcutta killings were headed. He could read the political pulse. It was, in his estimate, going to be something more messy and mischievous than a war. He had been warning everyone, Jinnah most importantly, to come to their senses. When leaders aren't in their senses, they can't read the outcomes of their in/actions. Gandhi also had a clear-headed view regarding the various strands of politics around him battling for power. He was also forthright about it. In reply to questions posed by the presidents and secretaries of various Provincial Congress Committees who had assembled in Delhi for the All India Congress Committee (AICC) session held on 23 and 24 September, Gandhi said:

> 'Today there are all sorts in the Congress. That is why I have suggested the removal of the words "peaceful and legitimate" from the Congress objective. That need not mean abandonment of truth and non-violence by Congressmen. The object is only to purge out hypocrisy. It jars. Let those who believe in the doctrine of the sword openly avow it. To take the name of non-violence when there is [a] sword in your heart is not only hypocritical and dishonest but cowardly.'[16]

On 9 July that year, Gandhi had spoken his mind at the AICC session in Bombay of 'the danger within'.[17] He warned against 'smug satisfaction'[18] that came from Congress members suffering prison sentences, and competing for posts during forthcoming elections. The two ends of a satyagrahi's life were 'the slaughterhouse even as that of the spotless lamb.'[19] Gandhi next asked: 'Who is responsible for the mad orgy in Madura and, coming nearer, in Ahmedabad? It will be folly to attribute everything evil to British machinations.'[20] The Congress had rejected the British proposal for an interim government that led to rioting in Madura, a place in the south, where five people died and a few sustained injuries.[21] On 1 July, the Jagannath Rath Yatra in Ahmedabad resulted in communal clashes where two men, one Hindu and the other Muslim, were killed.[22] The Congress was in power in both these provinces after the January 1946 elections.

Gandhi was categorical on the Muslim League position:

> 'The Muslim Leaguers have today raised the slogan that ten crores of Indian Muslims are in danger of being submerged and swept out of existence unless they constitute themselves into a separate State. I call that slogan scare-mongering pure and simple. It is nonsense to say that any people can permanently crush or swamp out of existence one fourth of its population, which the Mussalmans are in India . . . Therefore, those who want to divide India into possibly warring groups are enemies alike of India and Islam. They may cut me to pieces but they cannot make me subscribe to something which I consider to be wrong.'[23]

This preconceived fear—whatever its justifications—comes with a solution: the need for a state for Muslims, where only a handful of Muslims can be accommodated, and the rest will be thrown into the jaws of Hindu majoritarianism. The solution is clearly aimed at creating a rival nation where multiple fears (fears of the Hindu minority in Pakistan, and the Muslim minority in India) will be left to their fate. Gandhi's fears for both Hindus and Muslims were proved right.

Jinnah's partial fear for the Muslim community got worsened by his decision. Jinnah may have been good at legalese, but he was terrible at history.

Gandhi next took on the communists:

> 'The question of the Communists stands on a slightly different footing. They seem to have made trouble-making their profession. I have friends among them. Some of them are like sons to me. But it seems *they do not make any distinction between fair and foul, truth and falsehood.* They deny the charge. But their reported acts seem to sustain it. Moreover, they seem to take their instructions from Russia, whom they regard as their spiritual home rather than India. I cannot countenance this dependence on an outside power. I have even said that we should not depend even on Russian wheat in our present food crisis. We must have the ability and courage to subsist on what our soil can give us rather than depend on foreign charity. Otherwise, we shall not deserve to exist as an independent country. The same applies to foreign ideologies. I would accept them only to the extent that I can assimilate them and adapt them to the Indian scene. But I must refuse to go under them.'[24] [Emphasis mine]

Gandhi was referring to 1942. Indian communists (then, mainly comprising the Communist Party of India, CPI) stayed away from the Quit India Movement that was launched on 8 August 1942 at the Bombay session of the AICC by Gandhi in the thick of World War II, where he declared the famous slogan, 'Do or die'. Rudrangshu Mukherjee puts the communist response in perspective that bolsters Gandhi's complaint:

> 'The CPI was officially against the Quit India movement. What needs to be emphasized here is that this decision of the CPI was not based on any understanding of the Indian situation by Indian communists. The opposition

> to the clarion call of 1942 was the outcome of a diktat emanating from Moscow. When Hitler attacked his erstwhile ally, the Soviet Union, in 1941, the fight against Nazism became a People's War for all communists overnight. The directive from Moscow was carried by Achhar Singh Chinna, alias Larkin, who travelled from the Soviet Union to India with the full knowledge of the British authorities. In India, it meant that communists had to isolate themselves from the mainstream of national life and politics and see British rule as a friendly force since the communists' 'fatherland', Soviet Russia, was an ally of Britain.'[25]

By withdrawing support for a rejuvenating moment of the anti-colonial struggle to suit Soviet Russia's cause and to the detriment of India's, the CPI clearly behaved like a satellite party. This was the precise problem of communist internationalism in that era. An Indian communist party didn't mind losing its intellectual sovereignty and self-respect to its ideological bosses in another part of the world whose history, society and political culture were radically different. Sumit Sarkar lays out the context in a more supportive manner:

> 'After six months of hesitation and internal debate, the C.P.I. in January 1942 lined up with the rest of the international Communist movement in calling for full support to the anti-fascist "people's war" even while reiterating the standard Congress demands for an independence pledge and immediate national government (which were now considered as valuable but no longer indispensable preconditions for support).'[26]

Sarkar is offering a twisted defence of the CPI, and advancing a half-truth. The problem lay not with Indian communists supporting the Soviet Union in the war against Hitler, but rather in the compromise they were forced to submit to because of it vis-à-vis the Indian freedom movement. A few pages later, Sarkar acknowledges that the communist political line was out of sync with the national mood in 1942, but as a balancing act, he insists on a theoretical justification in favour of the CPI:

> 'What we have to understand are the deeper factors underlying the new popular mood of August 1942, which Gandhi certainly sensed and reflected *incomparably better* than the Communists with their theoretically not unjustifiable people's war line.'[27] [Emphasis mine]

Elsewhere, in an essay (responding to charges made on the CPI's role during the Quit India Movement by Arun Shourie in a series of articles in the *Illustrated Weekly of India* that year), Sarkar accepted that the communist line of 'People's War' was 'dubious and perhaps wrong-headed'.[28] Sarkar also mentions the significant detail that 'Savarkar, September 4, 1942, ordered Hindu Mahasabha members of local bodies, legislatures and services to "stick to their posts and continue to perform their regular duties."'[29] This was clear indication of the Hindu right's non-participation in the Quit India Movement.

In a letter from Panchgani on 30 July 1944, to the CPI General Secretary, P.C. Joshi, Gandhi reiterates the problem:

> 'I suggest that the title "people's war" is highly misleading. It enables the Government in India to claim that at least

> one popular party considers this as people's war. I suggest, too, that Russia's limited alliance with the Allied powers cannot by any stretch of imagination convert what was before an imperialistic war against that Nazi combine, into a people's war.'[30]

Apart from these two separate objections to the use of the phrase 'people's war' in the context of the war in Europe, Gandhi made a third one in the beginning of his letter. It is no guarantee, he argued, that if the Allied Powers won the war, it would boost the chances of the peoples of Asia and Africa fighting for freedom against colonialism. This was more than a logical argument, for Britain was a leading colonial power. The joint battle against fascist Germany and Japan was a matter of survival for the other European nations (compromised notoriously by Stalin in the Nazi–Soviet Pact of 1939). To imagine that collaboration with the British in its war would boost India's freedom because the war was being supposedly fought in the name of democracy for the whole world was ideologically wishful.

Also, why was India's freedom movement any less of a 'people's war' against imperialism than a world war fought by imperialist western powers? The problem lies in the assumption that the West stands for the universal emancipation of people, while the Indian freedom movement was specific to its own people. It can still be asked of such scandalous communist thinking whether an anti-colonial movement has less universal status in the emancipatory sense, compared to expansionist western powers going to war.

The Quit India Movement led to the leading men of the Congress—Gandhi, Nehru and Patel—getting arrested.

Gandhi was arrested for two years (9 August to 6 May 1944), and Nehru, three years (9 August to 15 June 1945). Nirad C. Chaudhuri makes a significant point on the political repercussion of these incarcerations:

> 'When the Congress leaders were in jail between 1942 and 1944 or 1945, and thus unable to influence political opinion in the country, two other parties which were free to carry on their activities had immensely extended their influence. These were, on the Muslim side, the Muslim League and, on the Hindu side, the Hindu Mahasabha, which was the political organization of the conservative and militant Hindus.'[31]

This observation was particularly true for Bengal as Janam Mukherjee notes, echoing Chaudhuri:

> 'With Congress leaders jailed and the organization in shambles, the Hindu Mahasabha, in particular, was able to gain a popular foothold in Bengal that had eluded them electorally.'[32]

Even as he prepared to go to these places, Gandhi kept giving statements on the riots in Calcutta and the Noakhali genocide. On 15 October, he said,

> 'During the recent blood bath in Calcutta, stories of Muslims having, at the peril of their lives, sheltered their Hindu friends and vice versa were recorded. Mankind would die if there were no exhibition any time and anywhere of the divine in man.'[33]

Such examples are often drawn to counter the overwhelming fact of interreligious strife. Every time they point to only one thing. Communal violence endangers those people within a community who can *dissociate their ethical responsibility* (coming from either religious, or secular sources, or a mix of both) *from their purely communal one.* The communal, in this sense, is not purely religious. It demands a violent action in the name of religious association that repels the ethical and moral sensibility of people (even as it excites those who like destroying morality in order to uphold political power). This is the reason why communalism and communal violence can't be easily blamed on religion. It is mass political violence by a community *in the name of* religious identity. That identity is always political, a religious identity used for political ends.

When Direct Action Day was declared, Jinnah was not the only person from the League who indulged in violent language. Other illustrious colleagues of Jinnah also aired what they had in mind. Pyarelal mentions Khwaja Nazimuddin, League leader from Bengal, saying in a press conference,

> 'There are a hundred and one ways in which we can create difficulties, especially when we are not restricted to non-violence.'[34]

Liaquat Ali Khan, speaking to the Associated Press of America said,

> 'Direct Action' meant non-constitutional methods that can take 'whatever form may suit the conditions under which we live.'[35]

A League leader from the North-West Frontier, Abdur Rab Nishtar (who was briefly in the Congress), went a step ahead and said that the shedding of non-Muslim blood couldn't be ruled out in the bid to achieve Pakistan. He added: 'Muslims are not believers in Ahimsa.'[36]

Jinnah's aversion to Gandhian methods ran deep and he spread it in the whole party. It was time to publicly demonstrate the idea of partition so far discussed and debated in closed rooms by the League with leaders of the Congress and British bosses. The historical and political claims made by Jinnah in the name of the Muslim community were not enough. Those claims had to be proven by a violent enactment of divisiveness to legitimize the demand for Pakistan. Khwaja Nazimuddin thought that non-violence introduced a lack of options. It placed too many restrictions on expressing oneself politically. Violence, on the other hand, could make a hundred flowers of expression bloom.

Jinnah had already argued the Muslim case by simultaneously endorsing the idea of Hindus as a nation (mentioned already, in the message to the Bombay Presidency Provincial Muslim League Conference in May 1940).[37] The Hindu right was, however, against the division of the nation, and the claim for Pakistan and declaration of Direct Action Day precipitated the difference between the League and Hindu right organizations.

The Killings Begin

The Great Calcutta Killings started on the morning of 16 August 1946. Suhrawardy (who was sworn in just four months ago, in April) and his colleagues in the League had already denounced the Cabinet Mission and made fiery speeches in the city demanding Pakistan. Keeping in mind his government's reputation, Suhrawardy asked for peaceful protests in a press statement on 7 August.[38] A few days later, he also declared 16 August a public holiday, arguing that it would help maintain public order. But it was clearly in solidarity with the Muslim League's call for 'direct action'.[39]

Suhrawardy's political background offers a good indication to his communal sensibility. When the 'United Muslim League' was formed in Bengal in 1936 to replace the provincial Muslim League (that had degenerated), Suhrawardy was one of its founding members. Before this move, during the Calcutta riots of 1936, Suhrawardy founded the Chamber of Labour, which he used as a platform to promote trade unions against communist labour organizations[40]. Joya Chatterji writes about Suhrawardy's communal propensities:

> 'It was in this period, when he defended the Muslims accused of crimes after the 1926 riots (including a notorious slum criminal) that Suhrawardy built up his connections with Calcutta's underworld.'[41]

Suhrawardy did something similar, and worse, in 1946. The other detail about him is interesting: 'Suhrawardy himself was hardly a pious Muslim. In the words of a contemporary acquaintance, he "was totally unscrupulous, but not communal or religious. He ate ham and drank scotch and married a Russian actress".'[42]

Being irreligious and communal at the same time suggests a rational distinction of the modern, political self where personal preferences can convey a semblance of secularity (in the sense of worldliness), but political interests are committed to a communal cause. Even as personal relationship with religion and community can have a degree of freedom and manoeuvre, there can be simultaneously a sense of political commitment towards religious and communal interests. There is a double instrumentality of the modern, political self at work here. Ashis Nandy made a pertinent point on this phenomenon:

> 'It is very strange that in South Asia, both, the leader of the Hindus, who produced the Bible of Hindu nationalism—Vinayak Damodar Savarkar, and the leader of Muslim nationalism who carved out a Muslim state in the subcontinent, Pakistan— Mohammad Ali Jinnah, were non-religious.'[43]

The ideology of religious nationalism does not necessarily emerge from a consciousness or life of deep religiosity. Religious nationalism is about competitive group interests and has to do more with political animosity against others, or other groups. Since hate is the primary mover of religious nationalism, even the language and sentiment of love shown towards one's own community is inevitably exaggerated, and suffers from historical and cultural blindness.

The Muslim National Guard, a youth organization of the League, founded by Jinnah in 1942, went on a recruitment drive. On 9 August, a few Muslim volunteers went around the city with slogans like 'Larke lenge Pakistan' (Will battle for Pakistan).[44] Irrespective of the nature of the claim and its justification, it is tragic how, on the verge of Independence when the anti-colonial movement was about to taste success, the focus shifted to the battle lines drawn between Hindus and Muslims. The option of the two communities living together was being sacrificed by the creation of a permanent state of political hostility with the demand for Pakistan.

Historian Joya Chatterji mentions that Syama Prasad Mookerjee was earlier a proponent of Bengal unity and had campaigned against Rajagopalachari's formula in 1944 of accepting Pakistan with Muslim-majority districts.[45] Suhrawardy's premiership demoralized Bengali Hindus. As a Minster of Civil Supplies during the Bengal Famine, he was held responsible for starvation deaths by the Hindu press and public opinion.[46] Mookerjee shifted his stance on a united Bengal in 1946, refusing to imagine Bengali Hindus 'under a permanent tutelage of Muslims.'[47] Mookerjee however added a casteist concern under Muslim rule: 'In order to placate a set of converts from low caste Hindus to Islam, very ancient Hindu culture will be sacrificed.'[48]

This was the cultural limit of the upper caste Hindu imagination and the social ethic. In one stroke, Mookerjee connects ancient Hindu culture to the twentieth century, as if historical time is uninterrupted and changeless. To claim the ancientness of culture in the middle of the twentieth century is a modern fantasy with no bearing on, or resemblance to, what was ancient. It is an ahistorical idea of culture.

The casteist designation of Muslim converts is the real anxiety that confirms Joya Chatterji's claim that for Hindus in Bengal, the political is cultural. Bhadralok Hindu Bengalis, Chatterji writes, 'promoted a powerful sense of cultural superiority over the Muslims of Bengal.'[49] This was behind the Hindu mindset that equated political power with the self-perception of being the cultured elite. Chatterji however stretches the point too far by drawing a comparison between the sense of cultural superiority in the Hindu elite and British racial pride as a source of legitimation to hold political power.[50] There is a qualitative political distinction between fractured societies with cultural hierarchies facing the brunt of colonialism, and the unmitigated and unscrupulous nature of colonial power. Chatterji's politics of equivalence wants to make colonial racism appear to be just another version of prejudices internal to 'native' societies.

Chatterji makes another wrong analogy, this time confusing the distinctness between a national and a cultural community. She argues that the idea of a singular identity under Brahmanic Hinduism as propagated by privileged caste Hindus undermined the diversity of numerous sects and cults that emerged in Hindu Bengali society during the nineteenth and twentieth centuries. So, to speak of a single 'Bengali Hindu community' was to 'invent' what Benedict Anderson called an 'imagined community'[51]. It is a fanciful misreading of Anderson whose definition is based on a spatially scattered national community held together by print capitalism and officially performed cultural rituals of memory. Chatterji forgets that Anderson clarified that an imagined community is not to be understood through a 'falsity/genuineness' binary but by its 'style'[52] of imagination. Brahmanic Hinduism is a political construct and all political constructs invent an identity for itself.

Chatterji nevertheless conceded the point that grants some legitimate ground to the political concerns of Hindus:

> 'The crude and heavy-handed measures adopted by Suhrawardy's ministry in its first months in office ensured that this was a future that many Hindus were determined to avoid.'[53]

This was not merely a bad mindset administratively, but more so, politically. The relationship between the government and the people was not yet—it couldn't be—sorted out under colonial rule. The interim government had the responsibility for instilling confidence in communities that were poised to become citizens of a sovereign nation–state.

The Muslim League in Bengal gave up that responsibility and communalized the idea of governmentality. In fact, if 'divide and rule' was the understated principle of British rule, it was being replicated by the League. For a new rule, or law of the sovereign nation–state to be established, a new reason and argument of division must be put in place. What was an understated policy of the British now came to be stated in explicit terms in the two-nation theory.

The Hindu nationalists first theorized their version of two-nation in the 1920s. But the League had the distinction of making a political claim on their version and managing to justify it successfully. The nature of colonial complicity in the League's demand also lies in how, unlike the Congress's and Gandhi's repeated desire and request that the matter of special rights for Muslims be sorted out between the leaders of two communities after the British left, was overridden by the League's insistence on making the British a party to negotiations, and finally, partition.

On 25 September 1946, Wavell met Sarat Chandra Bose after lunch. Wavell wrote in his journal that Bose tried to influence him with 'Hindu propaganda on the origins of the Calcutta riots.'[54] Wavell sums up the meeting:

> 'On the general political situation he [Bose] brought up the "divide and rule" insinuation. I said shortly that we were trying now to "unite and quit".'[55]

The viceroy does not hide his Empire's instrumentalist designs. The phrase 'unite and quit' reveals the callous paternalism of colonial language, the language of middlemen. Societies, or communities, are not mechanized units that are always readily amenable to manipulation, for good or bad ends. Having divided and ruled their subjects long enough to their advantage, the masters couldn't be trusted to have either will or method to patch up communal differences. Also, the Empire was dealing with elite leaders of both communities where political ambitions and other considerations would take precedence over prudence.

Calcutta witnessed unprecedented mass violence from 16–20 August 1946. Historian Anwesha Roy writes, the official report said 4000 were dead, and over 10,000 suffered serious injuries. Government figures put the number of deaths to 4000 and around 11,000 for people who faced serious injuries.[56]

Joya Chatterji cryptically mentions: 'More Muslims than Hindus died in the fighting'.[57] What is the significance of this point? How does it matter? The numbering and declaration of the dead along communal lines borrowed the logic and mindset of the colonial state. Such scholars writing on the riots reproduced the colonial design and contributed to the politics of death. The dead belong to a religion, but to count them or according to their religious identity is to give a communal shape to the agony of the tragic event.

Janam Mukherjee is alert to this problem and connects this official tendency from the time of the Bengal famine to the Calcutta killings:

> 'The violence in the streets of Calcutta in August 1946 was, in some definite sense, a very gruesome echo of the official truism, propagated in relation to famine and war, that bodies themselves—even corpses—should be understood as either "Hindu" or "Muslim." In other words it might also be said that famine and war had introduced the idea that the mass annihilation of bodies could be understood as a "communal" phenomenon.'[58]

Joya Chatterji mentions two of the social groups among those involved in the killings: 'While the Muslim rioters consisted mainly of up-country migrants, a surprisingly large number of bhadralok Hindus were arrested on charges of rioting.'[59] She says 'surprisingly', because in her analysis, the bhadralok Hindus understood themselves as a people for whom the 'elusive substance' called culture was symbolic of its communal identity, marked by the quality of 'gentility'.[60] The Muslim migrants included the '*kasais*',[61] or butchers of North and Central Calcutta, and the 'itinerant and expert boat-men', or '*khalasis*'[62] from Howrah. The Hindu groups involved in violence, in Chatterji's findings, were an 'improbable alliance' that included 'businessmen and ex-soldiers, Congressmen, Mahasabhaites, shopkeepers and neighbourhood bully boys'.[63]

The question of 'Hindu culpability' in the genocide, Chatterji points out, was however not recognized by the 'Hindu press' that laid absolute blame on the Suhrawardy government and the Muslim League.[64]

It is clear that the Muslim League government played an ideological and active role in organizing the riots. Public meetings by League members, including congregations in mosques, tried to motivate people, explaining the significance of Pakistan and Direct Action Day, and the Calcutta Muslim Student's League mobilized students.[65] A call for 'jihad' was circulated in copies of a Bengali leaflet titled '*Muslim League-er Sakriya Karmapanthar Ahban*' (Call for Direct Action by the Muslim League) on 14 August.[66] The League also used newspapers like *Asre-Jadid* and pamphlets for propaganda. These were read out to the non-literate sections.[67] There were reports by the Calcutta Police Commissioner and Intelligence Branch officials that League members had distributed methylated spirit, kerosene oil and knives to arm Muslim-run hotels.[68] 'Members of the League ministry also utilized government machinery,' writes Suranjan Das, to transfer Hindu police officers from key areas, issue coupons for gallons of petrol and also draw food rations for League activists.[69]

These were clear moves not just to prepare for mass violence but also to precipitate the mental and material conditions for it.

Two Accounts of Violence via Manto

To add another lens to the event, I will refer briefly to two accounts—one intellectual and long-distant one and the other a direct witness—of the killings in Calcutta, from Nirad C. Chaudhuri and Ashis Nandy. Chaudhuri had left Calcutta for good in 1942, but he had friends and relatives in the city that passed on information. Nandy was nine years old and new to the city.

In his memoir, *Thy Hand Great Anarch!* Chaudhuri writes with characteristic bluntness:

> 'The unwillingness of the Government of Bengal was certainly intentional, and if they at last asked for military intervention that was only to save themselves from the obvious charge of being behind the massacres. It is also possible that they asked for military help when they saw that the game of killing was going against Muslims.'[70]

The *fact* of a leader or government abetting crime often happens through carefully crafted acts of prevention of duty (which is prevention of law and justice). It is difficult in retrospect to hold them responsible as the motivational aspects behind such facts are clouded by claims that befuddle and confuse interpretation. Objectivity must negotiate with suspicion and good faith. This false challenge is deliberately created to withhold judgement. Chaudhuri blames Suhrawardy's intentionality from facts. Governmental dilly-dallying in taking decisions when there is an outbreak of mass violence and lives are at stake comes from political reluctance. This nefarious tradition became the norm in postcolonial India where minorities have been targeted. Here's a clinching detail from an official about Suhrawardy's delaying tactic to ensure that he had enough deaths for his cause:

> 'The Calcutta Police Commissioner, Donald Ross Hardwick, said that he had "very little time to study the situation" because Suhrawardy was constantly in the Control Room and entered into "discussions" with him. Other British officials also agreed that he caused unnecessary confusion by bombarding them with questions and impractical suggestions.'[71]

Janam Mukherjee's highly speculative reading of the situation argues, rather than Suhrawardy, or the state administration, allegedly controlling the riots from the Control Room, it was the *lack of control* that characterized the Calcutta riots.[72] Mukherjee however mentions that the chief minister, sitting in the Control Room with the police commissioner, was 'worrying incessantly about fellow Muslims'.[73] It is not a detail that instils confidence. Joya Chatterji writes: 'Suhrawardy's culpability is by now a well-established tradition. But Hindu leaders were also deeply implicated, a fact which is less well known.'[74]

What makes Chatterjee think public perception involving people who suffered the riots deserves to be treated with intellectual sarcasm? It is possible many among those who suffered the riots were communal. Does their being communal completely falsify their knowledge and opinion of the riots? People's mindsets do colour facts, but the fact that Suhrawardy was in power and his activities in the Police Control Room were fishy are corroborated by sources independent of Hindus who faced the riots in Calcutta. To call that informed opinion a 'tradition' with an air of disbelief is elitist disdain masquerading as the self-critical 'Hindu' scholar.

The fact that Hindu leaders were involved does not overturn the asymmetry vis-à-vis the responsibility of the Muslim League that was in power.[75] Administrative culpability is the established story behind all riots in postcolonial India whose template was set in 1946 Bengal and ruthlessly imitated the same year in Bihar.

Chaudhuri mentions an important detail about the massacres, which explains the ruthless and timid logic of how such riots are executed over a vulnerable people:

> 'It must not be imagined, however, that there were pitched battles between the communities. That would have resulted in fewer deaths and put a stop to the violence sooner by making it too costly. But what was carried out was the slaughter of Hindus by the Muslims where the latter were a majority, and *vice-versa*.'[76]

Chaudhuri offers his scathing criticism of the unreliable nature of social behaviour in an atmosphere of radical uncertainty:

> 'The immediate impact of the massacre in Calcutta was seen in an exhibition by both the communities which in its silly maudlinity should have been regarded as an insult to the dead, but was regarded by weak Bengalis as a 'miracle'. The Hindus and Muslims joined one another in processions, chanted that they were brothers, and embraced one another. This could not bring back the dead, although it served to wipe off some of the shame . . .
>
> The futility of weak repentance was demonstrated very soon. The violence spread at once to the villages of East Bengal, and in the district of Noakhali in the south the Muslim attacks on the Hindus were on a very large scale. This made Mahatma Gandhi go on a tour of the district on foot, preaching peace. I felt the Noakhali disturbances even in Delhi.'[77]

The politics of communalism seeks to manipulate grief and transform it into mass anger so that it can be prepared for violence.

Ashis Nandy describes living in a third-floor apartment of the Calcutta YMCA where his father worked.[78] He could see the slums of migrant North Indian Muslim labourers from his window. Beyond the slum were a couple of localities belonging to lower- and middle-class Bengali Hindus, and further away another slum of Muslim migrants. Before 16 August, people in the slums flew the Muslim League flag, beat drums and shouted aggressive slogans. On the 16th, the slum dwellers sharpened their knives, and by evening they resorted to violence. The police was 'openly partisan' in Nandy's observation. The workers at YMCA, comprising both communities, helped 200 Hindu families escape by putting up a ladder on the high wall of the compound. 'The radio worsened things,' writes Nandy, with officials censoring stories. When a government wants to lie to the people, it makes the media its accomplice, misusing the reputation (and also exposing the myth) of a neutral and truthful media. The tragedy is that people will still allow themselves to believe the news on the radio because it holds the mysterious power of a source that is legitimized by its existence as a singular, authoritative voice.

Nandy writes, after the Muslim charge, it took a couple of days for the Hindus to regroup and counter-attack. The atmosphere in the YMCA building, hosting Muslim families, surprised a young Nandy: 'Strangely, there was no hostility between the communities within the building, among either the riot victims or those serving them.'

This strangeness is sharply explored and explained by Sadat Hasan Manto in his autobiographical story, *Shyam: Krishna's Flute*.

During Partition, Manto and his friend, Shyam, met a family of Sikhs, refugees from Rawalpindi, who told them horrifying stories of Sikh victims in the riots. Later, when

Manto asked his friend if he felt hostile towards him after listening to the story of Muslim atrocities, Shyam said, 'Not now . . . but when I was listening to the atrocities the Muslims had committed . . . I could have murdered you.'[79] Manto reflects: 'I was deeply shocked by Shyam's words. Perhaps I could have also murdered him at the time. But later when I thought about it—*and between then and now there is a world of difference*—I suddenly understood the basis of those riots in which thousands of innocent Hindus and Muslims were killed every day.'[80] [Emphasis mine]

Manto understood the psychological basis of communal violence. There is a visible abyss between 'then' and 'now'. A feverish transformation takes place in the body, as it passes from a murderous state to a state of calmness. Manto realized the politics of hate as a politics of heat. The state of communal hatred is a state of heat. This heat is corporeal. Hatred is an emotion that is meant to stir your blood and raise your temperature.

Here, it is important to distinguish between those who carry out the agenda of hatred and commit hate crimes and those who are behind the scenes. The manufacturers of hate, the men who plan genocides and mass violence, are cold-blooded. They indoctrinate the executors and generate enough heat in them to carry out the mission. Communal violence creates an atmosphere where ordinary people who are not part of the mob are infused with hateful anger when they come to hear the gruesome stories. That is how Manto and Shyam were momentarily consumed by communal passion. In such situations, the heat takes on viral proportions.

Another important distinction needs to be made. Hatred is more of an emotion than a feeling. Emotion is an *inwardly directed* state of subjective intensity, acutely self-consuming, constrained by self-serving considerations, to give a literary expression, pulled by self-ward winds. Feelings, in contrast, are an *outwardly directed* state of subjective intensity, expansive and loose, unlike emotions, moved by other-centric affectations. I am not situating emotions or feelings in any specific place (self or other, inside or outside), but rather describing their direction.[81]

Hate is not about the self, so a philosophy of hate is not possible. Hate is identity reduced to itself, where identity is unable to think, or imagine its tensions and contradictions.

The politics of heat is an enemy of thinking, and considers thinking its enemy. The moment this heat subsides, and the person is back to his prior self, he faces the absurdity of his emotion (and actions, if he acts on those emotions). There is nothing natural about it. This heat is artificially produced in the body, and executed with an emotion of hatred that is biologically human. Manto reflects on the moment:

> '"Not now . . . but at that time, yes." If you ponder over these words, you will find an answer to the painful reality of Partition, an answer that lies in human nature itself.'[82]

The idea of 'human nature' holds an interesting paradox. Human is distinct to the human being, while nature is what humans share with other species. Human nature is thus a combination, or mix of what is human and non-human (or not-so-human) in us. The faculty of reason and imagination, the faculty that holds power or takes life, are human attributes, but as modes of thinking and action, they aren't bereft of nature. Reason and nature are not so apart in human beings. It depends on what aspect within the human gets manipulated and expressed at a certain moment. Time alone reveals what human beings in the world are, through their encounter with others.

If you experience an intense moment of desire to kill and, a little later, you experience a moment where you are shocked, ashamed or bewildered by it, it means a radical, unexplainable rupture has occurred in your relationship with time.

Manto and Shyam were forcibly thrown out of their own time and flung into an abyss of irreconcilable hatred. When they returned to their time, or, when their relationship with time was mended, they remembered their desire to kill in a detached, passive manner and articulated it as such.

The politics of communalism achieves this deadly rupture between people and time by creating the spectre of the enemy who must be annihilated *at once*. There is no time left, no time to waste. Pick up your weapons and rush for the nearest throat. Between the justification for murder and the act of murder, people inhabit a feverishly linear time, like a train going through a tunnel. When they come out of the tunnel, they are stunned by the light. The politics of communalism creates an artificial state of darkness that suffocates the light of human nature, not just reason.

Partha Chatterjee mentions a small book in Bengali with an English title, *Delirium*, published in April 1947 by a medical practitioner and social worker named Birendranath Chattopadhyay. He described the Calcutta riots as 'an assault from the outside, carried by powerful but anonymous forces, against which the carefully nurtured bonds of neighbourhood solidarity were no match.'[83] Chattopadhyay himself had made a door-to-door appeal for peace. Still, 'before the night was over, the slums were in flames and people were killing one another in astonishing brutality.'[84]

The outbreak of violence breaking apart social relations, reconfirms that human nature and human reason are deceptively entwined. It is difficult to predict when they may untwine and go their separate ways. When reason is yet to find a centre, it easily gives way. The rational myths of modernity do not hold.

To return to Nandy's account, he writes that being Christian, he and his family could afford to hold a 'distant, non-partisan, moral position', though his father narrowly escaped death twice (he was shot at!). He makes a larger political point on the Hindu retaliation: '[We] were treated to the spectacle of a Hindu nation emerging in Calcutta . . . What the Hindu nationalists could not do over the previous one hundred years, the Direct Action Day had done. Many years later, when I read that international wars created nations, it did not sound a cliché. I knew exactly what it meant.'

Noakhali Carnage

In an article on 17 August in the *Dawn*, Jinnah 'unreservedly' condemned the violence, and as Anwesha Roy quotes from the archives, he expected the guilty to be punished 'according to law'.[85] With a reference to Muslims who turned violent, Jinnah held that they acted 'contrary to expressed instructions' and 'played into the hands of the enemies of the Muslim League.'[86] In a press statement on 5 September, Jinnah blamed Gandhi and the Congress, probably as a tactical afterthought.[87]

It is revealing that hearing of a moral calamity, Jinnah first thought of the law. He felt that a juridical punishment was the most apt act of justice for a collective act of horror. He was looking to measure something without measure. In fact, it is revealing that he thought of punishment in the first place. The best way to deflect an act of horror and represent it as an act of crime is by evoking the law. A moral condemnation was expected for collective immorality. But Jinnah was not a scrupulously moral politician. He was incapable of moral condemnation, knowing he had masterminded the violence himself. His own judgement was equally revealing: Muslims had done what their 'enemies' expected them to do. Jinnah practised a politics of enmity. By saying that Muslims acted *against* 'instructions' he tried to distance the instruction-makers of the Muslim League and absolve them of any hand in the genocide.

Pyarelal writes on the Muslims in Noakhali in the aftermath of the genocide in a matter-of-fact manner like a seasoned anthropologist:

> 'The bulk of Muslims of Noakhali are converts from Hinduism. As a class they are illiterate and backward, by nature simple, affable and peace-loving; one might even say timid. "Their feuds," to quote W.H. Thomson, "take them to court instead of bringing them to blows." But they are extremely ignorant and excitable and can be easily misled, especially when their fanaticism is appealed to. Then they show an extraordinary capacity for organised mass action. To mention a small instance, during the non-cooperation days, they organised an "Allah- o-Akbar" chain-cry from Chittagong to Ghandpur, a distance of over 100 miles; and even the incredibly short time taken to traverse that distance was given us when we were in Noakhali. They

> thus provide ideal material for fabricating a highly efficient push-button machine for mob-violence.'[88]

Pyarelal was part of Gandhi's peace mission in the villages of Noakhali. He gives us a good impression of what made it possible for the Muslim peasantry to be easily manipulated by the Muslim League. Pyarelal goes ahead to offer a small history of how Noakhali was connected to the political stream of the Indian national movement, and how internal political shifts made the local peasantry move away from class to communal concerns, collapsing the two:

> 'During the non-cooperation and Khilafat days of the twenties, the Muslim workers of Noakhali including Pirs, Maulvis and Maulanas joined the Congress movement in large numbers and were in the first flush of Hindu–Muslim unity lionised by Congressmen. After the suspension of the mass civil disobedience movement in 1922 at Bardoli, and the collapse of the Khilafat movement following upon the abolition of the Khilafat by Kemal Ataturk, the bulk of them fell back and in the 1930 civil disobedience movement they took very little part. The Gandhi–Irwin Pact of 1931 gave a fillip to their waning enthusiasm. Noakhali district is a saltproducing area. As a result of the salt concession under the Gandhi–Irwin pact the peasant class took to salt manufacture extensively, the production and sale of tax-free salt being not less than five lakhs of rupees annually. Then came the 1932 civil disobedience struggle. It convulsed the whole district, and at one stage the British administration in the district seemed to be almost on the point of being paralysed. The bureaucracy were not slow to react to this challenge. They had not forgotten how in

> 1921 an illiterate Hindu cobbler and two illiterate Muslim hotelwallas standing on the Congress ticket had heavily defeated at the polls a Government pleader, who was a Rai Bahadur, and two Khan Bahadurs—all the three titled candidates forfeiting their deposit money! When all other means had been tried, the favourite one of communal division was resorted to. The district authorities rallied round them all the Pirs, Maulvis and Mullas who had deserted the Congress ranks. A Krishak Samiti (Peasants' Party) movement had been in existence for some time before. It was an agrarian movement to begin with. Under the new orientation, it was given a wholly communal and reactionary turn. Free use was made of the Government's "discretionary fund" to further its propaganda. The then Muslim District Magistrate of Noakhali wholly identified himself with the new movement and used himself to address the Krishak Samiti meetings. The speeches delivered at these meetings and the slogans raised during the processions were anti-Congress, rabidly communal, and defamatory of every class and section of the Hindus, not excluding Hindu women.'[89]

The point is not missed that the British administration was alarmed by the growing communal unity in the district of Noakhali and wanted to encourage division. The 'policy' of divide-and-rule has always been used to accentuate the question of rights along communal lines of representation. The Krishak Praja Party (KPP) was formed in 1936 with the help of Fazlul Huq as an effort to unify the krishak samitis and form a united front of peasants for the abolition of zamindari.[90] Ghulam Sarwar, an influential leader of the KPP, joined the Muslim League in 1937, around the time Huq did. Sarwar played a notorious role in the Noakhali riots.

Pyarelal adds an interesting detail about how Muslims monitored the entry points to the river around Noakhali to ensure that Hindus who travelled for work, or those Hindus who lived elsewhere and came to visit their relatives in Noakhali didn't get wind of their plans:

> 'A large proportion of the intelligentsia and well-to-do people in Noakhali have either jobs in Calcutta or do business or send their children for education there. During the Puja holidays in the month of October, people returning from Calcutta to their mofussil homes in Noakhali found to their surprise that boats were being searched at every bridge and at every turn of the khal by people styling themselves as "League volunteers", "Muslim National Guards", and so on. Boat-drivers in Noakhali are mostly Muslims. They were directed by the ring-leaders not to carry Hindu passengers. The latter were sometimes manhandled and their belongings snatched away from them. Muslims held secret nightly meetings from which Hindus were rigorously excluded. All Hindu newcomers on their arrival in a locality were interrogated, their movements shadowed, and their freedom of movement restricted. They were prevented even from meeting or calling on one another by their Muslim neighbours. There was an odour of something ominous, evil brewing in the air. In desperation the President of the Hindu Mahasabha of Noakhali and the Chairman-in-charge of the Noakhali Municipality approached the District Muslim League leaders and appealed to them for peace and security. The latter's answers were evasive.'[91]

Pyarelal's description is corroborated by Suranjan Das's archival work where he laid out details of the 'highly organized'[92] form of violence in Noakhali–Tippera. Ghulam Sarwar's men split into groups and ensured that Noakhali was cordoned off and a surveillance system put in order before the carnage: 'The rioters adopted extraordinary measures to prevent outside interference with their work. Villages were cordoned off, communications with the outside were obstructed by cutting deep ditches across the approach roads and blocking to boat-landing places. Muslim employees in Post and Telegraph offices held up Hindu telegrams asking for urgent help.'[93]

These details confirm the clear designs by the League to orchestrate a genocide in Noakhali–Tippera. One of the pamphlets bearing the stamp of the Muslim League circulated in Noakhali after the Calcutta riots issued the following advice:

> '"[Force] an intense communal feeling by breeding hatred against the Hindus," "to *learn the scientific method* of destroying Hindu properties and dislocating telegram communications, destroying railway lines and all other conceivable means of transportation and communication".'[94] [Emphasis mine]

It is instructive that the violence was termed 'scientific'. A chillingly clinical method was followed to identify the material means of life to be destroyed and to cut off technological means of escape. The victims had to be dispossessed and trapped. Modern forms of mass violence—war, genocide, riots—look to inflict maximum damage on the enemy.

A lot of modern violence has a strong internal dimension. Modern societies are structured in a manner that intensifies proximity. Ethnic, religious and social enmities are lived and experienced within neighbourly spaces which are not open and scattered like premodern times, but enclosed within the norms of jurisdiction and modes of infrastructure, including transportation. These norms and modes also enclose villages where sophisticated forms of urban life are missing. The intensification of space creates mental fields of social relations. If these relations are strained and troubled, then any violence that spills out is bound to include psychological trauma, as much as physical harm and material loss. The nature of power within unevenly placed groups (in terms of economic, social and political power) works surreptitiously, and often insidiously, across the shared spaces they inhabit, and the interactions (and transactions) of everyday life that binds them together. Any violence that is perpetrated in order to reconfigure power relations will look to tear apart this thick fabric. It is particularly true in cases where perpetrators of genocide (both people who conceive them and those who execute them) want to damage social relations in order to achieve political goals. The goal is often the reorganization of society to suit a new political imagination.

The carnage at Noakhali began on 10 October 1946, the day of Lakshmi Puja, the festival of the Hindu goddess of wealth. Ghulam Sarwar made provocative speeches at a school in the Ramganj police station area where the first sparks were lit with looting at the bazaar.[95] Anwesha Roy pulls out extracts from a telegram sent to the Bengal Provincial Committee on 15 October:

'Serious Communal Conflagration Destroyed Lives and Properties of Hindus
'Of Ramganj Thana Disturbance Affected Some Part Of Begumgunj and
Lakshmipur Thana . . . Hindus Compelled To Slaughter Cows and Eat Cooked
Beef . . . Hindu Houses Burnt On Mass Scale . . . Large Number Hindu Girls
Forcible Married To Moslems And Abducted All Hindu Temples And Images
Desecrated Helpless Refugees Coming To Tippera District . . .'[96]

Pyarelal mentions the cross section of people belonging to the Muslim community who took part in the genocide: 'Among those who took part in the disturbances, figured presidents and members of Union Boards, Muslim National Guards, Muslim schoolmasters and students of schools and colleges, local criminal dements of the community and a sprinkling of ordinary Muslim village-folk including women and children.'[97]

It is striking that a community as a whole is made to acquire a sudden and intense professionalization of hate crime. Such pathologies have occurred in the twentieth century in the cause of ethno-national passion. The participation of children can be read as a motivated effort by adults of the community to rinse itself of all vestiges of innocence. The dreadful honesty of communal/ethnic/fascist hatred is that no one shall be allowed to remain innocent of it. Yet, the equally dreadful paradox of this theatre is that all participants have an innocent sense of obligation to it. The human psyche—in its individual or collective form—is a nightmare of paradoxes.

At a press conference on 16 October in Calcutta, Suhrawardy spoke about the difficulty faced by troops in reaching Noakhali due to damaged canals and bridges and roadblocks. He acknowledged the plunder and conversions. But he pretended ignorance about the cause of the violence and did not consider visiting Noakhali yet.[98] Pyarelal mentions another important detail:

> 'The same day he [Suhrawardy] left for Darjeeling where the Governor was having a Cabinet meeting. "It seems odd," commented The *Statesman* on 18 October, 'that, despite evidence of administrative breakdown in a part of the Province for weeks notoriously menaced by just this sort of catastrophe, there should have been no movement yet of Governor or Chief Minister to the point of catastrophe. The one remains in Darjeeling, the other has gone to join him there.'[99]

The *Statesman* editorial registers its surprise at the curious activity of the Bengal chief minister. Suhrawardy demonstrably shirked responsibility. By running away from questions, Suhrawardy raised more questions about himself and his regime. Since the breakout of the Calcutta killings in August, there were plans afoot to engineer more riots in Bengal to cement the demand for Pakistan.

The anthropologist teaching at Calcutta University, Nirmal Kumar Bose, who took leave from teaching to be Gandhi's associate and Bengali translator in Noakhali, wrote in his famous journal *My Days with Gandhi* that as soon as news of Noakhali 'leaked through to the Press on the 17th of October' Satish Chandra Dasgupta received a telegram from

Gandhi to 'send a batch of volunteers into the interior of Noakhali'[100] to find out what had taken place. Dasgupta had met Gandhi for the first time in 1921 at Kakinada and had become a devoted Gandhian. He had set up an ashram called the Khadi Pratisthan in Sodepur in the early 1920s as part of Gandhi's constructive programme.

Gandhi boarded the train to Calcutta on 28 October 1946, and reached Sodepur at 5.30 p.m. on 29 October.[101]

'Tell Sparta, Here Her Sons Are Laid'

Gandhi chose a few people to assist him in his peace work in Noakhali. Having dissuaded a number of individuals and organizations from joining him, he however agreed to a few members of the Indian National Army (INA) led by Sardar Niranjan Singh Gill to accompany him. To the request made by INA members to send a thousand people, Gandhi agreed to a hundred, and Pyarelal says, the number remained within fifty.[102] Gandhi's personal team comprised seven people: besides Pyarelal, there was his sister, Sushila Nayar, who, after finishing her MBBS and MD from Lady Hardinge Medical College at Delhi and advanced courses in the US, joined Gandhi and Kasturba in Sevagram as their personal physician.[103] There was Gandhi's grand-nephew, Kanu Gandhi, and his wife, Abha Gandhi (daughter of Amritlal Chatterjee). Amtus Salam, a Muslim inmate of Gandhi's ashram, and his adopted daughter, Sushila Pai, a graduate of Bombay University, and Prabhudas completed the group. They were posted separately in different villages.[104]

On 30 October, when Gandhi was returning back to the ashram in Sodepur after meeting the governor, Sir Fredrick Burrows, on invitation, an iron ring was hurled at his car when he was passing through a Muslim locality.[105]

News reached Gandhi in Sodepur that communal riots had broken out in Bihar as a repercussion to Noakhali. He sent a wire to Nehru through the Bengal chief minister asking him for confirmation on the news on Bihar that he had read in the Muslim League run newspaper, *Morning News.*[106] Making Suhrawardy privy to his personal communication with Nehru, Gandhi wanted to establish trust. Nehru, who had rushed to Bihar to get first-hand reports, replied to Gandhi that the details were exaggerated, the Bihar government was doing its best, but the situation was tense.[107]

At the prayer meeting in Sodepur on 2 November, Gandhi said, lasting peace could only come from people's hearts. He made a rhetorical analogy: 'Supposing someone kills me, you will gain nothing by killing someone else in retaliation. And, if you only think over it, who can kill Gandhi except Gandhi himself? No one can destroy the soul. So let us dismiss all thought of revenge from our hearts.'[108]

But even as Gandhi addressed people in Bengal, news of Bihar had unsettled him. He wrote in a letter to Jaisukhlal Gandhi on 4 November:

> 'The happenings in Bihar have made me decide that if people's hearts do not change for the better I must not be a witness to them. These days I am observing something like a partial fast. The main reason for its being partial is my health. But Bihar will lead me on to a total fast. I will go to Noakhali the day after tomorrow.'[109]

This shaky ground of feelings torn apart by the disintegration of societies would pursue Gandhi throughout his stay in Noakhali. Being at one place, he was worried about the situation in another place. The long shadow of violence from Bihar was superimposed over the shadow of violence in Noakhali. Gandhi was caught in a web of shadows that overshadowed his intent to bring peace between Hindus and Muslims. He wanted to fast, despite his ill health, for the violence in Bihar even as he stationed himself in Noakhali.

In the prayer meeting in Sodepur on 4 November, Satish Chandra Dasgupta read out Gandhi's speech as it was his day of silence:

> 'If Congressmen fail to protect the Mussalmans where the Congress is in power, then what is the use of a Congress Premier? Similarly, if in a League province the League Premier cannot afford protection to the Hindus, then why is the League Premier there at all? If either of them have to take the aid of the military in order to protect the Muslim or Hindu minorities in their respective provinces, then it only means that none of them actually exercises any control over the general population when a momentous crisis comes. If that is so, it only means that both of us are inviting the British to retain their sovereignty over India. This is a matter over which each of them should ponder deeply.'[110]

Since members of the Congress and the Muslim League were running the Interim or Provisional government representing the newly elected Constituent Assembly formed on 2 September 1946, it was incumbent on their leaders to protect minorities in their provinces. Gandhi equated moral and political legitimacy of governance with the protection of minorities. The lack of administrative control, however, appeared to be a political ploy to foment communal violence. Gandhi felt that calling in the army to contain civic unrest further weakened the political effectivity of governance. What Gandhi did not realize was that by allowing genocide to happen in Noakhali and Bihar, the Interim government was establishing national sovereignty where minority communities would be treated the way the colonial state treated its subjects. Genocide was a way of establishing sovereign power by internalizing the motives of colonialism's original sin.

Bihar was bothering Gandhi and in a letter to Nehru, on 5 November, he wrote:

> 'The events in Bihar have distressed me. I can clearly see my duty. My bonds with Bihar are close. I cannot forget it. If half of what I hear is true, it means that Bihar has lost all humanity. To say that *goondas* were responsible for whatever happened there would be quite untrue. Although I have tried hard to avoid the fast, I shall not be able to do so. It is the seventh day today since I gave up milk and cereals. The cough and the boils were responsible for it, but also I was tired of the body. Then Bihar made matters worse. And the cry came from within: "Why should you be a witness to this slaughter? If your word, which is as clear as daylight, is not heeded, your work is over. Why do you not die?" Such reasoning has forced me to resort to fasting. I want to issue a statement that if in Bihar and other provinces slaughter is not stopped, I must end my life by fasting.'[111]

Gandhi had started his anti-colonial movement in India in 1917 with his satyagraha in the Champaran district of Bihar to support the peasant uprising against indigo farming enforced by the colonial regime. Gandhi refused to believe that the Bihar carnage was the handiwork of antisocial elements alone. Against the backdrop of the breakdown of civic peace, Gandhi also informed Nehru about the state of his body. The exasperating realization dawned on Gandhi that his clear and simple message of non-violence was not heeded.

In the extract from Pyarelal's 'Weekly letter', published in *Harijan*, we learn about a significant remark that Gandhi made in his prayer meeting on 5 November in Sodepur:

> 'Pandit Jawaharlal had told the guilty parties that the Central Government would never tolerate such barbarism. They would even use aerial bombing to put it down. But that was the way of the British. The Congress was an organization of the people. Was the Congress to use the foreign mode of destruction against the people whose representative it was? By suppressing the riots with the aid of the military, they would be suppressing India's freedom. And yet what was Panditji to do if the Congress had lost control over the people?'[112]

Gandhi spoke on the fresh wave of communal atrocities in Bihar where the Congress was in power. Gandhi knew that using colonial means of force would mean crushing the spirit of the people who were yet to taste the feeling and responsibility of freedom.

In the prayer meeting in Sodepur the next day, 6 October, just before leaving for Noakhali, Gandhi again turned his attention to Bihar:

> 'It is easy enough to retort that things under the Muslim League Government in Bengal were no better, if not worse

> and that Bihar is merely a result of the latter . . . I must confess, too, that although I have been in Calcutta for over a week I do not yet know the magnitude of the Bengal tragedy. Though Bihar calls me, I must not interrupt my programme for Noakhali. And is counter-communalism any answer to the communalism of which Congressmen have accused the Muslim League? Is it Nationalism to seek barbarously to crush the fourteen per cent of the Muslims in Bihar? The misdeeds of Bihari Hindus may justify Qaid-e-Azam Jinnah's taunt that the Congress is a Hindu organization in spite of its boast that it has in its ranks a few Sikhs, Muslims, Christians, Parsis and others. Bihari Hindus are in honour bound to regard the minority Muslims as their brethren requiring protection, equal with the vast majority of Hindus. Let not Bihar, which has done so much to raise the prestige of the Congress, be the first to dig its grave.'[113]

Being unable to prevent the genocide of Muslims in Bihar, the Congress lost its defence against Jinnah's accusation of it being a party for the Hindus. The violence in Bihar brought the Congress closest to the charge of being communal.

The other striking aspect in Gandhi's statement was that Bihar was already 'calling' him, even before he had set foot in Noakhali. Each place was a distress call, and Gandhi could hear it. Gandhi also addressed the sheer imbalance of numbers between the perpetrators and the victims that was mentioned by Nirad C. Chaudhuri:

> 'I do want, however, to tell you that what you are reported to have done will never count as an act of bravery. For thousands to do to death a few hundreds is no bravery. It is worse than cowardice. It is unworthy of nationalism, of

> any religion. If you had given a blow against a blow, no one would have dared to point a finger against you. What you have done is to degrade yourselves and drag down India.'[114]

About 11 a.m. on 6 October, Gandhi left Sodepur for Noakhali, along with his associates, by train. They reached Kushtia an hour later. Nirmal Kumar Bose mentioned the presence of a huge crowd at the station that Gandhi addressed on a microphone standing at the door.[115] Gandhi told the crowd that Suhrawardy was held up in Calcutta, or would have accompanied him to Noakhali. But the chief minister sent his Labour Minster Mr Shamshuddin to accompany Gandhi. During the days of the Khilafat, Gandhi said, no one spoke of dividing the country. But it was different now.[116]

Gandhi's next stop was Goalundo Ghat, where he reached on 6 November at 3 p.m.[117] The government had arranged for a special steamer, the *S.S. Kiwi*, to take Gandhi to Noakhali.[118] He spoke from the deck of the steamer to the large crowd that had gathered at the ghat. He said both Bihar and Bengal had disgraced India's name. If a thousand Muslims, Gandhi said, referring to Noakhali, looted homes and molested women, they had 'stabbed their own religion'.[119] Gandhi made a stinging remark, noted by Nirmal Kumar Bose:

> 'Let us pray that the Hindus and Mussulmans of Bengal should become one in heart. But to be of one heart does not mean that all of them should be converted to a common religion.'[120]

This hits hard at the conversion mentality propagated by the politics of the Muslim League. When the Muslim leadership encourages Muslims to convert by force, the practice gets legitimized as political logic and masquerades as religious morality.

Gandhi reached Chandpur, a river port that exported jute, in the evening and the steamer halted for the night in Chandpur. The next morning, on 7 November, Gandhi separately met relief workers from the Congress and a delegation of the Muslim League. He first met the workers and representatives of relief organizations in the dining saloon of the *Kiwi*. He tried to impress upon them that they must convince the Hindus of Noakhali not to leave despite tragic provocations. Gandhi invoked the epitaph composed by the Greek poet of Ceos, Simonides, and inscribed upon a memorial at Thermopylae on the epic battle of 480 BC where Leonidas and three hundred Spartans had defended the pass against the invading Persian army:

> 'They should not leave. 20,000 able-bodied men prepared to die like brave men non-violently might today be regarded as a fairy tale, but it would be no fairy tale for every able-bodied man in a population of 20,000 to die like stalwart soldiers in open fight. They will go down in history like the immortal three hundred of Leonidas who made Thermopylae:
>
> *Stranger! Tell Sparta, here her sons are laid,*
> *Such was her law and we that law obeyed.*
>
> I will proclaim from the housetops that it is the only condition under which you can live in East Bengal. You have asked for Hindu officers, Hindu police and Hindu military in the place of Muslim. It is a false cry. You forget that Hindu officers, Hindu police and Hindu military have in the past done all these things—looting, arson, abduction, rape.'[121]

History was an opportunity to die heroically. Not fight to kill, but resist to die was Gandhi's maxim in the face of battle. Non-violence was not without an ethic of chivalry. Gandhi demanded that helpless people must not surrender their post. It was a fallacy to expect the police and the army to sort out a civic conflict. Their past record shows that they can only abet communal violence, not stall it. Gandhi strongly believed that the state can't ensure peace during a communal war. Only the will of the people can bring an end to conflict.

Gandhi was also candid about his own intentions:

> 'No, I am not going to leave you in peace. Presently you will say to yourself, "When will this man leave us and go?" But this man will not go. He did not come on your invitation and he will go only on his own, but with your blessings, when his mission in East Bengal is fulfilled.'[122]

Until people guaranteed peace, Gandhi wouldn't leave them in peace with his peace mission. He told his audience that he was aware that his presence may not be welcome and may add to their agony, but they couldn't deter him from his public responsibility.

In response to a worker's statement, Gandhi agreed that the genocide in Noakhali was part of the logic to establish Pakistan, calling it 'midsummer madness.'[123] He believed that the people who instigated it had already begun to get sick of their handiwork. To the worker's question on why, in that case, the Muslim League leaders were not working to bring about peace yet, Gandhi replied, 'That stage will come. Sickness only marks the crisis. Convalescence must precede cure. You see I am a nature-curist.'[124] When the worker raised the question that a 'goonda does not understand reason', Gandhi responded: 'But he understands bravery. If he finds that you are braver than he, he will respect you.'[125] The Hindu worker next asked if Hindus had the right to retaliate after Noakhali. Gandhi reminded him that 'two can play at a game' and told him what he thought of his question:

> 'Biharis have behaved as cowards. Use your arms well, if you must. Do not ill-use them. Bihar has not used its arms well. If the Biharis wanted to retaliate, they could have gone to Noakhali and died to a man. But for a thousand Hindus to fall upon a handful of Mussalmans—men, women and children—living in their midst is no retaliation but just brutality.'[126]

Gandhi counters the calculating cowardice of communal genocide that picks on vulnerable populations to execute its vile designs. He exposes the exact nature of the justificatory rhetoric of retributive punishment (in the form of retaliatory violence) to call it by its real name: plain brutality.

What is Evil?

The Muslim League leaders who came to visit Gandhi argued that the real cause behind reports of Hindu refugees fleeing to Chandpur was due to panic caused by Press propaganda. They said that merely fifteen Hindus were killed in the genocide and a greater number of Muslims died in firing by the army who comprised mostly Hindus. One MLA said that some Hindus were obstructing the rehabilitation of the refugees, having encouraged them to migrate in the first place to discredit the Muslim League government. In their desperate bid to ridicule the truth, they probably did not anticipate that Gandhi had basic logical skills. He asked them, if there was no disturbance, why the military was summoned in the first place. Gandhi told them that he met delegations of Hindus and other Muslim League leaders who narrated to him terrible tales of violence. A Muslim member made another ridiculous attempt to argue that Hindu homes were looted after they were left empty by fleeing occupants. Gandhi reasoned,

> 'But why should people flee from their homes? . . . Everybody knows that an unoccupied and unprotected house is bound to be looted by someone or the other. Would anyone risk the loss of all he owns just to discredit the League?'[127]

Yet another member felt encouraged to argue that only 1 per cent of Muslims indulged in acts of hooliganism while 99 per cent behaved honourably. Gandhi did not have much trouble in pointing out that if the 99 per cent 'actively disapproved of what had taken place, the one per cent would have been able to do nothing and could easily have been brought to book.'[128] In the following paraphrased quote from Gandhi, he makes an important distinction between good and evil:

> 'Good people ought actively to combat the evil, to entitle them to that name. Sitting on the fence was no good.'[129]

The statement is reminiscent of Hannah Arendt. In *The Life of the Mind*, Arendt explores the problem of evil among other things. She considers Socrates's argument that evil comes from lack of thinking. Only people who are 'inspired by the Socratic éros, the love for wisdom, beauty and justice'[130] are supposed to be incapable of evil. Arendt does not think that 'Plato's "noble natures"'[131] are impervious to voluntary acts of evil. In other words, she refutes the assumption that people, whether they think and are addicted to éros or not, are prone to doing good. Arendt offers her own understanding of what produces evil: 'The sad truth of the matter is that most evil is done by people who never made up their minds to be or do either evil or good.'[132]

It is not so much thinking, or not thinking, but the *suspension of intentions*—where intentionality involves the desire to do good or evil—that produces evil in the world. To not make up one's mind about evil is to be lazy, or passive, or indifferent to the problem. It allows evil to exist as a possibility in time. But what is evil? Even though it has a religious connotation, the idea of evil has a secularized presence in modernity. In other words, we need not define evil in terms of a religious idea of morality—for instance the injunction that comes from the Book of Exodus, 'Thou Shalt not Kill'—but something that is post-religious. Evil is not a matter of belief today, but an understanding of a symptom. In religion, evil is a deed and/or a person. In modernity, the meaning has evolved according to the new technology of self and power. In other words, evil has acquired a new phenomenology. In a poem, 'Although It Is Night', Octavio Paz writes, thinking about the courage of the writer Alexander Solzhenitsyn who was sentenced to the Gulags for documenting the terrors of Stalinist Russia after World War II:

> 'I was a coward, I did not face evil,
> and now the century confirms the philosopher:
> Evil? A pair of eyes with no face,
> an abundant void.
> Evil: a someone no one, a something nothing.'[133]

Evil is not a person; it has no face. It is a state of depersonalization. The challenge of evil is *facing* it, facing the threat of its abyss. It is also a matter of the will (intentionality transformed into an act): to confront evil (within oneself and in the world). This is precisely what Gandhi is telling the Muslim Leaguers: the proof of being good lies in combating evil as an act of will, and not fence-sitting, which is Arendt's point on the undecidability of intention that allows evil to be.

The Dog That Bore Witness

Gandhi left Chandpur by train the next morning, on 7 November, around 10 a.m. At Laksam Junction, around 10,000 evacuees from riot-stricken villages came to see him.[134] Gandhi told them,

> 'I have not come on a whirlwind propaganda visit. I have come to stay here with you as one of you. I have no provincialism in me. I claim to be an Indian and therefore a Bengali even as I am a Gujarati. I have vowed to myself that I will stay on here and die here if necessary, but I will not leave Bengal till the hatchet is finally buried and even a solitary Hindu girl is not afraid to move freely about in the midst of Mussalmans.'[135]

Gandhi claimed a self-representation that provoked the Bengalis to see him not as an outsider but as one of their own. His claim was backed by a material gesture of living amongst them till peace was restored. He addressed the question of fear at length, and said that running away from danger was antithetical to having faith in the divine. Gandhi reached Chaumuhani the same day, early in the afternoon. He told the people during the prayer meeting, 'I have not come to excite the Hindus to fight the Mussalmans. I have no enemies.'[136]

Gandhi has been consistent on the question of the enemy in his politics. Speaking at the YMCA auditorium in Madras on 16 February, 1916, Gandhi had explained the politics of ahimsa to his audience:

> 'For one who follows the doctrine of ahimsa, there is no room for an enemy; he denies the existence of an enemy. But there are people who consider themselves to be his enemies, and he cannot help that circumstance . . . Another thought which comes out of this is that, under this rule, there is no room for organised assassinations, and there is no room for murders even openly committed, and there is no room for any violence even for the sake of your country, and even for guarding the honour of precious ones that may be under your charge.'[137]

Even if satyagrahis are charged with being enemies by their opponents, they must harbour no enmity with others. The politics of ahimsa is premised on the possibility of friendship, or fraternal love.

During his meeting with relief workers at Chaumuhani, Gandhi faced sharp questions. Someone asked, 'How can we create a sense of security and self-confidence?'

Gandhi replied, 'By learning to die bravely. Let us turn our wrath against ourselves. I am not interested in getting the police substituted by the military or the Muslim police by the Hindu police. They are broken reeds.'[138]

Probably the same person asked, 'To whom should we appeal—the Congress, the League or the British Government?'

Gandhi said, 'To none of these. Appeal to yourselves, therefore to God.'[139]

Dissatisfied with Gandhi's reply, the questioner shot back, 'We are men—made of flesh and blood. We need some material support.'

Gandhi said, 'Then appeal to your own flesh and blood. Purify it of all dross.'[140]

A woman worker asked Gandhi, 'What is your idea of rehabilitation?'

He said, 'Not to send them to Assam and West Bengal but to infuse courage in them so that they are not afraid to stay in their original homes.'[141] She asked how they could do that. Gandhi said,

'You must stay in their midst and say to them: "We shall die to the last person before a hair of your head is injured." Then you will produce heroines in East Bengal.'[142] In the end, the woman felt assured, 'You have opened up a new vista before us, Mahatmaji. We feel fresh blood coursing through our veins.'[143]

Gandhi knew that the Noakhali genocide was orchestrated to scatter and convert Hindus in order to create demographic changes that would facilitate the territorial logic of Pakistan. He wanted the thought and expectation of protection to be replaced by the thought of recovering lost strength within, turning inwards. He called it '*atmabal*'[144] or soul-force in *Hind Swaraj*. If faith in divine force was lacking, they could seek it in their corporeal self. Gandhi was not trying to minimize or ignore the role of administrative responsibility. He took up the matter himself. He wanted people to focus primarily on their own battered strength. The woman worker's response showed that he had the intended effect on his listeners.

Gandhi next reached Dattapara on 8 November. He wrote a letter to Suhrawardy on 10 November:

> 'The work here is more difficult than I had imagined. And the Qaid-e-Azam's statement given to the representative of the *Globe* which I saw in the *Morning News* of November 10, has rendered it even more difficult . . . Is co-operation between Hindus and Muslims an utter impossibility? If it is so, what will be the plight of Bengal and Hindustan? What will happen to Noakhali and Tippera? The refugees here do not get even half their rations and the rice they get is unfit for consumption. They have nothing to cover themselves with during winter. Their houses are damaged, the sanitation is unsatisfactory.'[145]

Communal lines were drawn in Bengal since the 1930s. There have been Hindu–Muslim riots on many occasions. But this was a moment of extraordinary crisis. Gandhi was pointing to the fact that Jinnah was still harping on what was wrong, and not on what needed to be mended and healed. It was not a moment to argue about the impossibility of Hindu–Muslim relations, but of life's material needs for people dispossessed by genocide.

Speaking at the prayer meeting in Dattapara on 10 November (where nearly 80 per cent of the audience comprised Muslims),[146] Gandhi referred to the Surdas bhajan[147] sung during prayer, and said, just as the poet 'likened God to the philosopher's stone' the same stone with alchemic properties 'is within us all.'[148] He told the Muslims that the Hindus could return to their homes not on government assurances but on neighbourly goodwill. He yet again distinguished between 'bravery' and 'cowardice'[149] in the context of the genocides in Noakhali and Bihar, where the many attacked the few. At the prayer meeting the next day, Gandhi spoke about hearing stories of looting and forcible conversions and meeting Hindu women 'without the auspicious vermilion mark on their heads and foreheads and without their conch-shell bangles.'[150]

On 11 November, Gandhi undertook a tour of three villages that fell under the jurisdiction of the Ramganj police station: Noakhola, Sonachak and Khilpara. In Noakhola, the team heard of a household whose eight members had been murdered. Many houses were burnt down. Pyarelal writes, even 'the betel-nut and the coconut trees surrounding the houses were scorched.'[151] There is an unforgettable scene described by Pyarelal after Gandhi emerged from inspecting a ruined building:

> '[A] Tibetan spaniel that was always seen roaming about the place in mournful silence came along and with a soft whimper tried to attract his attention. It would run a few steps, turn back and again beckon, if it was not followed. Gandhiji's companions were mystified by the strange behaviour of the animal and wanted to drive it away. Gandhiji stopped them, and said: "Don't you see the animal wants to say something to us?" He let the dog lead him. It brought him to three human skeletons one after another and several skulls and bones that lay scattered all over the ground! It had seen its master and seven other members of the family being done to death during the riots. Ever since it had hovered about the place and tried to bring to light the dark deed to which it had been witness.'[152]

The scandal of genocide is reflected in the animal tormented by the destruction of human life. A dog was in an animal state of shock having witnessed human violence.

There was nothing human about the dog's traumatized condition but there was something animal about the human violence the dog witnessed. It is permissible to animalize certain human actions. But you can't humanize animal sensibility. The animal alone is common to the animal and the human, while the human is either a possibility or a violent intrusion. It was possible for Frantz Kafka to imagine being dog in his famous short story *Investigations of a Dog (1922)*, but a dog can't imagine being Kafka. Kafka's artistic imagination brings matters close by making a claim: 'All knowledge, the totality of all questions and all answers, is contained in the dog.'[153] This knowledge however remains a secret: 'Every dog has like me the impulse to question, and I have like every dog the impulse not to answer.'[154]

The Noakhali dog used its dog-skills to bring to light merely the remnants of the crime. The dog's silence carries the secret animal surplus of genocidal memory.

The dog wanted people to register its animal state of destitution. Even though it couldn't speak, it conveyed its concern through the limited natural gestures at its disposal. The dog's sense of attachment towards its caregivers' went beyond the transactional economy of life, and spilled over into an exceptional sense of animal loyalty. The dog was loyal to the bone. The madness of human reason was beyond the dog's comprehension. But it could grasp the theatre of violence, and the fear it produced. It could smell the blood, and the dead bodies. The dog's animal memory was active about an incident that had occurred a month ago. Human brutality produced such horror that it horrified an animal.

In the prayer meeting on 12 November in Dattapara, Gandhi reiterated the desire for 'repatriation'.[155] He told his co-workers on 13 November that they needed to disperse and settle down in the affected villages and make themselves 'hostage for the safety and security of the Hindu minority of that village.'[156] He also had a clear, stern message for them:

> 'Those who have ill-will against the Mussalmans or Islam in their hearts or cannot curb their indignation at what has happened should stay away. They will only misrepresent me by working under this plan.'[157]

People hiding communal sentiments had no place in Gandhi's politics of trust, or the politics of restoration of ties. A worker said that the whole issue was religious and not political, and that the 'movement'[158] for Pakistan was not aimed at Hindus but against the Congress. Gandhi replied with clarity:

> 'Do you not see that they think that the Congress is a purely Hindu body? And do not forget that I have no watertight compartments such as religious, political and other. Let us not lose ourselves in a forest of words. How to solve the tangle—violently or non-violently—is the question.'[159]

Gandhi could see that modern politics, particularly of the communal kind, did not leave politics and religion as separate spheres but combined them into a tricky and dangerous cocktail. The politics of non-violence had to untangle this mesh. A worker asked Gandhi, 'How can you reason with people who are thirsting for your blood? Only the other day one of our workers was murdered.'[160] Gandhi replied, 'I know it. To quell the rage is our job.'[161] The worker's difficulty and point of concern was precisely what his political task was about, to face danger at the risk of death. There was no other way to establish peace non-violently.

Gandhi visited two more villages, Comatoli and Nandigram. Pyarelal notes, 'Nandigram was a heap of cinders; nearly 600 houses, a school building, a hostel and a hospital having been reduced to ashes.'[162] Before leaving Dattapara, Gandhi wrote in a letter to Vallabhbhai Patel:

> 'The work here may perhaps be my last. If I survive this, it will be a new life for me. My non-violence is being tested here in a way it has never been tested before.'[163]

Gandhi did not only seem to believe that his attempt to bring peace in Noakhali was difficult or near-impossible, but also that he was physically in danger. Even before he reached Noakhali, he had felt that the proportion of hostility was enormous.

Riot-affected villagers waiting for Gandhi, Noakhali, 1947

On 14 November, Gandhi was received by a small crowd at Shahpur, instead of the big gathering that he was expecting, as rumours reached people that he was accompanied by police personnel and a magistrate who might make arrests. He regretted it as a 'cruel joke', but the authorities insisted that he couldn't be left unprotected.[164] Gandhi said that he learnt on his way that the Muslims wanted to establish peace but were unable to do anything without the approval of League leaders.[165] This clearly showed that they were acting at the behest of the League, whose members had complete control of their sovereignty.

At the prayer meeting at Kazirkhil on 14 November, Gandhi observed that there was a disjunction between the peace of the landscape and the lack of peace on people's faces.[166] He said that, after Bihar, there was no need to dwell on which community was worse, or who started the trouble. He yet again reminded the Muslims about the depraved and pointless nature of forced conversion:

> 'One who is forcibly converted to Islam ceases to be a man. To recite the Kalma through fear is meaningless.'[167]

Gandhi makes a psychological and moral argument that forced conversion does not succeed in establishing religious power over the converted person. By committing violence upon the internal and moral sovereignty of the person, forced conversion achieves something contradictory. It inducts people into the fold after depriving them of free will and a sense of moral choice.

To get an idea of this politics, it is necessary to learn some detail. Anwesha Roy gives us a picture of the devious pattern of forced conversion from witness accounts in Noakhali:

> 'Conversions, according to eyewitness reports, followed a similar pattern everywhere. A *maulvi* generally accompanied the crowd of rioters. He administered the *kalma* and the to-be convert was made to touch one end of a *chadar* (cloth). New converts were taken then to the mosque to offer namaz, and on Fridays, they were brought there for *jumma* prayers. Often, the new converts were made to cook and eat beef in their own house. Even women were not spared and were converted behind the *purdah*.'[168]

Pyarelal describes the double-role of the maulvi in Noakhali: 'In all these cases the village Maulvis, who accompanied the mob, were ready with their services, thus acting at the same time as hooligans and priests.'[169]

For the maulvi, the theatre of religious politics assigns a variety of acts that may be ethically incongruous, but what matters is the effectiveness of the performance. Theatre is temporary and acts on stage are evanescent. Men of religion can be mischievous people who act without moral qualms. They will still be prone to a language of self-justification, where they can lie to themselves.

This premeditated design of conversion served the political logic of Muslim League's nationalism. If a surplus of reluctant and aggrieved converts can provide the numerical basis for political calculations, their inclusion into the community is not considered a moral issue. Forced conversions are political acts accomplished through the engine of fear.

The history of forced conversions, however, does not delegitimize the right to convert. Conversion by choice is not just to be considered a political right in a democracy, but also a spiritual right in any civilized society. Gandhi's justification for conversion is based, as I showed earlier, on the enhancement of moral character. Ambedkar's embrace of Buddhism in 1946[170] is considered a historic example of a modern 'exercise of individual choice based on reason, careful deliberation, and historical consciousness'.[171]

A Half-Burnt House

The next day, Gandhi spoke at a prayer meeting at Ramganj. Barely a month ago, the place had witnessed tremendous violence. Gandhi said that, though his heart wept, he could not afford to cry at sights of destruction for his task was to wipe other people's tears. He wanted to speak frankly to the Muslims and expected them to repent. It was the only way the Hindus could return.[172]

Back to Kazirkhil, Gandhi told his audience at the prayer meeting on 16 November that he had received threatening letters. Muslims thought (or were told) that Gandhi had come to suppress them. Gandhi was asked why he wasn't leaving for Bihar. He said that he would fast if the genocide in Bihar did not stop. While tensions remained, Muslims were returning home. Since Noakhali was a Muslim-dominated area, Gandhi wanted to live with a League member, rather than with Hindus. He added:

> 'My requirements are very few. All I want is cleanliness, clean water, permissible food and the freedom to pray to God in my own way. The Muslim friends will have an opportunity to examine me at close quarters and find out whether I am an enemy or a friend.'[173]

Physical proximity was the best means to lay the foundations of a politics of friendship. Trust is a matter of spending time together. It comes from realizing the common simplicity of daily chores. The freedom to pray your way is enough to establish communal friendship.

Speaking at the prayer meeting the next day, Gandhi informed the crowd that the district magistrate had issued orders that forced conversions wouldn't be recognized by law.[174] On 18 November at Kazirkhil, Gandhi returned to the problem of fear in a speech that was read out as it was his day of silence:

> 'What can I tell you on my silence day? The more I go about in these parts, the more I find that your worst enemy is fear. It eats into the vitals of the terror-stricken as well as the terrorist. The latter fears something in his victim. It may be his different religion or his riches that he fears. The second kind of fear is otherwise known as greed [or love of material possessions]. If you search [deeply] enough, you will find that greed is a variety of fear. But there has never been, and will never be, a man who is able to intimidate one who has cast out fear from his heart. Why can no one intimidate the fearless? . . . Till fearlessness is cultivated by the people there will never be any peace in these parts for the Hindus or for the Mussalmans.'[175]

The victim and the perpetrator are caught in an intense field of mutual fear. If the victim fears being harmed, the perpetrator too fears 'something' in the victim. What is this 'something'? It can be the fear of retaliation, or fierce resistance, in other words, the refusal to submit. Both violence and resistance to violence are fraught with risks. The vicious desire to possess the victim's corporeal and personal property induces fear. The point that Gandhi is perhaps driving at is that a certain fear of uncertainty lurks within the violent manifestation of greed. Perhaps this fear also psychologically propels—if not justifies—the act of violence. Any act of daring against violence tells the perpetrator that the fear they want to induce in the victim is not enough, and this makes the perpetrator turn even more violent. The politics of fear seeks to transform the human condition into one of predator and prey. Once that animal condition is established, violence exceeds moral limits. This is also one way to understand Gandhi's distinction between 'sensible' and 'senseless' violence. Sensible violence is juridical, social/structural and statist, involving institutions where coercive methods are normalized by power. Senseless violence is eruptive, 'abnormal', radically communal or revolutionary, unconstrained by any ethical appeal to the human, something that is not universalizable.[176]

Gandhi's argument is that in order to stop this mutual intensification of fear, apart from appealing for peace, people should mentally equip themselves to face danger and death. Violence, and the fear induced by it on both sides, creates a frantic state, where panic runs loose. If people under attack don't get intimidated, they can throw a fearless challenge to the perpetrators. This alone can set an honourable example of (non-violent) resistance and bring about the possibility of peace.

In the morning of 20 November, Gandhi and his associates left the house of Kashi Pandit in Kazirkhil and took a boat for Srirampur. The distance of four miles took two and a half hours, Nirmal Kumar Bose wrote, because 'the canal was choked tight in many places with water hyacinth and the boat had to be punted all along.'[177] As they travelled, Gandhi wrote a statement for the press:

> 'I find myself in the midst of exaggeration and falsity. I am unable to discover the truth. There is terrible mutual distrust. Oldest friendships have snapped. Truth and ahimsa by which I swear, and which have, to my knowledge, sustained me for sixty years, seem to fail to show the attributes I have ascribed to them. To test them, or better, to test myself, I am going to a village called Srirampur, cutting myself away from those who have been with me all these years, and who have made life easy for me.'[178]

Gandhi acknowledged that his method was facing defeat after sixty years. There was a web of lies around him. Perpetrators and officials were not prepared to tell the truth. Gandhi had chosen to camp in the village of Srirampur to assess the state of violence and untruth in others and himself. For Gandhi, seeking the truth warranted simultaneity, of putting yourself to the test as much as others.

The camp was an interesting contrast to Gandhi's idea of the ashram. Gandhi's ashram was an experiment to tackle modernity and its pervasive social imaginaries by occupying an *in-between place*: neither bourgeois family nor revolutionary commune, neither sect nor party. It was also a space to erase prejudices of caste and untouchability. The peace camp also occupied an in-between place, which was neither state nor civil society?. It did not represent a politics, or a community. Gandhi's peace camp was a small and dedicated band of volunteers. The Gandhian element in its public activities fundamentally involved a moral exchange or engagement with the crisis at hand. This moral exchange included conversation. Gandhi would speak, his audience would ask questions and he would answer them. Gandhi did not merely write a dialogic text in 1909 as a generic form to present his political views. He lived, pursued, experimented with the idea of a dialogic politics at the most crucial moment of his life and the life of Hindu–Muslim relations. Both commitments merged together and it claimed his life.

On 20 November, when Gandhi reached Srirampur, he was first greeted by a Hindu man whose house was burnt down. A Muslim farmer, Ismail Khondkar, and Maulvi Waliullah Kari also came to welcome Gandhi.[179] Manoranjan Chaudhuri, a Hindu Mahasabha member, was part of the discussion after prayers, on the Bengal government's proposal for setting up peace committees. He insisted that the arrest of those who indulged in violence must precede the formation of the peace committees in order to instil confidence. Gandhi disagreed, and tried to persuade Chaudhuri to agree that the approach should be reversed: place trust in the committee and entrust it to name and book the perpetrators.[180]

Gandhi told an audience of a thousand people in Srirampur during the prayer meeting that it was possible for him to settle down in Noakhali because of Satish Chandra Dasgupta's efforts, and that he would be there with Nirmal Kumar Bose, who would work as his interpreter and teach him Bengali, and Parasuram, who was from Malabar, and knew a little Hindustani and no Bengali. The rest of his troupe was spread across villages.[181]

In an interview to *The Hindu* on the same day, Gandhi said that he was imposing this isolation on himself. He added: 'People have been pampering me too much. I would not have felt free until I was severely alone.'[182] The peace mission was meant to be contemplative, undisturbed by too much attention and chatter. Noakhali was a place of mourning.

In his report, the correspondent from *The Hindu* described meeting Gandhi 'in the evening in his new abode in Srirampur, sitting calmly in a half-burnt house amidst ruins'.[183]

This description registers an unusually poignant moment at the heart of the twentieth century. Gandhi was playing watchman to an empty place that was in ruins. The half-burnt house reflected Gandhi's ruined expectations. He had the courage to sit inside the wreckage of his own dreams. Gandhi's choice to live in a destroyed home was also, paradoxically, a stubborn, symbolic gesture that signified that all was not destroyed yet.

'Kya Karun? Kya Karun?'

On the next day, 21 November, Gandhi had to postpone his early morning visit to meet Maulvi Waliullah during his walk due to rain. Later, he met some Hindu political workers where the Mahasabha leader, Manoranjan Chaudhuri, reiterated that Hindu demands be fulfilled before the formalization of a peace initiative. Gandhi said,

'Your proposal . . . virtually means a summary rejection of the peace offer. This will only succeed in embittering feelings still further. The Government offer should be accepted on grounds of expediency. I do not however plead for peace at any price, certainly not at the price of honour. Let us act on the square, and let us put them in the wrong.'[184]

Gandhi's method is based on political morality. The moral onus is on the government to betray the people who have invested their trust in it. Gandhi's politics of trust, or his political idea of trust, involves making governmental power responsible by exercising moral pressure. Gandhi confessed that he saw no 'change of heart' in the Muslim leadership, but he detected a 'change of plan'[185] that made him hopeful for the peace initiative.

Next Gandhi said something very significant, paraphrased by Nirmal Kumar Bose:

> '[Hitherto] our non-violence had been non-violence of the weak; but now that we had to apply it against a section of our own countrymen instead of against the British, it had to be non-violence of the strong.'[186]

Gandhi, in the figure of the editor of *Hind Swaraj*, had refuted the reader's observation that 'passive resistance is a splendid weapon of the weak'.[187] Gandhi in Srirampur seems to mean that even if earlier, people with lesser will and courage could give non-violence a try, the gravity of the current situation offered no luxuries. It is more difficult to maintain self-restraint with people with whom one shares social and cultural intimacy, than with foreigners with whom relations are more objective and distant.

Gandhi's diary entry for 22 November in Srirampur gives us a glimpse of the life he was beginning to lead in Noakhali:

> 'Rose at 4 a.m. The *Gita* recitation took two hours. Pronunciation of the reciter was very unsatisfactory.
>
> Wrote to R. that his son (who recently lost his wife) should not remarry, or marry a widow if he must.
>
> Visited a Muslim *badi* at 7.30 a.m. The way was long. It took full 20 minutes to get there—55 minutes coming and going.
>
> Gave myself massage like yesterday . . . At 10.30 a number of visitors came. After they had gone, had a short nap with mud-pack on the abdomen. Span for one hour. Abdullah (the Superintendent of Police) with some others came for

> the meeting at Ramgunj in the evening. Started at 4 p.m. with them for Ramgunj. Reached Ramgunj at 5.20 p.m. The meeting continued till 10.30 p.m. Addressed a few words at the end . . . Had evening prayer on the boat on the return journey and then some sleep. Had milk while proceeding to Ramgunj; hot water on return. Reached Srirampur at midnight.'[188]

There was nothing spectacular or dramatic about Gandhi's range of activities. But it was a lot for a man of seventy-seven. Gandhi was simultaneously dealing with his ageing body and the crumbling body politic around him with agility and attention. On 23 November, *The Hindu* reported Gandhi's speech at Chandipur:

> 'He could not say whether Suhrawardy Saheb was a good man or a bad one. But he knew that he was elected by the voters. Hindus and Muslims had to live under his Government just as those in Bihar had to live under the rule of the Congress Government. If people did not like a particular Government the electorate could change it. But it was not in his power to do so.'[189]

Gandhi strictly maintained this position during his Noakhali campaign. He did not absolve Suhrawardy of his moral responsibility for failing to quell the Noakhali genocide. Yet he appealed to his political responsibility and took his help. As long as Suhrawardy was in power, it was his job to protect people. Gandhi had come to ensure peace and heal wounds. But part of his job was also to remind the government of its duty. The fact that the interim government in Bengal needed Gandhi to remind it of its executive responsibilities shows the deep shadow of communal power corroding the origins of India's political sovereignty.

From Gandhi's diary entry of 23 November, we learn:

> 'Massage was given by N. [Nirmal Kumar Bose] so that I was able to have a 40 minutes' nap on the massage table. Leafy vegetable served at midday was very bitter. Took it with 1 oz. of coconut milk . . . Next unsuccessfully tried to have a little sleep—nausea and gripe. Gave myself enema . . . Dozed off with mud-pack on the abdomen while proceeding to Ramgunj . . . Had to stop the boat on account of violent diarrhoea and vomiting . . . Felt relieved . . . Reached Ramgunj at 5 p.m. Had another motion during the recess but was able to address the meeting at the end without difficulty. Started on the return journey at 8.15 p.m. . . . Reached Srirampur at 11 p.m. . . . Completed the daily quota of spinning, partly on the boat while proceeding to the meeting and the balance at the meeting itself.'[190]

Sleeping on a massage table, undergoing physical turbulence in the midst of his travel routine and keeping track of time were manifestations of Satyagraha that demonstrated the material stakes of its avowed principles. The insistence on spinning while journeying is not to be read only as an act of relentless productivity. It is also an act of calm against a volatile and gloomy atmosphere. Spinning was a slow activity in time, or a calm activity in a time that has slowed down.

On 24 November, Gandhi met Sarat Chandra Bose who arrived early in the morning at Gandhi's makeshift camp at Srirampur. Bose was accompanied by Chapala Kanta Bhattacharya, the editor of *Ananda Bazar Patrika*, Captain Razvi, Lieutenant Samson of the Indian National Army and others.[191] During the conversation, Bose observed,

'If the League leaders were to take the Noakhali situation as seriously as you and Jawaharlal took Bihar, order would be restored in a day.'[192]

Gandhi did not want to entertain that comparison, and called it a way to 'degrade oneself'.[193] He called for 'more introspection', clearly suggesting that they accept more responsibility, rather than harbouring any sense of moral superiority.[194] Gandhi then made the observation that 'Harijans and Namashudras'[195] showed more strength and courage during the carnage than other Hindus who lived by caste distinctions. The suggestion is that people living by customs of social hierarchy and distancing were incapable of bravery as they were more prone to protect their social position in times of calamity. Ironically, such a social attitude enabled upper caste Hindus to take advantage of their economic prosperity during the famine, but made them completely vulnerable during the genocide.

The group left after two hours of discussion with Gandhi on the situation in Noakhali and Bihar. Nirmal Kumar Bose mentioned in his diary entry for the day:

> 'Twice during the whole day, I heard him [Gandhi] muttering to himself, "*Kya karun*? *Kya karun*?", 'What should I do? What should I do'?'[196]

This little description offers an intimate window into the state of Gandhi's mind. There is a desperate desire to overcome the hurdles that he was facing in Noakhali. It is a moving expression of Gandhi's vulnerability. It is not easy to think when you are surrounded by widespread violence and distrust, when society has undergone a moral breakdown in existential and relational terms. It is easier to understand the reason behind the violence rather than the *condition* such violence has produced. The condition of life post-violence can't be grasped through a rational prism. It involves the feelings, emotions and sentiments not only of the people who faced brutality, but also of the people who perpetrated it.

Gandhi was faced with the impossibility of the moment, seeking rapprochement between two communities divided by violence. There has been irreparable damage done to the body and the soul. The method of non-violence faced its most formidable block. Gandhi was finding it difficult to locate the *space of recovery*, both within people's hearts and in their neighbourhoods.

Considering this unique moment in Gandhi's life, V.S. Naipaul in *India*: *A Wounded Civilization* makes note of Gandhi's heroic resolve in Noakhali without his usual touch of sarcasm and acerbic tone:

> 'Now, in Bengal, he has nothing to offer except his presence, and he knows it. Yet he is heard to say to himself again and again, '*Kya karun? Kya karun?* What shall I do?' At this terrible moment his thoughts are of action, and he is magnificent.'[197]

At the peace committee meeting at Ramgunj on 25 November, Gandhi informed the audience,

> 'The most important task is to restore the confidence among the Hindus so that they would be able to pursue their religious practices in freedom. Mr Akhil Dutta has lately sent me a cheque for Rs 850 and a letter stating that 200 pairs of conch-shell bangles and a pound of

> vermilion had been despatched to Noakhali. These are for distribution among women who had suffered during the riots. *The best part of the presents is that they were collected by eleven Muslim gentlemen and one Englishman.* I have met women who put on the vermilion mark indoors but wipe it off when they stir out in public. Such fear has to be removed by the Muslims. It is not a question of giving monetary aid, but of restoring confidence by respect shown to the culture of others. I will ask my Mussalman friends to treat this as their sacred duty. The prophet once advised Mussalmans to consider the Jewish places of worship to be as pure as their own and offer it the same protection. It is the duty of the Mussalmans of today to assure the same freedom to their Hindu neighbours.'[198] [Emphasis mine]

Be it Gandhi's presence or sheer soul-searching or both, the gesture of the Muslim men to distribute the bangles and vermillion among Hindu women was a promising gesture of rapprochement. Communal violence is violence not just against people, but against the marks and signs of culture. To work against such violence includes a certain restoration of culture. Culture, with its prejudices and oppressive forms, is also the lowest limit of people's relationship with the community. The significance of restoring culture in contexts like Noakhali is to heal what has been devalued by violence. An internal critique of cultural values within a community is meant for another time. In other words, social and political criticism of culture is a gradual historical process, which can argue for change, including the rejection of cultural markers of belonging (that act as signs of power). But the devaluation of those markers of belonging by coercion is an ethical violation of the right to cultural life.

On his morning walk on 26 November, Gandhi visited the house of Ismail Khondkar, the farmer who had come to meet him at Srirampur station, to help with a child suffering from 'kalazar' (leishmaniosis).[199] Later in the morning, he met members of the communist party and the Students' Federation who shared their apprehensions about fresh trouble after the Constituent Assembly commences on 9 December.[200] They suggested that Gandhi convene an all-parties' meeting and coordinate the work done by different organizations. Gandhi declined the suggestion without offering a good reason, hinting that he wanted to work separately by his own rules. He said that the best way in which the Hindus of Noakhali could come together was by 'utterly forgetting caste, not as mere lip-profession but in actual practice.'[201] Then he added in a dramatic manner:

> 'I do not want to retire from Bengal as a defeated coward. I would like to die here, if need be, at the hands of an assassin. But I do not want to court such death.'[202]

Gandhi was clearly wrestling with thoughts of defeat. But at the same time, it did not make him lose his patience, or his calm resolve.

In an interview later in the day, he was asked why he had decided to camp in one village alone (meaning, Srirampur). Gandhi made an analogy of a 'wise gardener' raising a single seedling with care to ascertain 'the exact conditions under which the plant will thrive'[203] (paraphrased by N.K. Bose). This explains an important aspect of the Gandhian 'experiment' of non-violence during a crisis where time and effort are invested in creating conditions where the will and strength of a beleaguered people can be restored.

During an interview with The *Bombay Chronicle* on 27 November, Gandhi was asked if Hindus who lived in areas where they were outnumbered by Muslims should be shifted to areas where Hindus had a comparatively bigger presence, to enable some form of resistance if they were attacked again. Gandhi's reply was clear,

> 'There is no such safety as you imagine in numbers in imagined conditions. Migration is no remedy whilst there is hope of co-operation. It will become a necessity when the majority party wishes it, if a clash is to be avoided. All this is a matter of mutual adjustment, not arbitrary action. What is needed is that barbarities must cease, if we are to survive as one nation or two, or many free nations still living in friendly co-operation.'[204]

Gandhi's firm view about the dislocation of people to create pockets of safety zones shifted from the fundamental responsibility of ending hostilities. To that effect, Gandhi's hopes were bleak. In a press interview to *Hindustan Standard* in Srirampur on 2 December, Gandhi confessed:

> 'I argued to myself that I must be on the scene of action and I find that my ahimsa does not seem to answer in the matter of Hindu–Muslim relations. This struck me forcibly when I came to learn of the events in Noakhali. The reported forcible conversions and the distress of the Bengali sisters touched me deeply. I could do nothing through pen or speech. I argued to myself that I must be on the scene of action and test the soundness of the doctrine which has sustained me and made life worth living. Was it the weapon of the weak as it was often held by my critics or

> was it truly the weapon of the strong? The question arose in me when I had no ready-made solution for the distemper of which Noakhali was such a glaring symptom.'[205]

Gandhi admitted that he was losing to his critics. His politics of love lay shattered in Noakhali. The only thing he could do was bring himself to test the technique of non-violence in a place shaken by violence. In other words, Gandhi was out to test the real ground of non-violence.

Gandhi wrote a letter to Suhrawardy on 3 December, updating the chief minister on the conditions prevailing in Noakhali, including his apprehensions:

> 'In spite of all my efforts exodus continues and very few persons have returned to their villages. They say the guilty parties are still at large, some finding a place on the Peace Committees, that sporadic cases of murder and arson still continue, that abducted women have not all been returned, that forcibly converted persons have not all returned, that burnt houses are not being rebuilt and generally the atmosphere of goodwill is lacking. How far these charges are true or can be proved I do not know. My object just now is to bring these to your notice. It might be that a summary impartial inquiry is necessary to restore confidence.'[206]

On 4 December, Professor Amiya Chakravarty, who taught English at Calcutta University, came to Srirampur, and suggested to Gandhi that the peace workers who were stationed at various villages should be brought together so that people could have a better sense of the method of non-violence at work in East Bengal. Gandhi replied,

> 'They are following not a beaten path but a trackless route. Their work lies in the midst of a Muslim population. They do not know the language and are not familiar with local problems. I myself don't know what the next step is and cannot guide them. They are unable to send reports now. If I made a chart for them, they would be able to keep a log-book. Even the great Thakkar Bapa, as old as myself, a seasoned worker and utterly selfless, is working away without knowing what he is doing'.[207]

This is a remarkable admission. The nature of the work undertaken by Gandhi and his associates was without precedence. The peace workers did not know the local language, nor were they aware of the specific nature of the problems that afflicted the people. The workers were guided by intuition rather than a firm grip on knowledge regarding their habitat. They worked for peace under a condition of radical unfamiliarity without fear (or by overcoming fear).

Chakravarty acknowledged the exemplary nature of what Gandhi and his associates were doing, holding it up as a universal standard for peace work:

> 'Noakhali has now become a laboratory where a crucial test is being made; the remedy will apply to situations all the world over where disputes arise between communities and nationalities and a new technique is needed for peaceful adjustment.'[208]

In a political context, the word 'laboratory' has had a sinisterly negative connotation. Writing in *Origins of Totalitarianism* on the concentration camps under the totalitarian regime run by Hitler and Stalin, Hannah Arendt called them 'special laboratories to carry through its experiment in total domination.'[209] Laboratories are spaces where you experiment on the validity of an idea. It is a space for scientific research in the modern world where even politics seeks to be science. The race theory of Nazism and the Marxist theory of historical materialism were presented and propagated as scientifically accurate blueprints for a perfect human society. Both these theories were supported by regimes that committed grave violence against countless people who were designated enemies of this scientific project of a new humanity.

Chakravarty goes against the established connotation to signify that Gandhi's peace mission was a laboratory. The word is not so out of place since Gandhi in his autobiography considered his historical mission as 'experiments with truth', which combined 'experiments in the political field' and 'experiments in the spiritual field'.[210] Comparing his task to that of a scientist, Gandhi upholds his approach saying that 'he conducts his experiments with the utmost accuracy, forethought and minuteness, never claims any finality about his conclusions, *but keeps an open mind regarding them*.'[211]

For Gandhi, the laboratory of peace is a place where an experiment is conducted not by insisting on establishing a truth he already possessed, but by allowing the possibility of being contradicted. To keep an open mind about truth is to acknowledge the worth of experience. The laboratory of peace is the ethical antithesis of the Gulags and concentration camps where political regimes experimented with horror.

Gandhi believed in acts of persuasion. Something Aristotle affirmed in *Rhetoric*. In his political career, Gandhi has always drawn attention to the political value of persuasion. He made a significant statement on how fundamental the value of persuasion is for him while speaking to Sikhs at Bhangi Nivas in Delhi on 12 April 1947:

> '[One] cannot bring about any change in a person by law, it can be done only through persuasion. Therefore, no one can ever become non-violent through law.'[212]

The spirit of non-violence can't be a juridical imposition. Its value is best imparted through the craft of persuasion. In *Rhetoric*, Aristotle argues that the 'means of persuasion come about not only through demonstrative argument but also through argument expressive of character (for we are persuaded by a speaker due to his appearing to be of a certain quality, that is, if he appears good, goodwilled, or both).'[213] Gandhi's insistence that the success or failure of his non-violent mission depends on the strength and weaknesses of his character is in tune with Aristotle's view on the political success of persuasion.

Chakravarty further said something in adulation:

> 'That Bengal should be chosen for this great task, that you should have made this your centre, is, to us, a supreme privilege though people have suffered and are suffering beyond description. The whole of Bengal is conscious of your arrival and of the fact that you have come to live and work with the suffering men and women who need you so much at this hour.'[214]

Given Gandhi's age, his physical limitations, the distance between Noakhali and Delhi, his own cultural distance from the people and despite the tremendous violence that separated them the most, Gandhi's presence was a significant event. It was only after Gandhi reached Noakhali that people—his own associates, the people of Bengal and Noakhali, the political leaders, the administrators, even the police—realized that this was real, someone had indeed arrived to be with the people in their darkest moment. It was an epic gesture, a great moment of the arrival of a messiah to heal the wounds of a people.

There were encouraging signs, as Pyarelal describes in *The Last Phase*:

> "By the end of his six weeks' stay at Srirampur, Gandhiji had won many hearts. Groups of Muslim men, women and children collected in front of their huts with presents of fruit to greet him when he went out for his morning and evening walks. There was an instinctive recognition that he was of them, united to them with bonds of common humanity that transcends all barriers of caste and creed. And the transformation was not confined to Muslims alone. The Hindus, too, began to revive under the message of love. Shortly before the prayer on the 4th December, a procession of about 600 Hindu men, women and children arrived from the neighbouring villages after walking a distance of six miles singing the *namasamkirtan* to the accompaniment of *khol* and *kartala*."[215]

This is nothing short of a miraculous transformation of the communal psyche. Even though this response to Gandhi's presence was partial and short-lived, he managed to stir people's hearts and extract fraternal gestures. In the two letters he wrote on 5 December from his camp at Srirampur, one to Agatha Harrison (an English peace activist from a nonprofit organization), and the other to his nephew, Narandas, Gandhi used similar language to express his condition. To Harrison, he wrote: 'I have never been in such darkness as I am in today.'[216] And to Narandas: 'I do not remember to have experienced such darkness in my life ever before, and the night seems long.'[217]

The same day, Gandhi also met Hindu Mahasabha leaders where the president, secretary and Naren Bose, brother of a Noakhali victim, shared their plan for segregating the Hindus of Noakhali to ensure their safety. Gandhi thought differently on the question:

> 'Put yourself in Mr Suhrawardy's shoes; do you think he would favour it, or even the Muslim residents of Noakhali? For it would be interpreted as a preparation for war. But if you believe that this is the only workable scheme, you can go ahead with it. For myself, the path is different.'[218]

Gandhi still thought rapprochement was possible. He also did not want to antagonize or alarm the state administration as they held power, and wanted to take them into confidence.

On 19 December, Manu reached Srirampur with her father, Jaisukhlal Amritlal Gandhi. She started writing her diary from her first day with Gandhi in Noakhali. It remains the most extraordinary testament of Gandhi's last years, offering us a unique glimpse into the everyday life of non-violence through the eyes and mind of a teenaged girl.

Manu's growing into maturity and India's descent into chaos happened together. This incomparable contrast, and that Manu lives it with bewilderment and resilience, remains the hallmark of her testament. The fact that she was part of the controversial 'experiment' of Brahmacharya has found singular focus among scholars and writers. It is far from the true measure of her work during these turbulent last years of Gandhi's life. Manu has been reduced to an overawed and vulnerable figure, negotiating with adult attention.

Apart from the fact that Manu handled that attention with remarkable balance, it is the nature of her work as a peace worker, and her witness-account of Gandhi's life and movement that remains her most significant contribution to history.

Crossing the Bridge

Manu's clock was put in motion the very next day, from the morning of 20 December. She took part in the morning prayers at 3 a.m. Since she was still tired from her journey and lacked sleep, Gandhi asked her to rest. After an hour, Manu took a walk with Gandhi who gave her, she noted in her diary, 'a picture of the grotesque acts committed in Noakhali.'[219] Manu also noted,

'Bapuji every day practices crossing a bridge.'[220] (The bridge is erected with a single bamboo.)

Troubled by news from Bihar, Gandhi wrote to the Bihar chief minister Srikrishna Sinha on 21 December:

> 'I read in some newspaper that the Bihar Ministry does not propose to hold any inquiry. I was sorry to note it. I want the ministries of both the provinces to hold an impartial inquiry by a joint committee to probe the incidents in both the provinces . . . It will be good if you can also let me know the true condition at present. What is the truth in the report that many Muslims have left Bihar and many are still leaving? There is also a complaint that representatives

of the Muslim League are not even allowed to visit the Muslim refugee camps set up by the Bihar Government.'[221]

On 24 December, Gandhi wrote to Suhrawardy, reminding him of their pleasant meeting in Faridpur (Dacca) where they met in the presence of Deshbandhu Chittaranjan Das. Suhrawardy had said that he felt like Gandhi's son. Gandhi wrote:

> 'I would like to think still that you are the same Shaheed and to feel proud that my son has become Chief Minister of Bengal . . .
>
> I wish you had Bengal on the brain rather than Bihar. Assume the truth of all that has been said in the Bihar provincial Muslim League's reports . . . You do not want to satisfy yourself by thanking God for Bengal being as bad as Bihar . . .'[222]

Against the light of an old memory where Suhrawardy conveyed his filial attachment, Gandhi reminded the Bengal chief minister not to lose his moral compass by indulging in comparisons between the killings in Bengal and Bihar, but rather address his own lack of responsibility.

The next day, lying on his wooden bedstead at 3 a.m., Gandhi dictated a disturbing but telling letter to Manu, addressed to Vallabhbhai Patel:

> 'The situation here poses many difficulties and problems. Truth is nowhere to be found. Violence masquerades as non-violence and heinous crimes are committed in the name of religion. But truth and non-violence can be tested only in such conditions. I know this and that is why I am here.'[223]

Gandhi's sense that violence was masquerading as non-violence can lie in a gamut of things. It can be in speech and intention, in the difference between what people say and what they mean, in the void between the visible and the invisible, the uncertainty beneath language and silence where you cannot trust either. This describes a moral breakdown of social ties, infected by the air of violence. Gandhi finds this condition the perfect ground to test the strength of truth and non-violence. Since truth and non-violence are what is *absent*—what there is a dearth of—in the world, it is in the state of their radical violation that their possibility can be most imaginatively explored. Truth and non-violence are possibilities in a world that negates them by its nature and reason. There is a nature of violence, but also, always, a reason behind violence. It is in their demonstrability that truth and non-violence exist as a possibility. Gandhi was in Noakhali to demonstrate that truth and non-violence were possible.

The next day, 25 December, Manu again noted in her diary: 'Bapuji "practices" crossing the bridge daily. The bridge is so constructed that a fall would certainly result in an injury.'[224]

Crossing the bridge was part of Gandhi's daily challenges, and he wanted to master the art. Behind it was also Gandhi's principle of maintaining an economy of time when he was out on his mission.

Gandhi with his peace mission crossing a slender wooden bridge, Noakhali, November 1946

The same day, Gandhi wrote to some sub-divisional members of the Muslim League in response to the postcard that he had received from them. This postcard had a copy of the resolution that they had passed, stating that Gandhi must leave Noakhali for Bihar, claiming things were currently normal in Noakhali. Addressing the leaders as 'Gentlemen', Gandhi wrote,

> 'I have just received your postcard scribbled out in ink and thank you for your advice. I am unable to follow your advice which is definitely based on ignorance of facts. In the first place, I know that the situation is not normal here and that in so far as I can contribute to the Bihar problem,

> I have to inform you that such influence as I have on Bihar can be and is being efficiently exercised from Srirampur.'[225]

The Muslim League was clearly uncomfortable with Gandhi's presence in Noakhali. It was a political and not moral discomfort because they had already sacrificed their morality to achieve their genocidal ambition. Gandhi was sternly forthright, telling them that their assessment of the situation wasn't correct and that he would not act on their advice.

On 27 December, Gandhi wrote a letter to Hamiduddin Ahmed, the Parliamentary Secretary to the Minister for Commerce, Government of Bengal, in response to his indictment of Gandhi in an article in the pro-League Bengali daily The *Azad* (published from Dacca) on 14 December. It is necessary to quote the letter at length to understand the political questions around Gandhi's camping in Noakhali:

> 'Why do you in common with many advisers advise me to leave Noakhali and go to Bihar or somewhere else?
>
> I have not come to East Bengal to hold an enquiry. I have come to make my humble contribution to a lasting and heart peace between the two communities. I think that I made this statement during the speeches I had made in your presence. Why then the sudden change betrayed by the article in question? Do you not think that after the exuberant regard you showed for me, I had the right to expect from you a friendly and personal enquiry from me, to inform me of the change and giving the grounds for the change? Perhaps, on reflection, you will discover in your very article valid reason for my longing to be in Noakhali in preference to Bihar. How can I test the efficacy and soundness of my ahimsa except in a place where even the

loudest protestations of trust in my professions can be so short-lived as in your case?

You are right when you say: "In Mr Gandhi's opinion, the condition in Noakhali is not yet such that Hindus can shoulder the responsibility of returning to their homes." I have chapter and verse to show why the Hindu refugees who proved themselves deficient in personal courage are reluctant to go back to their homes. The Peace Committees which you left in the process of formation are not in working order . . .

You say, again: "If he (Gandhi) had issued a statement about the real nature of the happenings, perhaps the atmosphere would have cleared to a large extent. His silence with reference to this matter raises suspicion in the minds of many." Why this insinuation when the fact stares you in the face that I am not in a position to speak in praise of what has been and is being done on behalf of the Bengal Government? If you will care to study the thing, you will appreciate restraint instead of coaxing me to speak.

You are again right when you say: "Mr Gandhi does not wish to leave for Bihar." But your reasons for reluctance are wholly wrong. My "trusted Bihari followers" have indeed kept me informed of the happenings there. The information they give is wholly contrary to what you believe. In common with all, the Bihar Government deplore the tragic happenings. But they claim that they have acquired control over the turbulent elements and are straining every nerve to give satisfaction to the afflicted.'[226]

From Suhrawardy to Hamiduddin, Muslim leaders in Bengal who had an amiable disposition towards Gandhi grew restless against him for poking his nose into their political affairs.

With admirable humility, Gandhi clarified that he had not arrived in Noakhali to seek political accountability for the genocide, but ethical accountability from the government to bring peace. Gandhi had arrived in Noakhali without any thought of *doing* politics but to find out the *state* of the politics.

Gandhi raised the question of trust as the basis of responsibility, exposing the utter lack of it in Hamiduddin who was single-mindedly serving the politics of suspicion. In fact, Hamiduddin clarified that the specific source of his suspicions was based on Gandhi not sharing his views publicly on what he thought had taken place (and was taking place) in Noakhali. He hinted that Gandhi was expected to absolve the state government from public accusation for its alleged role in orchestrating the genocide, and praise the League for the semblance of its relief work. Gandhi's silence on these issues made him a suspect in the eyes of the League ministers. For them, the way to establish peace lay in Gandhi assuring the League that he believed their every word and action. In other words, Gandhi must suspend his moral and political judgement to favour the League in order to buy their confidence. Any reluctance shown by Gandhi to do so would point towards secret hostility on his part, and force the League to question Gandhi's motives for coming to Noakhali.

The desperate anxiety of the League made them suspect Gandhi's *imagined* hostility towards them and led them to make their *real* hostility public.

This is a good illustration of how political power behaves when guilt turns into aggression. Gandhi altered his tone to remind Hamiduddin not to stretch his luck too far by looking for praise, but to feel grateful that Gandhi hadn't spoken his mind. To the insinuation that he was unwilling to go to Bihar and address the genocide against Muslims there, Gandhi gave a tactical response, putting his faith behind the Congress government but saying he was 'not anxious to give them a certificate of good conduct'.[227]

Hamiduddin had also raised concerns over Gandhi 'importing numberless volunteers'.[228] Refuting the accusation, Gandhi described the nature of the work that his volunteers did. It marked the fundamental distinction between people involved in a political movement and Gandhi's movement of peace:

> 'I hope that before the Government takes the adumbrated action they will depute an officer of their choice or trust to find out from me or them the kind of work they are doing. Their life is an open book. There is nothing hidden or underground about their activities.'[229]

Landing at Dum Dum airport on 27 December, Nehru left for Noakhali in the afternoon. He had come to urgently discuss the intricacies of the Cabinet Mission Plan with Gandhi ahead of the Congress Working Committee meeting to be held in Delhi in January the following year.

Bangladeshi journalist and columnist Syed Abul Maksud writes, a crowd of 2000, mostly comprising Muslims, had come to greet Nehru at the Feni aerodrome braving the severe cold.[230] The Feni aerodrome was temporarily built in Chittagong by the British for the United States Air Force during the Burma Campaign of 1944–45 (against the combined armies of Japan, Burma and the INA). Before leaving for Srirampur where Gandhi was stationed, Nehru spoke briefly to the audience that had gathered near the airport. As he began to speak, stones were hurled at Nehru and he was hit by a stone on the cheek.[231] Gandhi's followers, Maksud writes, believed that the stones were not thrown by Muslim League supporters (even Nehru thought so), but by members of either the Sarat Bose faction of the Congress or the Hindu Mahasabha to deliberately put suspicion on the League.[232] After Nehru had asked Sarat Bose to step down from the Executive Council of the Interim Government in October 1946 to accommodate League members, Bose's followers were disgruntled.[233] Nehru stayed with Gandhi in the partly damaged 'rajbari', a nineteenth century mansion that belonged to a zamindar but was abandoned during the genocide after it was looted and set on fire.[234] Nehru and other Congress leaders had formal discussions with Gandhi on 28 December.

In a closed-door meeting with Gandhi later, Maksud writes, Nehru shared his annoyance with the 'public utterances' of Congress leaders Kripalani and his wife Sucheta, which he construed as communal.[235]

Maksud writes that the Congress leadership took its final decision on partition 'on the night of 28–29 December 1946 in a small tin-shed house where Mahatma Gandhi was staying temporarily while conducting his Peace Mission in the riot-affected areas.'[236]

On 30 December, Gandhi's day of silence, Nehru left Srirampur for Delhi early in the morning. Gandhi accompanied him over the course of his own morning walk. Maksud sums up the moment of farewell:

> 'Nehru took leave of the Mahatma as far as the end of the bridge, half a mile from Srirampur.'[237]

It reads like the description of a longshot in a film. You can feel the quietness of the moment with its poignant uncertainty. The bridges of hope were breaking apart. Two powerful men in India's anti-colonial movement were bidding farewell to each other at the end of a tenuous bridge in a far-flung village in East Bengal. The moment is significant considering that it was nearing the end of 1946. On the one hand, there were political negotiations on independence and partition in Delhi, while a vicious 'final solution' of communal politics was at work in the eastern corner.

On 31 December, the last day of the year, Gandhi bared his gravest concerns in a conversation with his Malayali stenographer Parasuram and Nirmal Kumar Bose:

> 'If the Hindus and Muslims cannot live side by side in brotherly love in Noakhali, they will not be able to do so over the whole of India, and Pakistan will be the inevitable result. India will be divided, and if India is divided she will be lost forever. Therefore, I say that if India is to remain undivided, Hindus and Muslims must live together in brotherly love, not in hostile camps organized either for defensive action or retaliation. I am, therefore, opposed to the policy of segregation in pockets. There is only one way of solving the problem and that is by non-violence. I know today mine is a cry in the wilderness. But I repeat that there is no salvation for India except through the way of truth, non-violence, courage and love. To demonstrate the efficacy of that way I have come here. If Noakhali is lost, India is lost.'[238]

Gandhi's words are succinct and prescient. Noakhali was a far-flung district of Bengal, comprising a cluster of villages.

If the rural folk living in this area committed genocide, while falling for a contrived communal emergency, other areas, particularly more urban ones (where Hindu and Muslim populations were more concentrated) were prone to becoming successful laboratories of collective hate. Hate has a spiral effect, like an epidemic. The Muslim League realized that it wasn't possible to divide India by juridical strategies alone. A demand for Pakistan was not enough as a political argument. The logical justification of partition had to be cemented by demonstrating that Hindus and Muslims couldn't live together.

Before partition could be formalized in ink, it had to be decided by blood.

Gandhi was against camps. He saw them as furthering the logic of segregation and hostility. He wanted victims to retain their neighbourhoods, for neighbourhoods alone retained the possibility of rapprochement. If neighbourhoods were lost, the nation was lost. It turned out to be true when millions were displaced during partition and ended up in camps. India was lost for these displaced people. Gandhi's cry in the wilderness of politics was ignored by those busy making history.

On 2 January, Gandhi travelled to Chandipur with a dozen volunteers. The team left Srirampur at 7.30 a.m. and Nirmal Kumar Bose described how 'Gandhi walked across the paddy fields recently laid bare after the harvest had been gathered in'.[239]

Walking Alone, Walking with Others

Speaking at the prayer meeting in Chandipur on 2 January 1947, Gandhi emphasized the need to reorganize village life and improve economic conditions by improving the cottage industries. This would bring Hindus and Muslims together by engaging them in a common task.[240] The next day, speaking to Hindu women in Chandipur, Gandhi urged them to invite Harijans for dinner as a way towards erasing untouchability. Gandhi's diary entry of 3 January reads:

> 'While walking, saw the ravages in the colony of Namasudras. The mind started thinking: how could anyone stoop so low as to perpetrate such havoc in the name of religion or for selfish gain.'[241]

Namasudras, Bengal's Dalits, were not landowners like upper-caste Hindus. Muslims and Namasudras were both cultivators, and shared the status of the peasantry.[242] In the late 1920s, Namasudra and Muslim sharecroppers fought together against Hindu landlords.[243]

By the late 1940s, Namasudras and tribals in the northern and eastern parts of Bengal were influenced by the spread of the shuddhi and sangathan movements and began to assert their Hindu identity and got into clashes with the Muslims.[244] Since social and cultural status are as much a matter of political contestation as economic rights, both motivations (irrespective of, or despite, ideological influences) by marginalized groups have their legitimate place in political history. The genocide of 1946 clearly marked the triumph of communal sentiments over weakened class solidarity, which rules out the peasantry as necessarily fulfilling a prescribed role as agents of historical change.

Manu's diary also recounted the painful discovery of 3 January:

> 'In the forenoon we went to visit the Harijan locality they are called Namasudra here. The inhumanity perpetrated on them makes one quiver Devnath Das and Jiwan Sinhji of INA were with us'.[245]

She also noted in the entry for the same day: 'Bapuji applied a mudpack on his stomach and talked with visitors from Bihar including Bhai Sinha and Walton Sahib. Bihar's killings appear to be such that they would push Noakhali in the second place.'[246]

For Manu, who had just arrived in Noakhali, to make that definitive comparison may appear to be presumptuous. But she knew what we don't, at least not yet.

Manu wrote on 4 December of Gandhi telling her: 'Thousands have been killed here. And that should make us accountable for each wasted moment. Sleep only to sustain the body. Same with respect to food, thus we limit all our bodily needs.'[247] The active nature of a non-violent movement involves accountability of time. The time of violence is a time of crisis, and non-violence fills up that crisis with intense activity. Because non-violent activity is ethical, it is other-bound, and least focused on the needs of the self. *You live in the time of the other.* The plight of the other dictates your time. When violence has run deep, there must be deep engagement in order to restore lives and heal hearts. Gandhi had come to Noakhali to spend his time with the people. There is no greater material commitment to something you value.

Time is calculative if we think of clock-time. It is metaphysical if we think of life as such. Our experience of time is being in the world, including being body. Experience has two doors, or openings, one leading within, and another leading towards others. To experience the time of the other one must cross the second door. It is face-to-face time, the time of hearing, of learning something beyond yourself but what is intimately connected to you. It opens up the possibility of experiencing ethical time.

On 7 January, Gandhi was at Masimpur. They left for their morning walk at 7.30 a.m. Manu described the scene:

> 'The women of the house and other women from the neighbourhood did an *aarti* and applied a *tilak* on Bapuji's forehead. Bapuji's one hand rested on me and with the other he held his stick. He was bare foot. At precisely 7:30 a.m. the *Ekla chalo re* ["*If no one heeds your call, walk alone*", written by Tagore in 1905 inspired from a Vaishnava song] was sung and we began our walk. After that *Ramdhun* and other hymns were sung. Persons from the press and military accompanied us. The path on which we walked was very beautiful. It was wide enough only for two persons to walk and a canopy of coconut and areca nut trees bent down as if to bless Bapuji. Above the green canopy the sun god emerged in a crimson sky to bear testimony to this historic, pious, great man. The sunrise was grand. There were water bodies around and a carpet of green grass.'[248]

For Manu to find Gandhi historic in that setting is itself historic. There was nothing grand and imposing about their status. Gandhi and his team were a bunch of vulnerable people trying to address a more acute problem of vulnerability in people reeling from violence. The lovely description by Manu is reminiscent of Salman Rushdie mentioning in *Midnight's*

Children about 'the violence in Bengal and the long pacifying walk of Mahatma Gandhi.'[249]

Writing in *Young India* on 3 April 1930, Gandhi said, walking is 'justly called the prince of exercises.'[250] The term, peripatetic, is associated with Aristotle. 'To travel on foot', Jean-Jacques Rousseau writes in *Emile*, 'is to travel like Thales, Plato, and Pythagoras.'[251] Rousseau believes that anyone who has 'some taste for natural history'[252] will prefer walking. Since the body and its movements were a part of Gandhi's engagement with life, including political life, it gave him a sense of resistance against modern technologies of travel (which he otherwise used without hesitation for practical purposes). In a conversation with G. Ramachandran, a student of C.F Andrews in Shantiniketan in October 1924, Gandhi was asked if he was against all machinery. He replied, 'How can I be when I know that even this body is a most delicate piece of machinery? The spinning-wheel itself is a machine; a little tooth-pick is a machine. What I object to, is the craze for machinery, not machinery as such. The craze is for what they call labour-saving machinery.'[253] Then he added, in response to another question, 'The machine should not tend to make atrophied the limbs of man.'[254]

Gandhi acknowledges the body as a kind of technology. He highlights the distinction between the body's fragile technology and technology as a power over the body's fragility. Gandhi argues for a qualitative distinction between machinery as a fetish and machinery *as such*, and speaks against a cult of technology, a technology-driven cult. No wonder walking became an organic part of his political life. Gandhi walked against the British Empire using the simplest means to draw people along. With Gandhi, walking becomes a force in

India's political history. In Noakhali, walking merged with the idea of pilgrimage. It wasn't only a pilgrimage of mourning, but also of intimacy with people in the villages.

Gandhi with his peace mission on way to a riot-affected village, Noakhali, 1947

When they went for the prayer meeting later in the day singing *Ram Dhun* on their way, Manu paused over the sight before her: 'We saw a completely charred house on our way. It was burnt to cinders. There were bloodstains. Murders must have been committed therein.'[255]

During prayer, Gandhi was upset when a few Muslims left when the *Ram Dhun* was sung.[256] The reason behind their discomfort was believed to be political, not personal. Communal propaganda has a singular objective: it jams the mind with noises that do not allow you to hear the song of the world.

On 8 January, Gandhi wrote to Suhrawardy, requesting him to remove the men in uniform escorting him, as they created hindrances in the peace mission:

> 'All my attempts at bringing about real friendship between the two communities must fail so long as I go about fully protected by armed police or military . . . The fright of the military keeps them from coming to me and asking all sorts of questions for the resolution of their doubts. I do see some force in their argument. There would be none if either community was really brave. Unfortunately both lack this very necessary human quality. I would, therefore, like you to reconsider the position and, if you feel convinced, to withdraw this escort.'[257]

After passing through Daspara, Gandhi reached Fatehpur on 8 January. Manu noted: 'We arrived here at 8.30 a.m. Bapu saluted all the Muslim brothers that he came across but they did not respond to his greeting and went their way as if they had never heard of him.'[258] Manu asked Gandhi, why he persisted with his cordial gesture when the people were 'so indifferent, if not hostile?'[259] Gandhi replied that he believed in 'sincere humility', and that he was engaged in overcoming the hurdles to his politics of friendship:

> 'At present the one thought that occurs to them when they see me is, "Here comes our enemy", whereas I want to prove I am no enemy, but a friend.'[260]

Gandhi reached Jagatpur on 10 January. There was a dramatic moment in the women's meeting with Gandhi that took place in the afternoon.

Nirmal Kumar Bose narrated the incident:

> 'A gruesome sight was encountered in that meeting. A lady who had become slightly demented had come to attend the meeting. Her husband had been murdered during the disturbances along with several others, and then the bodies had been buried by the Muslims. She had recovered one long bone of her husband's body from the grave and carried this thing with her as she came to meet Gandhiji.'[261]

The woman was carrying the long bone as proof of her life having turned into horror. Apart from being the last vestige of her grief, she carried the bones like a memento of her horror. This incident led Gandhi to request that Bose take down witness-accounts. Some of the statements made by the Noakhali victims reveal the nature and pattern of the violence.

Testimony against Ghulam Sarwar

Noakhali testimonies were compiled by Nirmal Kumar Bose on Gandhi's instructions. The English translation by V. Ramaswamy, *1946 Diary* is a work in progress. It is a difficult read. The harrowing accounts pose a challenge to the readers to imagine a sober society that can outgrow and outlive their memory.

Upendrachandra Dey of Shibpur village, Khilpara (Noakhali) described how a few hundred Muslim men from nearby attacked their house on 13 October 1946, demanded money and said that they would torture the household if they didn't convert to Islam. They returned two days later, to change the names of the men and women and remarry them as Muslims and broke all the idols in the house. They even cut down the trees that symbolized a Hindu goddess.[262] A woman, Jyotirmoyi Das, narrated on 31 October, that Muslims came in hordes carrying fishing-harpoons, spears and guns, killed the men in the house and set it on fire. The women were spared after they promised to convert. A certain Rajen Babu (maybe her father-in-law) was made to stand under a mango tree where 'Golam Sarwar' (elsewhere Ghulam Sarwar, the KPP leader who later joined the Muslim League and was one of the main instigators behind the Noakhali genocide) himself shot at his chest and killed him (his head was severed as well).[263] This is the only account and an exceptional one where Sarwar was named participating in the violence himself. Das also discovered the heads of two other Bengali men, in two different cooking pots. Parimal Chandra Bose recounted[264] on 18 October that hundreds of Muslim men arrived at 2 a.m. and set fire to the house. After witnessing the killing of his three sisters, their husbands and six nephews, Bose hid in the pond overnight and fled on his horse (affordable because he was a zamindar). He travelled half a mile the next day carrying valuables with him, before a gang of men caught hold of him and took away his valuables. Bose was spared and after walking through a forest, he reached Nangalkot railway station. Mohanbashi

Banik narrated[265] a story about the attack on his house on 25 October by around 1500 men. A man named Tariq Ali was about to knife him when Banik handed over his money and gold to him. Banik narrated how another man, Nural Huq, directed the gang to loot the house, evoking Ghulam Sarwar's justification that 'God was on their side, nothing would happen.'[266] Labanyaprabha Majumdar, a rape victim, narrating her woes to Nirmal Kumar Bose, said that on the day after Lakshmi Puja (11 October 1946), a large number of Muslim men had entered the house early in the morning and set fire to the house. She and her sister-in-law had hidden in the garden behind the kitchen. She was discovered and taken to the house of someone named Kala Miya Sheikh. This is a particularly disturbing account: 'I encountered Muslims from many households on the way, they asked about which household this girl belonged to. When they found out, they said, don't let her go, take her away. Atar Ali and Mohammad were holding my hands, while Kala Miya was behind me, pushing me ahead. I did not scream. When I reached there, the womenfolk were laughing.'[267] Two men raped her twice and took her back to her house.

There was a letter in English, addressed to Gandhi at his Chaumuhani camp on 8 November, written by a widow, Binarani Roy Choudhury from Chandpur (Tippera), whose fifteen-year-old daughter Namita Roy (nickname, Khuku) was taken away by Muslim men on 11 October. One of the men, Abdul Quddus, was arrested and confessed to the crime. The letter ended with a helpless threat: 'I will not let you go away from this part of province until i get back my beloved daughter.'[268]

For the men, it was either death or conversion. For the women, rape or conversion. The fact that even Muslim women passively participated in the humiliatory violence against Hindu women shows a striking class divide and communal distance in the neighbourhood. Even if the caste snobbery of the wealthier Hindu households may have been partly responsible for this divide, it cannot be part of an explanation for the extreme masculinization of Muslim women. Though Hindus belonged to a dominant class, the genocide in Noakhali cannot be reduced to class vengeance. The subaltern Muslim violence was not about restructuring class relations and restoring class parity. It was to establish religious nationhood by brute force. The Muslim men in Noakhali shouted 'Allahu Akbar' and 'Pakistan Zindabad'.[269] The nature of perpetration defines the nature of victimhood. The nature of sentiments reflect the mirror image of the nature of horror.

Isvar Allah Tere Naam

While returning from his evening walk in Bhatialpur on 14 January, Gandhi met some Muslim youths who expressed their satisfaction with his work on Noakhali. They also offered their pledge for ensuring peace. The last question posed to Gandhi during his discussion with the youths was, now that the violent disturbances have ensured 'neither Pakistan nor peace' what was Gandhi's answer to the problem. Gandhi replied,

> 'That is exactly what I am searching for in Noakhali. As soon as I discover it the world shall know it.'[270]

Gandhi admitted that he was still clueless about how to tackle the issue of violence and bring about peace. At that time, he was battling the violence of a yet-undeclared partition as a lone voice in the wilderness of politics. During evening prayer at Bhatialpur, Gandhi reinstalled an idol, which had previously been removed, at the Thakur temple. Muslim men pledged to protect the temple at the cost of their lives.[271]

At the prayer meeting in Ramdebpur on 16 January, Gandhi told his audience about his conversation with a Muslim group at Narayanpur the previous day. They had asked him, since he claimed to belong to both communities, why he had been nursing back the Hindus alone in Noakhali for the past two months while the Muslims suffered in Bihar. Gandhi replied that he wasn't 'nursing back'[272] his own community. He said that he had no community of his own but belonged to both communities. He refuted the claim that he hadn't done anything for Muslims in Bihar. Some Muslims in Noakhali, with or without the instigation of local Muslim League leaders who also harped on the matter, kept reminding Gandhi of his responsibility towards the Muslims in Bihar, without addressing their own responsibility towards Noakhali Hindus. It was as if the onus of bringing peace was on the apostle of peace alone and not on everyone.

After staying in Parkote for a day, Gandhi was in Badalkot on 18 January. He wrote a letter to the barrister of Patna, Ali Hussain, who had cast aspersions on Gandhi spending time in Noakhali, instead of Bihar. Gandhi wrote that Hussain's attempt to lay down 'the law'[273] for him was an error in judgement regarding both Noakhali and Bihar. But Gandhi clarified his position on Bihar with honest accuracy:

> 'I am firmly of [the] opinion that whilst the Bihar Ministry may not be accomplices in the crime committed by the Bihar Hindus, to their shame and disgrace, as responsible Ministers they could not be acquitted of responsibility for the behaviour of crowds within their jurisdiction.'[274]

He made a significant point during the prayer meeting at Badalkot:

> 'Hindus and Mussalmans . . . should not look to the Muslim League or the Congress or the Hindu Mahasabha for the solution of their daily problems of life. For that they should look towards themselves; and if they did that then their desire for neighbourly peace would be reflected by the leaders. The political institutions might be left to deal with specifically political questions but how much did they know about the daily needs of individuals? If a neighbour was ailing, would they run to the Congress or the League to ask them what should be done? That was an unthinkable proposition.'[275]

Gandhi argues for a necessary separation between social and political life. This would establish distance between people and the machinations of political power and act as a bulwark against the possibility of mass violence in the social sphere.

The next day, 19 January, Gandhi left Badalkot for Atakhora early in the morning on foot. Manu described the path as being 'treacherous' and 'narrow' and that it was difficult for two people to walk side-by-side.[276] On top of it, Muslim boys had defecated on their path to discourage Gandhi and show their disapproval for the peace mission. Manu wrote about how Gandhi responded to the challenge:

> 'As I trailed behind, Bapuji began to clean the dirt with leaves. I became aware of it as the party came to [a] halt. The pathway was so narrow that we could walk only in a single file. I was angry with Bapuji, I told him, "Why are you intent upon shaming me? Why did you have to clean it? You could have told me." Bapuji laughed and said, "How are you to know what joy such work gives me? If you did, you would not have spoken in anger." The people of the village watched . . . Bapuji said, "You shall see that from tomorrow we would not have to clean soiled pathways, because everyone will get the lesson that such work is not lowly work. It would bother me if the pathways were to be cleaned only for my sake."'[277]

Gandhi made brief sojourns in Sirandi and Kethuri. At Kethuri, he wrote a letter to Dr Syed Mahmud, Minister for Development and Transport, Government of Bihar, 'Bhai Mahmud, Give me a clear picture of Bihar. I want from you detailed information. Is everything being done for the Muslims who have been ruined? Are those who were spared quite satisfied? Give me all the details.'[278]

The same day, 22 January, Gandhi reached Paniala. It rained during prayers, and Manu introduced a new stanza to the popular bhajan:

> *'Raghupati Raghav Raja Rama, Patit Pavan Sita Rama;*
> *Isvar Allah Tere Naam, Sab Ko Sanmati De Bhagvan'*[279]

Manu had heard this stanza from a *kathakar* in Porbandar where she had gone with her mother 'for a *katha* at a Sudama temple'.[280] This is how this famous stanza got added into Gandhi's version of the bhajan. The mention of 'Isvar' and 'Allah' together created a spiritual neighbourhood across religion in the stanza, which also came to be regarded as a secular cultural gesture. It was not Gandhi who introduced it but his teenaged grand-niece, who recollected it from memory. Its inclusion was purely accidental, but its spirit resonated with Gandhi. He congratulated Manu for bringing the stanza into the song, and outlined its significance to her:

> 'Such were the times gone by. A brahmin could naturally invoke the name of Allah in a Sudama temple. This poisoned atmosphere between the two communities has increased in the last two–four years only.'[281]

Darshan and Anti-History

After halting for a night at Dalta, Gandhi travelled 2.5 miles on foot and reached Muriyam on 24 January. The local Maulvi, Habibullah Sahib Patwari, offered his home to Gandhi and his team. 'The family is very affectionate',[282] wrote Manu in her diary. The Muslim women of the household were shy to meet Gandhi without observing purdah. Gandhi asked them to stop observing 'false purdah'.[283] The Maulvi supported Gandhi:

> 'We have been purified. There is a dark blot on our community of having killed the Hindus . . . We have sinned. God's angel has come to our home, we have to purify ourselves through his *darshan*, why then the purdah?'[284]

The Maulvi speaking of '*darshan*' (or divine sight) goes to show that the term did not, as part of 'the history of practice and habitus'[285] (to quote Dipesh Chakrabarty), belong to the Hindu community alone but that it also belonged to Muslims, and was part of a common spiritual culture.

Tofael Ahmed, the writer and academic from Bangaldesh, recollected in his 1992 book, *Mahatma Gandhi in Bangladesh (East Bengal)* that when Gandhi was touring Noakhali, he was a student of Class Five in Chatkhil Panchgaon Government High School. He summed up the experience:

> 'I have not seen any prophets or messengers but Gandhi.'[286]

This striking confession too falls under the rubric of darshan. There were Muslims in Noakhali who saw Gandhi as a prophetic figure in the form of a messenger of peace. Ahmed compares Gandhi to the figure of a messenger, or a prophet. We are familiar with descriptions of Gandhi's aura and the exceptional nature of his nonviolent work. In a mission where Gandhi's technique and dream were failing as he confessed publicly, for Ahmed to see the prophetic through Gandhi's vulnerability is striking.

The writer and old associate of Gandhi, T.K. Madhavan made the suggestive remark in his book on Gandhi, '[a] prophet... does not issue out of a vacuum; he is made. He is hammered out on the anvil of unexpected happenings. He has almost to walk over a bed of red-hot coals.'[287] Madhavan's book is on Gandhi's early experiments in the Phoenix Settlement near Durban in South Africa, but the description reads closer to Gandhi's peace missions in 1946-47.

The point is not to argue—or worse, trying to prove—whether Gandhi was god's angel, or messenger, or a prophet, but to wonder how, people belonging to a deeply religious society were sufficiently moved and convinced by Gandhi's spiritual status they recognized as exemplary. It is not an exaggeration to say that Gandhi's peace mission in Noakhali, Bihar and Calcutta has no parallel in the history of the violent twentieth century.

Gandhi reached Hirapur on the morning of 26 January. Muslim women expressed the desire to meet Gandhi. But when he approached them, they fled indoors. Gandhi visited each hut and offered *salaam*[288]. The ex-INA soldier Niranjan Singh Gill unfurled the tricolour flag in the presence of some women in the village[289].

Gandhi spoke at the prayer meeting in Bansa the same day. He reminded the audience of the day's significance as 'the day of our freedom'.[290] Gandhi, however, refrained from hoisting the tricolour because of 'the poisoned atmosphere prevalent here'.[291] He did not want to force respect for the flag upon the Muslims of the village.

After spending a day in Bansa, Gandhi reached Panchgaon on 29 January. In the meeting with a deputation led by the Secretary of the District Muslim League, Mujibur Rehman, Gandhi responded to the query on large numbers of Muslims being put behind bars, that even though as a reformer he believed in replacing 'corporeal punishment by awakening of the conscience', until culprits stepped up and acknowledged their guilt, 'ring-leaders should be arrested'.[292]

After stopping over at Jayag and Amki, Gandhi reached Nabagram on 31 January. At the prayer meeting, Gandhi said that he received solidarity from Muslim writers and that he had the right to speak on *purdah* and other matters of Islam.[293] A few workers informed Gandhi that Muslims were boycotting Hindu artisans and craftsmen and were taking up occupations like fishing, fir trade and pan cultivation traditionally associated with Hindus.[294] Another worker asked Gandhi about his views on the Tebhaga movement, where the landowner's share was reduced from half to one-third. Gandhi not only welcomed the demand but said he was willing to concede the share of the entire harvest to the peasants who tilled the soil.[295]

The next day, 1 February, Gandhi gave an early morning interview to *The Hindu* at Nabagram, where he said that ever since he had begun his walking tour of Noakhali, he had faced two kinds of people: 'a sullen population on the one side and a frightened one on the other.'[296] Gandhi was confronted by 'the dual task of infusing courage into the frightened Hindus and at the same time convincing the majority community of the right to protection of the minorities.'[297]

This is a telling predicament. Two communities separated by brutal violence faced each other as frightened victims on the one side and unrepentant perpetrators on the other. There was no sign of any possibility of compensation, healing or justice for the victims. Both victims and perpetrators anxiously waited for a larger political decision where the fate of victims would be altered forever: the declaration of partition. It is against the looming shadow of partition that this moment must be read, where a higher form of justice (the division of the nation in accordance to a religious logic) would overwhelm and supersede the injustices of an engineered genocide. Once Pakistan comes into place, new majorities and minorities will be formed, and the new law will erase crimes and silence grievances.

Tragic News from Bihar

Gandhi left Nabagram for Amishapara at 7.30 a.m. After the prayers at Amishapara, Gandhi was visited by four women who had been raped.[298] He travelled through Dasgharia[299] and reached Sadhurkhil on 3 February. Manu wrote on the evening prayers and more at Sadhurkhil on 4 January:

> 'Many Muslims and officials came to meet Bapuji. The evening prayer was held at a Muslim home . . . I went to meet the women [.] I recited for them the *Auzubillah*. A young girl said that we consider even talking to Hindus a sin. I said, "I came because you wanted to meet me. I believe Khuda and Iswar to be one and that all of us are his children. I recited the *aayat* from the Quran at your instance. But I want to learn from you, your way of reciting it. You show it to me, I have come to you as a student."[300] This had an impact on an elderly woman who had said that even talking to a Hindu was a sin. She also recited an *aayat*.'[301]

Gandhi reached Dharmapur on 5 February, passing through Srinagar. At the prayer meeting at Dharmapur, he picked up disparate issues, and addressed the sensation that walking barefoot caused in the Press. Gandhi said the grass in Noakhali was velvety and green like an exquisite carpet and that it reminded him of the grass in England. He added that this was also a pilgrimage for him, and that it had to be barefoot.[302]

Gandhi passed through Prasadpur and Nandigram to Bijoy Nagar, where he stayed for two days. At the prayer meeting on the first day, 9 February, Gandhi was told that Hindu cultivators and landowners who had suffered the loot of agricultural implements and bullocks and had been deprived of Muslim labour, missed growing long pepper, sesame and mustard seeds. Gandhi asked them to take help from the state to restart cultivation and also help fix the wages.[303]

After a day's silence, Gandhi faced unsavoury questions during the evening prayer meeting at Bijoy Nagar on 10 February. Muslims told him that his stay at Noakhali would gather world attention and give the impression that excesses were still being committed whereas Muslims have been peaceful.[304] Someone asked if a non-violent gesture warranted that cases against Muslims be dropped.[305]

Gandhi passed through Hamchandi, Kafilatali, East Keroa, West Keroa, Raipur—at Raipur, Manu noted in her diary on 15 February that a 'village temple has been converted into Pakistan club'—,[306] and reached Devipur on 17 February. At the prayer meeting, Gandhi brought up the issue that some Muslims complained to him about Hindus lodging false complaints against them.[307] Gandhi replied to these questions soberly, but these motivated questions were thrown at him to discourage his efforts and put pressure on him. On the evening of the 17, Gandhi was visited by a Maulvi, Khalijur Rahman. Rahman had reportedly converted a lot of Hindus in the October violence of 1946. Gandhi asked him if the reports were true. Rahman replied that it was done to save Hindu lives. Gandhi asked whether sacrificing life was better than sacrificing faith out of fear, to which the Maulvi said that false conversion was sanctioned by religion if it saved lives.

This made Gandhi lose his temper.[308]

From Devipur, Gandhi travelled to Alunia, Chardukhia, Birampur, Bisakhathali, Kamalapur, Char Krishnapur, Charsoladi and finally on 24 February, he reached Haimchar. After evening prayers on 18 February, Gandhi travelled from Alunia to Birampur by boat across the Dakaria River.[309] Gandhi spent the night at an old boatman's named Nalini Chandra Das.[310]

On the first day's prayer meeting in Haimchar, his audience comprised mostly Namasudras from the village.[311] Fazlul Haq came to meet Gandhi at 3.40 p.m. on 27 February. Haq began with the complaint that Gandhi's place was in Bihar rather than Noakhali, where Muslims, according to Haq, were victims of police repression rather than being aggressors.[312] Gandhi asked him about his earlier statement that if Gandhi visited Barisal (Haq's hometown) he would have him thrown into the *khal* (canal).[313] Haq laughed it off as a joke.[314] Haq had reduced politics and Gandhi's stature to a snide joke. It was a joke out of communal discomfort against the honesty of Gandhi's political challenge.

28 February brought grave news. Manu wrote in her diary:

> 'Mustaffa Sahib, the private secretary to Dr Syed Mahmud of Bihar came. He read the Bihar report. Dastardly acts have been committed. Women have been stripped naked and their breasts cut off. They have been pushed into wells and five to seven men have collectively raped girls of twelve and fifteen. *And the tragic aspect is that Congressmen have been involved.* Pregnant women's bellies have been cut open and mother and fetus killed. O' God! How can human beings be so cruel! Sushilabehn Pai and I wept copious tears. Bapuji's heart convulsed. Poor man, Mustaffa choked while reading the report, he could barely read.'[315] [Emphasis mine]

Manu described the details and the effects on the people hearing them in bare details before moving on to write something else. She was surrounded by grief but she did not make capital out of grief. She also always described the human and not its communal aspect. Manu's passage to maturity was strewn with such stories of gross violence. Despite the occasional agitations, she jotted down her daily life in her diary with remarkable calm.

The last few days of February were hard and depressive for Gandhi. Nirmal Kumar Bose wrote on the reasons behind the gloom:

> 'The opposition to Gandhi's stay in Noakhali began to take a vulgar turn towards the end of February 1947. The roads over which he walked from village to village were deliberately dirtied by human faeces every day, while Muslim audiences began to boycott his meetings more persistently. Gandhiji tried to bear all this with calmness and patience. For he held stubbornly to the view that it would never be right for him to surrender his own love for men even if they were erring.'[316]

Gandhi's peace movement could strike a chord only with a minority among Muslims. A few stepped forward to welcome him despite informal sanctions made by the League. Muslims attended his prayer meetings, and engaged with him. But the League ensured that Gandhi was largely shunned by the Muslim community. Using little boys to defecate on his path and not allowing him to walk is striking for two reasons. One, a community that did not hesitate in unleashing extreme brutality a few months ago to further its political self-interest had now resorted to repulsive but non-harmful efforts to literally stop Gandhi in his tracks. Two, the disarming nature of Gandhi's mission inflicted a measure of passive meanness on his opponents. The subaltern style of conveying hostility through public defecation was an act enforced by circumstances.

On 31 March, Gandhi wrote a long letter to Suhrawardy from Haimchar, telling him there was 'consternation among the Hindus'[317] when they learnt he was leaving for Bihar. He wanted the chief minister to allay their fears. There were rumours that ration might be stopped from 15 March. Gandhi gave a precise picture of the scene of material distress:

> 'Weavers have got no yarn for weaving. Fishermen have got none for making nets. Carpenters have got no tools. Agriculturists have no bullocks. There are no seeds for sowing.'[318]

Gandhi told Suhrawardy that he had heard that the Bengal Government was encouraging Muslims to boycott Hindus. He wished that what he had heard was wrong. Leaving Noakhali with a heavy heart, Gandhi gave Suhrawardy a clear picture and assessment of the situation, and left it to his conscience.

In a letter written to Vallabhbhai Patel on 3 March from the steamer at Chandpur, Gandhi wrote: 'I leave today for Bihar. There was a letter from __[319] and now there is another from Dr Mahmud. Both are shocking and so I am going.'[320]

Le bon Dieu est dans le détail

The Gandhi–Manu relationship became a matter of controversy as Gandhi made his 19-year-old grand-niece part of his Brahmacharya experiment. Its place in Gandhi's peace mission in Noakhali has been debated by Gandhi's associates during his time, and commented upon by scholars and writers later.

The popular idiom, *the truth is in the details*, and *the devil is in the details*, are later variations of an older idiom attributed to Gustave Flaubert (1821–80): *Le bon Dieu est dans le détail* or *God is in the details.*[321] It is a good idiom vis-à-vis the idea of a telos, or finality. There is no truth, or god, or devil to be found at the end of the text. They are part of the entire text. You meet them along the way. It is good to keep this in mind in this unusual story about Manu and her Bapu.

Manu came from a different world, not the kind of world we live in. It is important to understand that world in the way of understanding her and her relationship with Gandhi. Manu joined Gandhi and his wife Kasturba at Sevagram at the age of seventeen after her mother passed away, for literary training and *seva*, or service.[322] When Kasturba passed away at the Aga Khan prison on 22 February 1944, Manu was present. She had started writing her diary much earlier, since 11 April 1943. It was essential for Gandhi that all satyagrahis (who were also ashramites) keep a diary.[323] Explaining its importance, Gandhi told fellow ashramites:

> 'Thinking about a diary I feel that it is of priceless value to me. For a person who has dedicated himself to the pursuit of truth, it serves as a means of keeping watch over himself, for such a person is determined to write in it nothing but the truth.'[324]

Foucault traces the western genealogy and tradition of this practice of a 'self-technology' in relation to the 'discovery and formulation of the truth concerning oneself' to the *Delphic* precept, 'know yourself'.[325] The act of radical self-examination for the sake of what Foucault calls 'the obligation to tell the truth about oneself'[326] is akin to the Christian verbalization during confession. Writing the diary is an act of self-confession to oneself. In the Christian era, Foucault tells us, the practice involved confessing your thoughts to your spiritual guide and this transformation had an impact on modern subjectivity.

Gandhi, as Manu's spiritual guide, would read and sign her diary entries as 'Bapu'. However, unlike the private act of confession, Manu's diary was meant to be a public record for the future.

Gandhi wrote his first note in Manu's diary two days after she was into the practice: 'You must keep an account of the yarn you have spun. Thoughts coming into your mind should also be noted down. You should keep a record of all that you have read.'[327] On his day of silence on 27 February 1944, Gandhi wrote a note to Manu:

> 'I feel much worried about you. You are a class by yourself. You are good, simple-hearted and ever ready to help others. Service has become dharma with you. But you are still uneducated and silly also. If you remain illiterate, you will regret it, and if I live long, I too will regret it. I will certainly miss you, but I do not like to keep you near me as that would be weakness and ignorant attachment. I am quite sure that at present you should go to Rajkot . . . You will learn there besides music, the art of working methodically. You will learn Gujarati, too. There may be other benefits also. If you spend at least one year there, your slovenliness will disappear. If you go to Karachi or anywhere else you like after you have become more mature, you will get all that you want.'[328]

From Gandhi's letter to Manu's father, Jaisukhlal, on 12 June 1944, we learn that Gandhi wanted to send Manu to Rajkot, but she was reluctant to go there. She was excited by a letter she had received from a teacher in Karachi and Gandhi sent her there.[329] On 19 June, Gandhi wrote to Manu in Karachi, 'I have your letter. If you behave as you promise, I shall be very happy. I am glad that you did not go to the cinema.'[330] On 27 July, Gandhi's letter read, 'I have your letter. That your weight should go down to 87 lb. is a matter of shame. It is sinful to read up to 2 o'clock at night.'[331] These were the early correspondences between Manu and Gandhi.

On 4 November 1946, Gandhi wrote to Jaisukhlal from Calcutta, making an authoritative wish: 'Manu's place can be nowhere else but here by my side.'[332] Reading it on 1 December, Manu wrote, the sentence 'moved me deeply'.[333] Manu wanted to take care of Gandhi's personal needs, but since he had spread his associates across Noakhali, Manu wondered if that was possible. The thought made her 'sleepless.'[334] She woke her father in the middle of the night and he advised her to write to Gandhi. Manu wrote to Gandhi at 1.30 a.m. on 12 December, 'explicitly laying down the condition'[335] under which she was willing to join him. 'I do not wish to come, if you want me to work in some village away from you'.[336] She was willing to 'brave any dangers'[337] that might befall her.

Manu reached Srirampur with her father in the afternoon on 19 December. During the conversation, Gandhi told Jaisukhlal,

> 'I have had a regard for her ever since she came to me. Pyarelal also saw in her some great qualities, which he hoped to nurture and help blossom. It is for this reason that he had expressed to me his desire to marry Manu. I have never believed that they have done anything wrong. Even then, they would be tested here. I have described Hindu–Muslim unity as a *yajna*. And in this sacrifice, nothing

impure can subsist. So, if Manu were to be impure, even with a mere trace of it, she would be in a terrible state. You must understand this clearly, discuss it with Manu so that she could return with you if she so wants. It is better to return now, than later when one may be in a bad state.'[338]

Jaisukhlal departed the next day. Manu told Gandhi later in the day that as long as she was with him, 'I would accept any test that I was put to or any condition that was imposed.'[339] She said that her father gave her 'complete freedom since childhood' and never cast aspersions on her or had any doubts about her.[340] Gandhi asked Manu to read aloud from her diary. She objected, 'I am ashamed to read my confessions aloud to you.'[341] Gandhi replied, '*It is better to confess to one's own errors face to face.* One rises further through that. It is preferable to confess through writing compared to it being conveyed by a third person. For this reason, you should read it, it would also give me a measure of your comprehension and thereafter I would sign it.'[342] [Emphasis mine] For Gandhi, writing the diary as an act of confession and mode of truth-telling was simultaneously—in fact, fundamentally—documenting life's errors. This is directly related to Brahmacharya as well. Tridip Suhrud writes in the introduction to Gandhi's autobiography:

> 'An experiment in Truth is an experiment in Brahmacharya . An experiment with Truth cannot have any possibility of secrecy. As an experiment, it was important and imperative, Gandhi felt, to record the unusual, uncontrolled occurrences. It was essential to speak of the darkness within.'[343]

For Gandhi, experimenting with truth opens up a necessary task of recording his errors. Errors are the 'unusual, uncontrolled occurrences' that have to get faithfully, truthfully, without any temptation for 'secrecy', written on paper. The act of truth-seeking demands that there be no hiding place for errors. Gandhi's autobiographical task is the confession of errors. Writing on his errors is the only possible (and demanding) means to his experimenting with truth.

In his essay on Gandhi's sexuality, Vinay Lal made the point: 'In his aspiration to embody femininity . . . Gandhi may have been relying upon familiar idioms of Indian thought, though it is instructive how far he departed from Indian textual and customary traditions as well.'[344] On 28 September, while explaining Brahmacharya to Manu, Gandhi said, 'I do not believe in that *Brahmacharya* where the mind is filled with carnal desire but outwardly even the touch of a woman's body is eschewed.'[345]

Writing on 'How Non-Violence Works' in *Harijan* on 23 July 1938, Gandhi explained that *Brahmacharya* – Satyagraha's twin – "does not mean mere physical self-control" but "complete control over all the senses."[346] He goes ahead to write that "power comes from the preservation and sublimation of the vitality that is responsible for creation of life"[347]. By power Gandhi alludes to the retention of sexual vitality, which is part of spiritual culture. It attests Freud's observation of the sublimation of the sex drive as the "primary feature of cultural development"[348]. However, Gandhi offers a unique twist to this ascetic practise:

> 'A *brahmachari*, it is said, should never see, much less touch a woman. Doubtless a *brahmachari* may not think of, speak of, see or touch a woman lustfully. But the prohibition one finds in books on *Brahmacharya* is mentioned without the important adverb... Cupid's visitations are often unperceivable. Difficult though therefore *Brahmacharya* is of observance when one

freely mixes with the world, it is not of much value if it is attainable only by retirement from the world.'[349]

Gandhi's approach to Brahmacharya was uniquely his own, and not purely a product of Hindu or Indian tradition, though there are obvious and distinct traces of that tradition. Gandhi's notions of terms like 'experiment' and 'face-to-face' have roots in his familiarity with Judeo–Christian texts.

In *My Days with Gandhi*, Nirmal Kumar Bose mentions something important in this regard he subsequently includes in a letter to friends. On 14 March 1947, when Gandhi and his troupe were in Patna, two old associates of Gandhi, Swami Anand and Kedar Nath came to visit him, and they had private discussions. Anand told Bose later that Gandhi told them 'his ideas of Brahmacharya were not of the orthodox kind, and they had been modified by his long contact with the West'[350]. Gandhi specifically mentioned being 'partly influenced by the writings of some Western writers on this subject.'[351]

The influence of the West is inescapable for our understanding and engagement with the condition of modernity. Gandhi's profound antimodernity did not prevent him from welcoming western influences. He acquainted himself with different traditions of faith including Christianity by reading writers from those traditions. It is however important to note that such influence was restricted to what Ashis Nandy called Gandhi's wish to be a symbol of 'the other West'[352], meaning the Christian West. The books that Gandhi carried in his bag to Noakhali, as noted by Pyarelal, are revealing in this aspect: *The Sayings of Muhammad, Glances at Islam, The World Bible, The Book of Daily Thoughts and Prayer, Practice and Precepts of Jesus, A*

Book of Jewish Thoughts, Dhammapada, Thousand Names of Rama, Shri Ramacharitamanas among others.[353]

On 20 September, Gandhi told Nirmal Kumar Bose that having told Manu that he had reached the last chapter of his life where he was 'thinking of a bold and original experiment, whose "heat will be great."'[354]

On 21 December, Gandhi asked Manu at Srirampur about sleeping beside him. Manu replied, 'Why did you even ask? I have made you my mother and a child sleeping by her mother's side sleeps naturally, isn't it?'[355] Gandhi said,

> 'This effort to restore peace and unity among Hindus and Muslims is a *yajna*. And you are a partner in this *yajna*. Because wherever I am, you will be with me . . . In this *yajna* no one who is impure can be a partner. And I have hitherto never considered you impure . . . I am like a mother to you. But I am a man, and you are a woman. You are young. Can a young woman remain pure even when she sleeps by the side of a man? That is the question . . . Veena, Kanchan and Lilavati [ashram inmates] said that we will not sleep by your side. They were all young women. Today I took you by my side, and you were in deep sleep in about five minutes. This is very auspicious. You are pure and I had some glimpse of that today. We shall know more in the next two–four days. I have taught you geometry, have I not? The theorems require a proof.'[356]

Even though Gandhi uses the term 'yajna', he equates it with geometry and theorem, making it clear that his idea of tradition is mediated by the modern, scientific language of truth. Innocence is fundamental to Brahmacharya, but it also invites a paradox: innocence must be tested, tempted, to ascertain its depths. The name of the test is Brahmacharya.

Gandhi asked Manu about her health, and if she had a regular menstruation cycle. He scolded her for pulling the drawstrings of her salwar too tight. He also lectured her for wearing a tight bodice, and said it was a new fashion for women who were trying to attract men.[357] In a fateful manner, Gandhi stuffed Manu's head with anti-sexual views as an aesthetic mode of initiation into the world of *seva*.

On 28 September, Manu noted in her diary:

> 'Sushilabehn is displeased with me. I sleep by Bapuji's side, and she discussed this with me, and said, "Do you know that this would not end well?" She also asked me to reconsider the proposal of the relationship with Pyarelalji. I was very angry with her and told her clearly, "I have faith in Bapuji. Bapu is my mother and you should have mercy on me and not mention the possibility of any relationship with your brother. You have been preparing me for your family, and I understood this very late. I was under the misconception that you love me more than my sister does." I told her all this. She is very angry.'[358]

Later, Manu asked Gandhi why Sushila was jealous of her and why she was making a hue and cry about her sleeping next to Gandhi when she herself had done the same. Sushila, according to Manu, gossiped about her to other inmates and they were whispering against her. Gandhi told her, 'I wish to present, through you, a new ideal to the world. You are a granddaughter of mine, we share the same blood, I claim to be your grandfather as also your mother, and despite this if I harbour a carnal desire for you even in my thoughts, I am a false Mahatma. God will punish me for it. I shall die a painful death and maggots will crawl over my body.'[359] Gandhi seemed a bit desperate to convince Manu in the face of others trying to create discomfort and doubts in her head. Manu however needed no convincing. She wrote in her diary:

> 'In which all directions Bapuji took me? Will I be able to fulfil his aspirations? I do not see such capabilities in myself. I pray to god to grant me the strength to fulfil the tasks that he intends for me. I want nothing else.'[360]

Manu was willing to be led by Gandhi into the Brahmacharya experiment, but she was also curious and unsure about where it would lead her. However, she was committed to fulfilling Gandhi's expectations, which involved inculcating in her the ascetic mode of *seva* and sacrifice.

On the first day of the New Year in 1947, Gandhi shared questions raised by Parasuram with Manu, 'What was the necessity of inviting Manu here at this time! Your work is for Hindu–Muslim unity, and because Manu is here Pyarelal comes here daily as he believes that Manu's *darshan* is sufficient to sustain him. And for that reason, he is unable to do his work in the village.'[361] Gandhi acknowledged the exceptional work that Parasuram was undertaking in the villages and was upset by his stance on Manu. The same day, Manu wrote in her diary:

> 'I was between Scylla and Charybdis. I wondered what newer experiences were in store for me. I do not know what is happening. I had not imagined that my co-workers would experience such jealousy. I had convinced myself that since Bapuji has dispersed all the co-workers no

> one will feel jealous of me or have a heart burn. But my assumption proved to be false.'[362]

Gandhi woke Manu up the next day at 2 a.m. and said, 'Why do such things happen? I can see that I must be at fault. There must be a shortcoming in me and in my faith in non-violence which I am unable to either comprehend or locate.'[363]

Later in the day, Gandhi wrote to Parasuram: 'I have read your letter with great care . . . It contains half truths which are dangerous. You wronged me, the parties you mention, yourself and the cause by suppressing from them and me your opinion about them . . . I cannot concede your demands. The other points you raise do not make much appeal to me. Since such is my opinion and there is a conflict of ideals and you yourself wish to be relieved, you are at liberty to leave me today. That will be honourable and truthful. I like your frankness and boldness. My regard for your ability as a typist and shorthand writer remains undiminished and I was looking forward to taking a hand in bringing out your other qualities. I am sorry that it cannot be . . . Finally let me tell you that you are at liberty to publish whatever wrong you have noticed in me and my surroundings.'[364]

Manu reported to Gandhi about Abha's sarcastic behaviour towards her. Gandhi told her, 'How will you cope if you are perturbed by such petty barbs. You have a lot to do still, don't be so weak; or you will not last.'[365] At night, Manu noted in her diary: 'I have forbidden Bapuji from making any reference to my diary in his diary. His diary is public, and I do not want that he should write about my diary in his, and hence he makes no mention of my diary. I had made this condition on the very first day when he had spoken about me keeping the diary.'[366] Manu was not yet ready to share her thoughts with the world. On 7 January, she noted,

> 'I am determined not to listen to anyone except Bapu. Even if all the other associates were to hang me in their anger, I am not going to leave the side of the person I regard as my mother out of fear of anyone. What about the fact that she shared his bed? I am not going to be pressured by anyone.'[367]

On 18 January, Manu had an interesting conversation with Sushila,

> 'Sushilabehn tried a lot to engage me in a conversation, but not much came of it as I had no time to spare. Despite that she took me in her arms and said, "It is not good that you share Bapu's bed. Kishorlalbhai, Kanu and others are very displeased, and it affects their health and wellbeing." I replied, "I recognize no one other than Bapuji. And why do you hide the fact that hitherto you have shared his bed?" She said, "I did so with the sense of service as a doctor." I said, "One should refrain from doing a service that we consider sullied. Hindus kill Muslims and claim that they do so in service of India, why should then the Ministers suppress them?" She went away somewhat displeased.'[368]

Sushila met her match. Manu defeated her argument logically. The next day, seeing her deep in thought, Gandhi told Manu,

> 'You know that every fiery ordeal bears fruit. If I fail to win you over, I can never win the Muslims over. I place myself in the equation with you. And for that reason, you should share your mind with me. You know and you can also see that I am pouring immense love over you. The whole world will forsake me, but I will not forsake you, this is my covenant with you.'[369]

On 26 January, Manu noted in her diary:

> 'This chapter of my sleeping in the same bed has caused quite a storm. But for some reason I am not worried by that. Perhaps because he is my mother, though a male he is a mother to me. "Mother" bears all responsibility. Despite such angry letters I experience joy and walk about unconcerned. I have experienced the power of the mind and its capacity for work. Sometimes a person is ill because of the mind. And if there is mental resolve one can bring together the earth and the sky. Thus, the outcome depends upon the mental framework. In my case it has proved to be true. All women are scared, are afraid. There were discussions at Seagon also and that had frightened me as well. If I were to share Bapuji's bed, everyone will gossip about it. But here there is not even one hundredth of what I had feared. Oh God, let my faith in my mother—Bapu, my mother—remain undiminished till the very end . . . With what affection Bapuji helps me sleep! If the cover slips a little, he puts it back on me.'[370]

Manu could smell the difference between apprehension and reality. After midnight into the next day, Gandhi woke up a couple of times to urinate, and on one occasion he told her,

'[What] has convinced me about your purity is your sleep. You sleep like a dead body, which I like very much.'[371]

In his commentary on the monk and theologian John Cassian's writings on early Christian monasticism, Foucault mentions that among the spiritual battles for chastity, Cassian lays emphasis on 'the absence of erotic dreams and nocturnal pollution' a sign of 'the pinnacle of chastity.'[372] Manu's sleeping body was dead to any sign of sexual consciousness. It was proof of the purity of their yagna.

Gandhi was upset by Parasuram leaving his company over the Manu episode. He addressed it publicly at the prayer meeting in Amishapara on 1 February 1947, speaking about the general air of distrust and suspicion around him.[373] Referring to Christ, Gandhi said that he approached his act of Brahmacharya with 'the spirit of God's eunuch' (paraphrased by Nirmal Kumar Bose).[374] (Bose adds that he had left out this part when he translated it into Bengali for the audience. Gandhi caught the 'omission' and shared his displeasure with an unrepentant Bose.[375])

On 2 February, Gandhi responded to Kishorelal's letter. Kishorelal Mashruwala (1890–1952) was a lawyer and educationist, and also edited *Harijan*. His niece, Sushila, married Gandhi's second son, Manilal. Gandhi wrote to him:

> 'Your letter had [a] totally opposite effect on me. It is painful. It is my considered opinion that all of you fail to understand my work. You have no opportunity to understand it. You even lack the eagerness for it. Some things cannot be explained beyond a point. Perhaps this is one such thing. We must leave its resolution for the future. There are limits to arguments. Time is the biggest argument of all. That you blame Jaisukhlal is an injustice. He is a generous father. He has four daughters, whom he has raised like sons. He has placed his trust in me. Manu put forth the idea that she wanted to come serve me, which he supported and encouraged . . . Out of love for me, you wish to reduce my blame, you characterize Manu as *Maya* and decry Jaisukhlal . . . I have shown your letter to Manu. It was my duty to do so . . . According to me, her sleeping by my side does not violate this *yajna*, it is an integral part of it. It has become so.'[376]

Manu noted in the beginning of her entry on 17 February in Devipur that they slept separately last night. Gandhi had written (in his own diary):

> 'Manu slept separately. Every time I woke up, I checked, and Manu was fast asleep. I liked that very much. I woke up again at 3 o'clock and my thoughts were about Manu, which I did not like. It was unbecoming of one aspiring to detachment but could not stop the thoughts.'[377]

Gandhi admits missing Manu's comforting proximity. That she was severed from his yagna bothered him. Although Gandhi's attachment was not sexual, he felt anxious about Manu's absence beside him.

On 20 February in Bisakhathali, Manu wrote about the previous night:

> 'The night was extremely cold. For that reason, Bapuji drew me closer to him. He woke me up around 12:30 and said, "The soles of my feet have gone numb with cold, and I am feeling very cold." I checked and found that his feet and hands had gone cold. I held him close to me for warmth. I do not know as to when I fell asleep.'[378]

This is a poignant moment. A 78-year-old Gandhi drew warmth from his 19-year-old grand-niece on a cold night in Noakhali. Even though they were being harshly judged by associates, they made a circle of mutual trust around each other and bore the agony. Thinking of them lying beside each other, one may tend to forget their tired bodies labouring through the day, experiencing the impact of horror stories of violence, going about their mission with calmness and empathy. This is not to rescue Gandhi and his experiment from scrutiny, but to caution the critic that Gandhi's open politics of sexuality must be read *within* his mission in Noakhali. Vinay Lal emphasises, 'Gandhi takes us into that realm of the politics of the body where 'woman' and 'man' must be reconfigured'.[379]

On 22 February, Gandhi told Manu at Char Krishnapur,

> 'I have been a *brahmachari* . . . [When] a mature man and woman, although sleeping unclothed in close proximity, experience no desire in mind and body nor cast a covetous glance at each other, they then attain the condition of a child . . . You slept by my side. You are a daughter, my own blood. You even played as an infant in my lap. You have now, following laws of nature, become mature in body, your breasts have developed, and you menstruate, your body matured. Does that mean that by having you sleep by my side, I, a grandfather to you, indulging in carnal pleasure? That is the indirect accusation of Kishorelal and others. What kind of a demon that would make me? And if I were such a demon I would not last in this world for a moment . . . The innocence of the child is the innocence of the unaware. But the innocence and purity of the mature in body and mind is the true *Brahmacharya*.'[380]

This was an important clarification from Gandhi. Even though Manu had a point to prove about her own innocence, it was Gandhi's adult self that faced a tougher task to prove that even the shadow of lust did not reside in his body. That he chose his teen-aged grand-niece for the experiment was meant to be the starkest proof of his will to celibacy. It was the most prohibitive, and hence, the most challenging. Gandhi's idea of

Satyagraha and Brahmacharya was the recovery of innocence by doing the undoable, and thinking the unthinkable. The practice of non-violence was meant to push the limits of violence within, and in the world.

On 24 February, Gandhi had a discussion with Thakkar Bapa at Haimchar. Thakkar Bapa was Amritlal V. Thakkar (1869–1951) who worked as a civil engineer in East Africa, and joined Servants of India Society in 1914.[381] Thakkar asked him a simple but pertinent question, 'Why this experiment here?'

Gandhi replied, '[It] is not an experiment but an integral part of my *yajna*. One may forgo an experiment, one cannot forgo one's duty. Now if I regard a thing as a part of my *yajna*—a sacred duty—I may not give it up even if public opinion is wholly against me . . . Ever since my coming to Noakhali, I have been asking myself the question, "What is it that is choking the action of my ahimsa? Why does not the spell work? May it not be because I have temporized in the matter of Brahmacharya ?"'[382]

This was a significant argument. Gandhi had postponed the idea of mastering Brahmacharya while plunging headlong into the peace mission in Noakhali. But he attributed his failure to impress upon the people as a personal lack that had to do with his untested sexuality, which for him could be a source of libidinal violence. He felt that he could no longer postpone one for the other and had to face the double intensity of the moment. He went on further:

> 'On the lonely way to God on which I have set out, I need no earthly companions.
>
> Let those who will, therefore, denounce me, if I am the imposter they imagine me to be, though they may not say so in so many words. It might disillusion millions who persist in regarding me as a Mahatma. I must confess,

> the prospect of being so debunked greatly pleases me. Thousands of Hindu and Muslim women come to me. They are to me like my own mother, sisters and daughters. But if an occasion should arise requiring me to share the bed with any of them I must not hesitate, if I am the brahmachari that I claim to be. If I shrink from the test, I write myself down as a coward and a fraud.'[383]

In a poignant moment, Gandhi admitted that he was risking his stature in order to gain it. He was unperturbed, however, as the possibility of failure, instead of worrying him, would give him the satisfaction of intense loneliness. The man who spent a considerable amount of time in the midst of people was aware of the paradox of solitude. It was a paradox that death, or mortality, introduces to life, including the lives of the most public of men. It is also significant that Gandhi explained that he saw the act of sharing the bed with a woman as a provocative necessity to prove that he had no sexual feelings regarding them on all occasions. The situation of extreme sexual proximity alone could determine the truth of Gandhi's asexuality.

Bapa persisted, and this time he raised the question of the social aspect or repercussion of Bapu's yajna:

'What if your example is copied?'

Gandhi replied, 'If there is blind imitation or unscrupulous exploitation of my example, society will not and should not tolerate it. But if there is sincere, bona-fide honest endeavour, society should welcome it and it will be the better for it.'[384]

On 3 March, Manu took a decision at Haimchar:

> 'I told Bapuji that Bapa has been a witness, he has seen me sleep in the same bed with you and having seen it

> for himself, he does not regard it a violation of righteous conduct. It is my wish, to satisfy Bapa, that henceforth I sleep in a separate bed. Bapuji immediately assented to my wish. He gave me his consent.'[385]

We learn of Manu's awareness of the importance of consent through her expression of delight on Gandhi consenting to her wish. Such are the unexpected ironies of heteronomy. It was Manu who decided to end the experiment.

Nirmal Kumar Bose wrote to Gandhi from Masaurhi on 18 March regarding Manu:

> '[Last night] I first ascertained from you if she had had any connection with the experiment, and you replied in the affirmative. I had a suspicion when she told me some time ago that she had nothing to do with your prayog that she was screening facts . . . Personally, I have practised the Freudian technique of dream analysis on myself and have derived immense benefit, as it has helped to bring to the surface submerged desires which had been causing trouble, and thus helped me to deal with them satisfactorily . . . [As] I told you in the January letter, my charges against her was that she had become nearly neurotic and had been taking away a considerable portion of your time when all your services were needed almost exclusively in the national cause.'[386]

Bose added that Calcutta University where he taught had given him all the time to be with Gandhi in Bengal where he was helpful, translating his speeches into Bengali among other things. But his students suffered. His lack of knowledge of Hindustani also didn't make him an asset in Bihar. He wanted Gandhi's permission to take his leave and promised to serve Gandhi again if he returned to Bengal.[387] In his reply to Bose from Bir, Gandhi wrote on 19 March: 'What is Freudian philosophy? I have not read any writing of his. One friend, himself a professor and follower of Freud, discussed his writings for a brief moment. You are the second.'[388]

In the beginning of his diary, *My Days with Gandhi*, Bose wrote between October 1946 and January 1948, Gandhi reached 'two climaxes . . . simultaneously in his life; one in the personal, spiritual sphere, and the other in the sphere of his public and political relations. Although the two might seem to be unrelated, there was an underlying bond between the two.'[389]

There is an interesting division of labour (complimentary, not alienating) in Gandhi's life at Noakhali between the satyagrahi (by day) and the brahmachari (by night). The politics of politics and the politics of sexuality were intertwined. Both contained provocations to violent transgressions. Politics was public, sexuality was private. Politics was meant for the waking hours, and sexuality was a concern during sleep. To live one's truth, both had to be confronted by a method proper to each. The common element in Gandhi's method in both cases was intensification: If violence provokes, meet it with a disarmed body. If sexuality distracts, expose yourself to a bare body. Truth is not metaphysics. It had to be confronted daily *in the body*.

Foucault mentioned Cassian's preoccupation with constant vigilance in the battle for chastity that is akin to the Gandhian division of labour: 'To stay awake night and day—at night for the day and in the day thinking of the night to come.'[390]

On a strikingly similar note, during his discourse on the *Gita* on 6 April 1926, Gandhi explains Krishna's description of the *sthitaprajna* (a yogic state of repose associated with an enlightened state of being) from Chapter II of the text in his own words: 'The world will tell us that the senses cannot be controlled. We should reply that they certainly can be . . . The world's night is our day and the world's day is our night.'[391]

There is an interesting similitude between the mystic state of awareness in Christianity and Hindu practices. This involves a mental practice where you subvert the natural state of the senses in relation to time into its opposite, in order to overcome distraction. It involves a daily commitment to self-invigilation.

Bose found Gandhi's adoption as Manu's mother a 'rare . . . (but) established modes of the subordination of sex among spiritual aspirants in India.'[392] Bose wrote: 'It was by *becoming* [. . .] woman that he tried to circumvent one of the most powerful and disturbing elements which belong to our biological existence.'[393]

Manu gave Gandhi the right to put her at risk as much as he was putting himself to risk. Her trust in him was effortless. Yet, the question that persists is: Do *we* trust her? There may be questions on Manu's sense of autonomy because of her age. It is clear that the force of heteronomy was at work regarding Manu's reverential feelings for Gandhi. Trust at any stage of adulthood comes from a leap of faith that isn't decided by autonomy. The roots of trust therefore can't be determined (accepted or rejected) by the condition of maturity, and the power of objectivity.

Manu was apprehensive about the *public reception* of Gandhi's yagna with her, not about the yagna itself. The silent and verbal accusations and suspicions she faced among Gandhi's associates must have been traumatic. The silences in her diary on her experience might be provoked by her hesitation to feed public imagination and misunderstanding more than other factors.

The judgement of a sexualized world that inevitably must raise the question of Manu's (lack of) maturity can consider whether their sense of judgement is sensitive enough to not let their claims to objectivity be coercive upon someone else's subjectivity. If Manu's age makes her vulnerable to universal knowledge, her life is a testament to her cultural specificity that negates that knowledge.

The shadows will, however, remain.

After Gandhi's death, Manu lived life in obscurity, self-willed or dictated by others. The figure of Gandhi was too important for history. Manu, an obedient but perceptive witness to the most difficult period of Gandhi's life, was sidelined.

Gandhi didn't want to save Manu from the world, and risked his own reputation. The point about whether Gandhi should have invited Manu to take that risk, or why did he not consider the lifelong impact that the yagna may have on her mind and her social relations, will be open to debate. I have no wish to offer any defence or criticism here. The criteria of judgement must be carefully considered. *Le bon Dieu est dans le détail.*

The Historian's Task

Cambridge historian Joya Chatterji paints a dense sociological picture behind the violent communal face-off of 1946. She reveals the communal make-up of the bhadraloks, largely comprising upper-caste Bengali Hindu society, and shows how their cultural influence and social power had a big impact in shaping Hindu communal politics from 1932 to the second partition of Bengal in 1947. The Hindu communal attitude towards Muslims, Chatterji has shown, centred on intensifying a threat perception regarding the growing presence of Muslims, particularly in the mofussil areas, and the treatment of them as culturally inferior.

Chatterji's focus on the problem of communal relations, however, is starkly silent on the larger historical trends that shaped modern India's social and political history, intercepted by colonial modernity and enforced by colonial power. The problems of urbanization and new socio-economic relations precipitated communal rivalries. The 1932 Communal Award intensified the political competition between Bengal's Hindus and Muslims. The 1943 Bengal Famine was a gift of the anti-India British bully, Winston Churchill, who rejected Wavell's request to ship food grains to address the alarming shortage of food grains in Bengal. The British Cabinet blamed the crisis on 'Marwari supports of the Congress' who, the Cabinet felt, were out to embarrass the Muslim League government in Bengal, the colonial Indian government and Her Majesty's government.[394]

In the context of the Communal Award, Chatterji mentions Roland Inden's critique of the British understanding of Indian society being 'essentialist'.[395] She juxtaposes this critique with the colonial enterprise making the claim of playing 'arbiters between the conflicting interests in Indian society and, at the same time, as the guardians of the people against the rapacity and corruption of their leaders.'[396] By her exposition of the conflicting interests between Hindus and Muslims and the political corruption of the local leadership, Chatterji has eventually upheld the colonial claim. Commenting on the Bengal Famine, Chatterji quotes Nehru from *The Discovery of India* to spell out colonial plunder and the revenue system as being among the central reasons behind the famine.[397]

Quoting Inden and Nehru at critical junctures appears to be a technique to evade commenting on the question of the moral complicity of British rule towards fomenting communal divisiveness and thrusting famine on the Indian people under the war economy. British rule offers the determining factor behind both issues. Critical focus on Hindus and Muslims placed vis-à-vis each other in terms of power and resources, and how communal politics shaped the political relationship between them by absenting the colonial players who were manipulating this game, are attempts by Chatterji to maintain the unstated argument (like her Cambridge colleague, Perry Anderson) that Indians were responsible for all the mess they alone supposedly created.

Just as 'the bhadralok press', according to Chatterji, 'was curiously muted in its criticism of the British officials'[398] behind the Communal Award of 1932, Chatterji herself is curiously muted on how colonialism contributed to the story of Hindu communalism and partition. For instance, when dealing with the conflictual world of Indian politics and the 'embattled [Hindu] elite determined to pay whatever price it had to in order to cling to power and privilege'[399] there is a clear moral tone in Chatterji's language accompanying her political judgement. She is more careful and balanced when it comes to the Raj. Chatterji's tone of neutrality in this regard is a matter of concern. The criticism of India's religious societies is illuminating, but muting a robust criticism of the Raj is not. Chatterji knows very well that colonial power did not allow societies to carve out their destinies freely and negotiate their animosities without colonial meddling. Even if the focus of her work is the politics of Indian society under colonialism, there is no analytical or ideological reason for her to keep the British out of the game as far as possible, at least till 1947.

Janam Mukherjee has written on the 1943 famine and some of the sociological connections with the 1946 genocide, particularly the demographic shifts in Calcutta during the famine and the 'differential access to scarce resources'[400] that particularly affected poor Muslims. But Mukherjee goes overboard in his thesis, without being able to account for the key reason for the violence:

'About naked hatred and senseless murder there is very little that is interesting. What is more interesting is that this descent into carnage and communal blood-lust did not occur in a vacuum. It emerged in the context of a collective madness that had seized Calcutta, erupting on the day of a political demonstration. This demonstration and the politics behind it have already been detailed in some depth. Neither the demonstration itself, nor the politics behind it, can account for the carnage that ensued. The over-determining factor, even in politics, and more specifically in communalist politics, leading up to this event was famine. Politics had become deeply enmeshed in society's grief, and its attempt to come to grips with the avoidable death of at least three million of its citizens. It is one thing when an opposing party is accused of kick-backs or catering to its own constituency; it is another when they are accused of being responsible for the death of millions. Famine hardened the political discourse to a dangerous extent. It also hardened society at large.'[401]

Notice Mukherjee using the word 'senseless'. Gandhi made a distinction between 'senseless' and 'sensible' and informed us about what he thought were the dangers of senseless violence. Is senseless violence uninteresting to consider for thinking or dangerous enough to interest thinking?

There is a visible discomfort to explain the violence by dismissing it as intellectually uninteresting. Such a remark is possible only when the suffering produced by violence becomes a matter of magnitude and statistics. Mukherjee, and many others like him, live in a philosophical void where economic factors alone matter to our understanding of epic suffering. To be sure, this suffering is political, as much as the reasons that produced them. But if suffering were only political, it wouldn't be a value above politics, or a value against which politics is measured.

Politics lacks depth. To treat suffering only within a political realm of understanding is to reduce its depth. Suffering can't be summoned for an ideological critique of politics and left to subsist in the dark corners of history. Such a callous intellectual and public attitude contributes to the neglect of the human condition and its festering wounds that do not help the politics of the future. The claim of modern political thought to understand the human condition falls short if that condition does not pose a limit to that thought. At critical junctures of history, the human condition has contradicted the designs of political thought and ideology. These junctures mark the spaces which provoke us to think differently and anew.

Emmanuel Levinas is particularly despondent about commentators on historical events of mass grief, whom he calls 'revisers of history' who epitomized the discursive 'uselessness' of suffering.[402] The fact that there is no philosophical rumination on the violence of partition proves the banality of scholarship on it. There is ideological commentary and critique, but no philosophical engagement with the narratives of suffering.

Partition is a wasteland of mass death and grief, with no posthumous reflection on that grief. It is treated with a negative discomfort, as an event of unnecessary deaths, killings that don't make sense, so they remain unrecognized by intellectual efforts to mourn them reflectively and tell us why such tragedies dampen our claims to being human. Partition is India's holocaust and it warrants more than an ideological reading. Intellectuals and scholars who have housed their thinking in ideology are incapable of this gesture.

In *Remembering Partition*, Gyanendra Pandey makes the suggestion, taking from Paul Ricoeur, that historiography (what he calls, taking from Ricoeur, historian's history) seeks 'to produce the "truth" of the traumatic, genocidal violence of Partition and to elide it at the same time.'[403] The elision is unavoidable according to Pandey because, to begin with, 'such violence [is] non-narratable: the "limit case" of history, as it has been described in the instance of the Holocaust.'[404] He goes on to quote Paul Ricoeur that 'horror isolates events by making them incomparable, incomparably unique, uniquely unique.'[405]

Ricoeur's point on the untranslatability of the experience of horror (both individual and collective) is not an argument for elision. In the section from the third volume of *Time and Narrative* that Pandey refers to, Ricoeur defines historical horror as something that 'constitutes the ultimate ethical motivation for the history of victims.'[406] What is this motivation and how do we address it in language?

History's limitations involve the narrative of spectacular victimization that 'no cunning of reason can ever justify' and it is also something that 'reveals the scandal of every theodicy of history'.[407] In other words, the motivations of secular history that uses Hegelian tools of historical reason, or historical theology that uses the idea of evil to justify divine goodness, aren't adequate for the task. Horror can't be explained or, worse—justified—in the name of an ideological logic, teleological or not. Nor can the intrusion of evil be understood against a metaphysical idea of goodness. Ethics demands a difficult truth.

Ricoeur's focus is the memory of horror, particularly in the genre of fiction. He seems to be saying that since the discipline of history is not enough to address horror, fiction as a genre may fill up the gaps of memory. The limits of historiography are neither an invitation for elision, nor a move to throw history out of the game. On such occasions, history may need to work around its limits and be inclusive. The radical specificity of historical horrors will need diverse forms of writing to join the pieces together. Ricoeur feels that when it comes to horrible memory, or memory of the horrible, the fusion of history and fiction will carry both forms back to their origin in the epic, and such 'negative epic'[408] can address human suffering.

Pandey is concerned about the problem of individuation of the event in Ricoeur's idea of epic horror. It is a misplaced and unnecessary concern. When an episode in history is *not* generalizable and universalizable, when the horror it produced has a radical specificity, and the suffering is difficult to address, that is when we are faced with the question of a truth that may have universal resonance, but is radically (spatio-temporally, experientially) specific. It is also *un-representable*. Ricoeur's claim that the 'victims of Auschwitz are . . . the representatives in our memory of all history's victims'[409] is not just an overstatement but a typical tendency in the West to see European history as both central and universal. Auschwitz is a proper noun of an incomparable memory of horror.

Some lessons in history are also about history. The 'limit case' of history is first of all about (modern) history, that it cannot keep reading the meaning of events, and placing and justifying its arguments (tacitly or overtly), based on universal notions and categories. The modernist lens of universal history has exhausted its theoretical rubbish. The horror of partition is irreplaceable, and has no use for revolutionary plans or normative generalizations. Just because it is of no use to certain kinds of historians or scholars doesn't mean that horror has no use for reflection. When historiography is unable, or is scared, to make sense of something, it exposes its limits, and we are faced by an enormous ethical question. If horror produces a crisis *within* history, it is also a crisis *of* history.

Since Pandey raised the question of 'truth' in relation to history and historiography, what is the truth of partition's genocidal violence?

Gandhi's politics of truth was to make people understand, if you took history too seriously, you will come to face your own horror. Those who do not understand the profound nature of the Gandhian intervention are bound to miss its central ethical significance.

Many historians and scholars who have focused on Gandhi's notion of truth (and even non-violence) missed an important and integral corollary. Gandhi's search for truth was simultaneously, paradoxically, about finding (his) errors. He wrote in the introduction to his autobiography:

> 'I am not going either to conceal or understate any ugly things that must be told. I hope to acquaint the reader fully with all my faults and errors. My purpose is to describe experiments in the science of satyagraha, not to say how good I am. *In judging myself I shall try to be as harsh as truth, as I want others also to be. Measuring myself by that standard* I must exclaim with Surdas:
> *Where is there a wretch*
> *So wicked and loathsome as I?*
> *I have forsaken my Maker,*
> *So faithless have I been*.'[410]

What is the harshness of truth? It is the most rigorous ordeal to harshly judge one's errors. Truth-telling can thus also be read as error-telling, and the science of Satyagraha, the technique of revealing your errors to yourself and to the world. Gandhi's purpose is not to say good things about himself, but to risk the judgement of others in publicly recording his own errors. Error-telling is not an attractive job. What is the 'standard' for measuring truthfulness? It is measured by the ability to boldly record one's errors. *To tell the truth is to tell one's errors.*

The truth of facing partition's genocidal violence was, for Gandhi, the problem of error, of lies, including the lies of politics. There is no truth outside it. Pandey mentioned how partition meant 'face-to-face destruction, frequently involving neighbour against neighbour.'[411] That is the whole point, ethical, political and historical. Gandhi's truth was the face-to-face, and partition violence was its destruction. The destruction of a neighbourhood is the destruction of what constitutes society, its most primary ethical relation. Gandhi pointed out moral errors to everyone he interacted with in Noakhali, as much as he wondered about his own errors that may have led to the defeat of non-violence. The individuation of a 'negative epic' is also that of its error, the error of its horror, the horror of errors.

The truth and error of horror isn't non-narratable. This doesn't mean the necessity for either 'pathetic history' or 'objective history'. It is not a necrophiliac interest in the dead, or a scientific one. The unconsumable narrative alone is the truth. It is a narrative of death and humiliation, the stripping of life to the bone. In fact, this is exactly the ethical risk at stake: the risk of memory against horror, and the risk of the historian and the writer in taking a leap to understand what horror means. The 'limit case' is the most illuminating case, which tells us that human suffering is more valuable than history.

The dead, Walter Benjamin said, 'will not be safe from the enemy if he wins.'[412] Theoreticians who avoid the dead if it ruins their revolutionary imagination of history also betray the dead. *The dead did not die safely during partition.* The truths of history can't be elided for history's sake. The violence of partition is messy, but not non-narratable. It demands a narrative of truth and *otherwise*, which haunts us with a lucidity that lies beneath the mess. The mess does not lie in the violence alone, but in the politics behind it at every corner. To address this mess is to bring revolutionary and nationalist fantasies to a halt. Historiography must pass through that danger.

No one cares about the civil war that seized Russia soon after the October Revolution in 1917, where millions died. They are useless and un/necessary deaths with regard to the new mythological moment in history. What matters to communists is that Bolsheviks seized power.

There are no questions asked about why the revolutionary Workers' and Soldiers' Council decided that a defeated Tsar Nicholas, his family—wife Alexandra, the four daughters, Anastasia, Marie, Tatiana and Olga, the three servants, Ivan Kharitonov, the cook, Aloise Trupp, the footman, and Anna Demidova, the maid—and the family doctor, Yevgeny Botkin, were taken to West Siberia and slaughtered in the cellar of their confinement in July 1918.

There are no moral questions to brood over when the logic of war is accepted in the name of class or nation. The rope of retributive violence is as limitless as the fear and suspicion that run in the body. The suffocating source of fascist and communist paranoia (and insomnia) is: *You cannot sleep till the last enemy is exterminated*.

Mukherjee accepts famine as the over-determining factor behind the riots. By doing so, he reflects the problem that Pandey speaks of, a certain historiographical approach of 'transforming the history of the event into a history of its causes or origins'.[413]. For Mukherjee, famine is the extended historical event that becomes the existential ground for communal genocide. The problem with this view is that Mukherjee wants to place the reason behind the killings in something as agonizingly real as hunger. It is incredible to assume there can be an authentic and profound reason behind something as grotesque as mass murder.

Writing on the Rwandan genocide of 1994, Mahmood Mamdani takes up the economist's explanation of the tragedy as a problem of a 'resource crunch' that is understood as creating 'internally and externally generated constraints'[414] on ordinary people for a decade. To grasp the nature of the condition, he uses the simile of 'a growing sense of claustrophobia in a crowded commuter train'[415]. Mamdani rejects this economic logic of causality: 'No matter how depressing these facts may seem, we need to keep in mind that there is no *necessary* connection between a drastic reduction in resources and deadly human conflict.'[416]

There is nothing left to argue, no ethics to evoke or defend, if history (and ideological readings on it) overwhelms and decides everything *in advance*. Mamdani writes that genocidal violence may not be 'understood as rational', but it is still 'thinkable'[417]. If violence exhausts all meaning of the encounter, there is nothing thinkable on the encounter. The thinking on violence is to recover the damage caused by historical reason. Mass violence, genocide, are exceptionally brutal. Neither the experience of grief, nor the politics of grief, however communally expressed, and used as motivation for intercommunal antagonism, can logically translate into such proportion of violence.

Grief can be a source of violence only when mourning has been manipulated to an extent that its ties with grief have been severed.

Communal politics can act as a catalyst in this regard, using emotional resources for manipulation. But communal violence is constructed around discourses of hate whose. That this discourse can work as justification for violence is one thing, and the fact that it can actually unleash that violence is another. It takes certain conditions to precipitate the atmosphere of antagonism. Political violence is committed by party henchmen, social bullies or hooligans called goondas in India, and the class that is most susceptible to violence, the urban and rural subaltern.

The Class/Communal Conundrum

Bipan Chandra makes a class distinction between communal violence and communal politics. He argues, 'the urban poor and lumpen and *goonda* elements, though in a few cases the peasants' indulge in communal violence, whereas communal politics (which provides the ideological basis of such violence) is the mastermind of 'the middle classes, landlords and bureaucratic elements'[418] who act as the chief provocateur. Both the urban subaltern comprising the city's poor (or the non-urban peasantry) who take part in communal violence and the elite and the middle class that gulp down these crimes do so without a trace of guilt. There is a tacit fusion of sentiments across the class divide when it comes to communal violence. It stands as compensation for past crimes that is never enough. The vicious logic of retribution overpowers the strength—or lack of—juridical force. During communal violence, the clock is set back and there is a setback for finer, reconciliatory arguments. During times of political discordance, the sentiments of a community are enhanced. It is not the business of the secular state to amend these sentiments. Sentiments are not a matter of law.

The subaltern is revolutionary, or reactionary, according to circumstances and provocations suitable to the nature of passion involved in both.

The peasant rebellion in 1831, led by Syed Mir Nisar Ali (popularly, Titu Mir) against Hindu zamindars and British indigo planters, and the Tebhaga Movement of 1946–47 by the All India Kisan Sabha, affiliated to the Communist Party of India (CPI), to reduce the landlord's share of the harvest to one-third, were the two major moments of subaltern assertion in Bengal's modern history. In between, however, Bengal mostly experienced a sweep of Hindu–Muslim riots. As early as 1906–07, there were communal riots in Noakhali and Comilla.[419] Riots happened in 1926–27 all over Bengal after the Bengal Pact—a pact of amity between Hindus and Muslims in Bengal put in place by C.R. Das, who formed the Swarajya Party within the Congress—was duly invalidated by the Congress after the death of Das.[420] Sugata Bose mentions two 'major conflagrations'[421] of communal riots before 1946: in Kishoreganj (Mymensingh district) in 1931 and in Dacca in 1941. Though these riots were connected to 'economic conflicts',[422] the other fact of the matter was religion. Regarding Noakhali and Tippera, Bose says that the Muslim peasantry mainly comprised Sunnis of the Hanafi School.[423] It is interesting that most historians writing on the carnage of 1946–47 convey bewilderment on the sudden and overwhelming nature of the event. It appears as if the peasants acted out of character. There are also ideological attempts to dissociate the class and communal elements in the psyche of the peasantry.

Bipan Chandra approvingly quotes W.C. Smith's argument in *Modern Islam in India* (1943) that communal riots in India were 'isolated instances of· class struggles fought in communal guise'.[424] Chandra thinks that the 'overlapping of class division and religious division . . . explains why lower class communalism often led to violence.'[425] There is a problem of authenticity in Chandra's understanding that 'communalism was sometimes a 'substitute' for class struggle.'[426] Chandra's argument is that the 'social anger' of the urban poor—understood in Marxist terms as 'declassed, rootless, lumpen social strata'—was expressed through '*senseless violence* or in a tendency to loot and plunder'.[427] [Emphasis mine] He calls these instances of communal violence 'distorted class struggles'.[428] Chandra considers class struggle authentic and communal violence its distorted form but imagines elements of both present during communal violence. This is a convoluted argument made to desperately retain the conceptual purity of class. Chandra's view of 'community' in the Indian context reveals the basis of the problem. Chandra holds, 'the use of the word community with reference to Hindus or Muslims or Sikhs in India was, and is, entirely misplaced. To agree to do so was to accept one of the basic premises of communalism.'[429] For Chandra, the term 'community' used to designate 'a social grouping as an analytical or political category and for the identification and articulation of certain group interests'[430] is to validate communalism. Chandra is wary of the term community because it is attached to religion, or religious identity, which tends to homogeneously subsume elements of class, ethnicity and culture.[431] This is the sort of liberal/Marxist conjuring trick where concepts and their corresponding realities can be made to disappear by arguments where secularism works as ideological faith and accepts and rejects the world according to its binaries. Chandra's problem also stems from the left and liberal obsession with universality. Any sociocultural identity that is not universalizable is dangerous and must remain unacknowledged for fear of legitimizing it. The basis of such progressivist paranoia is ideology, not reality. Secular nationalists like Bipan Chandra who wanted to do away with community as an analytical category were indulging in a dangerous sort of wishful thinking.

Community is made of collective sentiment, group-memory, common habits, beliefs and mores. It is both real and constructed. Community can be both face-to-face and imagined, as *imagined* as Benedict Anderson's 'imagined community'. Community is location (the location of cultural life), a place on earth, a home of shared symbols and practices. Community is shared rituals of birth, death and prayer, in a certain language and its offshoots. Community is what you may leave, and return to. It is belonging, or a memory of belonging. It is concentric circles of difference, something that can accommodate 'a bundle of contradictions held together by strong but invisible threads'[432] (to quote Nehru's description of India). Nation and community are analogous. Community can include elements of class, caste and ethnicity, imbibe hierarchies. It is residual in people who migrate, or who transform themselves into a broader and wider world of living and thinking (what is understood as universal, or global, with invisible, dislocated, shifting centres and peripheries).

In his 1843 essay *On the Jewish Question* (that was published the following year), Marx's anti-culturalism identifies negative attributes of the Jewish character (ego, self-interest, desire and accumulation of property and capital) to traditional identity alone. Marx decried the modern human being in civil society as conceived by the liberal–bourgeois state as 'abstract, artificial man, man as an *allegorical, moral* person'[433] (in another translation moral is mentioned as 'juridical'). It was for him the persistence of religion in a secularized form. The duality in the citizen-cum-person-of-faith that Marx decried as the privatizing of religion in bourgeois civil-society is the best option for people to grapple with the terrors of the new beast called the modern nation–state, and the alienation of individuated life. This allegorical existence allows a desirable middle ground to civil society, caught between the oppressive state and community. It acts as a safety valve in spiritual and psychological terms for people faced with the demands of a modern Moloch.

A national community as a form of collective self-interest that can pose a majoritarian danger for 'others' was not considered. Even though the ideological motivations are different, fascists use and exploit the language of cultural essentialism against minorities. In his rational universalism, Marx's argument unwittingly lends itself to the majoritarian project and endangered the Jewish community. His radical prescription to make being Jewish impossible dangerously merges with the Nazi logic that the Jew must be eliminated because he can't be integrated. The argument for the destruction of any community of faith based on a rational and universal idea of human emancipation forgets the majoritarian potential of nationalism where minorities are under threat. Fascist thinking is not the opposite of Marxism in this regard. It is Marxism's double. The fascist and communist idea of the nation has one fundamental connection: no one can exist as the *other* within it, without being an enemy.

Doesn't matter what Hegel or Marx or some other great thinker of the modern West thought of community. The community can't be reduced to the articulation of group interests. To hold economic interests (connected to social status) alone to be real, and the cultural part of identity as an artificial and dangerous surplus, is worse than offering an ideological binary. Splitting the coherent and comprehensive meaning of the individual and society is an artificial move in the first place. To use a simple scientific analogy,[434] when a 1:2 ratio of hydrogen and oxygen atoms comes together, they form a compound we call a water molecule, where the internal properties of hydrogen and oxygen are lost to produce something new. Class and community fuse together in a similar manner during communal violence and it is impossible to objectively assess its property, as much as it is absurd to divide them into an authentic/inauthentic binary.

Partha Chatterjee believes that 'communalism' is a conception of 'liberal–bourgeois ideology', which is deployed to contrast and legitimize the statist ideology of secularism.[435] He finds this binary unsustainable in the study of the 'second domain'[436] of politics where political action doesn't flow from statist principles.

This is a false argument that uses the communal–secular binary in a wrong fashion to hide the peasantry's propensity for communal violence as it was repeatedly displayed in Bengal's history from the 1930s. The secular–communal binary is problematic when it seeks to establish a statist principle (secularism) that overlooks politics. That does not mean that there is anything wrong in the state promoting a secular standard where political culture and ideology need to be sensitive to diverse religious identities. Majoritarianism, after all, is a palpable threat within any national community.

The genocide in Noakhali perpetrated by the Muslim peasantry on the instigation of the Muslim League was communal, and it communalized both class and community relations. Any political reading of the event can simply base its criticism on an anti-communal perspective. The condemnation of genocide does not have to refer to any statist principle, secular or not.

The interim government in Bengal was under the colonial state with partial sovereignty. In fact, the Muslim League behaved like a political party that was most willing to subvert all principles of governance by allowing genocide to take place under its jurisdiction. The Congress, in the name of being a party for all communities (avowing a secular identity, if not principle), followed suit by failing to protect Muslims in Bihar.

Secularism was still not a state policy, or a principle of governance, or even a principle of politics before 1947. The term 'communal' was in vogue since the 1920s. Shabnum Tejani argued that the political formation (and formalization) of a 'corporate Muslim identity'[437] after the Muslims demanded separate electorates from Lord Minto in October 1906 (leading to the formation of the All India Muslim League in December that year), made scholars writing about this period (Tejani mentions Hindu scholars) use the terms 'communal' and 'anti-national' for Indian Muslims. It is interesting to note that the term 'secular' was introduced much later in the lexicon of Indian politics, most significantly during the Constituent Assembly Debates that took place from 1946 to 1950. But the term has been around since much earlier. For instance, Lala Lajpat Rai used the term 'secular power' in 1926, 'secularism' in 1927 and 'secular government'[438] in 1928. Partha Chatterjee retrospectively made an argument to critique the communal/secular binary that had no relevance in Bengal politics in the 1930s and 1940s. Whatever Tejani may think of the Muslim League, the party lived up to its communal credentials in the most vicious manner since the beginning of the 1940s, leading up to partition. Ambedkar, in his speech introducing the Draft Constitution in the

Constituent Assembly on 4 November 1948, reiterated that India's minorities saw Hindus as 'a communal majority and not a political majority.'[439] Clearly, the Congress did not enjoy the status of being seen as a secular party in 1948 by everyone. The debate here is not about statist principles, but about how the political nature of identity formation, related to the majority and minority communities (across class), could not shrug off the accusation of being communal.

The peasantry in Bengal indulged in many more instances of communal violence in the decade leading up to 1946 than the couple of upsurges against economic grievances that are considered revolutionist. It is also part of revolutionary mythology that peasants are capable of making a distinction between their 'real' (economic) interests and concerns considered unproductive, like communal passion and dominance. This distinction is untenable in the first place. Religion is as 'real' for the peasantry as it is for the ruling classes, as are economic issues. Religion and material concerns make an integrated sphere. The history of class struggle is not a universal phenomenon precisely because of cultural specificities and the question of religion that marks the struggle for better economic conditions, relations and rights. These two components are differentiated by Marxist theoreticians to suit an ideological argument which is not supported by history. Ranajit Guha considers religion 'negative consciousness',[440] but following Antonio Gramsci, he accepts it as a 'necessary'[441] moment in the history of class consciousness and struggle. Any mark of religion in the peasantry is proof of the limiting influence of the ruling class. This 'negative' part of peasant consciousness is sought to be overcome by communist intervention. But in Bengal, it was successfully intensified and overcome through communal intervention. It throws apart the political expectations of Marxist theoreticians and attests to the limits of scientific history.

Partha Chatterjee wants to maintain a complex and open understanding of peasant consciousness as he believes that the idea of 'friend' and 'enemy' in the peasantry that fluctuates between considerations based on class and community at different instances can be identified in the 'alternative ideological systems, brought to the peasantry from outside, from the organized world of politics.'[442]

Genocidal Violence

In *Victims Become Killers*, Mahmood Mamdani writes:

> "Hutu/Tutsi violence in the Rwandan genocide invites comparison with Hindu/Muslim violence at the time of the partition of colonial India. Neither can be explained as *simply* a state project."[443] [Emphasis mine]

Mamdani mentions the silences in the accounts of the Rwandan genocide by scholars which include "political analysis [that] presents the genocide as exclusively a state project and ignores its subaltern and "popular" character"[444]. Mamdani's invitation attests the genocidal nature of partition violence. From the organizational details of how violence was systematically planned and executed in Noakhali, it is evident that all cultural, religious and moral signs of life of a community was sought to be erased within a geographical space. Forced conversion inflicted psychological harm.

Scholars like Partha Chatterjee shifted the focus from the peasantry in the case of the 1946 Noakhali genocide and made it appear like elite politics was responsible. The peasantry's overwhelming participation is left out of analysis. Chatterjee leaves a window open to interpret the political action of the peasantry without implicating them for their beliefs, which is seen as the interest of class enemies. This standpoint shall, by ideological necessity, refrain from explaining genocide perpetrated by the subaltern class.

The general problem of this ideological reluctance lies concealed in the Marxist approach to war.

Simone Weil is pithy regarding this in her essay 'War and Peace: Reflections on War':

> 'It is obvious that, as far as war is concerned, the Marxist tradition offers neither unity nor clarity. But all the theories agree on at least one point: the absolute refusal to condemn war as such.'[445]

Marxist theoreticians would focus on the communal angle, but carefully keep away from offering a firm critique on genocide not only because they want to protect the peasantry, but also because they don't want to offer a clear political judgement against war, even if it is civil war.

The suspension of moral judgement is a moral failure on the part of Marxists who argue in the service of their doctrine. Despite the Marxist interest in history, it is history that must be fitted into the demands of ideology. History's contradictions don't necessarily get resolved into more progressive patterns, or serve theories of liberty. History moves in a zigzag manner, where forces of class, race and community are intricately, often inflammably, entwined. Time is an unpredictable factor in history, but its past can be read clearly if we refrain from attributing rationalist fantasies or cultural and intellectual hagiographies to the meaning of events. Events have liberating or tragic consequences, but they can't be turned into a series of explanations to suit a theory about a figure or a thing. History owes no fidelity to theory. At best, history is a series of fragments. Everything can't be put together to make a suitable frame for the ideologue's pleasure.

The subaltern is a victim of structural exploitation and violence where power is not in its hands. But the subaltern is capable of violence where it might smell the possibility of power, however short-lived and sordid. Structural violence is entrenched and long-drawn. It has a bearing on subaltern life and their political consciousness. The subaltern class is disallowed certain social privileges, and bears the brunt of exploitative economic relations. To indulge in communal genocide against a community that may largely represent class power rejects the material nature of the relationship. The communally constructed and justified nature of genocidal violence emanates from an ethnocentric or religious discourse of hate. The nature of what Marxists define as class enemy is transformed into the communal enemy. The movement turns ideologically fascist. In this situation, the subaltern can't be defended by class discourse, and arguments based on economic exploitation won't hold. The subaltern bent on communal genocide takes on a monstrous collective identity that creates disjunctions in the deterministic trajectory invented for it in left-wing theoretical models. Class is as contradictory as people and history.

In fact, subaltern violence will have fewer pretensions to morality because this class of people has experienced exploitation. Even if you relativize morality according to class, you must still account for the moral crisis during genocide. People must share the responsibility for collectively engaging in degraded acts. Society is divided across class and community, but to have a remotely possible egalitarian and fraternal condition of life—not just in the formal, even purely political sense, but something that is more deeply, culturally experienced—there has to be a shared sense of morality.

2

'Neither a Hindu nor a Muslim'

Before Gandhi's arrival in Bihar, it would be a good idea to give a brief introduction to Bihar's political history and situation at the advent of the 1946 riots. Communal history, or the history of communal politics and relations, is complicated as pre-partition narratives show. There are claims, fears, accusations, and often distinguished scholars take these claims, fears and accusations seriously, suggesting that they carry a degree of authenticity.[1]

Mohammad Sajjad offers us a brief history of how Bihar was engulfed by communal politics. Sajjad writes, during the 1920s and 1930s both the Muslim League and the Hindu Mahasabha constructed the idea of political community based on religious identity, until the League took a step ahead and declared the 'Pakistan Resolution' on 23 March 1940 in Lahore.[2] In a mass meeting in April 1940 in Jamui (then part of Munger district), Sir Khawaja Nazimuddin (chairman of the Muslim League in Bengal between 1945 and 1947, and the first chief minister of East Bengal in 1947) gave the slogan, "Pakistan is our birthright, and we have, once and for all, decided to achieve it".[3] On 19 April 1940, the League observed 'Independence Day' in every district of Bihar, and it was immediately followed by riots during the '*Mahbiri Jhanda* procession in Ballia (Begusarai), in Rajmahal, and on the *Ramnavami* procession in Hazaribagh'.[4] On the other side, Sajjad writes, the pro-communal faction in the Congress kept growing and Rajendra Prasad was instrumental behind Congress declaring an electoral alliance with the Hindu Mahasabha.[5] The Mahasabha was active in Bihar even before the declaration of Pakistan by the League. Mahasabha leader B.S. Moonje (Hedgewar's mentor, who had met Benito Mussolini on his visit to Italy in March 1931, and while in Rome on 19 March, he visited the Opera Nazionale Balilla, the Italian fascist youth organization, and got inspired to militarize Hindu society),[6] addressed a meeting in Hathuwa (Saran district) on 20 January 1940. Military training for Hindus was emphasized, and Moonje spoke of launching a movement of the Hindu Sangathan. There were processions with people on elephants, camels and horses.[7] Moonje also addressed conferences at Begusarai and Muzaffarpur on 24 and 25 January 1940, followed by processions where the Congress and Gandhi's Hindu–Muslim unity programme were denounced.[8] Jagat Narain Lal, a Congress member, was part of the Mahasabha activities.[9]

Bipan Chandra has explained the reasons behind the Congress Party slipping into the communal trap despite having 'sturdy secularists'[10] like Gandhi and Nehru. The

Congress tried to rely on 'negotiations with communal leaders'.[11] They did not undertake any 'mass campaign'[12] against communalism. The Congress failed to explain the 'analytical content'[13] of communalism, which had deep roots in the economic exploitation by the colonial regime. Instead, the Congress in the 1920s acted as 'a mediator or intermediary between different communal leaders, groups and parties, or, as during the late 1920s. 1930s and 1940s, to arrive at a compromise through top-level negotiations with Muslim communal leaders through conferences, individual negotiations, etc.' By doing so, Chandra writes, the Congress legitimized communal leaders as representatives of their communities. Crucially, the Congress failed 'to acquire a base among the Muslim peasantry and artisans'.[14] These are important critical remarks to keep in mind from a historian who championed the Congress as a secular political force.

Revenge for Noakhali

The Congress formed the first cabinet of Bihar in 1946 with Srikrishna Sinha as chief minister. Sajjad writes that Bihar was reeling from an economic crisis with food scarcity and unemployment, as well as rising crime, but the Congress regime wasn't able to address these problems efficiently.[15] In the summer of 1946, there was an agitation in eleven districts of Bihar for the restoration of 'bakasht' land (lands that originally belonged to tenants but were seized by zamindars for non-payment of dues) where Hindu and Muslim peasants collaborated against zamindars.[16] The situation changed by November, when communal riots engulfed rural areas.[17] Government officials, Sajjad writes, 'connived with the antisocial elements' who were 'allegedly also Congress workers'.[18] Sajjad mentions a particular incident:

> 'A prominent Congress worker, deputed by Rajendra Prasad, was reported to have told a gathering of Hindus at Fatuha High School on 27 September 1946, "I'm one of the 86 persons deputed by Dr Rajendra Prasad and this is the right time for us to destroy and annihilate our enemies".'[19]

In another reported incident, when Muslim residents of Rupahua village in Munger district, as prosecution witnesses, testified about the massacre of children, the police officer interrupted them saying, this was revenge for Noakhali.[20] In another report, Congress leaders, in a procession in Gaya, carried portraits of Gandhi and Nehru and 'shouted slogans such as '*Noakhali ka badla le kar rahenge* [We will take revenge for Noakhali],' and '*Hindustan Hinduon ka, nahin kisi ke baap ka* [Hindustan is for Hindus, it is not anyone's paternal property].'[21]

Political Complicity and Collective Responsibility

The train from Calcutta, with Gandhi and his associates, including Nirmal Kumar Bose, aboard, reached Fatwah station (near Patna) early in the morning on 5 March.[22] Abdul Bari, the President of the provincial Congress committee, and Srikrishna Sinha, the Chief Minister of Bihar, received them at the platform. Gandhi made a bleak joke upon seeing Bari: 'How is it that you are still alive?'[23]

Gandhi was accommodated in Syed Mahmud's bungalow near the Ganges. In a conversation with Rajendra Prasad and

Bihar ministers, Gandhi urged the government to appoint a commission of inquiry, or else it would mean admitting to the guilt that the Muslim League was trying to impose on the Congress. Chief Minister Sinha expressed his fear the League would make political capital out of the inquiry. Gandhi replied:

> 'My sixty years' experience has taught me nothing if not that. That is also the lesson of my three months of travail in Noakhali. I was groping in the dark but I said just what seemed to me to be the truth. Those who regarded me as their enemy could exploit it. But I had faith that sooner rather than later they would see their mistake.'[24]

This was Gandhi's unwavering ethical clarity, which had universal resonance. Compare this with the dissident Russian poet Yevgeny Yevtushenko writing in his autobiography in 1963 at the age of 31:

> 'Lenin once said that our enemies would always eat the crumbs of self-criticism that fall from our table. In fact, they clearly do. But what are we to do to stop them? Keep silent about our mistakes, about the failings of our society? A strong man is not afraid of showing his weakness. I believed then and I believe now in the spiritual strength of our people and I therefore regard it my duty to speak openly about whatever I think is wrong.'[25]

As if mutual suspicion and bitterness between the Muslim League and the Congress weren't enough, Congress ministers also regarded one another with suspicion. Gandhi had to convince the Congress leaders that Syed Mahmud, whose letter had brought him to Bihar, had replied to his queries and had not acted disloyally against his colleagues.[26] At the prayer meeting, Gandhi was categorically frank: 'At present I have no evidence to say that Congressmen have committed these crimes. Tomorrow I may have to admit so.'[27] He said that since the Congress claimed to represent all Indians, it must take moral responsibility 'for the misdeeds of all communities and all individuals.'[28]

Pyarelal describes the socialist leader Jayaprakash Narayan (who was part of the Congress Socialist party, a breakaway group, found in 1934) meeting Gandhi: 'His evidence was highly damaging to the Government and the Congress.'[29] Narayan's visit was followed by a delegate from the Muslim community that 'alleged that many people high up in the Congress had taken part in the riots.'[30]

In the prayer meeting on 6 March the following day, Gandhi said that Muslim Leaguers admitted that Nehru's arrival in Bihar had helped stop the violence and save lives. Nehru and Vallabhbhai Patel, accompanied by Liaquat Ali Khan and Abdul Rab Nishtar, had reached there on 3 November 1946.[31] Sajjad Mohammad writes on Nehru's visit:

> 'Jawaharlal Nehru visited many parts of Bihar and addressed several public meetings during 4–9 November 1946, and he wrote to Patel (on 5 November 1946) that some educated people of the Hindu Sabha variety were involved in the riots, and that "some landlords backed these disturbances partly to divert attention of their tenantry from agrarian problem, partly to discredit the ministry."'[32]

Nehru visited several disturbed areas in Bihar, including Jethli, Fatwa, Bakhtiarpur and Biharsharif, along with League members. In the course of his peace mission, Nehru addressed a meeting in Biharsharif despite 'the tense communal atmosphere and against the advice of local officials.'[33] Addressing a public meeting at Taregna, a small town in Patna district that witnessed a lot of killings and where a railway station was burnt, Nehru impassionedly said,

'If you want to kill a Muslim you must kill me first and proceed to do whatever you choose after marching over my dead body'.[34]

In the prayer meeting on 7 March, Gandhi referred to the communal procession in Gaya where slogans of retributive violence were raised:

> 'I have heard that these people shouted *Mahatma Gandhi ki Jai* while carrying out the massacre. I do not consider myself a Mahatma. But I cannot understand how people who consider me a Mahatma dragged in my name for committing such heinous crimes. I learnt of these terrible riots in Bihar while I was trekking the villages in Noakhali and attempting to unite the hearts of Hindus and Muslims. Now that I have come to Bihar, I think I must visit the scenes of actual massacre.'[35]

That the Hindus committing genocide in Bihar used Gandhi's name appears to be a depraved strategy to tarnish Gandhi and his peace mission so that there was no ethical space and figure left to challenge the communal war.

On 8 March, Muhammad Yunus, who was briefly Bihar's chief Minister from the Muslim Independent Party in 1937 before the Congress took over, came to meet Gandhi. Yunus and Gandhi were old friends writes Pyarelal, so Gandhi candidly raised the question if Jinnah could be 'left out of the picture' (to mean Jinnah had a role to play in the mayhem that engulfed Bengal and Bihar), and asked whether it was the responsibility of League members to correct him if they thought he was going in the wrong direction[36]. Yunus replied it wasn't possible to disagree with Jinnah and still be in the Muslim League. In response, Gandhi made an ominous remark, 'Then the future is dark indeed for Islam and for India — more for Islam than for India.'[37] Yunus asked Gandhi how long he expected to stay in Bihar. To which Gandhi said he had set no time for himself, and Bihar was his Karbala[38].

Speaking to Pradesh Congress Committee members on 9 March, Gandhi said that he had heard the government spokesperson's apologia (referring to his meeting with Binodanand Jha earlier in the day, where Jha told him that the disturbances occurred due to a 'joint conspiracy' between the Hindu Mahasabha and British officials).[39] He felt that everyone must look inwards. Gandhi also told them that many Muslims air Jinnah's accusation that the Congress does not belong to all. One Congressman got up to admit that some Congressmen had taken part in the riots. He was interrupted by another member who denied the allegation.[40] Next, the chief minister offered excuses on behalf of the government, saying that they were caught unawares. Sinha mentioned that the Governor, Sir Hugh Dow, was absent, and that the British chief secretary and the inspector general of police let them down.[41] Contrary to Sinha's claim, Sajjad spoke about the Viceroy's report on political complicity in the Bihar genocide:

> 'A.P. Wavell recorded that the outbreaks were planned by the lower rungs of the Congress. Some of them confessed to Gandhi for having joined the rioters. Nehru

> also reported that, notwithstanding the involvement of some Congressmen (who had *Hindu Mahasabha* inclinations), several other Congressmen did excellent work in 1946.'[42]

Curiously, neither Sinha nor Gandhi brought up the other significant detail that Sajjad mentions from Sir Henry Dow's report to Wavell, dated 26 October 1946:

> 'Shri Krishna Sinha "visited the scene, called for a detailed report from the Commissioner, and then went off to Simla on a month long holiday."'[43]

It is reminiscent of Suhrawardy's trip to Darjeeling on 16 October 1946 on the pretext of joining the governor in a Cabinet meeting, when Noakhali was on fire. This act of moral irresponsibility by the highest chair in office sets a historical precedent. Suhrawardy and Sinha fled from the task at hand as they wanted to avoid taking decisions that could have saved lives. Their failure to act allowed the perpetuation of violence, and many lives were lost. It is difficult to detect any other motivation behind their evasion of duty than communal partisanship. Take a holiday from killings taking place under your nose.

Pyarelal mentions an article in *The Statesman* of 8 November 1946 titled *Disgraced Also* on the Bihar genocide that read: 'A pogrom of such magnitude could hardly happen without premonitory signs. Yet... the local administration seems to have been caught unawares.'[44] Comparing Bengal with Bihar, another article in *The Statesman* on 13 November said:

> 'Not only does Bihar's tragedy resemble Bengal's worse one in severity. There can be found dismal similarity in other particulars. Governors slow-moving or not on the spot; Ministers apparently at the outset divided in mind whether some rioting would not be good or bad, and later, amidst the crisis of carnage, quite incapable of disciplining the mob.'[45]

There have been varying degrees of administrative complicity and/or neglect in previous occasions of communal riots in India (for instance, the Kohat riots in 1924). But the largescale, onesided violence in Noakhali and Bihar raised questions about the role of the state administration run by an interim government that belonged to a political party (the Muslim League in Bengal and the Congress in Bihar).

Gandhi's speech at the prayer meeting on 10 March evoked strong reactions.

> 'We do not know what is actually happening in the Punjab. As long as we do not get full and reliable reports, let us hope that they have not descended to the beastly level of slaughtering innocent women and children. But even at present we must admit that brutality is very much in evidence in the Punjab . . . Those who are burning houses, looting properties and slaughtering the innocent, do not even know why they are perpetrating these crimes and atrocities. In a regular war both the sides know what they are fighting for. We are all slaves and our civil war will harm only ourselves. We should realize the teachings of our religions and act according to them. Our politics also should be consistent with our religion.'[46]

At this moment, the crowd close to the dais became noisy and Gandhi had to cut short his speech. Why did people react? Were they looking for some justification for retributive violence?

Gandhi hinted that people indulging in civil war were not even aware of what they were killing for. Unlike war, civil war is violence without clear reasons, or boundaries, without the clear boundaries of reason. It is possible to imagine two nations at war over territorial and other strategic matters. Nations are still to be understood as nations when they go to war. War is a hazardous part of being a nation. If people within a neighbourhood are at war, the meaning of neighbourhood collapses. A neighbourhood at war is a neighbourhood against itself, against its own existence.

Gandhi found it inexplicable, and wondered if people knew what made them destroy their neighbourhood. For Gandhi, the difference between 'sensible' and 'senseless' violence was a difference between meaning and absurdity. This does not mean that 'sensible violence' is justifiable, but that it can be understood. Gandhi wanted to make his audience realize the absurd nature of the violence that had engulfed Bihar. He also brought in religion to say that such violence wasn't approved by religion. This hit straight at the heart of the violence because it was based on religious lines. Gandhi made his audience confront their own acts and those of others they approved which is why they probably reacted in the way they did.

The next day in his talk with members of the Muslim League, Gandhi agreed that what had happened in Bihar was 'deplorable', but reminded them that Hindus also lived in fear in Noakhali.[47] He asked them to send volunteers to Noakhali to tell the Muslims to quell violence and offer confidence to the Hindus. He said this would have an impact on Bihar and Punjab. Gandhi's method was founded on an ethical premise: *If the aggrieved were only against violence committed by the other community, they were not against violence in principle.*

When both sides committed genocide, there were no sides to be taken. People from both sides can best ensure the safety of their own community and a commitment to peace by ensuring the safety of people belonging to the other community. Intercommunity gestures of solidarity alone can form the most formidable bulwark against communal violence and best ensure a return to peace.

The prayer meeting on 12 March was held at Mangal Talav at Kumarahar (near Patna), where, Manu wrote, a mosque and a house in which 340 women had taken shelter were burnt down.[48] Gandhi said to the crowd,

> 'Today I visited a village where Hindus had caused great damage. An old Muslim showed me his own house and those of his relations with broken door-frames where bricks were removed from the door-sill. I was shocked and shaken to see that the Hindus had caused these depredations.
>
> I had wept when I saw the ruins caused by Muslims in Noakhali. Today also I might have wept. But my tears cannot render any succour to the sufferers. What I witnessed today does not behove human beings. *We are all responsible for this vandalism so close to the city of Patna. Even if you did not participate personally in the loot, you cannot escape the charge of abetting the marauders.* A mosque was also damaged in the village Kumarahar. This

> also I consider to be a devilish deed. It is no justification to argue that the Hindus damaged the mosque because the Muslims were desecrating the temples.'[49] [Emphasis mine]

Gandhi said what he hinted at earlier on 10 March: all those who passively took sides in the genocide were among its participants. He alludes to Arendt's point that those who do not make up their minds to resist evil and allow it to exist and have its day are part of the evil.

Evoking the history of his association with Bihar, Gandhi added:

> 'I do not want the bravery of swords or words. Today we need that non-violence which was exemplified by the people of Champaran in 1917.'[50]

Gandhi told the crowd during the prayer meeting at Patna on 13 March that people who took part in the violence should confess their guilt to Syed Mahmud or to him despite their fear of punishment. They would not be reported to the police. He said that while returning from his tour of violence-affected places, the people of Sipara had stopped his car and donated money for the relief fund in a purse. The purse also contained a letter of apology for the violence and an assurance that Muslims would be resettled.[51]

In his speech at Masaurhi (where most houses were razed to the ground during the riots and all but twenty-five out of a population of 1000 had fled from the village)[52] on 17 March, Gandhi said that people who 'committed robbery, arson or murder'[53] did own up their crimes to him. It is not clear whether these confessions were offered by individuals or groups. Their impact is not known. But Gandhi's thinking clearly was to create a semblance of morality in a society where moral relations between communities had broken down. The act of confession was important for Gandhi because feelings were central to his politics of friendship.

Gandhi travelled to Khusropur on 14 March. Manu wrote on their experience as they made a stopover midway through the journey:

> 'We stopped on the way at Shafipur, where we met the *daroga* and visited two burnt down homes of the Muslims. Here women had been pushed to death in a well. Their sarees and other pieces of garments could still be seen floating in the well. It was a terrible sight. Bapuji turned grave.
>
> Bapuji described the scenes in a very moving, tragic terms at the prayer. I wept at that time, so did many others.'[54]

Gandhi with Abdul Ghaffar Khan, Mridula Sarabhai, Manu Gandhi and others at a riot-affected place in Bihar, 1947

We get a sense of the Bihar genocide from the horrible description. This is probably why Manu wrote in her diary on 3 January that the killings in Bihar had pushed Noakhali to second place.

The difference between Hindu women in Noakhali being raped and converted, as opposed to Muslim women in Bihar being put to death, has to do with conversion. The act of converting Hindu women by force made the Muslim men enjoy a perverse sense of domination. It led them to spare the lives of these women. Since the pleasure of religious humiliation was absent for Hindu men, the only brutal option for Muslim women was death. However, there are reports of women and children being locked in a room and set on fire in Noakhali too.[55]

In fact, Hindus were also killed in Noakhali if they 'refused conversion',[56] so clearly conversion was used as a bargaining tool to spare lives. Suranjan Das mentions an English observer who commented that the object of the Noakhali riots 'had been conversions to Islam and not extermination of Hindus.'[57]

A Bird of Passage

Speaking at the prayer meeting in Khusropur, Gandhi conceded that in retrospect, the practice of ahimsa against the British was a weak force that crumbled in the face of intercommunity violence:

> 'People had adopted ahimsa in Champaran at my instance. I now feel that it was the ahimsa of the weak. The British, who were our adversaries, were a mighty power. That is why we seem to have adopted non-violence in facing them; but we could not remain non-violent in our dealings with one another.'[58]

On 15 March, Gandhi said in the prayer meeting at Patna,

> 'I have come to Bihar from Noakhali, but my heart is still in Noakhali. I used to say there that I was working for Bihar in Noakhali. Similarly, I have not lost sight of the work in Noakhali while I am in Bihar.'[59]

Gandhi was split between heart and body, and was in two places at the same time. Even though his body had shifted from Noakhali to Bihar, his heart lagged behind, still reeling from the previous experience. Feelings don't shift as quickly as the body travels. They lag behind and linger. Gandhi resided in Bihar, but his memory resided in Noakhali. But even when he was in Noakhali, his mind was already in Bihar. Gandhi experienced multiple splits within his memory of feelings. The body of the satyagrahi was holding itself with difficulty as the body politic was being torn apart. Speaking to Congress workers in Bir on 19 March, Gandhi said,

> 'I am a bird of passage. God has not allowed me to stay at one place.'[60]

The 'inner voice' kept Gandhi busy as communal relations were in shambles across the country. Each crumbling mess of a place demanded Gandhi's attention in the shape of his presence.

There was a larger predicament within this. In his meeting with Abdul Ghaffar Khan, or Badshah Khan, on 12 March where they discussed the violence spreading into the Frontier Provinces, Gandhi told Manu:

> 'If we try and douse fires elsewhere, we will spoil the condition here. But if we were to douse the fires here, the flames will not spread elsewhere. We might in fact succeed in stopping the conflagration.'[61]

The non-violent experiment of truth, the peace mission, needs to create an impact on a particular location for it to have a ripple effect across multiple locations. The 'here', the immediate, is a more crucial site of work than 'elsewhere'.

Gandhi does move from one location to another in his bid to address the genocides taking place in more than one place. But he spends considerable time in each place before making a move. Even as he left Noakhali for Bihar, he left volunteers in Noakhali to continue the work he had initiated. Gandhi was also constantly giving interviews to leading newspapers in the country and abroad. He was alert to the role and impact of the print media having been the editor of *Harijan and Young India*.

On 17 March, Gandhi left Patna in the afternoon for Masaurhi by train. In the prayer meeting at Masaurhi that evening, Pyarelal writes, 'thirty to forty thousand men and women were present. The verses from the Koran were listened to amid pin-drop silence. Could they be the same people who had indulged in all those acts of madness?'[62]

Gandhi's prayer meetings during partition were a mass expiation of wrongdoing and realization of suffering. In an article in *Navajivan* in 1919 on 'Fasting and Prayer', Gandhi writes:

> 'When an individual or a nation suffers because of a great calamity, the true awareness of that suffering is prayer... A nation is born when all feel the same sort of grief at the suffering of any one among them; such a nation deserves to be immortal.'[63]

These meetings were different from traditional forms of religious gatherings, and also did not resemble the secular form of condolence meetings. Neither traditional nor secular, Gandhi's prayer meetings created a unique space where a new political community (comprising people from different religions) could address its problems through an interfaith ethics.

Gandhi said at the prayer meeting in Bir on 18 March that it was 'wrong' to observe Noakhali Day on 26 October 1946.[64] He objected to his name being 'falsely dragged' into justifying Noakhali Day, whereas he 'would never have allowed such an observance in Bihar'.[65] Sajjad mentions that instead of addressing its inadequacies in handling the riots and allowing rumours to thrive, the provincial Congress government made 'political capital' out of the situation by authorizing Noakhali Day to mourn the death of Hindus in Noakhali.[66] It is all right for civil society to conduct a commemoration of such a kind. A community has the right to mourn its victims (or people collectively across religions can mourn acts of violence). However, a government representing all communities, in the middle of genocide, has no business conducting such programmes. It is a clear attempt to fuel the fire, and a violation of secular responsibility.

On 19 March, Gandhi had a discussion with Congress members. He brought up the question of truth:

> 'Is it or isn't it a fact that quite a large number of Congressmen took part in the disturbances? I ask this question because people are making this allegation. But the Congressmen assembled here can themselves tell the truth. How many of the 132 members of your Committee were involved? It would be a very great thing if all of you assert that none of you was involved. But this assertion cannot be made . . . I wish to ask you, how could you live

> to see an old woman of 110 years being butchered before your eyes? How could you tolerate it? I do not wish to talk about anything else . . . I will not rest nor let others rest. I would wander all over on foot and ask the skeletons lying about how all that had happened.'[67]

These words are a translation of what Gandhi spoke in Hindustani. He confronted Congressmen with their moment of truth, asking them to address their complicity in the violence. To tolerate violence is a kind of violence. To tolerate violence is an internal form of violence. How do people survive this moral catastrophe?

Gandhi transforms into the dramatis personae who will ask the dead to become their own witness. The living were too dead-by-conscience to speak of their crimes. Gandhi challenged the moral spine of the Congress members. He said, 'I will have to strive to the utmost to prove that Hinduism and Islam can exist side by side.'[68] This was all that Gandhi wanted from the two communities: a fraternal neighbourhood.

Gandhi travelled out of Bir early in the afternoon. On the way, Manu noted, they passed 'villages in ruins'.[69] The evening prayer was held in a place called Goriakharhi. It was a place in ruins, writes Pyarelal, and it was 'almost impossible to get into any of the houses as the entrances were all blocked by debris. The atmosphere bore the stench of decaying bodies.'[70]

They returned to Bir for the night, and left for Masaurhi early in the morning on 20 March. On the way, they halted at a village named Harla. Manu wrote about the experience:

> 'The road to this village was really bad. The car bumped along the way. Bapuji nearly had his head bump into the hood. The condition of this village is

> terrible. Homes had been burnt, women raped and dumped into wells by Hindus. One is stunned by the bestiality of the Hindus.'[71]

Gandhi told the audience at the prayer meeting in Masaurhi about his visit to the two damaged villages, Andari and Garriakhari, the previous day. He also mentioned that Harla had been deserted by its inhabitants: 'And how can the Muslims stay at a place where their brothers and sisters, parents and children have been slaughtered? The mere memory of the massacre will stun them.'[72]

In his morning conversation with Muslim refugees, who had come to meet him from neighbouring villages, in Hansdih on 21 March, Gandhi said,

> '*When a man turns into a devil, he is neither a Hindu nor a Muslim*.'[73] [Emphasis Mine]

Gandhi's moral logic was sharp: If you commit a crime in the name of religion, you lose your religion. The act of devilry is committed by people who, whether they are religious or not, have abandoned the moral prohibition of committing acts of violence. Gandhi felt that it was still possible to appeal to the moral sensibility of men.

In the afternoon, Gandhi met some village representatives, who asked him,

> 'Is it [not] difficult to stop riots so long as the system of zamindari continues? The landlords are the persons who incite riots and will continue to do so.'[74]

Gandhi replied,

> 'I think it is foolish to connect riots with zamindari. The problem of zamindari is very old. How is it rational to kill Muslims to solve that problem? And many of the zamindars are themselves Hindus. The Maharaja of Darbhanga is a very big zamindar. Should he and his wife be killed? I am very friendly with him. He respects me like a father because his late father was a good friend of mine. A Hindu zamindar from North Bihar has promised to provide land to the Muslims. It is not proper to link the problem of Hindu–Muslim riots with the zamindari system. The latter is an altogether different problem and we have to consider ways and means of abolishing the system.'[75]

Gandhi does not find it rational that a problem of class conflict should be resolved through communal violence. But then, there is an irrational slippage between the class issue and the communal issue, which are forced together by the devious logic and machinations of communal politics. It is, however, interesting to note that Gandhi does not find the two issues connected. He believes that the class problem needs to be addressed without resorting to communal logic. In response to the problem of people trying to draw equivalence between victims in Noakhali and Bihar and making the restoration of property in one place incumbent as criteria for restoration elsewhere, Gandhi said that no community can hold another hostage. In the context of Bihar, he said that the Hindus have no right to dictate terms to the Muslims, adding:

> 'I do not intend to suggest that nothing untoward happened in Noakhali. But there women, children and old persons were not murdered the way it happened here, nor was it on such a large scale.'[76]

Yet again, the point was made that violence in Bihar exceeded the violence in Noakhali. There were more murders in Bihar, while there were a large number of conversions in Noakhali.[77] As I have argued, mass conversion in Noakhali deflected some measure of violence towards humiliatory domination. In contrast, the singular pattern of killings in Bihar reveals the brutal resolve to numerically erase a community's presence.

The late Pakistani academic and anti-war activist Eqbal Ahmad recollected in his interview with David Barsamian how he travelled with Gandhi as a twelve-year-old boy 'for about six weeks'[78] in riot-torn Bihar in 1946. Gandhi had decided to take along Muslim and Hindu children to the destroyed villages as a mark of unity.[79] It is unusual to make children witness scenes of gory violence. Gandhi saw children were not spared in genocidal violence and were unprotected. Innocence was trampled by violence. Gandhi's taking the traumatized children with him to walk the streets and witness the scenes of violence was an act of overcoming fear and affirming the right of children to reclaim their space in devastated neighbourhoods.

On 24 March, Gandhi visited a place named Berhawan in the afternoon. There, Manu noted down: 'Hindu homes have been destroyed. It is surprising as Muslims are a minority in this village. All Harijan homes have suffered damage.'[80]

When Gandhi reached Jehanabad (one of the worst affected areas in Gaya district) on 26 March, there was a huge crowd at the railway station[81]. In the middle of stories of death and destruction was the shining example of a local Hindu headmaster who along with his students and some workers patrolled three villages—Daulatpur, Nagama and Rasalpur—till they managed to evacuate the Muslims to Jehanabad[82]. Pyarelal writes,

'A Muslim remarked to a member of Gandhiji's party touchingly that even a radish that he had left behind had dried undisturbed in its place.'[83]

Gandhi visited two villages, Amathua and Belai, on the morning of 27 March. Belai, Pyarelal writes, was attacked by Hindu mobs on 3 November 1946. Pyarelal's description of Belai during their visit is chilling:

'One had to tread through the village cautiously, as lanes were still strewn with rubble. Gaping walls and ruined roofs met the eye everywhere. Wells choked with decomposing corpses bore the tell-tale evil smell. Gandhiji stood like one transfixed as one sufferer pointed out the place where his beloved ones lay. Occasionally a stray bone crunched under the feet. A mosque had been damaged. A few books were found burnt to ashes in one of the rooms.'[84]

Gandhi with Khan Abdul Ghaffar Khan, Mridula Sarabhai, Manu and others during his visit to a riot-affected village, Bihar, 1947

Muslim refugees handed a written memorandum to Gandhi on 28 March in Jehanabad. They requested him not to bring up Noakhali in his speeches in Bihar as it would incite Hindus. Gandhi disagreed, saying that he had restricted himself from speaking much on Noakhali, but that Muslims should not expect him to keep silent on the atrocities in Noakhali. He said that the 'sins' of both communities were of the 'same magnitude and equally condemnable.'[85] Gandhi's aversion to communal electorates was also in crisis. The ethical basis of his civil expectations, as he tells the Muslim refugees, sounds more humane than the pragmatic logic behind that law:

> 'I told the Hindus of Noakhali, who also expressed lack of confidence in Mr Shaheed Suhrawardy, that they could not remove Shaheed Saheb from the Ministry as he was returned by the separate electorate system. So long as Shaheed Saheb enjoys the confidence of the community he represents, no one can remove him. Similarly, how can you remove the Ministers when they have been returned by the Hindu electorate? This unfortunate situation has been created by the communal electorate system which, you know, I have always condemned.'[86]

The consistency of Gandhi's position lies in how he insists on his politics of trust within the framework of communal electorates, even when the beneficiaries of this system favoured communal politics over the principles of democracy.

In the afternoon, Gandhi visited the villages, Malathi, Gangasagar, Bola and Allahgunj, where Muslims suffered. Manu wrote about what had befallen Muslims in these villages:

> 'Even here the women have been oppressed. Masjids have been sprayed with colours of *holi* and that has been the cause of deep displeasure. This also pained Bapuji deeply. He said,
>
> "As the new dawn approaches, people have gone mad."'[87]

The evening prayer meeting was held in Allahgunj.[88] Gandhi apologetically confessed to the audience that the repentance of the Hindus didn't strike him as sincere. Nirad C. Chaudhuri's phrase 'weak repentance' after the Calcutta Killings was precisely about such insincerity. It leaves space for future violence.

In the prayer meeting at Patna the following day, Gandhi told his audience that he was leaving Patna for Delhi and hoped to return within a week.[89]

Gandhi left Patna for Delhi at 9.30 a.m. on 30 March.

'My Writ Runs No More'

Gandhi met Mountbatten on the morning of 1 April. The Viceroy told him that British policy never yielded to force, but that Gandhi's non-violent struggle had made them decide to quit India.[90]

During the evening prayers in Bhangi Colony, something dramatic happened. Manu wrote: 'During the prayer as I started reciting the *Auzbillah* a youth shouted, "We will not allow the Quran to be read in our Hindu temple".'[91]

Manu does not mention the young man telling Gandhi, 'You have been repeatedly telling this thing to us but our mothers and sisters continue to be slaughtered. We cannot tolerate it any longer.'[92]

But Manu mentioned another crucial detail:

> 'The Hindu Mahasabha is very strong here; the students associated with it remain present. It is likely that they would obstruct Bapuji.'[93]

There was commotion followed by a scuffle. Gandhi admonished the man for disturbing the prayer and not allowing others to pray. He then admonished the crowd for throwing the man out of the prayer meeting, saying it would help him justify his sense of bravado to himself. Gandhi clarified in his 'sequence of prayers'[94] that the Muslim prayer is followed by a Parsi prayer followed by the Ramdhun. The young man meant to say prayers couldn't exist side by side if their believers were slaughtering each other. The demand of the hour, according to him, was to stand by one's community and to protest against the misdeeds of the other community. Communal sentiments demand fidelity, and more desperately during times of crisis. And this was a civil war.

At the end of a long speech, Gandhi spoke about his reduced importance:

> 'My writ runs no more. If it did the tragedies in the Punjab, Bihar and Noakhali would not have happened. No one listens to me any more. I am a small man. True, there was a time when mine was a big voice. Then everyone obeyed what I said; now neither the Congress nor the Hindus nor the Muslims listen to me. Where is the Congress today? It is disintegrating. I am crying in the wilderness.'[95]

Gandhi begrudged being sidelined by the people and politicians alike. He felt belittled. His voice no longer made an impact. Gandhi meant that the Congress was disintegrating, probably in relation to its communalization. Even though Gandhi had admitted to his failure several times since he had heard of the Calcutta killings, he had never laid out reasons for it. He suggested that something may have been lacking in his method, or even in himself, but he never specified what it could be and didn't elaborate on it. He did not meditate—so far and publicly—on the precise reasons for his failure.

Perhaps great men find it difficult or are unable to understand their failures. Failure is not just about finding oneself out of favour with people, or being defeated by one's enemies, or in Gandhi's case, his political opponents (since he did not believe in enemies). It is also about being outmanoeuvred by time. Gandhi had lost his authority over others. He was also fast losing grip over his frail body.

On 4 April, Gandhi met a delegation of Egyptians accompanied by Nehru. Someone asked him if he would adhere to the practice of non-violence after independence. Gandhi replied,

> 'Of course, *today non-violence is no more to be found*. But, I hope, when the hurdle of foreign domination is removed everything will be peaceful.'[96] [Emphasis mine]

The interesting admission is not Gandhi's hope that once the British leave peace will reign, but that there was no sight of non-violence at the moment. Gandhi was witnessing the end of non-violence. What does such a thing mean? Even though the Gandhian movement was avowedly non-violent, violence had a constant presence in India's modern political history over the decades. There had been numerous communal riots in India since the first decade of the twentieth century. But for the first time, an imaginary line moving upwards on the map of India could be drawn from Bengal to the Punjab, via Bihar and Delhi, connecting the places engulfed in mass violence. Even if violent events had taken place before, Gandhi still held the reins of India's anti-colonial mass movement at the centre. The reins had gone out of his hands, and he no longer occupied the centre. He was reduced to a voice in the wilderness. The limits of negotiation meant that new laws would be established by violence. Elite leaders among Hindus and Muslims who could not agree with each other ensured that their communities would perform the last rites of a diminishing relationship. Non-violence had disappeared once the trumpet of partition was blown.

On 6 April, Gandhi said at the prayer meeting in Delhi,

> 'Nationalist Muslims had been killed by Hindus there and Hindu friends of Islam had been done to death by Muslims.'[97]

These were tragedies within tragedies, and they didn't make sense the way mass violence is senseless. It is not that if a Muslim mobster knew that a Hindu was a friend of Islam or if a Hindu mobster knew a Muslim was an Indian nationalist, their lives would have been spared. In such situations it is not possible to know who you are killing. You are fine with why you are killing them. The 'who' is completely divorced from the 'why', where 'who' is reduced to a singular identity and the 'why' to a singular reason. In a civil war just as in class war, the enemy is reduced to a monstrous singularity which structures and impels the logic of violence. You are one and the enemy is one, and each is out to eliminate the other.

On 7 April, Gandhi sent a personal letter to Mountbatten, sharing information that he had received wires informing him that there were two attempts to roast people in Noakhali.[98] The same day, Gandhi informed his audience during the prayer meeting that he had heard from a Hindu man, who escaped with his son from Rawalpindi, about how fifty-eight of his companions had been killed there.[99] He also reminded people to eradicate economic inequality. He remarked that instead of embracing his 'constructive programme' (a detailed idea that Gandhi had proposed in 1941 that included communal unity, removal of untouchability, 'Nai Taleem', village industries and sanitation, education in health and hygiene, provincial languages, adivasis, lepers, students and civil disobedience, etc), people were 'leaning towards Russian communism which draws its strength from the pistol.'[100]

Gandhi shared his interaction with a correspondent with the people during the prayer meeting in Delhi:

> 'One of the correspondents asks why I should not be called 'Muhammed Gandhi'? And then he hurls the choicest abuses'.[101]

Even a man of Gandhi's stature and honesty was abused by a Hindu correspondent because he thought that Gandhi was being partial to Muslims. The expectation, in communally polarized times is that leaders must cease to be anything other than communal and get polarized. If they don't, they will be caricatured as enemies of the community. The communal Hindu machinery since then has propagated lies about Gandhi. Pseudo-religious nationalism is a toxic industry where admirable national figures are lampooned and hated for admirable qualities like generosity of spirit.

Gandhi told his audience on 11 April at the prayer meeting that he was returning to Bihar. He said that he had received a telegram from 'a Muslim friend from Bihar'[102] asking him to visit Bihar for reassurance. It was, however, he clarified, not the telegram that prompted his decision to suddenly leave for Bihar, but his overall commitment to 'do or die there'.[103]

On 15 April, Jinnah and Gandhi signed a joint statement suggested by the Viceroy. They deplored the 'recent acts of lawlessness and violence', denounced 'the use of force to achieve political ends' and appealed to people to refrain from violence and disorder.[104] It was issued to the press on 15 April. Whatever impact it had on the public imagination, the joint statement has a farcical side to it.

Jinnah's Libido

Mountbatten bringing Jinnah and Gandhi together to make a joint gesture for peace is ironic given that the proposal for partition was being seriously considered by the Raj. The double-faced audacity of colonial power is such that it can divide people and make appeals for peace at the same time.

Later, Gandhi, in a prayer meeting in Patna on 16 April, pointed out the political weakness of the gesture that was prompted by the intervention of the 'third party':

> '[It] would have been much better had Shri Jinnah and I drafted the appeal jointly and signed it. It would then have been a great thing. But the Viceroy who is an outsider had to initiate it. How good it would be if we agreed to act upon it!'[105]

The joint statement was even more ironic because Gandhi alone put his body on the line to bring peace whereas Jinnah was doing literally nothing, having not just demanded partition but also declaring 'Direct Action Day', which was a clarion call for unprecedented violence.

All political comparisons between Gandhi and Jinnah come to an end when you focus on the most significant detail that holds them apart on ethical grounds. This detail has to do with partition violence. It throws light on the absolute difference between Gandhi and Jinnah, not just as political leaders but also as men of character. Ishtiaq Ahmed has laid out that stark historical detail:

> '[The] riots which erupted in Calcutta, and which triggered similar reactions in Bombay, Noakhali and Bihar, brought out in sharp relief the diabolical nature of communalism. Liaquat Ali Khan and other League leaders visited Bihar and reported the tragedy to Jinnah. *Jinnah neither visited Calcutta nor any other disturbed area, not even Bihar, where a slaughter of Muslims had taken place.*'[106] [Emphasis mine]

The fact that Jinnah was neither morally nor emotionally provoked to visit Calcutta, Noakhali, Bihar or any other place that experienced the horror of partition shows that he was impervious to human suffering.

American journalist and war correspondent William L. Shirer wrote in his memoir on Gandhi that he had left India in 1931 with the impression that Jinnah and Gandhi 'were drifting apart.'[107] Apart from Jinnah's concerns regarding Hindu domination in a united India that distanced him from Gandhi, Shirer also felt that Jinnah had a personal dislike for what he called 'Gandhi's Hindu fads'.[108] Even Nehru showed discomfort with Gandhi's 'fads' light-heartedly. He wrote in his *Autobiography*: 'Often we discussed his fads and peculiarities among ourselves and said, half-humorously, that when Swaraj came these fads must not be encouraged.'[109] Nehru at least did not communalize Gandhi's fads. Shirer quoted Jinnah detailing his personal dislike:

> '"Why does Gandhi," Jinnah would say, "have to squat on my good Persian rugs when he comes to see me, and break our talk by sipping goat's milk out of a filthy cup he has preserved from prison? Why does he have to preach the evils of eating meat, drinking alcohol, smoking tobacco? I like a good cut of beef, the best Scotch I can find, a vintage wine, my cigarettes . . . I resent a Hindu feeling it's unclean to eat with me, a Moslem, or even to shake my hand. Of course, Gandhi doesn't go that far, I admit, but he has his Hindu peculiarities."'[110]

Gandhi's preachiness is evidently irritating. No one has any business to feed me and bore me with moral and healthy dietary prescriptions. Though I don't quite understand the elite touchiness about rugs, Persian or not, and what is particularly wrong about preserving a cup from prison kept as a memento of difficult days. It is good to have fine tastes. But petty snobbery is not fine.

Ultimately, when it mattered, the man who squatted on Jinnah's Persian rugs and sipped goat's milk from a filthy cup walked barefoot through the villages of Noakhali, cleaning the shit strewn in his path by mischievous boys to discourage him from carrying out his peace mission, calming victims and challenging perpetrators.

Jinnah, however, visited the camp of Bihari refugees on the outskirts of Karachi on 23 February 1947 and told them,

> 'The sufferings that the Muslims had undergone in Bihar and elsewhere only show more clearly that we should have a separate State of Pakistan [. . .] Nations are built through sacrifices, and I am really proud of the Bihari Muslims who have suffered so much.'[111]

This is a revealing speech. It shows Jinnah's parasitical mindset. His political ambitions lived off the sufferings of others. The manipulative politics of martyrdom creates volatile situations where people are thrown into the fire. Jinnah unabashedly made human capital out of a tragedy to further his political interest. Bihari Muslims suffered the communal repercussions of what the Muslim League engineered in Noakhali. Jinnah interprets the death of Bihari Muslims as a sacrificial donation to his cause of Pakistan. Such nations, contradictory to what Jinnah thinks, are built on lies.

Ahmed reiterates why Jinnah's statement was out of place:

> 'The statement was rather ironic because, while the Bihari Muslims had indeed suffered the worst atrocities, Jinnah had not even paid a formal visit to Bihar, nor had he ever suffered any hardship like a prison sentence'.[112]

The man who never suffers for his beliefs makes others suffer for them.

This becomes amply clear in what Francis Mudie, the Governor of West Punjab, wrote about his private conversation with Jinnah to one of Jinnah's biographers from New Zealand, Hector Bolitho. Jinnah was staying at Mudie's place in September 1947 when the cataclysm of partition was in full swing. Mudie describes the context and Jinnah's state of mind:

> 'Everything in Lahore and in the Punjab was chaos. Refugees were arriving daily in tens of thousands and Sikhs and Hindus going out. My niece and Jinnah and I were sitting having a drink before dinner, when he suddenly said, *"This is very tragic—but very thrilling"* and his eyes flashed with excitement. It was tragic, but very thrilling, like a battle. And particularly thrilling to Jinnah. Here was his Pakistan at last in being. Here was the exchange of population, which he had been ridiculed for suggesting, actually taking place.'[113] [Emphasis mine]

The violence of partition was Jinnah's erection, his libidinal experience, where the pleasure principle and death drive, Eros and Thanatos, collapsed into each other. People were losing their lives and taking the lives of others to fulfil Jinnah's dream. History could provide no greater occasion for such monstrous satisfaction.

Protection is Not Appeasement

Gandhi was at the Bankipur Maidan (now Gandhi Maidan) in Patna on 14 April1947, telling his audience that although people urged him to visit Punjab, he didn't go anywhere at 'someone's bidding', but only when 'the inner voice' tells him.[114] He said,

'I had said at Noakhali that I would either do or die. Maybe I will die, not in Noakhali but in Bihar, or, I might die not even in Bihar but in the Punjab.'[115]

Gandhi's state of mind reflected the disintegrating body politic. The violence had claimed his mind, and he anticipated it to claim his body. It was close to harbouring a reluctant death wish. Gandhi feared that the atmosphere of death, infected by communal violence and hatred, would take his life. He felt that a violent death was closing in on him, as much as he was drawing close to it.

The next day at the prayer meeting, Gandhi offered a public defence against questions raised on his coming to Bihar at the 'Muslim' request:

> 'Some persons have accused me of leaving Noakhali and coming to Bihar not at the request of a Hindu but at the behest of a Muslim so that the Muslims may do what they like in Noakhali. But you know I have come here at the invitation of Dr Mahmud . . . He has rendered great service to the Congress and has been a member of the Congress Working Committee . . . I have come here at his invitation for he is an old friend of mine . . . It is true I have come here at the instance of Muslims but it is sheer folly to say that Muslims are devils and have drawn me away from Noakhali to do what they please there.'[116]

Just like Muslims in Bengal, Hindus in Bihar displayed communal hypocrisy pointing fingers at Gandhi for listening to Muslims.

The problem in such situations is this: once two communities have indulged in mass violence, for people on both sides who have some capacity to think and reflect to still hold the other community absolutely responsible for everything, is to end up justifying the communal divide. It creates a moral impasse in the social sphere.

To blame Gandhi for listening to Muslims, for being able to cross the line and make a genuine effort at rapprochement, is to believe that Gandhi was supposed to be a communal bigot like everyone else. To expect Gandhi to be what he never was, and what he would never be, is quite a remarkable kind of idiocy. Instead of making efforts to quell the violence, the Hindus in Bihar were seeking scapegoats to suppress their own moral failure. Individuals suffer from the denial syndrome, but sections of a community can suffer it too.

Next, Gandhi said something valuable:

> 'Even if the Muslims in the Punjab, Bengal and Sind harm the Hindus there, and if Bihar shows true courage in protecting and comforting Muslims and their children, Bihar will have raised India in the estimation of the world.
>
> *To protect the minorities is not to appease them.*'[117] [Emphasis mine]

In a situation where violence had spread to many parts, Gandhi was desperate to set an example for others to follow. Saving lives was not an act of appeasement in the sense that an ethical act was not to be seen as an act of political concession. It is unfortunate that Gandhi had to make that comparison. Talking to a representative of the Jamiatul-Ulema in Patna on 17 April, Gandhi exhorted them to take the ethical path:

> 'Instead of being anxious to find out how many Muslims were killed by the Hindus, your primary duty is to find out how many Hindus the Muslims had killed and where and persuade them not to commit such atrocities . . . If out of the four crore Muslims I could have only a hundred such brothers and sisters, they would be able to render great

> service to the forty crore Hindus and Muslims of India. Now, tell me, is any one of you prepared to take up this mission?'[118]

Gandhi offered a first principle on ethical response at a time of genocide. The first task is to address the violence committed by your own community, to seek out the other community and heal its wounds. Communities are territories of sentiments and you have to break out of that territory to make an ethical gesture.

Ethics is breaking territories. Ethical acts take the risk of stepping across the line of control, lines that control our territorial sentiments, and seek out the other side. Gandhi asked Muslim members of the Ulema to reverse their direction of concern as a way to overcome the communal impasse. It is also an effective way to address (and counter) the source of shock. It is important to allow yourself to be shocked by the violent deeds of your own community as much as you experience shock at the misdeeds of the other community.

An ethical response to violence needs one to deflect oneself from the primal to the pensive. The primal is what your blood makes you feel something you understand as self-preserving. It has a narrow circle of concern. The pensive is what forces you to think about the repercussions of violence. It distances you from the circle of blood and makes you think about how you can stop it from heating up your brain and preventing you from thinking. You think about how you can stop it from flowing further into the world.

In such situations, Gandhi also made the point that a few courageous people who can risk the encounter with a larger mass of people who are consumed by the thought of violence can make a difference. It is a difficult political mission to work against the overwhelming tide of hate-emotions and reverse it. The same day during the prayer meeting, Gandhi shared what the Ulema had told him: Hindus in Patna were unrepentant of their crime and kept threatening Muslims.[119] It was getting more difficult to see the light.

Gandhi warned the zamindars in his meeting with them at the camp in Patna on 18 April, that they had been 'exploiting the labourers and peasants' since the beginning of the British regime and that if they kept behaving with them as masters and not as 'partners and friends' they wouldn't survive.[120] On the same day, speaking to peasants and workers, Gandhi told them to assert their rights through cooperation rather than using violence against the zamindars. He acknowledged that abolition of zamindari was no longer a difficult matter. Gandhi said that if the peasantry and the working class took the law into their own hands, they would be 'striking at the root' of their interests.[121]

Clearly, Gandhi was in favour of ushering in a peaceful, juridical change in class relations, rather than through a violent, revolutionary act. It was not in the interests of the peasantry and working class to subvert the law. If he had in mind the complexity of class relations intersecting communal ties, he did not mention it.

Speaking to local Muslim League members in Patna on 23 April, Gandhi was forthright that they must speak up against the leadership, namely, Jinnah and Liaquat Ali, for 'going in the wrong direction'.[122]

He said that both Nehru and he had condemned Hindu atrocities against Muslims in Bihar and made public appeals, but League members hadn't done the same over Muslim atrocities in Noakhali, Bengal and Punjab. Gandhi said that Jinnah's assurance that he would protect minorities 'has not been fulfilled.'[123]

This was a strong charge that made the complicity of the League in communal violence quite apparent. It also bared open the logic that the violence was in the interest of those who sought partition.

Gandhi said something interesting on 27 April at the prayer meeting in Patna,

> 'I felt that someone might now think that since Bihar has just 13 or 14 per cent Muslim population and the rest are Hindus, why placate the Muslims? But I say that if the Muslims invite me with love I shall go to them even barefoot.'[124]

The argument that minorities need not be appeased, giving a population-based logic, comes from a majoritarian mindset that has stayed on in India's political history after Independence. This idea has been particularly promoted by the Hindu right. Gandhi's commitment to Muslims was based on a disarming gesture of love.

At the same venue as that of the prayer meeting the following day, Gandhi reiterated the point,

'My non-violence bids me dedicate myself to the service of the minorities.'[125]

To make the minorities feel protected and loved was part of the ethic of non-violence. Gandhi announced to the crowd at the prayer meeting on 29 April that he was once again leaving Bihar for Delhi. He requested them not to come to the railway station in huge numbers as he couldn't take too much noise.[126]

'Don't Talk Rot!'

At the prayer meeting in Delhi on 1 May, Gandhi shared his report on his work in Bihar to the crowd. He gave details about the peace and rehabilitation work being done by ex-INA soldiers, led by General Shah Nawaz. Gandhi said that Muslims who were forced to flee to Asansol (in Bengal) had returned.[127] The Muslim League's mischievous role, with reference to Bihar's Muslim refugees, is revealing:

> 'The League obstructed relief and rehabilitation works, discouraging Muslim refugees, who had left Bihar due to the riots, from returning to their villages—rather they actively forced them to migrate from Bihar whereas, by late December 1946, the refugees wanted to leave the Asansol camps and return to their homes in Bihar. The League, in fact, was more interested in making a political capital out of this than in helping the evacuees.'[128]

Sajjad writes that the League played 'a leading role in organizing the exodus of Bihar Muslims', though, he adds, 'the Congress also cannot be absolved of this'.[129]

In a conversation with socialist leaders Aruna Asaf Ali and Ashok Mehta on 6 May, Gandhi informed them that he had decided to go to Calcutta despite being dissuaded from doing so out of the fear of thoughtless 'ruffians'[130]. Gandhi found his reason to go in the very possibility of facing violence:

> '[That] is the very reason why I want to go there. If in the course of it death comes, I shall welcome it. What better use can there be for this body that has already weathered seventy-eight winters? My death will immediately stop the fratricide.'[131]

Gandhi reiterated his belief that there was a metaphysical connection between his body and the body politic. He believed that the outpouring of grief over his dead body would pave the way to end the fratricidal war between Hindus and Muslims.

On 8 May, Gandhi left for Calcutta via Patna. In the train to Patna, Gandhi wrote to Mountbatten, urging him to stay out of the partition business:

> '[It] would be a blunder of the first magnitude for the British to be a party in any way whatsoever to the division of India. If it has to come, let it come after the British withdrawal . . . If you are not to leave a legacy of chaos behind, you have to make your choice and leave the Government of the whole of India including the States to one party.'[132]

At the Burdwan station, Gandhi met a few workers. A particular question put to Gandhi gives a good impression of how Hindus were feeling,

> 'After the British withdrawal from India, there is a likelihood of chaos and anarchy prevailing in the country. There is a fear that the nationalists, unless they immediately started learning self-defence with fire-arms, may suffer and ultimately find themselves under the heels of the Muslim League whose followers believe only in fighting. Pakistan or no Pakistan, the trouble is coming because there is the secret hand of imperialism working behind the scenes. Would you not modify your theory of ahimsa in the larger context of such a political situation overtaking the country for the sake of individual defence?'[133]

On 10 May, Gandhi met Abul Hashem, Secretary, from the Bengal Provincial Muslim League, along with two of his students, and Sarat Chandra Bose, who was then President of the All-Bengal Anti-Pakistan Committee. Hashem said, Bengalis, whether Hindus or Muslims, had a common language and culture and did not wish to be ruled by Pakistanis from a thousand miles away.[134] From this, we get the idea that all Bengali Muslims were not comfortable with the idea of Pakistan in 1947. The feeling of cultural difference was quite prominent. Gandhi also raised the problem about Jinnah's indifference with Hashem:

> '[You] must ask Jinnah Saheb why, after signing the peace appeal with Gandhi, he is sitting in Delhi when thousands of Hindus are dying in the Punjab, the Frontier Province and Noakhali and thousands of women are being raped. Why should every worker belonging to your party not stand by the Hindus and protect them? If you are keen on saving the Muslims you will have to give protection to all these Hindus.'[135]

On 11 May, Suhrawardy, along with Mohammad Ali and Abul Hashem, came to visit Gandhi at the ashram in Sodepur. Gandhi told Suhrawardy that he had a letter from N.K. Bose (who was present) that described a certain incident of violence that revealed 'the incompetence of the Government and the veiled connivance of police officers in encouraging Muslim rioters.'[136] Suhrawardy's reply was worthy of a politician, 'Yes, it is a bad case. But I am sure, you realize that this is an exception.'[137] Bose placed yet another case before Suhrawardy, the murder of Jadunath Sarkar's son[138] (his eldest son, Abani),[139] where the police did not take up any enquiry even after a week had passed. Suhrawardy reacted,

> 'Do you know, there are more than half a dozen versions of that event? One even accuses me of complicity in the murder.'[140]

Gandhi lost his cool and directed a blunt accusation at Suhrawardy,

> 'Yes, you are responsible not only for that murder but for every life lost in Bengal, whether Hindu or Muslim.'[141]

The pitch of the exchange got raised with Suhrawardy's desperate counter-accusation,

> 'No, it is you who are responsible for it, for you have denied justice to the Mussalmans.'[142]

'Don't talk rot!' Gandhi replied.[143]

Suhrawardy returned on the evening of 12 May to impress on Gandhi his idea of a united, sovereign Bengal. He aired his doubts about Hindus trusting him enough to accept his proposal. It was rather ambitious of Suhrawardy to expect Hindus to take him seriously after he acted with moral irresponsibility as chief minister. Gandhi made him the offer of acting as his secretary and living with him under the same roof to try to ensure that Hindus gave him a hearing at least.[144] Suhrawardy, in N.K. Bose's account, did not respond. As he made his way out, he muttered to himself, 'What a mad offer! I have to think ten times before I can fathom its implications.'[145]

The man who hesitated to accept Gandhi's word wanted Hindus to take him at his word, after abandoning them to their fate in Noakhali.

Two days later, on 13 May, Gandhi met Syama Prasad Mookerjee, President of the Bengal Provincial Hindu Mahasabha, in Sodepur. They discussed the fate of Bengal. Mookerjee had heard that Suhrawardy's proposal of a united, sovereign Bengal had Gandhi's blessings. Mookerjee's own view in 1944 of a united Bengal had shifted by 1946 to a partitioned Bengal. He told Gandhi that Suhrawardy's proposal was 'sponsored by the British commercial interests in Bengal'[146] as it would create problems for the jute industry (where raw materials have to be brought from other states.) Suhrawardy saw the idea of a united Bengal as a ploy by the League to use Muslim votes to pass a new legislative act that would merge Bengal with Pakistan.[147] Gandhi said that they must trust Suhrawardy's proposal even if they didn't trust him.[148]

The next day, Gandhi informed the audience in the prayer meeting in Sodepur that he was leaving for Patna and that he would proceed to Delhi and hoped to return to Calcutta.

The Colonel of Non-violence

On 15 May, Gandhi was back in Patna. In their early morning walk, he told General Shah Nawaz:

> 'You were decorated with the rank of Colonel while serving under Netaji. I wish to make you a Colonel of non-violence.'[149]

At the Bankipur Maidan, he said that his visit to Calcutta was unforeseen. His being at one place, however, did not mean that he was not working for peace to return in other places. Gandhi's logic was that if he could help bring peace in one place, it was bound to have repercussions elsewhere. Then he made a sarcastic remark to his audience,

> 'Affairs in Bihar moved slowly. The Biharis were, however, not slow when they committed acts of madness. There was no reason why they should be slow in making amends. The rains were coming. They were working against time.'[150]

If people indulged in massacres in uncharacteristic haste, they should not waste time and make amends for the violence before the monsoon set in. Imagine the desperation for social morality, making it a matter of seasonal urgency.

On 16 May at the prayer meeting in Gulzarbagh, Gandhi reiterated the same thing:

> 'They were innocent men and women, who had suffered at the hands of the Hindus who had gone temporarily insane. It was their duty, therefore, to make all the amends they could. They should go and visit the refugees in the camp, interest themselves in every detail of their lives, and seek to help them in every way they could. If they did that, Gandhiji said, it would be in part payment of the debt that they owed to the wronged refugees.'[151]

The same day, Gandhi wrote to Manu's father, Jaisukhlal, about his daughter's operation, and we learn:

> 'Last evening Manu was operated upon for appendicitis in a hospital. I was by her side. It is a little before six in the morning just now. A man came to inform me that Manu says she is all right. I had suspected even in Delhi that it was appendicitis. I had hoped that treatment with mud-pack would help her to get well. But it did not help her sufficiently. I, therefore, called in the doctors yesterday. They advised an operation, and I therefore got her operated upon.'[152]

Manu stopped writing the diary on 18 April 1947, in Patna, and resumed from 27 May 1947, at Bhangi Niwas, New Delhi. She did not mention her operation of 15 May in her diary entry, nor at any moment till she briefly discontinued writing.

Manu however complained of nosebleed for some time. On 5 April, she was examined by a doctor at Bhangi Nivas, Delhi, with an enlarged liver as the cause of her frequent nosebleeds.[153] On the same day, she had multiple nosebleeds, mild fever and lost her appetite.[154] On 15 May, she wrote that her nosebleeds had persisted, and that she weighed 87 pounds, which worried Gandhi,

> 'Do you remember that you weighed 106 pounds in Aga Khan. You have lost 20 pounds. It means that I belabour you like a ghost or you are careless.'[155]

At the prayer meeting on19 May at Barh, Gandhi said to his audience:

> 'If people justify their sins with the argument that by killing and punishing the Muslims of Bihar they had avenged the crimes committed in Noakhali, which were a sequence of the happenings in Calcutta, well, it is the law of the jungle; it is beastly behaviour. Have beasts ever attained freedom? If you have heard of it, please tell me—at least I haven't.'[156]

The Ulema had told Gandhi, almost a month earlier, that the Hindus of Bihar were unrepentant of their crime. If mass violence is momentary animal behaviour by a religious group, the lack of remorse and guilt, and even more disturbingly, a sense of communal pride on doing violence, turns that momentary collapse of humanity into a lingering condition, which is bereft of any moral compass. Gandhi contrasts it with the idea of freedom, which is a moral desire and condition of human society. The animal condition of a free society is unthinkable.

At the prayer meeting at Hilsa the next day, Gandhi said,

'You have all assembled here in large numbers to listen to me and we are having a huge meeting here. I would urge those who are able to hear me to follow my advice. In following it you will not be put to any inconvenience. We do welcome relatives coming from the Fiji Islands or from South Africa and accommodate them in our homes, don't we? In the present case we are the offenders. Let us now welcome the Muslims as our friends whom we had turned into enemies.'[157]

He made a last-ditch effort to persuade the Hindus to help rehabilitate Muslims in the city.

On 21 May, Gandhi wrote to his associates, Anand and Gangi Hingorani, that he was reaching Delhi on 25 May[158] and would stay in the city for a week at least before proceeding to either Patna or Calcutta.

3

'The Kohinoor of India's Freedom'

Gandhi was back in Bhangi Colony in Delhi. On 25 May 1947, he replied to a letter from Mirabehn (Madeleine Slade, the British woman who was Gandhi's associate) in Rishikesh. He had a conversation with C. Rajagopalachari, who was then Minister in the Interim Government for Industries and Supplies. He aired his hope that he may continue his work on Noakhali and Bihar from Delhi. He reiterated his belief in 'handspun yarn'[1] as a necessary component of swaraj.

In a letter addressed to women published in *Young India* on 11 August 1921, Gandhi wrote on spinning: 'There is an art that kills and an art that gives life.'[2] Spinning is a silent, life-giving art. It is an act of slowing down time in the era of speed. It can also be understood as a digressive act in relation to the idea of work as factory production. There is an imbalance in the equation between doing and producing, as much as between time and production. Gandhi was not merely producing cloth to sustain a home-grown industry and the idea of self-sufficiency, but producing a specific relation between time and work in the process. In a message from Sevagram, Gandhi had said,

> 'Spin. Spin with full understanding. Let those who spin wear khadi. Let those who wear khadi compulsorily spin. Full understanding means the realization that spinning symbolizes non-violence. Reflect on it. It will become apparent.'[3]

The act of spinning was a mode of deliberation, a slow act of the will. If spinning was an activity of deliberation, it was the opposite of the idea of provocation. Gandhi spun in the face of provocations during the anti-colonial movement not simply as a political message to his opponents and to colonial power. Gandhi realized that the only way to challenge modern (colonial) power was by creating a workspace where the self can announce its own sovereignty. It was not possible to meet violence non-violently without a certain practice that enunciates a peaceful mind. Spinning granted that mode of restraint against the news and provocation of violence, particularly in Noakhali.

During his speech at the prayer meeting on 25 May after he met Rajagopalachari, Gandhi was in a spirited mood. He began by telling the crowd,

> 'The gatherings in Bihar tended to be larger than those in Bengal. The people of Bihar knew me but still came round to have a look at me. We are 400 million people and how long can we remember an individual by seeing and hearing him only for a while? People are always eager to see me. They wonder what Gandhi looks like. They want to see if

> he is a creature with a tail and horns. Thus people used to gather in huge numbers.'[4]

Gandhi was aware of the biological curiosity people had regarding him. A frail man in a loin-cloth speaking of non-violence amidst a genocidal atmosphere must have been a rare spectacle in history. There was intense curiosity and enough wonder regarding Gandhi, but was there an equally adequate measure of commitment to his exhortations on communal friendship and gestures of peace? That question was the real matter of concern. Gandhi continued,

> 'The Kohinoor of India's freedom is not going to come to us from the hands of others. We can have it from our own hands. I am not referring to the Kohinoor which is kept in the Tower of London. I am referring to the Kohinoor of our freedom. This Kohinoor is coming to us. We may throw it away if we wish or keep it with us if we so desire. Whatever we decide to do is up to us, not others.'[5]

The Kohinoor, an old, exquisite jewel from south India that was taken away by the East India Company from the minor king Duleep Singh (son of Maharaja Ranjit Singh) in 1489 as a 'gift' of conquest via the provisions of the Lahore Treaty, is a symbol of impermanent attainability. The Kohinoor of freedom, unlike its status as the fetish object in history, meant an alchemical object produced from the body and spirit. Gandhi makes a reverse turn of meaning to rejoin the metaphoric jewel of freedom to its real, historical counterpart. Even as an alchemic object within people, the jewel can slip away from them if they fail to keep it.

Harsh Words Must Be Said

On 27 May, Jayaprakash Narayan and his socialist co-workers came to visit Gandhi in the afternoon. He told them that instead of calling for strikes, they should do 'constructive work'. That meant living and working in the villages, making them self-sufficient, eradicating untouchability, uplifting women and volunteers choosing their marital partners from the village.[6]

Gandhi reformulated his old issues against machinery, bringing up the problem of leisure, and blamed it for facilitating cinema. He forwarded his peculiar view against popular art.[7] He found the cinema hall suffocating and wouldn't mind converting them into 'spinning halls and factories for handicrafts'.[8] Gandhi's idea of public culture was –sometimes amusingly– ascetic and utilitarian.

Speaking to the audience at the prayer meeting on 28 May, Gandhi said that if one community remained sensible it would calm the madness of the other community. Referring to Mountbatten's arrival with the proposed plan that came to known as the Indian Independence Act 1947, Gandhi said,

'Let us not look up to him, nor watch for June 2; let us look at ourselves.'[9]

Manu made a small entry in her diary: 'Yesterday Jawaharlalji gave Bapu a copy of *The Discovery of India.* Bapuji glanced at it after the prayer.'[10]

The next day at the prayer meeting, Gandhi gave us the tragic piece of news that 'many villages of the neighbouring district of Gurgaon have been burnt down.'[11] He also hoped that Mountbatten would 'not depart by a hair's breadth from the letter and the spirit of the Cabinet Mission's statement of 16 May.'[12]

In the prayer meeting on 31 May, Gandhi equated the capitalist Hindu and the Muslim ruler of the princely state as obsolete figures of power in the face of the coming of democracy:

> 'We want neither Birlas nor the Nawab of Bhopal's raj[13] in India. There are many Birlas in the country. What is their power? They have to get their work done by labourers and they can get it done only when they pay for it. When the workers refuse to work, the millions would remain stuck with the rich. Similarly, all the swords and spears and horsemen of the Nawab of Bhopal are going to be rendered useless. After all, how many people can they kill? Over whom would he rule after killing his own subjects? He would be able to rule over his subjects only by becoming their trustee.'[14]

There was a poignant moment when Gandhi spoke of the death of a young Telugu boy, Chakrayya, who had been a co-worker at the Sevagram Ashram since 1935 and had died of a brain tumour in a Bombay hospital on 28 May: 'He was a hard-working craftsman . . . I feel like crying over his death; but I cannot cry. For whom should I cry and for whom should I refrain from crying? . . . He was a Harijan but knew no distinctions of Harijan and *savarna* and of Hindu and Muslim.'[15] His death was an antithesis to the deaths that Gandhi saw around him in the riot-affected areas.

Mountbatten brought partition to India's doorstep. After meeting Indian leaders on 2 June, Mountbatten announced the plan for partition on 3 June on All India Radio, with the Muslim majority areas of Bengal and Punjab making up Pakistan[16].

The Congress made a volte-face of its long-standing position of a united India, and accepted partition in principle. The Congress Working Committee ratified the plan. This made Mountbatten's job easy and he assumed the role of a neutral and fair arbitrator, representing the Raj. Nehru, Jinnah and Baldev Singh spoke on air after Mountbatten. Nehru expressed his regret at accepting partition, but accepted it without fuss[17].

In this whole process, Gandhi and his views were sidelined.

On 8 June, Gandhi wrote to Sarat Chandra Bose that he had discussed Bose's draft proposal for a United Sovereign Bengal with Nehru and Patel but that they had dismissed it. He told Bose to give up the idea.[18] Earlier, on 20 May, the Working Committee of the Bengal Provincial Muslim League had also passed a resolution rejecting Bose's proposal.[19]

On 9 June, Gandhi wrote an anguished letter to Nehru,

'The more I contemplate the differences in outlook and opinion between the members of the W. C. [Working Committee] and me, I feel that my presence is unnecessary even if it is not detrimental to the cause we all have at heart. May I not go back to Bihar in two or three days?'[20]

Gandhi's politics of friendship, his ever readiness to make concessions for the minority, was no longer of use in the most utilitarian moment of the anti-colonial movement. The Muslim League in Bengal was using Gandhi, and the Congress in Delhi ignored him. It signifies the brutal origins of nationalist politics. There was too much reason at stake to offer space for affective politics. Nehru and the Congress were right that Jinnah was not being prepared to take anything less than Pakistan. The Congress had hardened its position since the Cabinet Mission. Nehru could not see the problem beyond Jinnah and the Muslim League. The Muslim question was not a communal question, but a national one.

It is bewildering how Gandhi could not make Nehru understand this historical point. Nehru's secular lens failed to read the historical nature of the problem. Nehru's attitude was defined by the understanding that he had laid out in *The Discovery*: 'In political matters, religion has been replaced by what is called communalism, a narrow group mentality basing itself on a religious community but in reality concerned with political power and patronage'.[21]

Nehru's secular irritation and refusal to see political demands through a communal lens was justified in principle. In politics, however, principles need to be negotiated if the larger aims of secular politics face serious hurdles. If the fate of millions of lives was at stake, a Gandhian gesture of dogged persuasion was worth the effort. In the last analysis, only Jinnah apologists can turn the argument around to blame Nehru's personality traits for the failed negotiation to prevent partition in their bid to put a thick blanket over Jinnah's adamant communalism.

Gandhi raised new questions in the present scenario. On 12 June, he said at the prayer meeting in Delhi:

> 'Now Hindustan will imply that the country belongs to Hindus. And who among the Hindus? Only the caste Hindus. But as I have said the caste Hindus—Brahmins, Kshatriyas and Vaishyas—are a very small part of the population. The vast majority consists of untouchables and Adivasis. Will they be ruled by the few caste Hindus?'[22]

Gandhi clearly wanted the princely states to fall in line and join the new union. On 13 June. he said at the prayer meeting,

> 'Let the Princes not question the right of the Congress to say anything in the matter. The Congress has rendered much service to them . . . The Congress always considered the Princes as its own countrymen. What harm could they do? In time, it was thought, they would co-operate. If the Princes now stand up and say, "Well, we are the rulers", it would not be proper. They ought to come into the Constituent Assembly, rather they should send popular representatives there. If they do not do so then it seems that strife is going to be India's lot.'[23]

Gandhi added another perspective to the problem:

> 'We are hardly out of the Hindu–Muslim quarrel and we are faced with this new conflict with the Princes.'[24]

It is interesting to note here that as the sovereign nation–state was to come into existence, everything was seen against its fruition. Gandhi saw the Hindu–Muslim problem in relation to unity and not, for instance, rights. In fact, the idea of unity circumscribed the idea of rights.

Faisal Devji has argued that for Gandhi, rights were a kind of negative principle that paved the way for a 'moral relationship between enemies rather than friends.'[25] Rights were granted by the state, and for Gandhi, it meant that rights did not fully 'belong'[26] to us. For Gandhi, the desire for (and justification of) unity was a more fundamental quest for the community. Just as Hindus and Muslims had to give up everything that came in the way of their fraternal unity, the princes must give up their claims on the people and join the Constituent Assembly. The demand of unity and popular representation was essential to the formation of the nation–state. For Gandhi, the nation seemed to be a higher-order community that communities must accept and live under. But Gandhi keeps the nation conceptually absent, keeping its components real and present.

In the prayer meeting on 14 June, Gandhi laid out the historical context of the problem before his audience:

> 'During the reigns of Chandragupta and Ashoka, India had to a large extent become unified but even so a small bit in the South remained outside the empire. It was only when the English came that for the first time the country became one from Dibrugarh to Karachi and Kanya Kumari to Kashmir. The English did it not for our good but for their own. It is wrong to say that Travancore was free under the British regime. The Princes were never free. They were vassals of the British, they were subservient to them. Now when the British rule is on the way out and power is coming into the hands of the people, for any Prince to say that he was always independent and shall remain independent is wholly wrong and not in the least becoming.'[27]

This is an interesting argument. The sovereignty of pre-modern empires facilitated the birth of India as a unified political entity. The British Empire extended and strengthened that entity. Even though unity was so far forged by empires, it was desirable in itself. Now that the British were leaving, the people of India for the first time had the historic opportunity to redefine sovereignty in their name.

Referring to the news of violence pouring in from the provinces of Punjab granted to Pakistan, Gandhi made no bones about his bleak expectations:

> 'Mr Jinnah says that under the Muslim majority the minorities will live in peace. But what is in fact

> happening? If after Pakistan has come into being the conflict is further sharpened then it will only mean that we have been made fools of. It will mean that they will be masters and anyone following a different religion will have to stay there as a slave or a servant and admit that he is inferior to them.'[28]

Gandhi shared a startling piece of news at the prayer meeting on 20 June:

> 'Today someone has sent a letter to this little girl Manu warning her that if she recites verses from the Koran at the prayer she will be killed. To threaten someone thus is not in keeping with our traditions and Manu is only a little girl. If she recites verses from the Koran she does so under my instructions. I myself do not have a good voice. If it is a joke, it is not a good joke.'[29]

On 27–28 June, Gandhi wrote a stern letter marked 'urgent' to Mountbatten. He wrote that it wasn't 'humanly possible' that the Congress and the Muslim League were 'equally in the right'.[30] Gandhi told Mountbatten that if he felt (as he suggested, according to Gandhi) that Jinnah was 'more reasonable'[31] than the Congress, he should consult them for everything from now on. He blamed the British for 'being party to spitting India into two'.[32] Gandhi reiterated that he thought that Mountbatten had made a 'grave mistake' by assuming that if the British left, Hindus would have disallowed partition and put Muslims 'under subjection'.[33] He put a few things for the Viceroy's consideration: 1) the Congress wouldn't force any province to subjugation, 2) it was not possible for a caste-ridden Hindu society to hold Muslims to ransom, and a controversial statement that

3) 'Muslim dynasties have progressively subjugated India by exactly the same means as the English conquerors later did.'[34]

The Congress did enforce military might against the princely states in the name of nationalist/territorial calculations and even the principles of political modernity. Gandhi's last statement lacks historical investigation and conceptual clarity. He compares medieval dynasties with a modern Empire. To say, for instance, that the Mughals (the Muslim dynasty that ruled India the longest) and the British used 'exactly the same means' to subjugate people in India is to misrepresent historical distinctions. The Mughals did not make India a colony like the British. They enjoyed direct imperial sovereignty within the loose geographical landscape of India. The British deployed 'long-distance rule',[35] or rule by means of faraway control by a sovereign nation–state. But administrative power in civil and military terms, and corporate monopoly over trade and resources was exercised within the body of the colony. Power was two-pronged. By 'subjugation', Gandhi could have been referring to a combination of military might and religious/cultural and political hegemony. Mughal and British conquest of India involved all these factors. It must be borne in mind that during medieval times, modernist values like political and social equality, the idea of liberty and individual freedom, were not part of the world-view of those who ran empires; they were also missing in the societies that were ruled over. Mughal subjugation was felt by a far-flung, diverse community of pagans. The Mughals, as descendants of Timur the conqueror (a Sunni dynasty of Turko–Muslim origin), were ethnoculturally other who integrated themselves with the local community. The Afghans were closer home. India was not a nation before the British administration marked its territorial sovereignty, aided by its cartographical ventures, when the East India Company's surveying team comprising engineers drew India on an imaginary map in the latter part of the eighteenth century. The Mughals and other Muslim dynasties did lord over and often coerce the local population, levy taxes, and occasionally loot temples (sometimes maintain them) to stamp their political and religious authority. Tagore drew a comprehensive picture: 'We had known the hordes of Moghals and Pathans who invaded India . . . with their own religions and customs . . . we had never known them as a nation . . . we fought for them and against them, talked with them in a language which was theirs as well as our own.'[36] The British, on the other hand, helped in the restoration of historical sites, including religious architecture.

Gandhi's statement on subjugation by the 'same means' is therefore not accurate.

The Bugbear

Gandhi also emphasized in the letter that Hindus are a fragmented social unit that posed no threat to Muslims in terms of the power equation:

> 'The caste Hindus who are the bugbear are, it can be shown conclusively, a hopeless minority. Of these the armed Rajputs are not yet nationalists as a class. The Brahmins and the Banias are still untrained in the use of arms. Their supremacy where it exists is purely moral. The Sudras count, I am sorry, more as scheduled class than anything else. That such Hindu society by reason of its mere superiority in numbers can crush millions of Muslims is an astounding myth.'[37]

At the prayer meeting on 29 June, Gandhi returned to his critique of the princes:

> 'Some Indian Princes are offended. They believe that so long as there are the sun and the moon in the sky, they ought to remain on their thrones. They argue that it was not the people who installed them as the rulers, it was the British or the sun or the moon. This does not show that they are doing their duty. This bespeaks pride and arrogance. So long as they were protected by the British these Princes squandered crores of rupees in England and America. They indulged in wild orgies. Now it cannot continue. Now they can remain rulers only on the sufferance of the people and as their servants.'[38]

The time for the theory and argument based on natural rights of sovereignty was over. It was time for the establishment of popular sovereignty, and the rulers of the princely states must conform to the new law. It was a modern, democratic justification for annexation. Older forms of power, based on the economy of material and cultural excess, had to pave the way for the supposedly liberating, new beast in history called the nation–state, or be devoured by it.

At the prayer meeting on 10 July, Gandhi countered the misinterpretation of the meaning of political appeasement and contrasted it with his politics of friendship:

> 'My humanity tells me that the whole world is my friend. Cutting each other's throats will not bring good to anyone. Friendship does not mean appeasement. A friend does not seek to appease another friend. If harsh words have to be said, they must be said. I have been asked, if I am against appeasement, what else have I been doing? When in 1944 I trudged my way in the sun on eighteen successive days to the Qaid-e-Azam's house I was doing my duty. I did not

> seek to appease the Qaid-e-Azam. Had he accepted what I went to offer him all this blood that has now been shed would never have been shed. And all this poison would not have been spread. Also there would have been no third power in India and even after the formation of Pakistan, India would have been one. My talks with Mr Jinnah were friendly. Appeasement today has a bad connotation. When Germany and England were hostile to each other, Chamberlain, who was the Prime Minister at the time, had sought to appease Hitler. It is not my view but that of many Englishmen that, had Chamberlain not chosen the path of appeasement, history would have been different. But since I do not consider anyone my adversary why should I go out to appease anyone?'[39]

There can be no gesture of appeasement in the politics of friendship. Appeasement is demeaning and contrary to the idea of friendship. To engage in dialogue with your political opponent is not appeasement but a political ethic, a duty of friendship. To be harsh in opinion or judgement of the opponent is a necessary part of that ethic. In fact, Gandhi turns the argument around that the politics of hostility may succumb to appeasement the way the British premier Chamberlain signed a peace pact called the Munich Agreement with Hitler in September 1938, hoping to calm down the Nazi zeal for world conquest. The same could be said of Stalin signing the Non-aggression Pact with Hitler in August 1939. These would be considered strategic necessities in the discourse of realpolitik. In hindsight, such acts were proof that ideological principles (liberal–democratic or communist) are only meant to be upheld in favourable conditions, but are easily abandoned when power is at stake.

Hitler's importance lies in the fact that he exposed the limits of ideological politics and its principles by threatening it with the question of survival. A peace accord with a dictator is a desperate attempt at self-preservation, knowing the costs of risk are high.

The next day, Gandhi shared disturbing reports that he was receiving from Bengal with his audience at the prayer meeting:

> 'A co-worker writes from Noakhali: "When you came to Noakhali you talked so much about doing or dying. Now if you do not come here before the 15th of August, you will repent." I admit that if I do not go to Noakhali before August 15, I shall repent. Why am I in Delhi? I ought to be either in Bihar or in Noakhali. I am restless here. I was not so in Noakhali. I walked long distances every day, visited ever new villages and met an immense number of people both Hindus and Muslims. I did some work in Noakhali, also in Bihar. There is a fire raging inside me. That fire will not rage after I go to Noakhali. I ask you to pray that God may quickly send me to Noakhali.'[40]

Noakhali is Gandhi's ordeal by fire. The scene of violence, of mass human crime, demanded Gandhi's presence. Nationalist politics has immense room for violence. Gandhi was caught in a paradoxical situation: he was part of the movement for the nation's freedom, but the politics of freedom included opposing strands of nationalism that split freedom into half. The most deplorable disservice that Jinnah and the Muslim League did to the subcontinent is tearing neighbourhoods apart along religious lines. There was a political rupture between land and body.

Gandhi was trying to stitch back torn neighbourhoods.

On 25 December 1946, a few days after she had joined Gandhi in Srirampur, Manu wrote in her diary that the woollen pashmina shawl that Gandhi had wore around his head as a protection against the cold was torn and that Manu had replaced it with a new one. Gandhi refused to be indulgent about wearing a new shawl and patched up the old one himself. Manu was impressed by Gandhi's skill, and wrote: 'The man who knitted India into a nation, the man who patched up quarrels and joined sundered hearts was equally at home patching a piece of cloth.'[41]

There was a fire raging inside Gandhi's body, being away from the arena of violence and not being able to put out the fire. To genuinely embody the body politic within one's self one must intensely internalize it. Gandhi has been understudied as a character of feelings. He had the ability to feel and empathize deeply. Many of his political efforts were not just outcomes of his thinking, but also issued from his affective sensibilities.

On 22 July, Gandhi read out news of indiscriminate violence that he was receiving from Bengal to his audience during the prayer meeting,

> '[A] telegram received from Sylhet is very disturbing. The referendum there is over but harassment of the people continues. Why have the Muslims there gone crazy? Nationalist Muslims are being killed and the telegram says that someone should be sent there as an observer. The sender has signed his name too. It is reported that after the referendum Muslims burnt down a Harijan colony. It is a matter of shame.'[42]

Gandhi took a trip to Kashmir on 30 July to recuperate from health issues. The Frontier Mail with Gandhi, Manu and other associates left Delhi at 10.00 pm.[43] On the morning of 31 July, the train halted at Amritsar station where Hindu students shouted slogans, 'Gandhi go back, Gandhi go back'.[44] At Rawalpindi station, Manu wrote, 'Prayer could not be said. There was just far too much noise.'[45] They reached Srinagar at 4.30 p.m. Manu noted down: 'There were crowds on the road. There were many who shouted "Sheikh Abdullah Zindabad" and "Gandhiji Zindabad." But there were also a few who chanted slogans for Pakistan. Here it is difficult to distinguish between Hindus and Muslims.'[46]

On the three days on which Gandhi stayed in Srinagar, Sheikh Abdullah's wife was with him. Gandhi also met Maharaja Hari Singh[47] and Kashmir's chief minister, Ramchandra Kak. On 2 August, Manu wrote in her diary that they had gone sightseeing with Khan Abdul Wali Khan[48] (Khan Abdul Ghaffar Khan's second son). Wali Khan 'explained the political situation of Kashmir' that Manu paraphrased in her diary:

> '[The] reasons for Sheikh Sahib's imprisonment, the reasons for the reluctance to join the Union and the machinations of Kak. He further said that Kak was a clerical functionary in the Kashmir state with a salary of Rs 35/month. Both his sons have been sent to Pakistan and he has obtained some guarantees from Jinnah and Bhopal. He is a scoundrel. The Maharaja is afraid of him. Kak tells him that the people would kill him if he were to join the Union and that joining the Union would imply that Sheikh Abdullah would have to be released.'[49]

Gandhi left Srinagar for Jammu on 4 August after early morning prayers. Manu jotted down her impressions of the passing landscape: 'On the way we saw the spring from which Jhelum emerges. It is a very attractive and beauteous spot. I felt like staying at that place. There is a Shiva idol there.'[50]

On the morning of 5 August, Gandhi and his associates left Jammu for Rawalpindi. On the way, they visited 8000 refugees at the Wah refugee camp. Manu wrote: 'Bapu met all the patients with care and gave them solace with tender love.'[51] From the camp, they visited the Panja Saheb Gurudwara, and finally reached Rawalpindi. Manu noted:

> 'The Hindu Mahasabha supporters shouted slogans at the Rawalpindi station; *Hind ki Zubban Hindi, Hind ka Naara Hindu, Hindi, Hindustani.*'[52]

They reached Lahore on 6 August. In a discussion with Congress workers, Gandhi said that he would refuse to salute the flag of the Indian Union if it did not have the emblem of the charkha in it.[53] He told them that his 'heart has always been with the Punjab and the sad tales of woes and sufferings' but added cryptically that there were 'certain forces . . . were against my coming to this province.'[54] Gandhi said that he was aggrieved to learn that people were fleeing West Punjab and that Hindus were fleeing Lahore, and exhorted them against doing so:

> 'If you think Lahore is dead or is dying, do not run away from it, but die with what you think is the dying Lahore.'[55]

Gandhi has an epic idea of fate for the witnesses of destruction. The self is part of a place. If the place is being destroyed by an uncivil war, the self has no other option but to defend the place against that destruction and die in the process.

The same evening, Gandhi left for Calcutta. They reached Patna at 3.30 p.m. on 8 August. Gandhi attended a prayer meeting. Speaking to the audience, he called 15 August the 'day of our trial', and added: 'The independence we are going to get is not of the kind we can celebrate by having illuminations.'[56]

4

'A Short-Lived Nine-Day Wonder'

Between Two Swords

Gandhi reached Sodepur on 9 August.

Manu wrote in her diary entry after reaching Sodepur:

> 'I kept thinking about the condition of India. In Calcutta now the Hindus kill the Muslims because they think that it is their government that rules now.'[1]

She notes that the wife of the soon-to-be-chief-minister of West Bengal, Prafulla Chandra Ghosh, told Gandhi that there would be peace in Noakhali only if peace prevailed in Calcutta. To which Gandhi responded:

> 'I am being crushed between two swords.'[2]

The next day, the secretary of the Calcutta District Muslim League, Syed Mohammad Usman, came to visit Gandhi and requested him to stay on in Calcutta and not proceed to Noakhali for at least two days, making an effective statement that Muslims had 'as much claim'[3] upon Gandhi as Hindus. Gandhi accepted their claim but not without making a counter-demand on them:

> 'I am willing, but then you have to guarantee the peace of Noakhali. If I do not go to Noakhali before the 15th on the strength of your guarantee and things go wrong there, my life will become forfeit; you will have to face a fast unto death on my part.'[4]

This was Gandhi's style of ethical bargaining. If the Muslims wanted to use his services to end violence in Calcutta, they have to make their leaders commit to peace in Noakhali. On 11 August, Muhamad Usman came to visit Gandhi with Suhrawardy who wanted him to stay on in Calcutta to bring peace in the city. Gandhi repeated the offer he had made to Suhrawardy on 12 May: he and Suhrawardy would stay together and work together to ensure peace.[5] He shared the proposal with his audience at the prayer meeting the next day.

Gandhi met some Hindu demonstrators at Hydari Mansion in Beliaghata on 13 August. One of the demonstrators began by accusing Gandhi of not coming to the rescue of Hindus on 16 August 1946 when Direct Action was launched, and now he had promptly arrived to help the Muslims. He bluntly told Gandhi that he wasn't welcome.[6] Gandhi responded with sincere humility:

> 'But what is the use of avenging the year 1946 on 1947? I was on my way to Noakhali where your own kith and kin desired

> my presence. But I now see that I shall have to serve Noakhali only from here. You must understand that I have come here to serve not only Muslims but Hindus, Muslims and all alike. Those who are indulging in brutalities are bringing disgrace upon themselves and the religion they represent. I am going to put myself under your protection. You are welcome to turn against me and play the opposite role if you so choose.'[7]

Gandhi was also pursued by violence since India was engulfed in violence after the declaration of Direct Action Day. Since October 1946, Gandhi was always arriving at the scene, a bit too late for the violence that had already occurred, but in time to stall the violence that could not occur due to the force of his presence. Gandhi's explanation amounts to a real predicament that you can never arrive on time to stop violence. The time of violence always precedes the arrival of any response to it, to any gesture or possibility of peace. He was always late to arrive, because you can only arrive late to violence. Violence erupts in its own time, without warning, and you have no time, never enough time to respond. Yet, Gandhi is telling the demonstrator that he had responded to it in his own time. Even though he was late to arrive, he had arrived.

Some people, probably among the demonstrators, Manu noted in her diary, broke the glasses in Gandhi's room.[8]

The Zero Hour

In the prayer meeting on 14 August at Hydari Manzil, there was a 10,000-strong crowd. Manu and others rendered Tagore's song *Sankocher bihwabalata nijere apomaan.*[9] Written in 1929, the song translated in English reads: '*Do not insult yourself with scruples of doubt, / do not lower your spirits from imagining danger, / free yourself from fear, / summon your strength, win over yourself.*'

At the advent of Independence, two Gujaratis, Gandhi and Manu, were reminding Bengalis of the words of their bard in the face of fear and violence.

The crowd demanded the presence of Suhrawardy. He appeared soon and spoke,

'Let us all put behind what has happened. It is our good fortune that a great man like Mahatmaji is among us in Bengal. How long shall we continue to fight? All of us want peace. We wish to demonstrate that Hindus and Muslims can live together amicably. If the Hindus of this area were to provide a guarantee that they would not kill the Muslims we would certainly go next to Park Circus, to Zakaria Street.'[10]

Someone in the crowd asked Suhrawardy if he wasn't responsible for the violence raging since 16 August 1946. He replied, 'We are all responsible.'[11] The questioner was dissatisfied and asked Suhrawardy to reply to his question regarding personal responsibility. The ex-chief minister accepted the charge. It had a terrific effect on the crowd, as they cheered the statement. Suhrawardy's calculated gesture to pacify the questioning crowd elicited a favourable response.

As if to complement the scene, Manu noted in her diary, news poured in that around 5000 Hindus and Muslims decided to bury the hatchet and embraced each other in the streets of Calcutta and took out a procession. Suhrawardy said Gandhi's presence and penance was responsible for making such a thing happen.[12]

Around midnight, people poured out in the streets and celebrated the coming of Independence. Crowds came to meet

Gandhi. Manu recited the *Gita* in the memory of Mahadev Desai, who had passed away on 15 August 1942. Manu noted in her diary that they went out by car in the afternoon to witness the celebrations. The crowd shouted *Jai Hind* and they shouted back. Manu wrote,

> 'Hindus were in Muslim localities and Muslims were in Hindu areas, as if nothing had ever happened! Everyone said that all this was due to Gandhi Baba.
>
> As if the very air of Calcutta changed within 24 hours.'[13]

On the night of 16 August, Gandhi wrote the short piece 'Miracle or Accident' that was later published in *Harijan*. He also wrote a letter to Amrit Kaur:

> 'This is not for me a new experience. It reminds me of old days in South Africa and the Khilafat days here. For the moment I am no enemy. Who knows how long this will last? Hindus and Muslims have become friends practically in a day. Suhrawardy has become transformed, so it looks. His association was the condition of my stay in the disturbed area of Calcutta.'[14]

There was a tone of both relief and disbelief in Gandhi's language. The situation was too unreal to be true. Suhrawardy's transformation too was beyond expectations. Gandhi felt that he managed to inspire an atmosphere of peace by his presence, and orchestrate a temporary truce that stood on shaky ground.

On the 18th, Gandhi visited Barrackpore and held the prayer meeting at the Mohammedan Sports Club. There were around four to five lakh people. Manu wrote that the Hindu National Guard and the Muslim National Guard attended the prayer together, and they sang Tagore's *Ekla Chalo Re.*[15] On the 19th, Gandhi visited Kanchrapara, where police firing had killed people after a dispute over playing music in front of a mosque turned violent.[16] Manu noted in her diary about the incident that followed after they returned from the prayer meeting:

> 'A wounded Hindu came. He had gone to cut grass. Muslims attacked him from behind with sticks. He had injuries on his nose and forehead. He wept a great deal. I cleaned and dressed his wounds and gave him Rs 20/-. I also gave him lemon water mixed with glucose.'[17]

It is clear from these descriptions that the peace that had descended upon Calcutta was fragile and the atmosphere was still raw. On 20 August, the prayer meeting was held at Bara Bazar (a place that had a mosque, temple and church on three sides) where the Calcutta violence had begun and where truce was declared on 14 August.[18] At dinner, Manu confronted Suhrawardy on his not sleeping at the Hydari Mansion with Gandhi and his associates as decided but that he preferred the comforts of home. Manu disparaged him with striking intimacy and boldness,

> 'I have no faith in you. You don't keep your word. You have a new excuse every day.'[19]

That a young girl could say such a thing with conviction to Suhrawardy to his face shows his insincerity towards keeping his word. Even though Gandhi was making life easier for him by ensuring peace in the city, Suhrawardy did not want to sacrifice small pleasures even as a momentary obligation. It is a clear weakness of character that did not go unnoticed by a maturing Manu.

On 21 August, the prayer meeting at Park Circus started with the singing of Iqbal's *Sare Jahan se Achchha*, with Gandhi recollecting that a fellow Muslim prisoner had sung it, and also on his request, Sarala Devi Chowdhurani (the daughter of Tagore's sister, from Jorasanko, Calcutta).[20] He tried to pacify the Muslims of Murshidabad and Malda for being left behind in India, the Hindus of Khulna and Gopalganj and the Buddhists in the Chittagong Hills.[21] On the 23rd, at the prayer meeting in Woodlands, the Alipore residence of the Maharaja of Cooch Behar, Gandhi told his audience that although *Allah-o-Akbar* was used on occasions as a war cry by Muslims that terrified Hindus, the original meaning is soul-stirring and noble, and should be adopted by the Hindus too. He also remarked that *Vande Mataram* was not a religious but a political cry. He wished it to be 'sung together by all on due occasion', but cautioned that it should 'never be a chant to insult or offend the Muslims.'[22]

Suhrawardy was alarmed at Gandhi's mention of *Vande Mataram* and felt that it might be 'misconstrued' and people might be 'coerced' into singing it.[23] Gandhi gave him his characteristic assurance,

> 'If Muslims are coerced into saying that, I would face that challenge.'[24]

On 24 August, Gandhi informed at the prayer meeting that Khwaja Saheb Nazimuddin, the then chief minister of East Bengal, had written to him for help in procuring 500 tons of rice from the shipment coming from Burma. He was willing to help and asked Dr Rajendra Prasad to allow that amount from the cargo to be delivered at the Chittagong post. Gandhi hoped that rumours that officials involved in flood relief would only distribute the rice to Muslims weren't true.[25]

A report by Nikhil Chakravarty, the Calcutta correspondent of *People's Age* (published from Bombay), appeared in the weekly's 24 August issue, titled Day One in Calcutta. Some excerpts from the report are worth noting:

> 'Everybody felt nervous about August 15. Weeks ahead authorities were on tenterhooks; more police and military were being posted to ensure peace . . . East Bengal Hindus were nervous that one little spark in Calcutta might throw the entire province into the flames of a civil war; Muslims were panicky that they might be finished off in Calcutta and many had left the city . . .
>
> Gandhiji had already moved his camp to one of the most affected areas—Belliaghata—and cancelling his East Bengal trip, had decided to spend a few days here with Suhrawardy. But even he was disturbed by rowdy goondas, backed by communal groups, accusing him of being an enemy of Hindus . . .
>
> Discordant voices there were, but they did not matter. The Hindu Mahasabha first raised the slogan of black flags, but then piped down and declared non-participation. But all the prestige of Shyamaprosad [Syama Prasad Mookerjee] could not make any impression on the very people whom he had swayed during the Partition campaign.
>
> Forward Bloc and Tagorites also opposed the celebration on the ground that real freedom was yet to be won . . .

> As the zero hour approached, the city put on a changed appearance. On the streets, people were busy putting up flags and decorating frontage. Gates were set up at important crossings, bearing names of our past titans like Ashoka or our martyrs in the freedom movement . . .
>
> The first spontaneous initiative for fraternisation came from Muslim bustees and was immediately responded to by Hindu bustees. It was Calcutta's poor toilers, especially Muslims, who opened the floodgate . . .
>
> [The] very storm-centres of most gruesome rioting of the past year—Raja Bazar, Sealdah, Kalabagan, Colootolah, Burra Bazar—Muslims and Hindus ran across the frontiers and hugged each other in wild joy. Tears rolled down where once blood had soaked the pavements.'[26]

It is striking how arbitrarily ordinary people respond to political moments that have a bearing on their fate. When Jinnah declared Direct Action, the Muslims were instigated into committing violence and drawing the Hindu community into it, without any material or political benefit for either. At Independence, after futile bloodshed, people expressed equally exaggerated emotions of fraternity. Did they really repent, or was it all what Nirad C. Chaudhuri called 'weak repentance'?

History is a trail of unresolved emotions and feelings. People don't always act according to self-interest, but interests manufactured by political leaders and ideologies. The ideological machinery creates the people they want to lead, control and use. Politics is a field of manipulation. Politics has the unique ability to transform genuine grievances (related to forms of exploitation and oppression) into a discourse of conflict that often intensifies the problem with the claim to solve it from the root. Often doctors make a similar claim to patients about their medication. Liberation theologies, including the secular kinds, often pretend to deliver people from historical suffering using radical methods. The precise nature of the original grievance is lost in ideological fire and smoke.[27]

It is noteworthy that despite dedicating his body to the service of peace, Gandhi was suspected of partiality by people and politicians from both communities. These were largely motivated suspicions because each side wanted Gandhi to turn his eyes away from the crime committed by them and focus on the other side. Does such hypocrisy disappear through non-violence?

To Gandhi's credit, he raised the question of hypocrisy, telling his detractors that his decisions couldn't be dictated, and that they should focus on their duty towards the fraternal relationship they expected from the other side. Despite provocation, Gandhi held his poise.

The discordant voices that did not want to be part of the Independence celebrations made it a point to endorse their feelings, rather than give in to the grand opportunism of the moment. It is people's right to be unhappy about freedom, if it brought an unbearable heap of hatred and death in its trail.

The name of Ashoka being inscribed on the gates, along with the names of freedom fighters who gave up their lives for the cause of national liberation, seems to be an attempt to draw a historical arc across time. Ashoka's remorse and disgust with war and his abandoning of warfare were mentioned in eloquent terms by Nehru in *The Discovery of India.*[28]

At the prayer meeting in New Delhi on 28 September 1947, Gandhi remarked:

> 'There is no doubt that in modern history there is no instance which can be compared with the transfer of power by the British. I am reminded of the sacrifice of Priyadarshi Ashoka. But Ashoka is incomparable and, moreover, he does not belong to modern history.'[29]

Though Gandhi had refused to bow to the Indian flag if the charkha wasn't part of it, he made peace with the fact that the charkha was 'reduced to a wheel [with] . . . a different interpretation', acknowledging that the 'interpretation is not bad.'[30]

There are two more significant descriptions by Chakravarty. The migrant Muslim working class of Calcutta made the first gesture of embracing the Hindus. They were drawn into the cycle of violence by the propaganda of the League and they realized that they had the most to lose from it now. Violence and rapprochement happen at a calculative level when the dubious engine of history is on the move. The streets and pavements of blood being overwritten by tears is testimony to the often comic madness of history.

At the Lake Maidan prayer meeting in Calcutta on 26 August, Gandhi brought up the question of special treatment and singular territorial claimants. The focus was slowly shifting to political issues that would confront the new nation–state.

Gandhi said that the Anglo–Indian community was entitled to rights and justice like the rest of the country, but wouldn't enjoy special privileges as they did under colonial rule. He criticized the growing provincial spirit within the country. He took the example of the Assamese community making a sole claim over Assam. It was reported that Biharis were against the presence of Bengalis in Bihar, and that the Gurkha League resented the entry of plainspeople into Darjeeling. Gandhi acknowledged that people within the country should not exploit, rule or injure the interests of provinces they migrate to, but however felt that the demand for exclusive rights of belonging by communities of a region was lack of national imagination.[31]

Gandhi arriving for the reunion meeting at the Calcutta Maidan, August 1947

Gandhi told his audience on 28 August, at the University Science College in Calcutta, about his differences with Subhash Bose. Bose did not see eye to eye with Gandhi on the question of complete non-violence. He was a man, Gandhi said, of unequalled daring, scraping together an army from different provinces and religious backgrounds to fight the mightiest empire in the world. *The Azad Hind Fauj soldiers who worked with Gandhi in his peace mission told him that Bose wanted them to carry out what Gandhi suggested to them as the course of action.* Gandhi felt that it wasn't practical for some time for the soldiers to be absorbed in the ranks of the military, or become separate units. Rather, Gandhi suggested, that they either replace the sword with the ploughshare and till the land, or work among civilians. He thought that the dictum 'once a soldier always a soldier' did not suit India, furnishing the example of the Boers in Africa who were excellent soldiers as well as farmers.[32]

On 30 August, Gandhi shared with his audience at the prayer meeting on Tollygunge Police Ground that the Gurkha League had written to him that he was misinformed by the correspondent. The League contended that Gurkhas considered themselves to be Indians like everyone else, and they had no repugnance against Bengalis and Marwaris settled in Darjeeling, but they had apprehensions of these communities trying to 'lord over them' instead of Bengalis sharing their art of letters and Marwaris their craft of business.[33] Gandhi appreciated and agreed on their expectation of 'perfect equality', and expected the migrant settlers in the 'beautiful hill' to live as friends and not as exploiters.[34]

In response to an anonymous questioner on 31 August, on whether his experiment with ahimsa succeeded in Noakhali and Calcutta, Gandhi made a distinction between the idea of ahimsa (which was 'infallible') and the practitioners of ahimsa who could suffer from ineptitude.[35] Even though the experiment of ahimsa entailed the sum of activities by Gandhi and his associates, success or failure couldn't be ascertained immediately. With humility, Gandhi played down the popular belief that he had performed any 'miracle' in Calcutta, pointing to the fact that circumstances of a growing friendliness between Hindus and Muslims were ripe and that he and Suhrawardy were present at the right time to take credit.[36]

The Lynch Law

On the night of the 31st, an injured man was brought to Hydari Mansion. Gandhi narrated the incident to Patel in his letter on 1 September:

> 'Someone received knife wounds in Machhva Bazaar. No one knew who stabbed him. People brought him here for demonstration. Perhaps they wanted to attack Shaheed Suhrawardy, but they could not find him; so their anger was turned on me. There was an uproar in the front yard. Both the girls [Manu Gandhi and Abha Gandhi] went out among the crowd. I was in bed about to go to sleep. Our Muslim landlady came in to have a look as she was afraid I might come to harm. I sensed danger and got up. I broke my silence. My vow permits me to break it on such occasions. I went to face the crowd but the girls would not leave my side. Other people also surrounded me. Glass windows were being broken and they started smashing the doors also. There was an attempt to cut the wires of the electric ceiling fans but only a few were snapped. I started shouting at the crowd, asking them to be quiet. But who would listen? I could, moreover, speak only Hindustani and they were Bengalis. There were also some Muslims nearby. I asked them not to strike back. So they merely stood around me. There were two groups; one trying to

incite the crowd, the other trying to pacify it. There were two policemen also. They also used no force.'[37]

Peace in Calcutta was as fragile as the glass windows of Hydari Mansion.

The description was followed by a note of suspicion: 'Everyone suspects the Hindu Mahasabha [was behind the attack].'[38]

Gandhi asked the superintendent of police not to hurry and to meet the two Hindu Mahasabha leaders Syama Prasad Mookerjee and N.C. Chatterji before arresting the culprits involved in the attack. The incident rattled Gandhi. On the night of the 31st, he told Pyarelal who had come to meet him from Noakhali with an associate, Charubhushan Chowdhary, to apprise him of the situation, 'My resolve to go to Noakhali has collapsed after this evening's happenings. I cannot go to Noakhali or for that matter anywhere when Calcutta is in flames. Today's incident to me is a sign and a warning from God. You have for the time being, therefore, to return to Noakhali without me.'[39]

Just as Independence dawned and the control of the League shifted to the Muslim part of Bengal, the Hindu right wing wasted no time in fomenting trouble. That they attacked the residence that Gandhi was staying in showed they were intensely uncomfortable with his presence in Calcutta and also that they probably resented his collaboration with Suhrawardy to bring peace. Gandhi's use of Suhrawardy was strategic. He wanted the efforts of his mission in Calcutta to be reciprocated by the League in Noakhali so that Hindus in Noakhali were protected from violence, and there was communal calm in Calcutta. It was fated to be a short-lived bargain. But it was timely, during the most turbulent days of the transfer of power.

In Gandhi's statement to the press on 1 September, he emphasized the concern that 'these young men tried to become judges and executioners.'[40] After narrating the story in detail, Gandhi wrote:

> 'What is the lesson of the incident? It is clear to me that if India is to retain her dearly won independence all men and women must completely forget lynch law. What was attempted was an indifferent imitation of lynch law. If the Muslims misbehaved, the complainants could, if they would not go to the ministers, certainly go to me or my friend Shaheed Saheb. The same thing applies to Muslim complainants. There is no way of keeping the peace in Calcutta or elsewhere if the elementary rule of civilized society is not observed.'[41]

India has been experiencing an alarming rise of the 'lynch law' since 2014.[42] Lynching is mostly a form of majoritarian barbarism where gangs claim social power by indulging in criminal activities subverting both civil and state law. This can be called vigilante law, where self-styled gangs bolstered by political affiliations operate in the name of community sentiments and interests. By 'indifferent imitation of lynch law', Gandhi probably had in mind racial lynchings in America. The history of terror lynchings in the history of the United States against African–Americans is dated from the Reconstruction Era of the late nineteenth century till World War II and beyond. It was racist violence reacting against the integration of blacks into the social, political and labour systems. In India, it was a spillover from the politics of partition.

The Miracle of Non-Violence

Gandhi wrote further in the press statement:

> 'From the very first day of peace, that is 14th August last, I have been saying that the peace might only be a temporary lull. There was no miracle. Will the foreboding prove true and will Calcutta again lapse into the law of the jungle?'[43]

On 14 August 1947, when it was reported that 5000 Hindus and Muslims came out together in celebration mode and that, in a certain corner of Calcutta, Hindus were trying to put up a national flag and the Muslims extended their support to put it up, Suhrawardy had remarked, 'Look at the miracle that Mahatmaji has wrought in a single day.'[44] On 15 August, C. Rajagopalachari, who was appointed the new governor of Bengal, met Gandhi and congratulated him on the 'miracle which he had wrought'.[45] Gandhi said he wouldn't be satisfied until Hindus and Muslims felt safe in each other's company and lived together as before.

How does an event become a miracle? Is the event political, or is it anti-political, against the machinations of communal politics?

The politics of friendship may not be strictly secular. Communal friendship can be practised and affirmed by religious people. The dominant political theme and atmosphere of the time was communal hatred. To achieve a sudden wave of fraternal feeling had an anti-political touch to it. If it nevertheless had an effect on politics, it must be considered a powerful force. If the force of the miracle is not political but interrupts the political, it appears close to the idea of truth that Gandhi sought in political conflict.

For Gandhi, love and truth were interchangeable terms: truth emerged from the spirit of love, and love emerged from the spirit of truth. The experiment with ahimsa was to enable people to reach and experience this moment of truth. For Gandhi, the possibility of truth was outside the instrumentality of politics. Politics was a battlefield of interests whereas truth was an imaginary space–time of reconciliation. Through ahimsa, it was possible to establish truth within politics. Truth was a liberating clarity that could cut through the mesh of politics and help people see the light.

The triumph of the politics of truth and love was momentarily achieved in Calcutta. To experience this moment was a miracle. A miracle gives the impression of being outside time, which momentarily stalls the movement of history. But the grand design of nationalist history was already established and for that reason, any miracle that resisted the tide was bound to remain momentary.

Miracle is temporary, politics is permanent.

In a fresh letter to Patel over two days (1 and 2 September), Gandhi wrote:

> 'I have just returned after seeing the dead bodies of two Muslims who had died of wounds. I hear that riots have broken out in many places. *Thus what was regarded as a miracle has proved a short-lived nine-day wonder*. Now I am thinking what my duty is in the circumstances. I am writing this at about 6 p. m.'[46] [Emphasis mine]

He ended the letter saying,

> 'May God keep all of you safe. In this holocaust, no one else can do anything.'[47]

The short-lived miracle of nine days ended with the re-entry of politics and the smothering of truth. News poured in of hell breaking loose in the city just after Abha left to visit her relatives early in the afternoon. Fresh riots were reported from Park Circus, Bada Bazar and Bau Bazar among other areas.[48] Some migrant Muslim refugees had returned to their homes in Beliaghata upon Gandhi's assurance that they would be safe. Nirmal Kumar Bose sent his driver to take the refugees in a truck to safety in another locality. The open truck was passing by a graveyard close to Hydari Mansion when a hand grenade was thrown at the truck from a nearby building and two refugees died on the spot.[49] Gandhi visited the scene of the crime, and exclaimed, 'The people have gone mad.'[50]

Abha, who returned at 6 p.m., reported that brickbats and soda bottles were hurled at her car when she passed by a Muslim locality.[51] She escaped unhurt.

Manu wrote in her diary: 'Bapu had diarrhea today. He passed stool five times. I asked him about food. He wrote in reply, "I am disturbed and cannot eat . . ."'[52]

In the middle of the night, Gandhi woke Abha and Manu and informed them that they wouldn't have to cook for him from the next day. He had decided to fast.[53] Manu asked him for how long he contemplated fasting. Gandhi replied,

> 'So long as the fires rage, either peace should be restored, or I shall die.'[54]

Gandhi's fast began at 8.30 p.m. on 1 September. During prayers early the next morning, Manu sang Tagore's *Jibon Jakhon Sukay Jai, Korunadharaay Esho*[*When life withers, come in the tides of mercy*].

In a letter to Nehru, Gandhi wrote: 'If the Calcutta friendship was wrong, how could I hope to affect the situation in the Punjab?'[55]

Calcutta was the current testing ground for the politics of ahimsa. If the mood for fraternal ties was missing, ahimsa wouldn't succeed anywhere. There was no point running from one place to another. Peace brigades were patrolling Calcutta as riots refused to ebb despite heavy showers in the city.[56]

Nirmal Kumar Bose came back from meeting Sarat Chandra Bose and reported that Sikhs and Biharis were behind the riots, with Hindus joining them.[57] When Sarat Chandra Bose came to meet Gandhi later that day, Gandhi told him the Mahasabha alleged that Bose's Forward Bloc was behind the fresh round of riots. Bose blamed the Mahasabha behind it, and said that they had instigated the Sikhs to retaliate against what was happening in the Punjab.[58] They were joined in the evening by Dr Prafulla Chandra Ghosh who straightaway complained to Gandhi that he was unfair to declare a fast without taking his new ministry into confidence. Gandhi acknowledged Ghosh's problem but said the violence was spreading fast and he had had to take a quick decision.[59]

Gandhi with Sarat Chandra Bose on way to a meeting, Calcutta, 1947

Syama Prasad Mookerjee arrived along with other Mahasabha leaders after Ghosh left. Mookerjee stated there was fear of a repercussion in East Bengal and reports from Dacca were disturbing. He also said Hindustan National Guards [belonging to Hindu Mahasabha] would patrol the streets from the next day along with Muslim National Guards. Mookerjee asked Gandhi when he will end the fast. Gandhi replied, 'When you give me the 'report' that Calcutta is entirely peaceful, I shall break my fast.'[60] The heavy rain returned to the city[61].

During prayer the next day, 3 September, Manu sang Tagore's composition of 1887, *Tumi Bandhu, Tumi Nath, Nishidino Tumi Amaro* [*You friend, you lord, day and night, you are mine*].[62]

Later in the day, two representatives each from the Hindu and Muslim communities met Gandhi. One of the Muslim representatives from the Bengal Muslim League pleaded with Gandhi in tears to give up his fast. He said that he was part of the Khilafat movement and was willing to undertake the responsibility that Muslims wouldn't disturb the peace again. The Hindu representatives gave similar assurances.[63] Gandhi was not willing to give up his fast till the condition of peace returned in letter and spirit. After the representatives left, he said,

> 'Let the evil-doers desist from evil, not to save my life, but as a result of a true heart-change. Let all understand that a make-believe peace cannot satisfy me. I do not want a temporary lull to be followed by a worse carnage.'[64]

Truth and politics were at loggerheads. The fraternal lull could not be trusted, for even though the mass heat of violence had subsided, the cold-blooded machinations of communal politics might be still lurking in the background.

Hope was playing hide-and-seek with Gandhi. He was no longer going to be moved or convinced by appearances. He was no longer going to be lured and duped by assurances.

Hannah Arendt and Étienne Balibar

It was a mad ordeal to suffer for establishing peace, or non-violence, in history. Gandhi thought he held in his hands the reins of an invisible thread of love that ran through the body politic. He had transformed himself into a metaphor of what he represented. It was a saintly endeavour to make people realize that it made no sense for the heart to dwell in hate. But hate was the order of the day. It was established by political leaders to achieve a new political order. It was not possible to sustain the politics of love against a successful hate campaign. Perhaps the politics of love and fraternity needs to argue love as the best means of self-preservation rather than as an ethic alone. The politics of hatred succeeds because it is based on using the instinct of self-preservation to develop fear. Hate is often a consequence of fear.

Gandhi's psychological and ethical battle against communal hatred was based on a challenge for people to elevate themselves morally. It was a challenge to rise against the order of the day. The winds of hate were blowing hard, produced by the windmills of communal politics. The politics of hate managed to inflict the logic of self-interest on people's heads. It was easily understood because a history of communal and class antagonism and instances of violence could be selectively picked from the last decade of history and served to enhance that logic. Religion was the icing on the cake of bitterness.

This is how the poor are mobilized and turned into an army that is ready to kill in the name of defending their interests and securing their political future. The violence of history is the triumph of exaggerated falsehoods paraded as truth. The only thing that is true about this violence is the loss and destitution of lives. This fact is used to feed the politics of retribution. As long as people keep counting their dead, the history of this violence will refuse to die. The last war to come will perpetually remain history's apocalyptic utopia.

The strength of Gandhi's non-violent movement has been acknowledged (even unintentionally) by thinkers—in fact, *precisely* by thinkers—who have pointed out its limits.

In the second section of Hannah Arendt's essay, 'On Violence', she famously wrote:

> 'If Gandhi's enormously powerful and successful strategy of nonviolent resistance had met with a different enemy—Stalin's Russia, Hitler's Germany, even prewar Japan, instead of England, the outcome would not have been decolonization, but massacre and submission. However, England in India and France in Algeria had good reasons for their restraint.'[65]

This passage has often been cited as Arendt's critical remark on the limits of the Gandhian intervention. Arendt acknowledges the Gandhian movement but unnecessarily pits it against worst-case scenarios. It is true that the restrained nature of British rule generated the scope for a movement like Gandhi's. The accommodative structure of British colonial power over its subjects helped frame strategies of resistance. In a pithy commentary on Gandhi in 1969, considered one of his last, Karl Jaspers did not miss the point:

> 'Gandhi could speak in public. Even from this prison he was allowed to act. The English liberality and legal attitude provided scope for Gandhi's activities. It was the result as much of the English political conviction as of Gandhi's own.'[66]

Even though Gandhi was wary of the British legal system, it allowed space for a Gandhian movement that chose non-violence instead of terror. However, British liberalism is not to be read as colonial generosity. It was rather a combination of caution and intimidation.

In a dramatic article in *Young India* titled 'The Death Dance' (9 March 1922), a day before he was arrested in Ahmedabad on charges of sedition for articles he wrote in his own publications (under Section 124, Indian Penal Code), Gandhi wrote: 'It would be a thousand times better for us to be ruled by a military dictator than to have the dictatorship concealed under sham councils and assemblies. They prolong the agony and increase the expenditure.'[67] The legal and bureaucratic system of colonial power was a liberal façade. It allowed Gandhi's acts of civil disobedience at the cost of frustrating his spirits.

During the trial on 18 March, Gandhi, in his written statement, pleaded guilty to the charge of promoting dissatisfaction toward the government established by law in India and proceeded to offer the reason:

> 'Affection cannot be manufactured or regulated by law. If one has no affection for a person or thing one should be free to give the fullest expression to his disaffection so long as he does not contemplate, promote, or incite to, violence.'[68]

Gandhi told the colonial court that the relationship between people and the law is founded not on a liberal contract based on interest, but on an obligation based on sentiment, the sentiment of affection. Hence, the law must take into account non-violent expressions of collective disaffection. The judge passing the sentence began by categorizing Gandhi as a unique subject under the law, '[It] will be impossible to ignore the fact that you are in a different category from any person I have ever tried or am likely to have to try.'[69]He ended on a condescending note:

> 'I do not forget that you have consistently preached against violence and that you have on many occasions, as I am willing to believe, done much to prevent violence. But having regard to the nature of political teaching and the nature of many of those to whom it was addressed, how you could have continued to believe that violence would not be the inevitable consequence, it passes my capacity to understand.'[70]

The judge posed a consequentialist problem against non-violence, probably with reference to Chauri Chaura where a crowd of peasants set fire to a police station on 4 February 1922, killing twenty-two police officers. It led Gandhi to call off his non-cooperation movement.

Colonialist limits and its sham liberalism apart, the colonized subject could dialogue with the law. In contrast, Stalin's Russia and Hitler's Germany brutally clamped down on all civilized forms of protest and resistance. That Gandhi's movement would have failed to take off under such regimes is not a comment on the possibilities of ahimsa, but on the limits posed by barbaric political regimes.

Étienne Balibar has compared the 'universalist scope' of Gandhi's model of politics as an organized mass movement with communism that includes 'struggles for national independence and autonomy by minority peoples, but also and everywhere, as we know, for the movements for civil rights and racial equality.'[71] Balibar argued that Gandhi 'systematized' Thoreau's concept of civil disobedience to deploy 'a set of tactics of struggle'[72] in the quest for political reform that tested the limits of the state's avowed principles.

On the evening of 4 September, a deputation of prominent citizens, including Suhrawardy, N.C. Chatterjee,

Niranjan Singh Talib, C. Rajagopalachari, J.B. Kripalani and Dr P.C. Ghosh, visited Gandhi. They tried to impress upon him that the disturbances weren't overtly communal but instigated by goondas, and that he should consider breaking his fast.

Gandhi heard them and said, 'My fast should make you more vigilant, more truthful, more careful, more precise in the language you use.'[73] He told them they had to assure him in writing that there was a change of heart among the citizens and that they wouldn't cause trouble again in the city. Suhrawardy tried to argue that stray incidents couldn't be avoided in a big city and surely Gandhi didn't need to fast for it. Gandhi replied that Suhrawardy had missed the point. He did not imagine Calcutta to be rid of all crimes, but for the mad frenzy of communal violence to end.[74] The deputation handed over a note of assurance to Gandhi in writing.[75]

Gandhi gave a speech, where he announced he was breaking his fast so he could concentrate on doing something for the Punjab. He warned that any disturbance in Calcutta was bound to impact Noakhali and the Panjab. He ended, saying,

> 'These girls have just now sung *Ishwar Allah tere nam, sabko sanmati de Bhagwan.* And, of course, above all, there is God, our witness.'[76]

He broke his fast at 9.15 p.m. with a glass of diluted orange juice.[77]

In the morning on 5 September, rioters visited Hydari Mansion (despite police trying to chase them away) on their own volition to surrender their arms—'Sten-guns, guns, spearknives, arrows, cartridges, bombs'—to Gandhi.[78] This exemplified the psychological force of guilt (and 'weak repentance'?) Gandhi could produce on people who indulged in violence.

On his last day in Calcutta, 7 September 1947, Gandhi spoke to the crowd at the prayer meeting, congratulating the 'Shanti Sena' for doing a wonderful job of maintaining peace in the city. He said that even though he was leaving, he would keep himself informed about the city. Gandhi exhorted the Sena to risk their lives for peace, reminding them that their battle was not with swords, but love.[79]

Gandhi's train departed for Delhi at 9.30 p.m.[80] He would never return to Calcutta.

5

'A Fist Full of Bones'

The Act of Truth

Gandhi reached Delhi early in the morning on 9 September, and later released a statement to the press, reacting to stories about atrocities that he had heard from his Muslim friends: 'I must do my little bit to calm the heated atmosphere. I must apply the old formula "Do or Die" to the capital of India.'[1]

Gandhi could not stay in his usual place in Bhangi Colony as it was 'up in flames' and there were incidents of firing, so he stayed in Birla House.[2]

Manu wrote in her diary the previous day that 3000 Muslims were killed in Delhi. Nehru blurted out in anger: 'The Sikhs take revenge here, they loot, how are we to say anything to Pakistan? We die at our own hands. The refugees have unleashed riots.'[3] This was too late a note of despair after partition was declared. There was a clear lack of anticipation regarding the repercussions. Leaders take big, objective decisions that affect people's lives, and when those decisions go awry, it affects the people more than it affects the leaders. When the ground beneath your feet is taken away and life is in survival mode, the moral compass gets unsettled.

Devdas Gandhi and Amrit Kaur reported that the hospitals in Delhi were overflowing, they had run out of rations and people were served khichdi on paper.[4]

The next day, Abul Kalam Azad shared his account of events in Delhi with Gandhi. Azad said,

> 'We are responsible. Partition should not have taken place . . .'[5]

After lunch, Gandhi, Manu and others visited 500 Meos (a tribal community of 'Rajput–Muslims' from the Mewat region of Rajasthan) from Alwar at a refugee camp near Humayun's Tomb. Gandhi heard their stories.[6] They next went to Jamia Millia where Gandhi consoled the refugees. At the Anand Hall camp, the Punjabis expressed their anger at Gandhi for being partial to Muslims. They said his heart was made of stone. Gandhi was happy that they unburdened their hearts by abusing him.[7]

On 10 September, Gandhi spoke at the evening prayer meeting taking the names of Nehru, Patel, Jinnah and Liaquat Ali to hold both the Congress and the League responsible for failing to fulfil their word and protect minorities:

> 'Did the leaders of these Dominions make such a declaration to please world opinion or was it their intention to prove that there was no difference between their words and deeds and that they would be ready to lay down their lives in order to fulfil their promises?'[8]

Gandhi was the last great political leader in modern India who made a moral demand from politics that was not possible for politics to fulfil. The violence of partition was too large-scale for the administration and even the police to handle. The political intent, however, was missing. Partition was a failure of leadership.

Gandhi narrated his experience at the camp near Humayun's Tomb and Jamia Millia. At the camps in Diwan Hall, Wavell Canteen and Kingsway, he met angry Hindu and Sikh refugees:

> 'I noticed some angry faces in all those camps. Those people can be forgiven. They talked to me in sharp tones for being harsh to the Hindus. They said that I had not undergone the hardships that they did, and not lost my kith and kin. They said I had not been compelled to beg at every door. They asked me how I could comfort them by saying that I had been staying at Delhi to do my utmost to establish peace in the capital of the country. True I cannot bring back the dead.'[9]

Peace is not an easily desirable emotion for those who have experienced personal horror. It is difficult, and can even be hypocritical, to mention peace to people whose bodily organs are still shaking with the effect of violence. Victims of violence who refuse comfort need it the most. Gandhi's calming presence can only be imagined, not argued. Only those who experienced it can tell us what it meant to them.

Zahid Husain, the first Commissioner of Pakistan to India, met Gandhi in the afternoon. He said that Muslims had nothing to complain after what Gandhi did for them. Husain asked Gandhi to summon Suhrawardy.[10]

On the morning of 12 September, the leader of the Rashtriya Swayamsevak Sangh (RSS), M.S. Golwalkar, came to meet Gandhi and they had a fifteen-minute conversation. Gandhi asked him whether what he had heard was true that the RSS was behind the riots and disturbances. Golwalkar denied the charge, saying that they stood for peace and that their policy was to rescue people who were stranded.[11] Gandhi asked him to issue a statement in this regard. Golwalkar wanted to use Gandhi's stature, requesting him to issue the statement on his behalf. Gandhi said he would but Golwalkar should also issue one.[12] Gandhi mentioned the conversation at the prayer meeting that day. He also told the crowd that he had visited Jama Masjid and that Muslims taking shelter there had gathered in large numbers to hear him. Seeing the women weeping, Gandhi wondered if it would serve anything, telling them what the Hindus and Sikhs faced in the Punjab and the Frontier Province:

> 'The people of Pakistan resorted to ways of barbarism, and so did the Hindus and Sikhs. And so, how could one barbarian find fault with another barbarian?'[13]

The crowd at the Masjid had heard of his peace work in Noakhali and Bihar. They asked him how he could help them. Gandhi described a poignant moment to his audience: 'A mother said her child was dead and she did not know what to do.'[14] Maybe Gandhi meant to say, he felt as clueless as that mother.

On 14 September, a Muslim delegation requested Gandhi to shift to a house belonging to Asaf Ali in Daryaganj. 'Bapu' they said, 'just as you lived in a Muslim home at Calcutta, do the same here as well.'[15] Gandhi readily agreed. Later however, Gandhi's wish was vetoed by Manu who said that Delhi wasn't Calcutta, where Suhrawardy had taken personal responsibility for Gandhi's stay at Hydari Mansion. Patel too was against the idea of Gandhi staying in Daryaganj where it was 'raining bullets', and it would mean 'cutting our noses.'[16]

On 15 September, the signs of a maturing Manu were evident in her diary. She did not often indulge in passing judgements. Sometimes she did so carefully and fleetingly. But her young mind was thinking. She was trying to make sense of the various fissions around her:

> 'From all that I have seen, it seems to me that we do not deserve our freedom. Wherever we go there is only one talk, if the Muslims have to be driven out something must be done. It seems to me that we are not united, no one subscribes to one idea. Jawaharlalji and Sardar differ from each other. Sardar and Bapu differ as well. In Pakistan, Jinnah is the sole leader. We speak openly. But we should see what secrecy Jinnah keeps. His "policy" is amazing. It seems that we are in a slumber. We work ourselves to death to no avail. God knows what will happen. Those thoughts are gnawing away at Bapu. People are unhappy at his prayer speeches. They say that it is easy to make such prayer speeches, but the true test is whether the government can establish control and function out of East Punjab! Everyone has an opinion.'[17]

Manu detected that despite differences, the political conversation in India had more internal equality and openness in contrast to Jinnah's Pakistan. Yet, she felt, freedom was undeserved when there was so much difference and disunity among people.

Early in the morning on 16 September, Gandhi made an important speech at the RSS rally in Bhangi Colony. He told them that he was taken to the RSS Camp at Wardha by the industrialist Jamnalal Bajaj when Hedgewar was alive. Gandhi said that he was impressed by their discipline and simplicity and that there was no trace of the practice of untouchability among their ranks. He said that if Hindus believed that Muslims had to live subserviently to Hindus in India, and if Muslims in Pakistan felt that only they could rightfully belong to Pakistan, Hinduism and Islam would die.[18] Gandhi told them of his meeting with Golwalkar and that he shared the complaints he had received regarding the RSS in Calcutta and Delhi. Golwalkar clarified: 1) the RSS was a protectionist organization for the Hindus but not at the cost of others, and 2) the RSS did not believe either in aggression or ahimsa, but in self-defence. Gandhi said that only the RSS could refute the allegations against them by their behaviour.[19] Whether Golwalkar was truthful about his organization's motivations and deeds or not, Gandhi told him that the best way to prove it: *truth does not lie in self-proclamations, but in the act.*

Gandhi met Congress workers at 4 p.m. while spinning. The workers said that they were one with Gandhi's sentiment that Muslims shouldn't be allowed to leave but Hindus wouldn't allow them to live there. Gandhi's response was cold and blunt, 'You have changed. I say that I am all alone and will die alone.'[20] The workers suggested that they run special trains to send the Muslims to Lahore and let them fend for themselves. Gandhi lost his cool, "Where will they go? Those whose home and hearth are here, where can they go?'[21]

Later, during the prayer at Kingsway refugee camp, the moment the *Auzubillah* was sung, people protested, 'We will not permit the recitation of the Koran. They force our mothers and sisters to say the same *kalama* in the Punjab . . . This Koran has killed us.'[22] Finding her voice, Manu was considerate about people's sentiments and weighed Gandhi's expectations critically:

> 'On one hand Bapu's insistence seems right but on the other hand I recognize that their sisters and daughters have been stripped naked and forced to recite the same Koran . . . The wretched people have left their millions behind and have come with only the clothes on their backs. Women cover themselves with cloth torn from men's *dhotis*. In such tragic circumstances Bapu urges them that evil needs to be met with goodness. This is a very difficult task.'[23]

Manu's thought is based on an important dilemma. Gandhi went a step beyond his own (and Arendt's) commandment of actively countering evil with good deeds. Gandhi expected people of a destitute community, who had just suffered extreme atrocities from another community, to not just respect but also embrace a certain religious content of that community that was part of the symbolic violence used against them. Why did Gandhi insist upon such a crazy demand?

Gandhi wanted people to behave as if nothing had happened. As if gestures of synthetic culture could freely circulate in public spaces despite mass violence. Was it an act of resisting evil, or altogether ignoring it? When human relations have slumped to a barbaric level, shared cultural symbols get tainted. Gandhi was making a difficult demand on a grieving people. It didn't make sense. But it made sense to Gandhi. Why should evil be met with goodness? What will it serve?

Let me offer a Gandhian response for consideration: The point of goodness, the proof that there is goodness in the world endangered by evil, faces its severest test, its proof, in the fierce moment of encounter. In ordinary, peaceful times, goodness has a quiet, almost invisible presence. Only when conditions (and relations) are strained does goodness begin to be visible. In other words, it is as a *political act* that goodness is experienced as a real possibility in the world.

Gandhi is trying to tell his audience to demonstrate that even if you can't love the enemy, at least love his prayer. If the prayer has been instrumentalized by evil, let it be rescued by those who suffered it. What is ethics if not visible in the heart of the battlefield? Gandhi wants society to shame evil with its least available resources of goodness. The desire for every finding is most acute at the brink of losing, every healing at the brink of madness, every life at the brink of death. Gandhi is trying to tell people at the Kingsway refugee camp, to shame evil when evil is at the height of its powers. That is the only way to rescue the future, the future of goodness.

On the drive back home, Gandhi shared his feelings about what he had encountered at Kingsway Camp:

> 'I must admit that I liked this very much. People need some place where they can express their rage, and they brought out their rage on me. And if people do not want, we must not offer prayers. We should go and meet them. What they do is understandable. I am reminded of the French Revolution.'[24]

Suhrawardy reached Delhi from Calcutta on 18 September. He boasted that Jinnah offered him three posts but he declined and he would act on Gandhi's wishes.[25] At the evening prayer, Gandhi returned to the question of death and honour:

> 'I have heard that many women who did not want to lose their honour chose to die. Many men killed their own wives. I think that is really great, because I know that such things make India brave. Not that their lives were not dear to them, but they felt it was better to die with courage rather than be forcibly converted to Islam by the Muslims and allow them to assault their bodies. And so those women died . . . When I hear all these things, I dance with joy that there are such brave women in India. But where is the place for those who have already fled? They must return and return with honour. Let there be justice at least on our side. Let us keep our hearts and hands clean. Then we can ask for justice before the whole world.'[26]

On 20 December 1946, a few days after Manu joined him at Srirampur, Gandhi told her that if she was captured by goondas and died at their hands, he 'would dance with joy'.[27]

It is tempting to borrow Žižek's hypothesis partly here. He suggests that if evil is an eternal, cyclic force, good can triumph over evil and escape its obscenity only by dying and returning to its original innocence.[28]

For Gandhi, the death of women at the hands of violators is an unparalleled symbol of cultural honour. By dying, the women forever erase the 'assault' on their bodies. Gandhi's idea of a moral community cannot afford the assaulted bodies of women. They are a disturbing and unwanted surplus with a complicated problem for the moral social order. Gandhi may not have thought in those terms, but we have the liberty to think in these very terms. If Gandhi's ideal community is raised to great heights by women who offer their lives to save their honour, it must at least have the decency to leave the choice to women to do what they want with their bodies, once men couldn't protect them. Once protection becomes impossible, women are free to live or die. To choose death as a morally superior option over life is the Gandhian limit of morality.

It must however be understood that Gandhi thought about the problem of dis/honour, bravery and death in epic terms. For him, the only idea that could match—and triumph over—the overwhelming idea of evil was the idea of sacrifice.

The next morning, there was a long discussion with a Muslim delegation. Suhrawardy suggested that the Muslim minority in the capital be given weapons to protect their lives and there should be no search orders in their localities. Gandhi vehemently disagreed with the idea of arming people and turning them into private militias. It was state responsibility: 'There is a government. If the government were to admit that they are incapable of providing protection, they may do so.'[29]

On 21 September, Gandhi had a half-hour conversation late in the afternoon with the socialist leader, Ram Manohar Lohia, while spinning. At 5 p.m., he visited a Muslim locality at Library Road. A crowd of around 5000 Muslims greeted him. Manu wrote her impression in memorable words in her diary:

> 'Muslims, at some point, considered Bapu as an enemy, but today they wish him victory. Bapu's work is such

> that he has won the hearts of those who had constituted themselves as enemy and he continues to win them over. In the present condition no Hindu has the courage to be among Muslims, but an old man made of nothing but a fist full of bones goes amidst them every day.'[30]

The Act of Listening

That Gandhi became the focal point of the communal conflict was both a success and a failure. On the one hand, he retained the moral authority to speak to Muslims and Hindus as one of their own, after Noakhali and Bihar. On the other hand, both communities were willing to listen to Gandhi more than each other. Both communities were abandoned by their political leaders, uprooted from their homes, forced to face a calamity that was bewildering and lethal. Only a seventy-eight-year-old fragile but spirited man was listening to their woes, reproaching them, receiving their abuse and anger, insisting on love and peace, reminding them of the moral precepts of their own (and even the other's) religion.

Gandhi's listening is part of his politics. In other words, his politics involves listening to others. Just as he listens to his 'inner voice' that helps him take important decisions, he also listens to the world when it demands his attention. Simone Weil writes:

> 'Those who are unhappy have no need for anything in this world but people capable of giving them their attention. The capacity to give one's attention to a sufferer is a very rare and difficult thing; it is almost a miracle, it *is* a miracle.'[31]

Gandhi's stay in Calcutta, which he called a nine-day wonder, or even his sojourns in Noakhali and Bihar, can all be considered miracles from Weil's perspective. History and politics don't run by miracles. But a miracle is not to be measured—and dismissed—vis-à-vis realism. The need for a miracle occurs during moments of crisis. The nature of the crisis is most often accentuated by the politics of realism (in this case, communalism). Gandhi responded to that crisis and produced a moment that could overcome the logical and psychological constraints of that realism and exhibit an intensity of fraternal relations. In this, the act of listening played a part. Weil's statement is not only true in an everyday social context. It has political and historical dimensions.

The miracle of Gandhi's peace mission lies in the manner in which he reversed the most entrenched political impulse in modernity where leaders and ideologues meet people to preach and lecture, not to listen. The politics of truth, which is also the politics of the face-to-face, is premised upon the recognition of what you hear from the other side. It exemplifies the truth of learning from others, and learning from others as part of the truth. Gandhi shared his ideas in his prayer meetings, but he heard the victims in Noakhali and Bihar and replied to their questions. This Gandhian ethic is contrary to the dominant principle of modern politics, a rare occurrence in twentieth century history.

Weil also has a unique take on what she means by 'attention'. In an essay titled, 'Attention and Will', Weil writes: 'We should be indifferent to good and evil but, when we are indifferent, that is to say when we project the light of our attention equally to both, the good gains the day'.[32]

Attention, for Weil, comes from a negative responsibility. You must be able to distance yourself from good and evil alike to pay attention to both. Weil's proposal is a way to understand

Arendt's point about evil being a lack of judgement between good and evil. By paying attention, you realize what has caused suffering. It tilts the balance in favour of human understanding. By paying equal attention to what is good and what is evil, we recover the reflective property of goodness.

Listening to victims and perpetrators, Gandhi often tells them what they don't expect to hear. Despite his sense of responsibility and affection, he wouldn't hesitate to say something harsh to a victim. When Gandhi tells people to give up their lives courageously rather than fear death, it may appear that he is being indifferent to the plight of sufferers. He is however trying to work against their fear—something he learns from listening to them—and impels them to overcome it.

On 26 September, Gandhi asked Suhrawardy, 'Have you returned as the king of the forest or as a jackal?'[33] This was in reference to Suhrawardy's self-motivated mission on 21 September to bring about rapprochement between the two new dominions. Due to his close association with leaders of the League, Suhrawardy hoped to make an impression while meeting them in Karachi.[34] In reply to Gandhi's question, Suhrawardy jested,

> 'Sir, only as a mouse. The mouse is a very discreet creature.'[35]

Gandhi went ahead to narrate Aesop's fable of the mouse setting the lion free from the hunter's net. There was so much strain on human trust that political leaders had to take recourse to fabulist tales to exchange concerns.

On 27 September, after taking his bath, Gandhi suddenly remarked,

> 'What a pitiable condition! Not a Hindu can sit in a train to Pakistan and if they were to, they would be killed and the same applies for the Muslims in India. I have never heard of such savagery.'[36]

Gandhi found himself in a pitiable state where all he could do was despair the dark times. Trains running between India and Pakistan were bringing the dead. It was a partition of death, and the transfer of population included the transfer of death bodies. It was a pandemic of hate and butchery.

On the afternoon of 1 October, as they were travelling back from meeting Hindu and Sikh refugees, Manu told Gandhi that they had heard him speak in his sleep. Gandhi shared the dream,

> 'It must be so. Because when I woke up from sleep I felt as if I was in a dream. In my dream I was reasoning with the Muslims. I saw Muslims being slayed. These days whether I am awake or asleep, while eating and drinking the same thoughts whirl around me. This is not a good sign.'[37]

The chasm between the constant preoccupation of a gruesome reality and the failure of any conceivable means to intervene meant that the concerns were getting deposited into the dark caverns of the unconscious. The preoccupation with reality had passed over into nightmare. All exit doors were closed.

On 2 October, Chaudhry Khaliquzzaman, the man whom Jinnah made president of the Muslim League in December 1947, accompanied Suhrawardy and General Ismay to Karachi to meet Jinnah. Jinnah was upset with Khaliquzzaman for refuting the jurist and Pakistan's first foreign minister Muhammad Zafrullah Khan's charges against the Indian government at the United Nations. Khaliquzzaman's statement had a special word of praise for Gandhi which must have irked Jinnah even more:

> 'Mahatma Gandhi is straining every nerve to impress upon the people in India where that independence would not be worth anything if the present inhuman and barbarous killing of one community by the other does not immediately end.'[38]

It was Gandhi's birthday on 2 October. Nehru came to visit with Indira and her two sons. When Ghanshyamdas Birla observed that Gandhi wasn't cured of his cough yet, he said that he had no desire to live. Birla joked, 'So you have come down to zero from hundred and twenty-five?'[39] He mentioned his birthday at the prayer meeting with grave sorrow:

> 'Today is my birthday . . . I would say that on this day we must fast, spin and pray . . . For me today is the day of mourning. I am surprised and also ashamed that I am still alive. I am the same person whose word was honoured by the millions of the country. But today nobody listens to me.'[40]

Gandhi was mourning two things together, the violence of partition and his own irrelevance. He and his people were both abandoned by the scriptwriters of history. But between them, he was the one abandoned by the people. Gandhi felt a double abandonment. The 'word' of Gandhi was a simple commandment: participate in a movement non-violently to make a demand or appeal or simply to break the law. From Gandhi's first major movement in India, the 1917 Satyagraha with peasants in Champaran against forced indigo cultivation, to 1919 on the Khilafat question, and the Salt March of 1930, he was in top form. By the time he reached Noakhali in the winter of 1946, the fate of Indian politics was no longer within his grasp. Non-violence was no longer the guiding principle. If there were members of the Congress who didn't care much for it, or the Hindu right and the Indian left that did not adhere to it, the Muslim League dealt the death blow to it.

Gandhi's cough kept worsening. On 7 October, he said at the prayer meeting,

> '[Something] has happened and I should not keep quiet about it. It has happened not here but at Dehra Dun. A Muslim gentleman was murdered. As far as I know, he had committed no crime. Nor had he taken the law into his own hands. But he was killed because he happened to be a Muslim. I was pained about it and wondered where we would stop if we went on at this rate.'[41]

This uncannily speaks to the deteriorating condition of India's civil society and its spaces since the last decade. Muslims have been targeted by Hindu right-wing vigilantes on some pretext or the other, but beneath the pretext, the reason has always been the same: they were Muslims. There has clearly been a conscious political attempt to turn the clock back to 1947.

The problem with the politics of retribution is that the score is never even. It can never catch up with the spectre of violence in the psyche. Retributive violence can dream of killing the spectre only by recreating it. You can kill the other, but never its spectre. The repeated failure of this terrible dream creates an agonizing sense of defeatism. Retributive politics turns memory into ideology. The phenomenology of retributive politics, or the politics of hate, is not natural but ideological. Its psychic component is constantly renewed through material forms (textual, oral) and feeds into modes of action.

In the prayer meeting on 8 October, Gandhi addressed some structural manifestations of a society engulfed by hate, for instance how the media becomes a propaganda machinery. To begin with, Gandhi returned to the subject of friendship:

> 'We don't want to go into the question of who is more guilty and who less, or who started it. In my view that would be sheer ignorance. That is not the way of becoming friends. If those who were enemies till yesterday want to be friends today, they should forget the past enmity and start behaving as friends. What is the point of remembering animosity? There can be no friendship if people think that they would be prepared to fight if necessary but would remain friends if they could. That is not how true friendship grows.'[42]

Gandhi holds that looking for the origins of a quarrel in order to hierarchize guilt was an ignorant way to propose the possibility of friendship. The second criterion for a possible friendship is the forgetting of past enmity. The memory of strife does not serve the cause of friendship. In fact, memory can only cause hindrances. Forgetting is the price to pay in the politics of friendship. Gandhi adds a strict third criterion: friendship can't be based on a vacillatory promise.

Gandhi took on the press next. First he laid down the general principles and limits of the freedom of press:

> 'When there is freedom, there can be no restrictions on the Press regarding the reports and the news to be published. But public opinion can be very useful at such times. When the newspapers do dirty propaganda or publish unfounded reports or incite people, the Government should come down on them to put an end to these or take legal action against them. But in doing so the riot situation worsens and there is more trouble. The Government cannot resort to that course . . . Today all the correspondents, editors and owners of newspapers must become truthful and serve the people. No false information should appear in the newspapers nor should they publish anything that would incite the people. Today, when we have become independent, it is the duty of the public not to read dirty papers but to throw them away. When nobody buys those papers they will automatically follow the right path.'[43]

Gandhi was a journalist besides being a political leader and reformist. He does not think of setting limits to media freedom through constitutional law, but through public opinion. The morality of public culture must be able to judge any deviance in media guidelines. Gandhi considers governmental intervention through legal action necessary if media indulges in propaganda that may disturb social peace. But he does not find it a useful deterrent during moments of social or political crisis. Curbs on the media in such situations might worsen the circulation of fake news. Gandhi lays a lot of onus on public responsibility.

His thoughts are extremely relevant today as press freedom in India is currently mired in propaganda for the ruling regime. Media ethics has been compromised by efforts to turn readers and audiences into collaborators of power.

Gandhi described the specific issue he was responding to that caused him consternation:

> 'I feel ashamed at the fact that today people have got into the habit of reading dirty and undesirable things. Such newspapers are widely circulated. I read about an incident at Rewari. A newspaper published a report saying that the members of the Meo community killed all the Hindus, set fire to their houses and looted their property and cattle. I was shocked to know that the Meos had indulged in such terrible things. The next day there was no information about Rewari in the papers. It was all a cooked-up story. I wondered how that news about Rewari ever came to be published in the paper. I would like to say that the man who wrote about the Rewari incident should give an explanation. He must explain whether he had written that story on wrong information or it was deliberate mischief. He is guilty of great crime before God.'[44]

Spreading misinformation either by publishing unverified facts or motivated by a political agenda is a crime, particularly in situations of strife. Journalists indulging in such activities are accountable to their job as well as to the people.

Manu, in her diary entry on 9 October, writes that Gandhi's cough was worsening. His private physician, the renowned naturopath Dr Dinshaw K. Mehta (who first met Gandhi in 1932) advised milk. Gandhi was given an enema to pass stool. Saifuddin Kitchlew, the Congress member from Amritsar who was back from a visit to Kashmir, informed him that Sheikh Abdullah had reiterated in his speeches, that among Kashmir's options of remaining independent, joining Pakistan or joining India, the one of joining Pakistan must be rejected due to the country's policies. This prompted the Pakistan government to hinder the supply of petrol and food grains by blocking the routes under Pakistani control. India sent the supplies by air.[45] The next day, Gandhi's throat condition improved. He took a walk with Horace Alexander.[46]

Self-Hating Hindus

In the prayer meeting on 18 October, Gandhi touched upon the question of languages, and the different political histories in India between Urdu and English:

> 'Urdu was born out of this fusion [between Muslim invaders and the local Hindus] and it acquired a distinct form as in course of time they crammed Arabic and Persian words into the language. They even put a new garb on it. Its grammar also comes from those languages. That is not the case with Hindustani whose grammar belongs to this soil. Whatever Persian words there are in Urdu have been there for ages. It is not for us to pick out those words and remove them from the language. The people who came as invaders settled down here and adopted local customs. *I think if we hate them now it will be as good as hating ourselves.* As far as the English language is concerned it was different. The British came here to build an empire. They

> had no intention of settling here. *They never came to belong to India.* They always considered themselves outsiders here . . . Later they also introduced the English language. Slowly they gave it a particular shape. Nothing happened to English similar to what happened in the case of Urdu. Urdu came into being from Avadhi or other languages spoken at that time. But that is not the case with English. Now the British rule has ended in India. But what will be our fate if the English language continues to dominate us and we cannot carry on our administration without that language?'[47] [Emphasis mine]

There was a clear distinction of motives between the Mughals and the British. The Muslims introduced a double transformation where their own culture and that of the Hindus produced a shared language of expression. This common language is part of our historical selves and to hate the Muslim for it would be an act of denial and a symptom of self-hate. But even though the British did not believe in such cultural integration, English took over as the dominant language. Gandhi's worries were ironic, as he was known as a fluent speaker of the language.

On 21 October, Gandhi said something to describe the culture of violence around him. It had an uncanny resemblance with what he would face on 30 January:

> 'All that I wish to say is that we have got into the habit of killing. It is just the beginning of our independence, and right from now such are the thoughts that have come to possess us. We want to kill simply because we possess a revolver. It is like a person aiming at a flying bird and killing it. Great hunter that he is, he aims at a flying bird.'[48]

On 31 October, Gandhi spoke at the prayer meeting of the rich among all communities, including upper-caste Hindus who managed to leave their homes during the genocide and found an occupation to maintain their livelihood, while the poorer sections found themselves trapped with no such luxuries:

> 'I found in Noakhali that the rich had run away from there, leaving the poor behind. The villages in that area are full of people whom we, in our foolishness, call untouchables. As I have toured the area, I know that the people there are very much in distress. The women in that place had even forgotten to wear bangles or apply sindoor. Even among the people who have come here from the Punjab and elsewhere I have found that the people with financial resources somehow carry on some occupation or the other. They have money and they also acquire friends. But what can the poor do? Where can they go?'[49]

Gandhi publicly spelt out every aspect of the crisis. He maintained proximity with the people as he visited the camps in Delhi and in his interactions with them in his prayer gatherings. This material access gave him enough scope to have a first-hand understanding of the situation. On 2 November, Gandhi asked the bewildering existential question on behalf of his people:

> 'Right now people in the refugee camps are shivering in cold. They ask why they have been treated thus. They want to know why their Government did this to them. What was their fault that they have to face such hardships?'[50]

This was an unanswerable question. No matter what the leaders of the Congress and the Muslim League (and their spokespersons, apologists and the theoreticians on their side) say to justify their moves and decide on partition, for the beleaguered people who suddenly for no fault of theirs lost everything in the blink of an eye, all the political leaders involved in the game of chess were to blame.

Speaking at the prayer gathering on 5 November, Gandhi praised Sheikh Abdullah for putting up a 'brave fight'[51] against the Afridis and other tribesmen (about 2000 of them had invaded Kashmir on 23 October and indulged in loot, arson and murder).[52] However, Gandhi wished Abdullah had fought them non-violently, prepared to die rather than kill. Gandhi lamented that he was no longer powerful enough to dictate to others on a method that had failed:

> 'In his time Mr Churchill could not say, but today, Sheikh Abdullah and the army which has gone there can tell me that my non-violence has failed in Delhi where acts of barbarism are being committed and what they are doing is not barbaric. And I must admit that they have a right to say that . . . [Today] I am helpless.'[53]

On Diwali, 12 November, Gandhi spoke to refugees at the Kurukshetra Camp (more than 170 kilometres northwest of Delhi) live from the All India Radio studios. This was, he told his audience, the second time that he was on radio, after his experience in October 1931 during the Round Table Conference in London where he made a broadcast to America on the Columbia Broadcasting Service (CBS) from Kingsley Hall. He shared his concerns with them:

> 'I was distressed when I heard that over two lakhs of refugees had arrived at Kurukshetra and more were pouring in. The moment the news came to me, I longed to be with you but I could not get away at once from Delhi because the Congress Working Committee meetings were being held and my presence was required . . . Yours is not an ordinary camp where it is possible for everyone to know each other. Yours is really a city and your only bond with your co-refugees is your suffering. I was sorry to learn that there is not that co-operation with authority or with your neighbours that there ought to be in order to make the Camp a success.'[54]

Gandhi advised them to cultivate community kitchens.[55]

At the important AICC meeting on 15 November, Gandhi spoke sternly to the Congress members and made his apprehensions clear:

> 'The Congress is held responsible for whatever happens today. The situation has changed since August 15. I am leaving out of consideration what happened *before* that date. I do not wish to hear what part you played in the events that have happened since August 15. I have not the right to sit here. I have much work to do outside this hall. That is why I had requested that I might be allowed to have my say and then take your leave.'[56] [Emphasis mine]

Gandhi meant to tell the Congress they had the chance to redeem past mistakes by honestly taking charge of the human crisis at present. He made it clear what he had in mind regarding Congress's role in the coming days:

> 'Though it is not true of the whole of India, yet there are many places today where a Muslim cannot live in security. There are miscreants who will kill him or throw him out of a running train for no reason other than that he is a Muslim. There are several such instances. I will not be satisfied with your saying that there was no help for it or that you had no part in it. We cannot absolve ourselves of our responsibility for what has happened.'[57]

As if reading the minds of the members, Gandhi did not leave anything unsaid:

> 'You may blame the Muslim League for what has happened and say that the two-nation theory is at the root of all this evil and that it was the Muslim League that sowed the seed of this poison; nevertheless I say that we would be betraying the Hindu religion if we did evil because others had done it.'[58]

Gandhi reminded them that India must not 'copy'[59] the misdeeds of their new neighbour and must not get provoked by the warring gestures of Pakistan. He made them feel privileged about Nehru's international stature and indicated that they should strengthen his arms:

> '[Nehru] is respected outside India as one of the world's greatest statesmen. Many Europeans have told me that the world has not known such a high-minded statesman. I have known Americans who hold Jawaharlal in higher esteem than they hold President Truman.'[60]

Gandhi next turned his attention to the two Hindu political groups in India and shared his precise apprehensions:

> 'The mission of the Hindu Mahasabha is to reform Hindu society, to raise the moral level of the people. How then can the Sabha advocate the compulsory evacuation of all Muslims from India, as I am told it does? . . . I hear many things about the Rashtriya Swayamsevak Sangh. I have heard it said that the Sangh is at the root of all this mischief. Let us not forget that public opinion is a far more potent force than a thousand swords. Hinduism cannot be saved by orgies of murder. You are now a free people. You have to preserve this freedom. You can do so if you are humane and brave and ever-vigilant, or else a day will come when you will rue the folly which made this lovely prize slip from your hands.'[61]

Gandhi told the Congress in his last meeting with them that they had to measure bravery with humaneness and vigilance, not murder, if they wanted to enjoy the fruits of freedom. It remained Gandhi's parting message to the grand old party he was once a member of.

On 28 November, Guru Nanak's birth anniversary, Gandhi first spoke at the special function organized by the Sikhs, where he was accompanied by Sheikh Abdullah. Later at the prayer meeting, Gandhi spoke about Nanak:

> '[The] Sikhs have a duty to consider all the rest as their brethren. Guru Nanak taught no other thing. He even went to Mecca and has written quite a lot [about communal harmony]. There are many such references in the *Guru Granthsaheb.* What did Guru Govind do? Many Muslims were his disciples and he even killed some people to accommodate them and protect them. He never killed anyone just for the sake of saving a Sikh.'[62]

The Neighbour and Anti-History

On 2 January in the New Year, in a fragment of a letter that Gandhi wrote to an unknown addressee, you find these unforgettable lines:

> 'Man today is afraid of man, afraid of his neighbour. How can I then talk about national issues? We deliberately bring suffering on ourselves, deceive ourselves. No one can harm another. In my view man is himself the cause of his sufferings. This city which is the metropolis of the country has the appearance of a dead city. No one trusts anyone. Such peace as one finds is to be attributed to the fear of the police. Why is it that the freedom achieved through non-violence is sought to be sustained by violence? I have been searching my heart. I find despair there. Maybe it was the will of God that I should witness this day.'[63]

This is a sea-in-a-pitcher kind of passage.

The primacy of concern on the destruction of neighbourhoods and fear of the neighbour would have resonated with Buber and Levinas. Like these philosophers, Gandhi posed the ethical question *outside* the universal categories of class (Marxism) and the individual (liberalism). The figure of the neighbour that Gandhi alludes to in the above passage (as well as in *Hind Swaraj*) comes from the Judeo–Christian injunction 'love thy neighbour'. Levinas extracts an open phenomenological reading of the injunction. In *Otherwise than Being*, Levinas writes that the 'exposure' to the neighbour is marked by 'disinterestedness, proximity, obsession by the neighbor, an obsession despite oneself, that is, a pain'.[64] In other words, the neighbour doesn't let the relationship *be* from the moment of inception. The encounter is unstable, where lack of interest or its excess is part of the process of familiarity. Later, Levinas adds, 'the obsession by the neighbor is stronger than negativity.'[65] It is difficult to allow historical perceptions (and judgements) to colour the encounter with a definite meaning. We are thrown into an open possibility and response vis-à-vis the neighbour that is dictated by the neighbour's presence and lies prior to our judgement. The discomforts of identity and its relation with others are open to contrary possibilities. It is true that peaceful possibilities turn out to be exceptions in history. But the brief histories of peace are seldom written, or find place in the historiography of strife.

As Gandhi wrote in *Hind Swaraj*, 'History is really a record of every interruption of the even working of the force of love or of the soul'.[66] The force of the soul is interrupted by history. The politics of ahimsa, (and its corollaries, Satyagraha, non-cooperation, friendship, love, brotherhood) based on soul-force, is meant to interrupt, in turn, the history of conflict. It is, to use Derrida's phrase, 'messianic interruption'.[67] The everyday history of love is not to be found in the record books. Gandhi's politics of Satyagraha is an interruption of the old politics of conflict and enmity with a new politics of love and non-violence. It remains silenced by history, but is capable of reasserting its lost dignity. The Gandhian moment during partition is a profoundly anti-historic one. It tells us that non-violence can't match history because it can only—bravely, but inadequately—respond to what history destroys conclusively.

We enter the story of the devastated neighbourhood comprising Hindus and Muslims in Noakhali *after* genocide has already taken place. Our beginning of understanding is not their beginning. There is an origin that may not have been pointing (by a perverse, consequentialist logic) to a historical moment interrupted by communal politics leading to genocide.

Ajay Skaria paid attention to Gandhi's use of the word *itihaas*[68] in *Hind Swaraj*'s original Gujarati version. In Chapter XVII, the Reader asked the Editor if there is 'any historical evidence'[69] of Gandhi's idea of Satyagraha or soul-force. In response, the Editor made a distinction between *itihaas*, meaning "thus it happened" in Gujarati, and history 'which concerns the doings of emperors' . . . where 'we find only the noise of the world'[70]. Skaria clarifies: 'The focus in this argument is on happening: if history cannot take note of satyagraha, this is because satyagraha is a happening'[71], whereas history is all about the noise of strife.

Itihaas is the other history, whose origins *within history* lies somewhere else. The historicity of *itihaas*, rooted in the everyday life of the neighbourhood, is a departure from the historicity of history, thus opening up a possibility of another history within historicist history[72].

To return to Gandhi's passage, for him there was no other 'national issue' worth considering and discussing other than the fear of the neighbour, and the mass fear that has overtaken neighbourhoods. There is no nation worth its existence if neighbourhoods have been trampled by marauding mobs. A fearful nation is a petrified nation where the blood runs cold. Even the semblance of peace is maintained by fear of the police. It is necessary to understand and tackle the roots of this fear by engaging with modern thinkers on the subject.

In the fifth section of *Civilization and Its Discontents*, Sigmund Freud writes that the Christian injunction that makes an ideal demand of civilized life, 'Thou shalt love thy neighbour as thyself', is older than Christianity. Freud dismisses the possibility of loving the neighbour by using the argumentative technique of subtraction. The neighbour doesn't deserve your love if there is nothing special about him. Since the neighbour is a stranger, he can't be at par with your family and friends. Though Freud skips the question of where does the friend appear from. Hence, the 'universal love' that the neighbour can at best receive is 'a modicum of love'.[73] In *Hind Swaraj*, Gandhi had made a clear distinction between the '*immediate neighbours*' and 'every individual' in the world. The neighbour represents the figure of a fraternity that cancels universality. Levinas calls it 'exclusive singularity'.[74]

Freud next draws a historical picture of the hostile neighbour: 'Whoever calls to mind the horrors of the migration of the peoples, the incursions of the Huns, or of the people known as the Mongols under Genghiz Khan and Tamerlane, the conquest of Jerusalem by the pious Crusaders, or indeed the horrors of the Great War, will be obliged to acknowledge this fact.'[75] History can always be successfully summoned as an argument against neighbourly fraternity from either side. Historical hostilities continue to persist and dictate national and international politics. These hostilities have proven way more powerful than Karl Marx's thesis on proletarian revolution. In his book *Violence*, Žižek juxtaposes the Judeo–Christian injunction of 'love thy neighbour' with Freud's and Lacan's notion where the figure of the neighbour 'resists universality' by its '*inhuman* dimension',[76] by being a figure of hostility. In this context, Howard Caygill has pointed out that Levinas's ethical principles crack when he came to consider non-Abrahamic Asians as prying hordes of intrusive migrants in Europe who lie outside 'holy history'.[77] Such people are not just others but *outsiders*. When it came to the Israeli–Palestinian encounter, Levinas cryptically said: 'There are people who are wrong.'[78] Caygill finds this shift that 'reduces ethics to the problem of knowledge'[79] disturbing. Caygill reminds us that the roots are present in Levinas's *Otherwise than Being* where he connects the State of Israel to the Jewish people, thus accepting the idea of 'political Zionism that the Jews constitute a *Volk*'.[80] The justification of the nation is bound to be mired in the idea of the enemy and war. It is not enough to reject the universalism and secular nationalism of Marxism. The tougher task is to imagine a world of neighbourhoods without nation.

Freud goes ahead to make an important point against the conceit of neighbourly love in the Christian West. Invoking the massacres of Jews in the Middle Ages, Freud writes that despite St Paul's proclamation of brotherly love, the 'extreme intolerance of Christianity towards those left outside it was an inevitable consequence.'[81] The example that intrigued Freud was that the desire to establish the 'new, communist culture in Russia should find psychological support in the persecution of the bourgeois'.[82] Every idea of brotherhood—ethnic, religious, national, ideological—in the name of universalism simultaneously names its others. *This is why the genuinely fraternal is not universal.*

Freud thinks that despite the 'methods' used to encourage fraternal love, the whole project runs contrary to human nature, and therefore he believes that 'for all the effort invested in it . . . this cultural endeavour has not achieved very much.'[83]

Freud does not discuss guilt in this context, but picks it up separately in the eighth and last section of the book. In the beginning, Freud clarifies that his intention in this section is 'to present the sense of guilt as the most important problem in the development of civilization and to show how the price we pay for cultural progress is a loss of happiness, arising from a heightened sense of guilt.'[84] Basing the idea of the super-ego as an authority on individual selves, Freud considers guilt and remorse as effects of human aggression, expressed or unexpressed. Guilt and remorse are proof of conscience.

This leads Freud to the question of ethics 'as an attempt at therapy'.[85] And as a way to deal with the 'greatest obstacle to civilisation'[86] which is human aggression, we are back to the Christian commandment. Freud does not deal with collective guilt from collective violence. But if communities don't follow the ethical commandment and engage in violence, it shall return as neurosis and therapy. Recall the various instances of people who took part in the brutal violence in Noakhali, Bihar and Calcutta confessing to their crime (and their guilt) to Gandhi. Also, despite animosity and suspicion, people everywhere attended Gandhi's prayer meetings in large numbers. Those people had found a soothing way to deal with their fear, guilt and neurosis. Gandhi's prayer meetings were a historic demonstration of mass spiritual therapy.

Internal Rot

Gandhi shared an unexpected decision in the prayer meeting on 12 January: to undergo his fifteenth fast after breakfast the next day. He said: 'I have been brooding over it for the last three days. The final conclusion has flashed upon me and it makes me happy.'[87] It was particularly surprising as he had met Nehru and Patel a few minutes before the prayer meeting, but had not said anything to them.[88] His aim, as he put it, was 'a reunion of hearts of all communities brought about without any outside pressure.'[89] After the prayer meeting, Manu wrote in her diary: 'Bapu has been here for four months. The internal rot is terrible. Sardar and Jawahar have differences. Bapu and Sardar have differences.'[90] On 13 January, Tagore's *Ekla Chalo Re* was sung. Gandhi explained its meaning to the crowd: 'The song these girls sang was composed by Gurudev. We sang it during our tours in Noakhali. A man walking alone calls to others to come and join him. But if no one comes and it is dark, the Poet says, the man should walk alone because God is already with him.'[91] Later, Manu mentioned in her diary that the issue of India's obligation to send Rs 55 crore from the colonial fund that was due to Pakistan was discussed at Birla House. The money was sent the next day. On 15 January, on Gandhi's third day of the fast, Manu wrote in her diary: 'A man made of a fist full of bones is undergoing an ordeal to establish unity for the benefit of humanity.'[92] The fact that Gandhi continued his fast even after India sent the money to Pakistan shows that it was not his primary motive. On the evening of 18 January, Gandhi broke his fast. It was later learnt that Nehru had secretly fasted with him.[93]

Ten Minutes Late

On 20 January, in the middle of Gandhi's speech at the prayer meeting, there was a sudden bomb explosion. Gandhi thought it was some military training going on nearby. To a visibly shaken Manu, he said, 'Will you be scared by something so little?'[94] Gandhi resumed his speech and finished it.

Later, it turned out to be a conspiracy hatched principally by Hindu right-wing extremists (mostly from Maharashtra) to assassinate Gandhi. The explosion was meant to divert attention, while a man named Digambar Badge was supposed to throw a hand grenade at Gandhi. Badge's courage failed him. One of the conspirators, Madanlal Pahwa, was arrested, while the others—Nathuram Godse, Narayana Apte, Vishnu Karkare, Gopal Godse, Digambar Badge and Shankar Kistayya—escaped in a waiting cab.[95] In his statement in court on 8 November 1948, Nathuram Godse denied that he or other members of the gang were behind Pahwa's failed effort.[96] Whether he was present at Birla House on the 20th or not, Godse successfully executed the assassination of Gandhi a few days later.

Godse acknowledged that he had been part of demonstrations against Gandhi in Delhi, along with Apte, and had taken out a procession of refugees, interrupting the prayer meeting at Bhangi Colony.[97] He believed that the 'real motive'[98] behind Gandhi's last fast was not Hindu–Muslim unity but to make India pay Rs 55 crore to Pakistan. For Godse, this was the third significant moment (he says, 'period') in Gandhi's political career.[99] Godse found this altruistic gesture intolerable and decided to kill Gandhi in 'the purest interest of our nation.'[100] In Godse's understanding, ahimsa would lead to 'the emasculation of the Hindu Community', and in order to 'counteract this evil'[101] he formed a band of propagandists. His project was the retrieval of Hindu masculinity. He clarified however that more than ahimsa, he and his men were more opposed to Gandhi's 'bias' towards Muslims, which, they felt, was 'prejudicial and detrimental to the Hindu community and its interests.'[102]

These views echo that of his political mentor, Savarkar, not just on Hindus and Muslims, but on their common quarrel with Gandhi.

The two had first met in a gathering in London on 24 October 1909 to celebrate *Vijaya Dashami* (Dussehra) where Savarkar, it was reported, 'delivered a spirited speech on the great excellence of the *Ramayana* and said that every Indian should realize the significance of the fact that *Vijaya Dashami* is preceded by *Navratri* (*Roza*).'[103] It is not clear if Savarkar connects the nine-day fast that precedes Dussehra with the fasting of Ramzan that precedes Eid.

During his discourses on the *Gita* on 4 March 1926, Gandhi mentioned meeting Savarkar and others in London who did not agree with his interpretation of the *Gita* and the Ramayana[104]. They met a second time when Gandhi paid a visit to an ailing Savarkar at his home in Ratnagiri on 1 March 1927, where they discussed shuddhi and untouchability. Registering the many differences between their opinions, Gandhi most generously called Savarkar 'a lover of truth and as one who would lay down his life for the sake of truth.'[105] It is instructive that between 1927 and 1930 'Savarkar wrote twenty-three articles in Marathi commenting on current affairs, almost all of them targeting Gandhi and Muslims.'[106] In one such article titled 'Way to Freedom', written on 11 August 1927 a (little over five months after Gandhi met him), Savarkar indulges in the polemics of ridicule:

> 'Well, enough of this demoralization of the nation, becoming only of a sworn enemy of the nation, under the glib garb of self-sacrifice, atmabala, Satyagraha, ahimsa, satya et al. enough of this mockery of politics. Enough of this Gandhian confusion!'[107]

Savarkar was speaking more for himself. He was clearly confused by Gandhi's politics. He exhorted his readers to believe that Gandhi's politics of truth was the antithesis of politics and detrimental to the interests of the nation. Savarkar's gesture against Gandhi's generosity is legitimate by the rules of ideology. The problem is that he was unwilling and incapable of understanding any language of politics that did not emanate from the logic of violence.

As India was heading towards a partitioned freedom, in a conversation with American vice consul Thurston on 8 February 1944, Savarkar crudely dismissed Gandhi's policies as 'dreamy nonsense' and Gandhi's philosophy of non-violence as 'stupid'[108].

In his statement to the court, Godse mentioned after being with the RSS for several years, he joined the Hindu Mahasabha just when Savarkar was elected its President[109]. Godse however did not share anything about his ideological affinity with Savarkar in court. He was busy refuting Badge's testimony about Savarkar's complicity in Gandhi's murder. He said the insinuation that Savarkar instigated and blessed them for the task was 'pure concoction'[110]. Godse highlighted his current differences with Savarkar to impress upon the court that the prosecutor's impression on him being 'a mere tool in the hands' of Savarkar was untrue[111].

Godse assumed that by murdering Gandhi he would secure the interests of his community. He acknowledged that Gandhi had unselfishly undergone 'sufferings for the sake of the nation', and brought about 'an awakening in the minds of the people.'[112] But it pained him to believe that Gandhi 'was not honest enough to acknowledge the defeat and failure of his principle of non-violence on all sides.'[113] Godse seems to have either not read or pretended ignorance about anything Gandhi said since the Calcutta riots began in August 1946. Fanatics like Godse suffer from tunnel vision in their thinking. The impassively unrepentant face in the courtroom photographs and the banal and noxious statements in court make Godse resemble a man whose personhood shrinks into a shadow.

In his critical reading of Attenborough's *Gandhi*, Salman Rushdie made a sharp political observation on the scene of Gandhi's murder. Rushdie objected to how Godse was 'not differentiated from the crowd', which can make the audience believe 'he *represents* the crowd—that people turned against Gandhi, that the mob threw up a killer who did his work; that Godse was "one lone nut" . . . But Godse was *not* representative of the crowd. He did *not* work alone. And the killing was a political, not a mystical act.'[114] This is an important reminder. Godse's appearance on screen can't be sudden. He was not fiction. His political associations were an integral part of his ideological makeup and it led him to justify his crime.

The most interesting point—at once ethical and political—that remains is that it is possible for all critics of Gandhi across political ideologies to articulate or justify their problems with Gandhi only through the radical nature of his non-violent movement. To make non-violence central to a political movement with no equivalent parallels (in terms of scale and context) in modern history differentiates Gandhi's politics from all leading political movements around the world.

The questions posed to Gandhi were never posed (and will never be posed) to a Lenin, and those political leaders of the twentieth century who were not against violence. Gandhi made it possible for the world to ask demanding questions on the strengths and shortcomings of non-violence. When he put forth the idea, it evoked laughter from the colonial regime and his own people. To Gandhi's credit, he ensured, by example, that even those who dismissed him could not scoff at the idea.

The next day, 21 January, at the prayer meeting, Gandhi apologized to the crowd for being ten minutes late.[115]

Gandhi with Abha and others during his visit to the Mosque of Khwaja Qutbuddin, Mehrauli, Delhi, on 27 January 1948

Gandhi along with Manu and other associates visited the Dargah of Qutbuddin Aulia at Mehrauli to take part in the festival of Urs. Manu notes in her diary:

'No one had the slightest hope that there would be a celebration of amity at such a scale. Miscreants have broken the marble latticed windows of Moti Masjid.'[116] Addressing the gathering, Gandhi said,

> 'Several days ago I had heard that it might not be possible to hold the Urs at Mehrauli as in the previous years. Had it been so I would have been deeply distressed. I request you—Hindus, Sikhs and Muslims who have come here with cleansed hearts—to take a vow at this holy place that you will never allow strife to raise its head, but will live in amity, united as friends and brothers... I have seen life. This is nothing new. Even now somewhere or other fighting is going on.'[117]

Gandhi's presence and appeal at the Urs is the reiteration of lived social relations. Even at the worst moment of communal strife, people must try to recover the spaces of cultural fraternity that were being ruthlessly erased.

On 30 January, Gandhi was yet again late by ten minutes for the evening prayer.

There was a moment of banter between Gandhi and the two young women close to him, Abha and Manu. Manu told Gandhi his watch was feeling neglected.[118] Gandhi replied that he did not need a watch in the company of his 'time-keepers'.[119] 'But you do not look at the time-keepers'[120] came the rejoinder, and Gandhi laughed. They cleared the steps, walking towards the prayer meeting with Manu to Gandhi's left and Abha to his right. Gandhi's mind was still stuck on time, 'It is your fault that I am ten minutes late . . . It irks me if I am late for prayers even by a minute.'[121]

The prayer meeting remained incomplete. Godse fired three shots at Gandhi from point-blank range with his Beretta M1934.[122]

Gandhi breathed his last at 5.17 p.m. He was ten minutes late for death.

Acknowledgements

In the winter of 2004, I submitted my PhD thesis at the Centre for Political Studies in JNU, comparing Gandhi's and Nehru's ideas of nationalism. I presented a paper comparing Gandhi and Emmanuel Levinas at the French Cultural Centre's 'Annual Series of Lectures on French Thought' (February 2004). My next paper on Gandhi was at the '*Hind Swaraj* Centenary International Seminar', organized by the Council for Social Development, in February 2010. I presented a paper on Gandhi in Noakhali for a workshop on 'Rethinking Power in Modern India' at the Centre of Political Studies in JNU in April 2012.

In early 1995, after my parents retired from their respective jobs as employees of the Northeast Frontier Railway in Maligaon (Assam), we shifted to Sodepur, a nondescript town on the outskirts of Kolkata. While reading Manu Gandhi and Nirmal Kumar Bose's Noakhali diaries for my 2012 paper, I came to know that the town my parents lived in was Gandhi's important station during his 1946–47 sojourn. In my next visit home from JNU, I visited the Khadi Pratisthan Ashram in Sodepur (near the Sodepur railway station), which was built by Satish Chandra Dasgupta in 1927. The caretaker was an old Dalit man who had seen Gandhi as a child.

During my first trip to Ahmedabad in April 2024, I visited the Sabarmati Ashram just before the renovations began. The courtyard, the simple tools in the kitchen, the spinning wheel, the windows, the birds and the Sabarmati River cast a moving spell.

I am grateful to Ramesh for introducing me to Emmanuel Levinas during my MPhil. It helped me understand the Judeo–Christian roots of Gandhi's political ethics.

In a conversation below a tree on a street corner in JNU, Avijit Pathak explained why Gandhi would often retreat to the mountains when facing a difficult question. Listening to Tridip Suhrud at the bar in India International Centre (IIC), I could measure the tone of Gandhi's life. Ashis Nandy's insights on Gandhi are always unexpected and revealing.

I am grateful to Tridip for sharing the unpublished manuscript of the second collection of Manu's diaries (1946–48) before it got published in October 2024. I am also grateful to V. Ramaswamy for sharing the unpublished English translation of Nirmal Kumar Bose's Noakhali testimonies. I owe Nikhil Chakravarty's historic article on the Calcutta Killings to Ramnik Mohan.

I tend to write fast by habit and temperament. Abir told me not to hurry with the writing. I kept his wise suggestion and adjusted myself between the hare and the tortoise.

I thank Ananya for speaking to me with clarity early one morning from Ghent on Gandhi's *Brahmacharya* experiment. I also thank Trina for sharing her views from Kolkata on Gandhi's connection with Indian patriarchy.

I am very indebted to my endorsers: Talal Asad, Ashis Nandy, Judith M. Brown, Howard Caygill, Tridip Suhrud and Faisal Devji. Their reading of the manuscript has added much value to it. Their words of appreciation are my life's takeaway.

I owe a warm thanks to Premanka, my editor at Penguin Random House India. He showed instant keenness on the idea of the book and helped me pass the litmus test of convincing the editorial team about the manuscript. I heartily thank all the editors at Penguin who welcomed the book. I must thank Milee for clearing the way for the proposal. Neeraj, my cover designer, chose the most expressive image of Gandhi that reflects the spirit of the book. The overall design is most elegant. Aninda and Cynthia were alert and meticulous copy editors of this manuscript that is full of twists and turns. I also thank my proofreader Devaki Khanna. I thank S. Padmanabhan, the knowledgeable and helpful librarian at the National Gandhi Museum and Library near Raj Ghat.

To friends, for conversation and time: Bidhan, Mohinder, Prasanta, Babu, Rajarshi, Vanya, Toy, Navdeep, Avinash, Nidhi, Kshipra, Urvi and always, Richa. I must thank my quiet little house in Masjid Moth. Its ambiance and windows help me reproduce my silences, my days and nights, into words.

Notes

Preface

1 *Collected Works of Mahatma Gandhi*, Vol. 59, The Director, The Publication Division, New Delhi, 1974, pp. 61-62.

Introduction: 'Rift in the Lute'

1 *Collected Works of Mahatma Gandhi*, Vol. 85, The Director, The Publication Division, New Delhi, 1982, p. 186 (Hereafter referred to as CWMG). Source: Gandhi Heritage Portal (gandhiheritageportal.org)
2 *CWMG*, Vol. 8, 1962, p. 373.
3 Ishtiaq Ahmed, *Jinnah: His Successes, Failures and Role in History*, Penguin Random House India (Gurgaon, 2020), p. 350.
4 Ibid.
5 Anwesha Roy, *Making Peace, Making Riots Communalism and Communal Violence, Bengal 1940–1947*, Cambridge University Press (New Delhi, 2018), p. 137.
6 Pyarelal, *Mahatma Gandhi: The Last Phase* Vol. 1, Navajivan Publishing House (Ahmedabad, 1956), p. 212.
7 Ibid.
8 Ibid. Pyarelal explained the analogy: 'To the Congress it offered a common Centre, though in an attenuated form, and

"freedom" of choice to Provinces to form groups or not. To the Muslim League it held out the prospect of 'Muslim zones', to be formed in the north-west and the north-east of India by making it obligatory on the representatives of the Provinces to sit in Sections to settle the Provincial constitutions. To the Princes it offered release from Paramountcy which was not to be transferred to the successor Government. To the Sikhs it held out the prospect of preserving intact the integrity of their homeland' [Ibid].

9 Ayesha Jalal, *The Sole Spokesman: Jinnah, the Muslim League and the Demand for Pakistan*, Cambridge University (New York, 1994), p. 189.
10 Ibid., p. 245.
11 Ishtiaq Ahmed, *Jinnah: His Successes, Failures and Role in History*, Penguin Random House India (Gurgaon, 2020), p. 352.
12 Ibid., p. 357.
13 Ibid., p. 358.
14 Ibid., p. 359.
15 Jawaharlal Nehru, *Selected Works of Jawaharlal Nehru*, Vol. 15, Orient Longman (New Delhi, 1982), p. 196.
16 Ibid.
17 Ibid., p. 234.
18 Ibid., p. 235.
19 Ibid., p. 242.
20 Ibid.
21 Ibid., p. 243.
22 Abul Kalam Azad, *India Wins Freedom*, Orient Longman (Madras, 1988), p. 164.

*Here, it is important to mention that Kalam's quote of Nehru's statement that Nehru said that the Congress would enter the Constituent Assembly 'completely unfettered by agreements and free to meet all situations as they arise' (*India Wins Freedom*, p. 164) is not supported by his complete statement at the press conference as published in *Selected Works of Jawaharlal Nehru Volume 15* (1982). All quotes of that statement, including Ishtiaq Ahmed's, are taken from Azad's book. Gandhi also mentions 'Maulana's letters' in that letter. [*CWMG*, Vol. 85, pp. 5*n*, 6]. I could not find any primary source that carries that statement.

23 Ibid., p. 165.

24 *CWMG*, Vol. 85, 1982, p. 5.

25 Ibid., p. 6.

26 *CWMG*, Vol. 84, 1981, p. 122.

27 A. G. Noorani, 'Review: Collapse of the Cabinet Mission's Plan', *Economic and Political Weekly*, Vol. 14, No. 47 (24 November 1979), p. 1918.

28 Ishtiaq Ahmed, 'The 1947 Partition of India: A Paradigm for Pathological Politics in India and Pakistan', Asian Ethnicity, Vol. 3, No. 1, March 2002, link: http://www.sacw.net/partition/IshtiaqAhmed2002.html

29 Ahmed, Ishtiaq, *Jinnah: His Successes, Failures and Role in History*, Penguin Random House, New Delhi, 2020, p. 354

30 Ishtiaq Ahmed, *Jinnah: His Successes, Failures and Role in History*, Penguin Random House India (Gurgaon, 2020), p. 354.

31 Ayesha Jalal, *The Sole Spokesman: Jinnah, the Muslim League and the demand for Pakistan*, Cambridge University, New York, 1994, p. 186.

32 Ibid.

33 Mohammad Ali Jinnah, *Jinnah: Speeches and Statements 1947–1948*, Oxford University Press (Oxford, 2000), p. 117.

34 Ibid.

35 Ibid., p. 118.

36 Jawaharlal Nehru, *The Discovery of India*, Oxford University Press (New Delhi, 1964), p. 50.

37 Homi Bhabha, (ed.), *Narrating the Nation*, Routledge (London, 1990), p. 1.

38 Jawaharlal Nehru, *The Discovery of India*, Oxford University Press (New Delhi, 1964), p. 62.

39 Mohammad Ali Jinnah, *Jinnah: Speeches and Statements 1947–1948*, Oxford University Press (Oxford, 2000), p. 148.

40 Ibid., p. 146.

41 M. K. Gandhi, Mohammad Ali Jinnah, (preface) C. Rajagopalachari, *Gandhi–Jinnah Talks: Text of Correspondence and Other Relevant Matter*, The *Hindustan Times* (New Delhi, July–October, 1944), p. 9.

42 Ibid., p. 11.

43 Ishtiaq Ahmed, *Jinnah: His Successes, Failures and Role in History*, Penguin Random House India (New Delhi, 2020), p. 284.

44 Wavell, *The Viceroy's Journal*, (ed.) Penderel Moon, Oxford University Press (Delhi, 1973), p. 91.

45 In July 1943, Lord Irwin (then Lord Halifax) told Wavell, Gandhi was not 'a practical person to deal with' (Wavell, *The Viceroy's Journal*, p. 14).

46 Ibid., p. 91.

47 Faisal Devji, *Muslim Zion: Pakistan as a Political Idea*, Harvard University Press (Cambridge, Massachusetts, 2013), p. 24.

48 The Lahore resolution 1) categorically rejected the federal scheme enacted by the Government of India Act 1935, 2) demanded that any revised plan must seek approval of the Muslims, 3) urged the formation of autonomously governable units in the north-western and north-eastern zones of British India where Muslims had numerical majority and 4) 'tacitly'

proposed, according to Ishtiaq Ahmed, 'a hostage theory to ensure that minorities are not mistreated by the respective states.' Ishtiaq Ahmed, *Jinnah: His Successes, Failures and Role in History*, Penguin Random House India (Gurgaon, 2020), pp. 216–17.

49 M. K. Gandhi, Mohammad Ali Jinnah, (preface) C. Rajagopalachari, *Gandhi–Jinnah Talks: Text of Correspondence and Other Relevant Matter*, The Hindustan Times (New Delhi, July–October, 1944), p. 12.

50 Sebastian C. H. Kim, *In Search of Identity: Debates on Religious Conversion in India*, Oxford University Press (New Delhi, 2003), p. 29.

51 Laura Dudley Jenkins, *Religious Freedom and Mass Conversion in India*, University of Pennsylvania Press (Philadelphia, 2019), p. 48.

52 M. K. Gandhi, (ed.) Anthony Parel. *Hind Swaraj*, Cambridge Text in Modern Politics, Cambridge University Press, 1990, p. Iiii.

Gandhi writes in the *Hind Swaraj*: 'What do you think could have been the intention of those far-seeing ancestors of ours who established Shevetbindu Rameshwar in the South, Juggernaut in the South-East, and Hardwar in the North as places of pilgrimage?... [They] saw India was one undivided land and so made by nature. They, therefore, argued that it must be one nation. Arguing thus, they established holy places in various parts of India, and fired the people with an idea of nationality in a manner unknown in other parts of the world.' Phrases like "undivided land" and "one nation" are politically loaded terms coming from a nationalist of the modern era.

[M. K. Gandhi, (ed.) Parel, Anthony, *Hind Swaraj*, Cambridge Text in Modern Politics, Cambridge University Press, 1990, p. 49-49. The annotated version clarifies:

'"*Shevetbindu*" clearly a misprint. Corrected in the 1939 edition: "*sethubandha*". In the 1939 edition: "*Rameshwar*" within brackets, i.e. *Sethubandha* (*Rameshwar*). In the 1939 edition the geographic description of Jagannath changed from "South-East" to "East". The British spelling "Juggernaut" discontinued in the 1921 edition in favour of "Jagannath", close to the prevalent spoken form. The original Gujarati does not specify the geographical markers of the places of pilgrimage.' [M. K. Gandhi, *Hind Swaraj*, (ed.) Suresh Sharma, Tridip Suhrud, Orient Blackswan, New Delhi, 2010, p. 42].

53 Ibid., p. 115.

54 M. K. Gandhi, Mohammad Ali Jinnah, (preface) C. Rajagopalachari, *Gandhi–Jinnah Talks: Text of Correspondence and Other Relevant Matter*, The *Hindustan Times* (New Delhi, July–October, 1944), pp. 12–13.

55 Faisal Devji, *Muslim Zion: Pakistan as a Political Idea*, Harvard University Press (Cambridge, Massachusetts, 2013), p. 78.

56 Ibid., p. 112.

57 Ibid., p. 113.

58 Muhammad Iqbal, *Stray Reflections: The Private Notebook of Muhammad Iqbal*, (ed.) Dr Javid Iqbal, Iqbal Academy Pakistan, 2008, p. 37.

59 Ibid.

60 Faisal Devji, *Muslim Zion: Pakistan as a Political Idea*, Harvard University Press (Cambridge, Massachusetts, 2013), p. 115.

61 Ibid.

62 Ibid., p. 48.

63 Ibid., p. 96.

64 Ibid., p. 97.

65 'The most blatant lie in Pakistan Studies textbooks is the idea that Pakistan was formed solely because of a fundamental conflict between Hindus and Muslims. This idea bases itself on the notion of a civilizational divide between monolithic Hindu and Muslim identities, which simply did not exist. The stress on religion ignored other factors that could cut across both identities. For instance, a Muslim from most of South India had far more in common, because of his regionally specific culture and language, with Hindus in this area than the Muslims in the north of the subcontinent. Similarly, the division of the historical narrative into a 'Hindu' and 'Muslim' period, aside from the ironic fact that this was actually instituted by the British, glosses over the reality that Islamic empires also fought each other for power. After all, Babar had to defeat Ibrahim Lodhi, and thus, the Delhi Sultanate, for the Mughal period to begin. Therefore, power and empire building often trumped this religious identity that textbooks claim can be traced linearly right to the formation of Pakistan.' Anushay Malik, 'The fundamental divide between Hindus and Muslims', from 'What is the most blatant lie taught through Pakistan textbooks?', *Dawn*, 15 August 2014. [https://www.dawn.com/news/1125484] Ayesha Jalal's *The Struggle for Pakistan*: *A Muslim Homeland and Global Politics* (2014) also heavily critiqued Pakistan's official history that single-mindedly and uncritically justifies the two-nation theory based on Islamic ideology.

66 Ibid.

67 Muhammad Iqbal, *Stray Reflections: The Private Notebook of Muhammad Iqbal*, (ed.) Dr. Javid Iqbal, Iqbal Academy Pakistan, 2008, pp. 24–25.

68 Salman Rushdie, *Shame*, Vintage (London, 1995), p. 87.

69 Mohammad Ali Jinnah, *Jinnah: Speeches and Statements 1947–1948*, Oxford University Press (Oxford, 2000), p. 73.

70 Ishtiaq Ahmed, *Jinnah: His Successes, Failures and Role in History*, Penguin Random House India (Gurgaon, 2020), p. 373.

71 Ibid., p. 378.

72 Ayesha Jalal, *The Sole Spokesman: Jinnah, the Muslim League and the Demand for Pakistan*, Cambridge University (New York, 1994), p. 213.

73 Ibid., p. 383.

74 Ishtiaq Ahmed, *Jinnah: His Successes, Failures and Role in History*, Penguin Random House India (Gurgaon, 2020), p. 378.

75 Shabnum Tejani writes, 'Jinnah had left Congress over differences with Gandhi's Non-cooperation campaign.' That is all the cryptic reason she offers, to avoid uncomfortable and revealing details. She could have at least provided what those differences were, for us to make a critical assessment. [Shabnum Tejani, *Indian Secularism: A Social and Intellectual History 1890–1950*, Permanent Black (New Delhi, 2007), p. 186].

76 Ishtiaq Ahmed, *Jinnah: His Successes, Failures and Role in History*, Penguin Random House India (Gurgaon, 2020), p. 72.

77 Ibid., p. 54.

78 Ibid., p. 73 [Faisal Devji writes that Jinnah opposed Gandhi on the Khilafat issue because it would turn the Muslim masses 'less political' and 'more religious' That is Jinnah's elitist misunderstanding, as mass movements are primarily political, even if they involve a religious matter. Faisal Devji, *Muslim Zion: Pakistan as a Political Idea*, Harvard University Press (Cambridge, Massachusetts, 2013), p. 84].

79 Ibid., p. 103.

80 Ibid., p. 102.

81 Ibid., p. 106 [The assumption that the Nehru Report was a blueprint for a unitary state and that the League wanted a federal structure is a simplistic rumour based on biased reading. Like this one from Shabnum Tejani: 'Iqbal's and Jinnah's proposals for a corridor of Muslim states and provisions for Muslims at the centre flew in the face of models of unitary nationalism that many found persuasive.' A proposal for a 'corridor' and 'provisions' for Muslims under the shadow of a demand for a separate nation based on religion is too deceptively vague for consideration. [Shabnum Tejani, *Indian Secularism: A Social and Intellectual History 1890–1950*, Permanent Black (New Delhi, 2007), p. 194].

82 Ibid., p. 110.

83 Ibid., p. 201.

84 Ibid.

85 Ibid.

86 Faisal Devji, *Muslim Zion: Pakistan as a Political Idea*, Harvard University Press (Cambridge, Massachusetts, 2013), p. 104.

87 Ibid., pp. 104–05

88 Ibid., p. 105.

89 Ibid., p. 106.

90 Mohammad Ali Jinnah, *Quaid-I-Azam Muhammad Ali Jinnah (Speeches, Statements, Writings, Letters, etc.)*, (edit.) Muhammad Hanif Shahid, Sang-e-Meel Publications(Urdu Bazar, Lahore, 1976), p. 25.

91 Faisal Devji, *Muslim Zion: Pakistan as a Political Idea*, Harvard University Press (Cambridge, Massachusetts, 2013), p. 103.

92 Ishtiaq Ahmed, *Jinnah: His Successes, Failures and Role in History*, Penguin Random House India (Gurgaon, 2020), p. 203.

93 Ibid., p. 207.
94 Ibid., p. 209.
95 *CWMG*, Vol. 72, 1978, p. 66.
96 Mohammad Ali Jinnah, *Quaid-I-Azam Muhammad Ali Jinnah (Speeches, Statements, Writings, Letters, etc.)*, (edit.) Muhammad Hanif Shahid, Sang-e-Meel Publications (Urdu Bazar, Lahore, 1976), p. 28.
97 *CWMG*, Vol. 72, p. 77.
98 Ibid.
99 Ibid., pp. 77–78.
100 Faisal Devji, *Muslim Zion: Pakistan as a Political Idea*, Harvard University Press (Cambridge, Massachusetts, 2013), p. 171.
101 Ibid., p. 191.
102 Ishtiaq *Ahmed, Jinnah: His Successes, Failures and Role in History*, Penguin Random House India (Gurgaon, 2020), p. 243.
103 Dr B. R. Ambedkar, *Pakistan or the Partition of India*, Thacker and Company Limited (Bombay, 1945), Preface to the Second Edition (No page number).
104 Ibid.
105 Ibid., p. xiii.
106 Partha Chatterjee, *The Politics of the Governed: Reflections on Popular Politics in Most of the World*, Columbia University Press (New York, 2004), p. 20.
107 Ibid.
108 Dr B. R. Ambedkar, *Pakistan or the Partition of India*, Thacker and Company Limited (Bombay, 1945), p. 11.
109 Ibid., p. 12.
110 Ibid., p. 15.
111 Ibid.
112 Ibid.
113 Ibid., p. 17.

114 Hegel writes: 'A principle, a law is something implicit, which as such, however true in itself, is not completely real (actual). Purposes, principles, and the like, are at first in our thoughts, our inner intention. They are not yet in reality. That which is in itself is a possibility, a faculty. It has not yet emerged out of its implicitness into existence. A second element must be added for it to become reality, namely, activity, actualization. The principle of this is the will, man's activity in general. It is only through this activity that the concept and its implicit ('being-in-themselves') determinations can be realized, actualized; for of themselves they have no immediate efficacy.' [Georg Wilhelm Friedrich Hegel, *Reason in History, a General Introduction to the Philosophy of History*, (trans.) Robert S. Hartman, A Liberal Arts Press Book, The Bobbs-Merrill Company, Inc. 1953. Link: https://www.marxists.org/reference/archive/hegel/works/hi/introduction.htm].

115 Dr B. R. Ambedkar, *Pakistan or the Partition of India*, Thacker and Company Limited (Bombay, 1945), p. 18.

116 Ibid.

117 Ibid., p. 30.

118 Ibid., p. 20.

119 Ibid.

120 Ibid., p. 21.

121 Ibid., p. 131.

122 Ibid., p. 133.

123 Ibid., p. 133.

124 Ibid., p. 132.

125 Ibid., p. 101.

126 Ibid., p. 102.

127 Venkat Dhulipala, *Creating a New Medina: State Power, Islam, and the Quest for Pakistan in Late Colonial North India*, Cambridge University Press (New Delhi, 2015), p. 56.

128 Dr B. R. Ambedkar, *Pakistan or the Partition of India*, Thacker and Company Limited (Bombay, 1945), p. 135.
129 *CWMG*, Vol. 19, 1966, p. 20.
130 Mahatma Gandhi, *Swaraj in One Year*, Ganesh and Co., Madras, 1921, p. 117.
131 Dr B. R. Ambedkar, *Pakistan or the Partition of India*, Thacker and Company Limited (Bombay, 1945), p. 136.
132 Ibid., p. 137.
133 Ibid., p. 140.
134 Ibid., p. 142.
135 See Jyotirmaya Sharma, *Elusive Non-violence: The Making and Unmaking of Gandhi's Religion of Ahimsa*, Context (Westland Publications Private Ltd.), Chennai, 2021.
136 Martin Buber, 'Gandhi, Politics and Us', *Pointing the Way*, (trans. and edit.), Maurice Friedman, Harper & Brothers (New York, 1957), p. 129.
137 M. K. Gandhi, *An Autobiography or The Story of My Experiments with Truth* (A Critical Edition), (trans.) Mahadev Desai, Yale University Press (New Haven and London, 2018), p. 46.
138 Ibid., p. 769.
139 Damien Casey, 'Levinas and Buber: Transcendence and Society', Sophia Vo1. 38, No. 2, 1999, September–October, p. 83.
140 Ibid.
141 Étienne Balibar, 'Lenin and Gandhi: A Missed Encounter?', (trans.) Knox Peden, *Radical Philosophy* 172, March/April 2012, p. 14.
142 Adriaan T. Peperzak, et al (ed), *Emmanuel Levinas: Basic Philosophical Writings*, Indiana University Press, 1996, p. 24.
143 Ibid.
144 Mahatma Gandhi, (ed.) Parel, Anthony, *Hind Swaraj*, Cambridge Text in Modern Politics, Cambridge University Press (New York, 1990), p. 67.

145 Ibid., p. 73.
146 Ibid.
147 Ibid., p. 118.
148 M. K. Gandhi, *An Autobiography or The Story of My Experiments with Truth* (A Critical Edition), (trans.) Mahadev Desai, Yale University Press (New Haven and London, 2018), p. 348.
149 Mahatma Gandhi, *Swaraj in One Year*, Ganesh and Co., Madras, 1921, p. 32.
150 *CWMG*, Vol. 16, 1965, p. 207.
151 *CWMG*, Vol. 17. 1965, pp. 46.
152 *CWMG*, Vol. 16, p. 308.
153 *CWMG*, Vol. 71, 1978, p. 132–33.
154 Jacques Derrida, *The Politics of Friendship*, (trans.) George Collins, Verso (New York, 2005), p. 183.
155 Jacques Derrida, 'Force of Law: The 'Mystical Foundation of Authority'', *Acts of Religion*, (ed.) Gil Anidjar, Routledge (New York, 2002), p. 244.
156 Dr B. R. Ambedkar, *Pakistan or the Partition of India*, Thacker and Company Limited (Bombay, 1945), p. 136.
157 *CWMG*, Vol. 17. p. 59.
158 Ibid.
159 Faisal Devji, *The Impossible Indian: Gandhi and the Temptation of Violence*, Harvard University Press (Cambridge, Massachusetts, 2012), p. 75.
160 Ibid., p. 70.
161 *CWMG*, Vol. 21, 1966, p. 319.
162 Faisal Devji, *Muslim Zion: Pakistan as a Political Idea*, Harvard University Press (Cambridge, Massachusetts, 2013), p. 84.
163 Mahatma Gandhi, (ed.) Parel, Anthony, *Hind Swaraj*, Cambridge Text in Modern Politics, Cambridge University Press (New York, 1990), p. 51.

164 *CWMG*, Vol. 13, 1964, p. 219.

165 Faisal Devji, *Muslim Zion: Pakistan as a Political Idea*, Harvard University Press (Cambridge, Massachusetts, 2013), p. 85.

166 Ibid.

167 Mahatma Gandhi, (ed.) Parel, Anthony, *Hind Swaraj*, Cambridge Text in Modern Politics, Cambridge University Press (New York, 1990), p. 60.

168 Ibid., p. 61.

169 Ajay Skaria, *Unconditional Equality: Gandhi's Religion of Resistance*, University of Minnesota Press (Minneapolis/London, 2016), p. 69.

170 Dr B. R. Ambedkar, *Pakistan or the Partition of India*, Thacker and Company Limited (Bombay, 1945), p. 144.

171 *CWMG*, Vol. 23, 1967, p. 343.

172 I have mainly consulted two essays for my views. (1) Robert L. Hardgrave Jr, 'The Mapilla Rebellion 1921: Peasant Revolt in Malabar', *Modern Asian Studies*, II, I (1977), pp. 57–99. (2) E. Ismail, 'Peasantry and the Malabar rebellion of 1921', *Proceedings of the Indian History Congress*, Vol. 67 (2006–07), pp. 488–99.

173 E. Ismail, 'Peasantry and the Malabar rebellion of 1921', *Proceedings of the Indian History Congress*, Vol. 67 (2006–07), p. 495 [Hardgrave offers his reasons: 'A multiplicity of explanatory factors may be identified in the analysis of the Mappilla rebellion: agrarian discontent, the perceived threat to Islam, the Congress–Khilafat agitation, inflammatory newspaper reports, and provocation by Government officials and police. Each of these (and, no doubt, others yet unidentified) may well have contributed to the explosive combination that produced the rebellion.' Robert L.

Hardgrave Jr, 'The Mapilla Rebellion 1921: Peasant Revolt in Malabar', *Modern Asian Studies*, II, I (1977), p. 98].

174 Bipan Chandra, *Communalism in Modern India*, Vikas Publishing House Pvt. Ltd. (New Delhi, 1984), p. 59.

175 Annie Besant, 'Malabar's Agony', *New India*, 29 November 1921, from Nair, Sir C. Sankaran, *Gandhi and Anarchy*, Tagore & Co., Madras, 1922 [https://www.gutenberg.org/files/52903/52903-h/52903-h.htm#Page_132].

176 Ibid.

177 Dr B. R. Ambedkar, *Pakistan or the Partition of India*, Thacker and Company Limited (Bombay, 1945), p. 153. ['Beginning with the year 1920 there occurred in that year in Malabar what is known as the Mopla Rebellion. It was the result of the agitation carried out by two Muslim organizations, the Khuddam-i-Kaba (servants of the Mecca Shrine) and the Central Khilafat Committee. Agitators actually preached the doctrine that India under the British Government was Dar-ul-Harab and that the Muslims must fight against it and if they could not, they must carry out the alternative principle of *Hijrat*. The Moplas were suddenly carried off their feet by this agitation. The outbreak was essentially a rebellion against the British Government The aim was to establish the kingdom of Islam by overthrowing the British Government.']

178 Ibid., p. 146.

179 Ibid., p. 147.

180 Ibid., p. 148.

181 Ibid., p. 149.

182 *CWMG*, Vol. 21, p. 7.

183 Ibid., p. 152.

184 Ibid., p. 112.

185 Ibid.
186 Ibid., p. 113.
187 Ibid.
188 Mahatma Gandhi, (ed.) Parel, Anthony, *Hind Swaraj*, Cambridge Text in Modern Politics, Cambridge University Press (New York, 1990), p. 74.
189 Ibid., p. 89.
190 Ibid.
191 *CWMG*, Vol. 21, p. 113.
192 Ibid.
193 Ibid.
194 Faisal Devji, *The Impossible Indian: Gandhi and the Temptation of Violence*, Harvard University Press (Cambridge, Massachusetts, 2012), p. 29.
195 Ibid., p. 69.
196 Octavio Paz, *In Light of India*, (trans.) Eliot Weinberger, Harcourt Inc. (New York, 1997), pp. 113–14.
197 Jawaharlal Nehru, *An Autobiography*, Allied Publishers Private Limited (Delhi, 1962), p. 160.
198 Ibid.
199 Neeti Nair, *Changing Homelands: Hindu Politics and the Partition of India*, Harvard University Press (London, 2011, p. 53.
200 Dr B. R. Ambedkar, *What Congress and Gandhi did to the Untouchables* in *Writings and Speeches*, Vol. 9, (ed.) Vasant Moon, Education Department, Govt. of Maharashtra (Bombay, 1991), p. 23.
201 Marcia Hermansen, 'A Twentieth Century Indian Sufi Views Hinduism: The Case of Khwaja Hasan Nizami (1879–1955)', p. 163.
202 Ibid., p. 166.
203 Ibid.

204 Ibid., p. 165.

205 Ibid., p. 159.

206 Yoginder Sikand, 'Shuddhi and Tabligh: New Forms of Religious Preaching in India [Part 1]', [link: https://www.newageislam.com/interfaith-dialogue/yoginder-sikand-newageislam/shuddhi-tabligh-new-forms-religious-preaching-india-part-1/d/3535].

207 Ibid., p. 175.

208 Christophe Jaffrelot, *The Hindu Nationalist Movement and Indian Politics 1925 to the 1990s*, Hurst and Company (London, 1996), pp. 6, 16.

209 Dayanand Saraswati, *The Light of Truth: Satyarth Prakash in English*, Vijaykumar Govindram Hasanand (Delhi, 2018).

210 Max Weber, *The Protestant Ethic and the Spirit of Capitalism*, (trans.) Talcott Parsons, Scribner (New York, 1958), p. 117.

211 Peter van der Veer, *The Modern Spirit of Asia: The Spiritual and the Secular in China and India*, Princeton University Press (Princeton, 2014), p. 51.

212 Ibid., p. 48.

213 Ibid., p. 30.

214 Gauri Viswanathan, 'Colonialism and the Construction of Hinduism', in (ed.) Gavin Flood, *The Wiley Blackwell Companion to Hinduism: Second Edition*, Blackwell Publishing Ltd (Oxford/U.K, 2023), p. 27.

215 Christophe Jafferlot, *The Hindu Nationalist Movement and Indian Politics 1925 to the 1990s*, Hurst and Company (London, 1996), p. 14.

216 Ibid., p. 17.

217 Raziuddin Aquil, *In the Name of Allah: Understanding Islam and Indian History*, Penguin Viking (Delhi, 2009), p. 73.

218 Ibid., p. 5.
219 Ibid., p. 12.
220 Ibid.
221 Bipan Chandra, *Communalism in Modern India*, Vikas Publishing House Pvt. Ltd. (New Delhi, 1984), p. 9.
222 *CWMG*, Vol. 24, 1967, p. 45.
223 Ibid.
224 Ibid.
225 Ibid.
226 Ibid.
227 Ibid.
228 Ibid., p. 148.
229 Ibid., p. 149.
230 The movement to convert Malkana Muslims (that reached its peak in 1927 when a large number of them got converted) is considered the primary reason that incited Abdul Rashid to murder Shraddhanand.
231 Ibid.
232 Ibid., p. 149–150 [Nizami later sent a telegram to Gandhi (for 'the sake of Islam, Hindu–Muslim Unity, and your beloved personality') that in view of Gandhi's statement of his pamphlet to the press, he has already amended portions of the pamphlet in later editions that were regarded objectionable and was willing to amend further. Later, Nizami visited Gandhi to deliver his assurances in person. Gandhi appreciated Nizami's gesture and published the telegram upon the author's request. But he maintained that Nizami must 'see the error of his thought' and 'recognize that he has really done an ill-service to Islam by suggesting questionable methods of propaganda'. He insisted that Nizami 'revise the pamphlet radically.' *CWMG*, Vol. 24, pp. 297, 298].

233 Maulana Mohamed Ali, *Presidential Address: Thirty Eighth Annual Session of the Indian Congress Held at Cocanada*, 26 December 1923, Jamia Milia Press (Aligarh, 1923), p. 97.
234 Ibid., p. 98.
235 Ibid.
236 Ibid.
237 Ibid.
238 Ibid.
239 Ibid.
240 *CWMG*, Vol. 32, p. 452.
241 Ibid., p. 454.
242 Ibid., p. 460.
243 Dr B. R. Ambedkar, *Pakistan or the Partition of India*, Thacker and Company Limited (Bombay, 1945), p. 147.
244 Ibid.
245 Vanya Vaidehi Bhargav, *Being Hindu, Being Indian: Lala Lajpat Rai's Ideas of Nationhood*, Penguin, Viking (Gurgaon, 2024), p. 367.
246 *CWMG*, Vol. 24, p. 261.
247 Ibid.
248 *CWMG*, Vol. 32, 1969, pp. 474–75.
249 Vanya Vaidehi Bhargav, *Being Hindu, Being Indian: Lala Lajpat Rai's Ideas of Nationhood*, Penguin, Viking (Gurgaon, 2024), p. 367.
250 *CWMG*, Vol. 32, p. 475.
251 Slavoj Žižek, *Violence*, Picador (New York, 2008), p. 61.
252 Dr B. R. Ambedkar, *Pakistan or the Partition of India*, Thacker and Company Limited (Bombay, 1945), pp. 146–47.
253 Vanya Vaidehi Bhargav, *Being Hindu, Being Indian: Lala Lajpat Rai's Ideas of Nationhood*, Penguin, Viking (Gurgaon, 2024), p. 365.
254 Ibid., pp. 365–66.

255 Ibid., p. 366.

256 Ibid.

257 Ibid., p. 367.

258 V. D. Savarkar, *Hindutva*, Veer Savarkar Prakashan (Savarkar Sadan, Bombay, 1969), p. 24.

259 Ibid., pp. 43–44.

260 By the modern idea of the Hindu religion, I mean a confluence of things. Peter Van der Veer and others have mentioned the orientalizing of Hinduism by European Indologists in the eighteenth and nineteenth centuries that resulted in the unified idea of a diverse tradition. One of the ways of standardizing the idea of Hinduism was by paying special attention to, or privileging, certain Sanskrit texts (the *Gita*, for instance) by orientalist scholars that made them central even for modern Hindus. It came to be understood critically by scholars later as the modernizing of the Hindu tradition. Veer makes terminological translation part of imaginative transformation: 'The translation of Hindu traditions into the English-language category of Hinduism, being the religion of Hindus, has been of immense significance for Hindu understanding of their own traditions.' [Veer, Peter van der, *The Modern Spirit of Asia: The Spiritual and the Secular in China and India*, Princeton University Press (Princeton, 2014), p. 67]. The other aspect is the further transformation of the orientalized idea into a nationalization of the Hindu religion. Here, the othering by European Christians gets reversed as Hindus assert their new-found modern identity against Christian missionaries (ironically, based on what the Europeans themselves fostered and established). The reverse othering also came to include Muslims. Separate ideas of nationhood (by Hindus, and later, Muslims) based

on modern ways of imagining religious identity came to be asserted since the late nineteenth century.

261 V. D. Savarkar, *Hindutva*, Veer Savarkar Prakashan (Savarkar Sadan, Bombay, 1969), p. 99.

262 Veer, Peter van der, *Religious Nationalism: Hindus and Muslims in India*, University of California Press (Berkeley and Los Angeles, 1994), p. 2.

263 Sri Aurobindo, *Nationalism, Religion, and Beyond: Writings on Politics, Society, and Culture*, (ed.) Peter Heehs, Permanent Black (Delhi, 2005), p. 180.

264 Ibid.

265 Ibid.

266 Ibid.

267 Ibid., p. 182.

268 Ibid.

269 M. K. Gandhi, *Hind Swaraj*, (ed.) Anthony J. Parel, Cambridge Text in Modern Politics, Cambridge University Press (New York, 1990), p. 57.

270 Aurobindo, Sri, *Sri Aurobindo and India's Rebirth*, (ed.) Michel Danino, Rupa Publications (New Delhi, 2018), p. 160.

271 Ibid., p. 161.

272 Ibid.

273 Ibid., p. 163.

274 Ibid., p. 167

275 See Jyotirmaya Sharma, *Hindutva: Exploring the Idea of Hindu Nationalism*, Harper Collins (New Delhi, 2015). I totally disagree with Sharma slotting Dayanand, Aurobindo and Vivekananda with Savarkar.

276 See Jyotirmaya Sharma, *A Restatement of Religion: Swami Vivekananda and the Making of Hindu Nationalism*, Yale University Press (New Haven & London, 2013).

277 Swami Vivekananda, 'Addresses at the Parliament of Religions', link: https://ramakrishna.org/vivekanandaparliament.html.

278 'RSS chief in US: Hindus don't unite . . . wild dogs can hunt a lion', 9 September 2018, link: https://indianexpress.com/article/india/rss-chief-mohan-bhagwat-world-hindu-congress-chicago5346831/.

279 M. S. Golwalkar, *We or Our Nationhood Defined*. Bharat Publications (Nagpur, 1939), pp. 51–52.

280 If Savarkar's book was a *Hindutva* manifesto, defining the central precepts of the Hindu right-wing imagination, Golwalkar's was a 'What is to be done' manual for action. My allusion to communist history is deliberate. In *Society Must Be Defended*, Michel Foucault mentioned Marx's letter to Engels in 1882, where Marx confesses: 'we found our idea of class struggle . . . in the work of the French historians who talked about the race struggle.' [Foucault, Michel, *Society Must Be Defended: Lectures at the College De France, 1975–76*, (ed.) Mauro Bertani and Alessandro Fontana, (trans.) David Macey, Picador (New York, 1997), page 79].

281 M. S. Golwalkar, *We or Our Nationhood Defined*. Bharat Publications (Nagpur, 1939), p. 87.

282 Govind Krishnan V., *Vivekananda: The Philosopher of Freedom*, Aleph (New Delhi, 2023), pp. 105–06.

283 Swami Vivekananda, *The Complete Works of Swami Vivekananda Vol IV*, Advaita Ashram (Calcutta, 1958), p. 126.

284 Ibid.

285 Javeed Alam finds an 'underlying consistency' behind Vivekananda's 'contradictions' (p. 112), and holds Vivekananda responsible for trying to denigrate Islam. For a rationalist ideologue like Alam, contradictions are not real and trustworthy. But just like the history of religion,

the nation, the human self and life is full of contradictions, so is our understanding of them. Vivekananda's lack of consistency is not a matter of ideological duplicity, but a manner of religious and political discourse that does not suffer from the constraints of a disciplinary framework and protocol. It is open to contradictions, and is to be judged as such. Alam finds Vivekananda too focused, and arbitrary, on what he considers a 'marginal aspect' (p. 116) of Islamic history that involves religious violence. Marginal or not, Vivekananda, however, did not make violence an 'essence' (p. 116) in Islam or its history, as Alam claims. There is always a secular discomfort towards what is deemed communally-driven criticism. There is exaggeration in Alam's misreading Vivekananda's supposedly consistent bias towards Islam. there is also a touch of sentimentality.

I do, however, agree with Alam on three important issues he raised. One, that given Vivekananda's stature, his words were bound to 'gain credence among the expanding middle classes within the Hindu community' (p. 116). Vivekananda's negative remarks on Islam and Muslims, because he used language in an impassioned style, can be prone to mistreatment. Two, Alam is right that in Vivekananda's treatment of Hinduism (unlike his occasional outbursts against the excesses of Islam and Christianity), all sense of 'history evaporates' and it is given an 'ideal form' (p. 116). Three, I *partly* agree with Alam's reading of the oft quoted remark of Vivekananda that India's future lay in the 'Vedanta brain and Muslim body' (p. 125). There is certainly a privileging of the mind over body, between 'thinking' and 'muscle' as Alam puts it (p. 125). I would risk a different argument. I would lay emphasis on the simple aspect that has been ignored here. Vivekananda used the phrase 'Vedanta brain' and not 'Hindu brain'. He championed Vedanta as a future basis of a world religion, where there is thinking without the necessity of god. It is something that should interest any secular mind.

There is a problem of sentimentality in Jalalul Haq's approach to Vivekananda and Islam. Haq makes three significant statements countering Vivekananda's negative remarks on Islam, Mohammad and Islamic history. One: 'Nearly all the wars fought by Muslim rulers were the wars of conquest not conversion, and if at all there were forced conversions or persecutions, they were not in accordance with but against the principles of Islam' (p. 186). Two: 'The killing of non-combatants, especially the religious leaders, or destruction of religious places and other properties in war times was forbidden whereas protecting the lives of non-Muslims in an Islamic state during peace time was made into an absolute obligation. The Prophet himself set an example when he triumphantly returned to Mecca and declared a general amnesty for his persecutors.' (p. 186) Three: 'Muslims have ruled over a large part of the civilized world for over a thousand years and are presently in power in countries with significant non-Muslim populations. But with all their failings, there is no more than sporadic incidents of violence and always much less in number than the persecution and prejudice they suffer at the hands of non-Muslims' (p. 187).

I do not wish to get into too many historical or empirical details to counter Haq's claims. But I want to simply point out a few things regarding Haq's defence of his religion. The wars and conquests that helped Islam establish its power are well documented. Muhammad expelled Jewish clans like the

Banu Qaynuqa from Medina for not supporting his cause, and had the Qurayẓah clan of Jews executed for failing to help him in the Battle of the Ditch in 627. The point is not whether Islamic power followed the principles of the *Quran* or not. Whether it did, or did not, the question of moral and political legitimacy will remain for non-believers (both within and outside the fold) and even for believers who may interpret political acts of religion differently. Political violence (conquest, forced conversions) happen *in the name of* religion. Religions can't be exempted from the patterns set by their origins. To say 'sporadic incidents of violence' is to reduce political history to newspaper reports. Even such reports may be unreliable if these Muslim nations are not democracies, with a secular-democratic press. It is poor apologia. Haq, however, concedes: 'But even as Vivekananda was reckless in his observations on the place of violence in Islam, he cannot be accused of being uniformly unfair or prejudiced. At places he makes every attempt to appreciate what he finds appreciable and is polite enough while disagreeing with what he considers to be disagreeable' (p. 187–188). Haq's conclusion on Vivekananda is exactly the opposite of Alam's. He finds Vivekananda's critical issues with Islam unevenly balanced with his more consistent gesture of appreciation.

Quotes from Javeed Alam, *India Living with Modernity*, Oxford University Press (New Delhi, 1999). Quotes from Jalalul Haq, *Hindu Tolerance Myth and Truth: A Study in the Thought-Systems of Ramakrishna and Vivekananda*, Institute of Objective Studies (New Delhi, 2014).

286 Swami Vivekananda, *The Complete Works of Swami Vivekananda Vol IV*, Advaita Ashram (Calcutta, 1958), p. 121.

287 Ibid., p. 134.

288 Paavo Havikko, *The Power Game*, 'A Time of Eternal Peace: A List of Allies, Short and Sweet', (trans.) David Barrett, Books from Finland 2/1984, Helsinki University Library. Vol. XVIII No. 2 1984, Helsinki/Finland, p. 66.

289 Ibid., p. 67.

290 Isaiah Berlin, *The Proper Study of Mankind: An Anthology of Essays*, (ed.) Henry Hardy and Roger Hausheer, Pimlico (London, 1998), p. 17.

291 Pierre-Joseph Proudhon, *What is Property? An Inquiry into the Principle of Right and of Government*, (trans.) Benjamin R. Tucker, Humboldt Publishing Company c. 1890. [link: https://www.marxists.org/reference/subject/economics/proudhon/property/ch05.htm].

292 Raul Zurita, 'Nicanor Parra: The Worst Is Behind', (trans.) Anna Deeny, *Bomb Magazine*, 1 January 2009 [link: https://bombmagazine.org/articles/2009/01/01/nicanor-parra-the-worst-is-behind/].

293 Rabindranath Tagore, *Letters from Russia*, (trans.) Dr Sasadhar Sinha, Vishva-Bharati (Calcutta, 1960), p. 64.

294 Walter Benjamin, *Illuminations: Essays and Reflections*, (trans.) Harry Zohn, Schocken Books (New York, 1969), p. 256.

295 The American political scientist Norman Finkelstein wrote *The Holocaust Industry: Reflections on the Exploitation of Jewish Suffering* in 2020, exposing the powerful American Jews who commodified the Holocaust (1941–45) to lobby for Israeli interests. The tragic surplus of historical memory was used to gain political profit. This industry is currently at war with world opinion against Israel's genocidal war against Palestine's Gaza.

296 Paavo Havikko, *The Power Game*, 'Speak, Answer, Teach', (trans.) David Barrett, Books from Finland 2/1984, Helsinki

University Library. Vol. XVIII No. 2 1984, Helsinki/Finland, p. 65.

297 Yannis Ritsos, *Repetitions Testimonies Parenthesis*, (trans.) Edmund Keeley, Princeton University Press (Princeton, New Jersey, 1991), p. 92.

298 'Servius, the late 4th and early 5th century Latin grammarian from Rome (called 'Servius the Grammarian'), who wrote a commentary on Virgil's Aeneid in the 4th century AD, tells us in a text that Arces, an Illyrian bandit, uprooted the tree sacred to Zeus but unfortunately doesn't give a date. But the poem says, they've 'turned everything upside down—altars, / churches, graveyard'. Now 'churches' here is the modern meaning of the word, post-dating it to an ancient historical event. The poem is anachronistic': Greek–Canadian poet Evan Jones shared this important detail on the poem.

Chapter 1: 'To Die a Beautiful Death'

1 *CWMG*, Vol. 86, 1982, p. 3.

2 Ibid., p. 6.

3 George Joseph was part of the Rowlatt Satyagraha launched by Gandhi in September 1920, in charge of the activities in Madurai, where he was also an important member of the trade union movement and played a role in the organization of textile mill workers. Joseph was also the editor of Motilal Nehru's newspaper *The Independent* in 1920–21, and succeeded C. Rajagopalachari as editor of *Young India* in 1923.

4 *CWMG*, Vol. 53, 1972, p. 483.

5 *CWMG*, Vol. 55, 1973, p. 255.

6 Immanuel Kant, *Groundwork of the Metaphysics of Morals*, (trans.) Mary Gregor, Cambridge University Press, U.K, 1997, p. 43.

7 Ibid., p. 46.

8 Emmanuel Levinas writes: "Pure reflection cannot have the first word: how could it arise in the dogmatic spontaneity of a force which moves by itself? Reflection must be put into question from without. Reflection needs a certain kind of heteronomy." (Levinas, *Philosophical Writings*, p. 21).

9 Emmanuel Levinas, *Totality and Infinity: An Essay on Interiority*, (trans.) Alphonso Lingis, Duquesne University Press (Pittsburgh, Pennsylvania, 1969), p. 199.

10 M. K. Gandhi, *Hind Swaraj*, (ed.) Anthony J. Parel, Cambridge Text in Modern Politics, Cambridge University Press (New York, 1990), p. 85.

11 Ibid., p. 90.

12 *CWMG*, Vol, 86, p. 16.

13 Ibid., p. 27.

14 *CWMG*, Vol. 85, 1982, p. 244.

15 Ibid., p. 282.

16 Ibid., p. 365.

17 *CWMG*, Vol. 84, 1981, p. 426.

18 Ibid.

19 Ibid.

20 Ibid., p. 427.

21 'Gandhi Stops British Plan; Riots Kill 5', *The Washington Post*, 24 June 1946. [link: https://www.washingtonpost.com/wp-srv/inatl/longterm/flash/june/india46.htm].

22 1.) 'Ahead of Rath Yatra, Ahmedabad cops set to promote communal harmony with street play on local heroes', The *Indian Express*, 6 June 2023 [link: https://indianexpress.com/article/cities/ahmedabad/ahead-of-rath-yatra-

ahmedabad-cops-set-to-promote-communal-harmony-with-street-play-on-local-heroes-8647411/], 2.) Peter Nazareth, 'When riots at rath yatra irked Gandhi', The *Times of India*, 25 June 2009 [link: https://timesofindia.indiatimes.com/city/ahmedabad/when-riots-at-rath-yatra-irked-gandhi/articleshow/4698905.cms].

23 *CWMG*, Vol. 84, 1981, pp. 366–67.

24 Ibid., p. 367.

25 Rudrangshu Mukherjee, 'The Red blunders: The communists have consistently betrayed national interests', The *Telegraph*, 21 August 2007, link: https://www.telegraphindia.com/opinion/the-red-blunders-the-communists-have-consistently-betrayed-national-interests/cid/1027877 [In response to Prabhat Patnaik's 10 March 2012 essay in the *Economic and Political Weekly*, 'The Left in Decline: A Response', N. Madhavan Kutty wrote from Thiruvananthapuram agreeing that Patnaik's assertion that the CPI's decision on the 1942 Quit India Movement being 'a decision entirely of its leadership is technically correct' but added that 'the decision was certainly influenced by the Comintern documents on the second world war that were prepared following the Nazi invasion of Soviet Union on 22 June 1941, which were transmitted to the CPI leadership in jail by Achar Singh Chinna who returned to India from Moscow under the instruction of the Comintern leadership headed by Stalin.' *Economic and Political Weekly*, Vol. XLVII, No. 15, 14 April 2012, p. 4].

26 Sumit Sarkar, *Modern India 1885–1947*, Palgrave Macmillan (New York, 1989), p. 384.

27 Ibid., p. 391.

28 Sumit Sarkar, 'The Communists and 1942', Social Scientist, Vol. 12, No. 9 (September 1984), p. 46.

29 p. 50.
30 *CWMG*, Vol. 77, 1979, p. 434.
31 Nirad C. Chaudhuri, *Thy Hand Great Anarch*!, The Hogarth Press (London, 1987), p. 808.
32 Janam Mukherjee, *Hungry Bengal: War, Famine, and the End of Empire*, Oxford University Press (New York, 2016), p. 176.
33 *CWMG*, Vol. 85, 1982, p. 459.
34 Pyarelal, Mahatma Gandhi: *The Last Phase Vol 1*, Navajivan Publishing House (Ahmedabad, 1956), p. 252.
35 Ibid.
36 Ibid.
37 '[We] propose that the Hindus and Mussalmans should be provided with their homelands which will enable them to live side by side as two honourable nations, and as good neighbours' [p. 23 of *Gandhi: The End of Non-Violence*].
38 Janam Mukherjee, *Hungry Bengal: War, Famine, and the End of Empire*, Oxford University Press (New York, 2016), p. 209.
39 Ibid., pp. 209–10.
40 Joya Chatterji, *Bengal Divided: Hindu communalism and partition 1932–1947*, Cambridge University Press, U.K. 1994, p. 81.
41 Ibid.
42 Ibid., p. 84.
43 Ananya Vajpeyi, 'Ashis Nandy: Why Nationalism and Secularism Failed Together', Reset Dialogues, 18 October 2016, link: https://www.resetdoc.org/story/ashis-nandy-why-nationalism-and-secularism-failed-together/.
44 Anwesha Roy, *Making Peace, Making Riots Communalism and Communal Violence, Bengal 1940–1947*, Cambridge University Press (New Delhi, 2018), p. 150.

45 Joya Chatterji, *Bengal Divided: Hindu Communalism and Partition 1932–1947*, Cambridge University Press, 1994, pp. 230–31.

46 Ibid., p. 230.

47 Ibid., p. 231.

48 Ibid.

49 Ibid., p. 16.

50 Ibid.

51 Ibid., pp. 42–43.

52 Benedict Anderson, *Imagined Communities: Reflections on the Origin and Spread of Nationalism*, Verso, London, 1983, p. 6.

53 Ibid., p. 232.

54 Wavell, *The Viceroy's Journal*, (ed.) Penderel Moon, Oxford University Press (Delhi, 1973), p. 352.

55 Ibid.

56 Anwesha Roy, *Making Peace, Making Riots Communalism and Communal Violence, Bengal 1940–1947*, Cambridge University Press (New Delhi, 2018), p. 159.

57 Joya Chatterji, *Bengal Divided: Hindu Communalism and Partition 1932–1947*, Cambridge University Press, 1994, p. 233.

58 Janam Mukherjee, *Hungry Bengal: War, Famine, and the End of Empire*, Oxford University Press (New York, 2016), p. 240.

59 Ibid., p. 239.

60 Ibid., pp. 176–77.

61 Anwesha Roy, *Making Peace, Making Riots Communalism and Communal Violence, Bengal 1940–1947*, Cambridge University Press (New Delhi, 2018), p. 167.

62 Janam Mukherjee, *Hungry Bengal: War, Famine, and the End of Empire*, Oxford University Press (New York, 2016), p. 229.

63 Joya Chatterji, *Bengal Divided: Hindu Communalism and Partition 1932–1947*, Cambridge University Press, 1994, p. 239.

64 Ibid.

65 Suranjan Das, *Communal Riots in Bengal 1905–1947*, Oxford University Press (New Delhi, 1991), p. 166.

66 Anwesha Roy, *Making Peace, Making Riots Communalism and Communal Violence, Bengal 1940–1947*, Cambridge University Press (New Delhi, 2018), p. 152.

67 Suranjan Das, *Communal Riots in Bengal 1905–1947*, Oxford University Press (New Delhi, 1991), p. 168.

68 Ibid., p. 177.

69 Ibid., p. 178.

70 Nirad C. Chaudhuri, *Thy Hand Great Anarch*!, The Hogarth Press (London, 1987), p. 810.

71 Anwesha Roy, *Making Peace, Making Riots Communalism and Communal Violence, Bengal 1940–1947*, Cambridge University Press (New Delhi, 2018), p. 165.

72 Janam Mukherjee, *Hungry Bengal: War, Famine, and the End of Empire*, Oxford University Press (New York, 2016), p. 237.

73 Ibid.

74 Joya Chatterji, *Bengal Divided: Hindu Communalism and Partition 1932–1947*, Cambridge University Press, 1994, p. 233.

75 The Bengali Hindu refugees who faced persecution during the Anti-Foreigners Agitation in Assam between 1979 and 1985 were also not exempt from communal feelings. That does not weaken their witness-accounts and experience. It is true that in Assam, the violence was one-sided, perpetrated by the majority Assamese community against Bengali Hindus and Muslims. But that is beside the point in my argument.

76 Nirad C. Chaudhuri, *Thy Hand Great Anarch*!, The Hogarth Press (London, 1987), p. 810.

77 Ibid., p. 812.

78 Ashis Nandy, 'Death of an Empire', Sarai Reader, no. 2 (2002), pp. 14–21 [link: https://southasia.ucla.edu/history-politics/independent-india/death-empire-ashis-nandy/].

79 Sadat Hasan Manto, *Stars from Another Sky: The Bombay Film World in the 1940s*, (trans.) Khalid Hasan, Penguin Books (New Delhi, 1998), p. 73.

80 Ibid.

81 British–Australian scholar Sara Ahmed does not make a distinction (as I do) between feelings and emotions. But she describes both in ways which relate to the way I have distinguished between the two. Ahmed goes beyond psychological theories of emotions and feelings to offer what she calls the 'sociality of emotions' (p. 9). She considers emotions not 'as coming *from within and moving outwards*' but rather something that comes 'from without and move inward.' (p. 9) Ahmed grants emotions the quality that allows us to distinguish between 'an inside and an outside'. (p. 10) Ahmed uses the idea of feelings as part of emotions. She describes pain as feelings 'that open bodies to others' (p. 15). Ahmed also refers to American sociologist Norman K. Denzin describing emotions as 'self-feelings' (p. 18 *n*). These specific formulations come close to my argument that even as feelings and emotions are part of each other, and both can be pleasant and fulfilling, or unpleasant and disturbing, feelings are nevertheless more open than emotions and retain better affective possibilities towards the outside, and the other. [Sara Ahmed, *The Cultural Politics of Emotion* (Second Edition), Edinburgh University Press (Edinburgh, 2014)].

82 Ibid.

83 Partha Chatterjee, 'The Second Partition of Bengal', in (ed.) Ranabir Samaddar, *Reflections on Partition in the East*, Calcutta Research Group (Calcutta, 1997), p. 50.

84 Ibid.

85 Anwesha Roy, *Making Peace, Making Riots Communalism and Communal Violence, Bengal 1940–1947*, Cambridge University Press (New Delhi, 2018, p. 164.

86 Ibid.

87 Ibid.

88 Pyarelal, Mahatma Gandhi: *The Last Phase Vol 1*, Navajivan Publishing House (Ahmedabad, 1956), pp. 297–98.

89 Ibid., pp. 298–99 [In this connection, Sugata Bose writes: 'The strong religious overtone to the Noakhali and Tippera riots is intriguing when seen in the light of a long tradition of militant protest by krishak samitis which tended to operate on 'class' lines.' Sugata Bose, *Agrarian Bengal: Economy, Social Structure and Politics, 1919–1947*, Cambridge University Press (London, 2008), p. 182].

90 Anwesha Roy, *Making Peace, Making Riots Communalism and Communal Violence, Bengal 1940–1947*, Cambridge University Press (New Delhi, 2018), p. 30.

91 Pyarelal, Mahatma Gandhi: *The Last Phase Vol 1*, Navajivan Publishing House (Ahmedabad, 1956), pp. 301–02.

92 Suranjan Das, *Communal Riots in Bengal 1905–1947*, Oxford University Press (New Delhi, 1991), p. 199.

93 Ibid.

94 Anwesha Roy, *Making Peace, Making Riots Communalism and Communal Violence, Bengal 1940–1947*, Cambridge University Press (New Delhi, 2018), p. 185.

95 Ibid., pp. 186, 188.

96 Ibid., pp. 188.
97 Pyarelal, Mahatma Gandhi: *The Last Phase Vol 1*, Navajivan Publishing House, Ahmedabad, 1956, p. 307.
98 Pyarelal, Mahatma Gandhi: *The Last Phase Vol. 1*, Navajivan Publishing House (Ahmedabad, 1956), p. 293.
99 Ibid., pp. 293–94.
100 Nirmal Kumar Bose, *My Days with Gandhi*, Orient Longman, Calcutta, 1974, p. 30.
101 Ibid., p. 31.
102 Pyarelal, Mahatma Gandhi: *The Last Phase Vol. 1*, Navajivan Publishing House (Ahmedabad, 1956), p. 408.
103 Manu Gandhi, *The Diary of Manu Gandhi (1946–1948)*, (edited) Tridip Suhrud, Oxford University Press.
104 Pyarelal, Mahatma Gandhi: *The Last Phase Vol. 1*, Navajivan Publishing House (Ahmedabad, 1956), p. 432.
105 Nirmal Kumar Bose, *My Days with Gandhi*, Orient Longman Limited, Calcutta, p. 31.
106 Ibid., p. 35.
107 Ibid.
108 *CWMG*, Vol. 86, p. 69.
109 Ibid., p. 72.
110 Ibid., p. 75.
111 Ibid., p. 78.
112 Ibid., p. 80.
113 *CWMG*, Vol. 86, p. 81.
114 Ibid., p. 82.
115 Nirmal Kumar Bose, *My Days with Gandhi*, Orient Longman Limited, Calcutta, p. 39.
116 *CWMG*, Vol. 86, p. 85.
117 Nirmal Kumar Bose, *My Days with Gandhi*, Orient Longman Limited, Calcutta, p. 39.

118 Ibid.
119 *CWMG*, Vol. 86, p. 86.
120 Nirmal Kumar Bose, *My Days with Gandhi*, Orient Longman Limited, Calcutta, pp. 40–41.
121 *CWMG*, Vol. 86, p. 89.
122 Ibid., p. 90.
123 Ibid.
124 Ibid.
125 Ibid., p. 91.
126 Ibid., p. 92.
127 Ibid., p. 94.
128 Ibid. (paraphrased quote).
129 Ibid.
130 Hannah Arendt, *The Life of the Mind*, Harcourt Inc. (Florida, 1978), p. 179.
131 Ibid., p. 180.
132 Ibid., p. 180.
133 Octavio Paz, *The Collected Poems 1957–1987*, (trans.) Eliot Weinberger, Indus (Harper Collins) (New Delhi, 1992), p. 525.
134 Nirmal Kumar Bose, *My Days with Gandhi*, Orient Longman Limited, Calcutta, p. 41.
135 *CWMG*, Vol. 86, p. 96.
136 Ibid., p. 98.
137 *CWMG*, Vol. 13, 1964, pp. 228–29.
138 *CWMG*, Vol. 86, p. 100.
139 Ibid.
140 Ibid.
141 Ibid.
142 Ibid.
143 Ibid.

144 Mahatma Gandhi, (ed.) Parel, Anthony, *Hind Swaraj*, Cambridge Text in Modern Politics, Cambridge University Press (New York, 1990), p. lvi.
145 *CWMG*, Vol. 86, p. 105.
146 Pyarelal, Mahatma Gandhi: *The Last Phase Vol. 1*, Navajivan Publishing House (Ahmedabad, 1956), p. 379.
147 The song isn't mentioned, but going through all the bhajans from Gandhi's prayer meetings only one fitted the bill in relation to the context. Surdas' 'प्रभु मोरे अवगुन चित न धरो' ('Lord, don't take my shortcomings to heart'). The words go: 'One piece of iron is used for worship, another in the hands of a thief for stealing, the *paras* makes no distinction and turns by its touch either to gold.' Source: https://www.gandhi-manibhavan.org/gandhi-comes-alive/aashram-prayers.html.
148 *CWMG*, Vol. 86, p. 106.
149 Ibid., p. 107.
150 Ibid., p. 108.
151 Pyarelal, Mahatma Gandhi: *The Last Phase Vol. 1*, Navajivan Publishing House (Ahmedabad, 1956), p. 380.
152 Ibid., p. 180.
153 Franz Kafka, *The Complete Stories*, (ed.) Nahum N. Glatzer, Schocken Books, New York, 1971, p. 289–290.
154 Ibid., p. 293.
155 *CWMG*, Vol. 86, p. 113.
156 Ibid., p. 114.
157 Ibid.
158 Ibid., p. 115.
159 Ibid.
160 Ibid.
161 Ibid.
162 Pyarelal, Mahatma Gandhi: *The Last Phase Vol 1*, Navajivan Publishing House (Ahmedabad, 1956), p. 382.

163 *CWMG*, Vol. 86, p. 119.
164 Ibid., p. 120.
165 Ibid.
166 Ibid., p. 121.
167 Ibid., p. 122.
168 Anwesha Roy, *Making Peace, Making Riots Communalism and Communal Violence, Bengal 1940–1947*, Cambridge University Press (New Delhi, 2018), p. 198.
169 Pyarelal, Mahatma Gandhi: *The Last Phase Vol 1*, Navajivan Publishing House, Ahmedabad, 1956, p. 307.
170 In 'Away from the Hindus' (which is part of *Untouchables or the Children of India's Ghetto*, published in 1989), Ambedkar made a series of remarks on conversion that are necessary to keep in mind. He writes, 'History records cases where conversion has taken place as a result of compulsion or deceit.' (p. 404) This is an interesting corollary to Gandhi's claim that history only records the 'interruption' to the history of love. The messy history of forced conversion interrupts the otherwise legitimate history of genuine conversions. Ambedkar points out the tradition of passive conversion by people belonging to the same religion as a matter of 'inheritance'. (p. 404) Rejecting the idea that conversion can help untouchables gain politically, Ambedkar looked for reasons within the Hindu religion. The missing idea of fraternity in Hinduism (due to its caste structure and the practice of untouchability) ensures a lack of normative ethic, which become conditions, or reasons, for conversion. Ambedkar makes two strong statements in this regard. He writes, 'In Hinduism, there is no hope for the Untouchables' (p. 412). The fate of untouchable life, which is marked by ostracization and a degrading social designation, won't change

in Hindu society. In other words, the spirit of the life of the untouchables is damaged under Hindu religion. Ambedkar reiterates the point: 'That Hinduism is inconsistent with the self-respect and honour of the Untouchables is the strongest ground which justifies the conversion of the Untouchables to another and nobler faith.' (p. 412) Keeping out the political question from conversion, Ambedkar hinges upon the moral question. Quotes from: Dr. Babasaheb Ambedkar, *Writings and Speeches Vol. 5*, Education Department, Government of Maharashtra, 1989.

171 Gauri Viswanathan, 'Religious Conversion and the Politics of Dissent', in Veer, Peter van der (ed.), *Conversion to Modernities: The Globalization of Christianity*, Routledge (London, 1996), p. 102.

172 *CWMG*, Vol. 86, p. 123.

173 Ibid., p. 126.

174 Ibid., p. 127.

175 Ibid., p. 131.

176 Revolutionary ideas can be universal, but revolutionary violence is always contentious, contextual or historical, and attempts are made to explain or legitimize, the illegitimate use of violence taking recourse to its universal ideas.

177 Nirmal Kumar Bose, *My Days with Gandhi*, Calcutta, Orient Longman Limited, 1974, p. 46.

178 *CWMG*, Vol. 86, p. 138.

179 Nirmal Kumar Bose, *My Days with Gandhi*, Calcutta, Orient Longman Limited, 1974, p. 51.

180 Ibid., p. 52.

181 *CWMG*, Vol. 86, p. 140.

182 Ibid., p. 141.

183 Ibid., *The Hindu*, 24 April 1946.

184 Nirmal Kumar Bose, *My Days with Gandhi*, Calcutta, Orient Longman Limited, 1974, p. 53.

185 Ibid., p. 54.

186 Ibid.

187 Mahatma Gandhi, (ed.) Parel, Anthony, *Hind Swaraj*, Cambridge Text in Modern Politics, Cambridge University Press (New York, 1990), p. 93.

188 *CWMG*, Vol. 86, pp. 146–47.

189 Ibid., p. 150, *The Hindu*, 28 November 1946.

190 Ibid., p. 152.

191 Nirmal Kumar Bose, *My Days with Gandhi*, Calcutta, Orient Longman Limited, 1974, pp. 59–60.

192 *CWMG*, Vol. 86, p. 155.

193 Ibid.

194 Ibid.

195 Ibid.

196 Nirmal Kumar Bose, *My Days with Gandhi*, Calcutta, Orient Longman Limited, 1974, p. 63.

197 V. S. Naipaul, *India: A Wounded Civilization*, Picador (London, 2002), p. 99.

198 *CWMG*, Vol. 86, pp. 160–61.

199 Nirmal Kumar Bose, *My Days with Gandhi*, Orient Longman Limited, 1974, p. 65.

200 Ibid.

201 *CWMG*, Vol. 86, p. 164.

202 Ibid.

203 Nirmal Kumar Bose, *My Days with Gandhi*, Calcutta, Orient Longman Limited, 1974, p. 66.

204 *CWMG*, Vol. 86, p. 167.

205 Ibid., p. 182, *Hindustan Standard*, 4 December 1946.

206 Ibid., p. 185.

207 Ibid., p. 192.

208 Ibid., p. 193.
209 Hannah Arendt, *Origins of Totalitarianism*, Harvest, Harcourt Brace & Company (New York, 1973), p. 392.
210 M. K. Gandhi, *An Autobiography or The Story of My Experiments with Truth* (A Critical Edition), (trans.) Mahadev Desai, Yale University Press (New Haven and London, 2018), p. 45.
211 Ibid., p. 46.
212 *CWMG*, Vol. 87, p. 261.
213 Aristotle, *Rhetoric*, (trans.) C.D.C. Reeve, Hackett Publishing Company, Inc. (Indianapolis, Cambridge, 2018), p. 19.
214 *CWMG*, Vol. 86, p. 193.
215 Pyarelal, Mahatma Gandhi: *The Last Phase Vol 1*, Navajivan Publishing House, Ahmedabad, 1956, p. 409.
216 *CWMG*, Volume 86, p. 196.
217 Ibid., p. 197.
218 Ibid., p. 199.
219 Manu Gandhi, *The Diary of Manu Gandhi (1946–1948)*, (edited and translated) Tridip Suhrud, Oxford University Press (New Delhi, 2024), p. 12.
220 Ibid., p. 16.
221 *CWMG*, Vol. 86, p. 251.
222 Ibid., p. 260.
223 Ibid., pp. 263–64.
224 Manu Gandhi, *The Diary of Manu Gandhi C (1946-1948)*, (edited and translated) Tridip Suhrud, Oxford University Press (New Delhi, 2024), p. 30.
225 *CWMG*, Vol. 86, pp. 265–66.
226 Ibid., pp. 274–75.
227 Ibid., p. 275.
228 Ibid.

229 Ibid., p. 276.
230 Syed Abul Maksud, *Gandhi, Nehru and Noakhali*, Mahatma Gandhi Smarak Sadan (Dhaka, 2008), p. 35.
231 Ibid., p. 36.
232 Ibid., p. 37.
233 Ibid.
234 Ibid., p. 40.
235 Ibid., p. 59 [Maksud writes: 'It was alleged by the local Muslim leaders that unlike other Gandhi Mission workers Sucheta had been spreading communal venom among the Hindu population'. Ibid., p. 75].
236 Ibid., p. 83.
237 Ibid., p. 75.
238 *CWMG*, Vol. 86, p. 294.
239 Nirmal Kumar Bose, *My Days with Gandhi*, Orient Longman Limited, 1974, p. 117.
240 *CWMG*, Vol. 86, p. 301.
241 Ibid., p. 306.
242 Sugata Bose, *Agrarian Bengal: Economy, Social Structure and Politics, 1919–1947*, Cambridge University Press (London, 2008), p. 19.
243 Joya Chatterji, *Bengal Divided: Hindu Communalism and Partition 1932–1947*, Cambridge University Press, 1994, p. 39.
244 Ibid., pp. 202–03.
245 Manu Gandhi, *The Diary of Manu Gandhi (1946–1948)*, (edited and translated) Tridip Suhrud, Oxford University Press (New Delhi, 2024), p. 55.
246 Ibid.
247 Ibid., p. 57.
248 Ibid., p. 66.
249 Salman Rushdie, *Midnight's Children*, Vintage (London, 1995), p. 112.

250 *CWMG*, Vol. 43, 1971, p. 169.
251 Jean-Jacques Rousseau, *Emile or On Education*, (trans.) Allan Bloom, Basic Books (USA, 1979), p. 412.
252 Ibid.
253 *CWMG*, Volume 25, pp. 250–251.
254 Ibid., p. 251.
255 Manu Gandhi, *The Diary of Manu Gandhi C (1946-1948)*, (edited and translated) Tridip Suhrud, Oxford University Press (New Delhi, 2024), p. 78.
256 *CWMG*, Vol. 86, p. 323.
257 Ibid., p. 330.
258 Manubahen Gandhi, *The Lonely Pilgrim (Gandhiji's Noakhali Pilgrimage)*, Navajivan Publishing House (Ahmedabad, 1964), p. 81.
259 Ibid.
260 Ibid.
261 Nirmal Kumar, *My Days with Gandhi*, Calcutta, Orient Longman Limited, 1974, p. 126.
262 Nirmal Kumar Bose, *1946 Diary*, (ed.) Abhik Kumar Dey, (trans.) V. Ramaswamy, [Work in Progress, kindly shared by the translator with author on 19 September 2023].
263 Ibid.
264 Ibid.
265 Ibid.
266 Ibid.
267 Ibid.
268 Ibid.
269 Ibid.
270 *CWMG*, Vol. 86, p. 355.
271 Manu Gandhi, *The Diary of Manu Gandhi (1946–1948)*, (edited and translated) Tridip Suhrud, Oxford University Press (New Delhi, 2024), p. 83.

272 *CWMG*, Vol. 86, p. 362.
273 Ibid., p. 367.
274 Ibid.
275 Ibid., p. 369.
276 Manu Gandhi, *The Diary of Manu Gandhi (1946–1948)*, (edited) Tridip Suhrud, Oxford University Press, p. 91
277 Ibid.
278 *CWMG*, Vol. 86, p. 378.
279 Manu Gandhi, *The Diary of Manu Gandhi (1946–1948)*, (edited and translated) Tridip Suhrud, Oxford University Press (New Delhi, 2024), p. 91.
280 Ibid., p. 97.
281 Ibid., pp. 97–98.
282 Ibid., p. 101.
283 Ibid.
284 Ibid.
285 Dipesh Chakrabarty, *Provincializing Europe: Postcolonial Thought and Historical Difference*, Princeton University Press (Princeton and Oxford, 2000), p. 175 .
286 Parvez Rahaman, 'Gandhi's sojourn in Noakhali', *The Daily Star*, 3 October 2022; Rahaman, Parvez, 'The Retrieving Memories of Gandhi's Peace-mission: Noakhali Riots 1946, East Pakistan', *Scientia et Humanitas: A Journal of Student Research* (Middle Tennessee State University, Spring 2023), p. 170.
287 T. K. Madhavan, *Dvija: A Prophet Unheard*, Affiliated East-West Press Pvt. Ltd., New Delhi/Madras, 1977, p. 35.
288 Manu Gandhi, *The Diary of Manu Gandhi C (1946-1948)*, (edited and translated) Tridip Suhrud, Oxford University Press., New Delhi, 2024, p. 103
289 Ibid., p. 104
290 *CWMG*, Vol. 86, p. 396.
291 Ibid.

292 Ibid., p. 402.
293 Ibid., p. 412.
294 Ibid.
295 Ibid., pp. 412–13.
296 Ibid., p. 417.
297 Ibid. (Gandhi's words paraphrased in report)
298 Manu Gandhi, *The Diary of Manu Gandhi (1946–1948)*, (edited and translated) Tridip Suhrud, Oxford University Press (New Delhi, 2024), p. 118.
299 Wrongly mentioned/spelt as 'Satgharia' in *CWMG*. Manu corrected it in her diary.
300 Manu Gandhi, *The Diary of Manu Gandhi (1946–1948)*, (edited and translated) Tridip Suhrud, Oxford University Press (New Delhi, 2024), p. 123.
301 Ibid.
302 *CWMG*, Vol. 86, p. 440.
303 Ibid., pp. 450–51.
304 Ibid., p. 455.
305 Ibid.
306 Manu Gandhi, *The Diary of Manu Gandhi (1946–1948)*, (edited and translated) Tridip Suhrud, Oxford University Press (New Delhi, 2024), p. 138.
307 *CWMG*, Vol. 86, pp. 471–72.
308 Nirmal Kumar Bose, *My Days with Gandhi*, Calcutta, Orient Longman Limited, 1974, p. 130.
309 Manu Gandhi, *The Diary of Manu Gandhi (1946–1948)*, (edited and translated) Tridip Suhrud, Oxford University Press (New Delhi, 2024), p. 145.
310 Braja Kishore Sinha, *The Pilgrim of Noakhali*, The Photographer (Calcutta, 1948), p. 148.
311 *CWMG*, Vol. 87, 1983, p. 16.
312 Ibid., p. 24.

313 Gandhi had mentioned it in his prayer meeting on 16 February at Raipur. *CWMG*, Vol. 86, p. 469.
314 *CWMG*, Vol. 87, p. 25.
315 Manu Gandhi, *The Diary of Manu Gandhi (1946–1948)*, (edited and translated) Tridip Suhrud, Oxford University Press (New Delhi, 2024), pp. 161–62.
316 Nirmal Kumar Bose, *My Days with Gandhi*, Calcutta, Orient Longman Limited, 1974, p. 132.
317 *CWMG*, Vol. 87, p. 31.
318 Ibid.
319 In all probability, it was Niranjan Singh Gill [mentioned in Nirmal Kumar Bose, *My Days with Gandhi*, Orient Longman Limited, (Calcutta, 1974) p. 132].
320 Ibid., p. 37.
321 Gregory Titelman, *Random House Dictionary of Popular Proverbs & Sayings*, Random House (New York, 1996), p. 119.
322 Manu Gandhi, *The Diary of Manu Gandhi 1943-1944*, (ed. trans.) Tridip Suhrud, Oxford University Press (New Delhi, 2019), p. xi.
323 Ibid., p. xii.
324 Ibid.
325 Foucault, Michel, *The Politics of Truth*, Semiotext (E), United States of America, 1997, p. 183.
326 Ibid., p. 225.
327 *CWMG*, Vol. 77, p. 74.
328 Ibid., p. 240.
329 Ibid., p. 311.
330 Ibid., p. 324.
331 Ibid., p. 426.
332 Manu Gandhi, *The Lonely Pilgrim (Gandhiji's Noakhali Pilgrimage)*, Navajivan Publishing House (Ahmedabad, 1964), p. 4.

333 Ibid.
334 Ibid., pp. 4–5.
335 Ibid., p. 5.
336 Ibid.
337 Ibid.
338 Manu Gandhi, *The Diary of Manu Gandhi (1946–1948)*, (edited and translated) Tridip Suhrud, Oxford University Press (New Delhi, 2024), p. 5.
339 Ibid., p. 12.
340 Ibid.
341 Manu Gandhi, *The Lonely Pilgrim (Gandhiji's Noakhali Pilgrimage)*, Navajivan Publishing House (Ahmedabad, 1964), p. 14.
342 Manu Gandhi, *The Diary of Manu Gandhi (1946–1948)*, (edited and translated) Tridip Suhrud, Oxford University Press (New Delhi, 2024), p. 14.
343 M. K. Gandhi, *An Autobiography or The Story of My Experiments with Truth* (A Critical Edition), (trans.) Mahadev Desai, Yale University Press (New Haven and London, 2018), p. 8.
344 Vinay Lal, 'Nakedness, Non-violence, and Brahmacharya: Gandhi's Experiments in Celibate Sexuality', *Journal of the History of Sexuality*, Vol. 9, No. 1/2. (January–April 2000), p. 130.
345 Manu Gandhi, *The Diary of Manu Gandhi (1946–1948)*, (edited) Tridip Suhrud, Oxford University Press.
346 *CWMG*, Volume 67, p. 195.
347 Ibid.
348 Sigmund Freud, *Civilization and its Discontents*, (trans.) David McLintock, Penguin Books, New York, 2002, p. 34.
349 *CWMG*, Volume 67, p. 196.

350 Nirmal Kumar Bose, *My Days with Gandhi*, Calcutta, Orient Longman Limited, 1974, p. 150.

351 Ibid., pp. 149-150.

352 Ashis Nandy, *The Intimate Enemy: Loss and Recovery of Self under Colonialism*, Oxford University Press, new Delhi, 1983, p. 48.

353 Pyarelal, Mahatma Gandhi: *The Last Phase Vol 1*, Navajivan Publishing House (Ahmedabad, 1956), p. 495.

354 Nirmal Kumar Bose, *My Days with Gandhi*, Calcutta, Orient Longman Limited, 1974, p. 101.

355 Manu Gandhi, *The Diary of Manu Gandhi C (1946-1948)*, (edited and translated) Tridip Suhrud, Oxford University Press (New Delhi, 2024), p. 21.

356 Ibid., p. 22.

357 Ibid., p. 23.

358 Ibid., p. 41.

359 Ibid., p. 43.

360 Ibid., p. 45.

361 Ibid., p. 48.

362 Ibid., p. 50.

363 Ibid., p. 51.

364 *CWMG*, Vol. 86, p. 299.

365 Manu Gandhi, *The Diary of Manu Gandhi (1946–1948)*, (edited and translated) Tridip Suhrud, Oxford University Press (New Delhi, 2024), p. 52.

366 Ibid.

367 Ibid., p. 67.

368 Ibid., p. 90.

369 Ibid., p. 92.

370 Ibid., p. 106.

371 Ibid., p. 107.

372 Foucault, Michel, 'The Battle for Chastity', *Ethics: Subjectivity and Truth,* (Ed) Paul Rabinow, The New Press (New York, 1994), p. 192.

373 Nirmal Kumar Bose, *My Days with Gandhi*, Calcutta, Orient Longman Limited, 1974, p. 133.

374 Ibid.

375 Ibid.

376 Manu Gandhi, *The Diary of Manu Gandhi (1946–1948)*, (edited and translated) Tridip Suhrud, Oxford University Press (New Delhi, 2024), p. 117.

377 Ibid., p. 140.

378 Ibid., p. 148.

379 Lal, Vinay, "Nakedness, Non-violence, and Brahmacharya: Gandhi's Experiments in Celibate Sexuality", *Journal of the History of Sexuality*, Vol. 9, No. 1/2. (Jan. - Apr., 2000),, p. 110.

380 Ibid., p. 150.

381 Gandhi, Manu, *The Diary of Manu Gandhi C (1946-1948)*, (edited and translated) Tridip Suhrud, Oxford University Press, New Delhi, 2024, p. 25.

382 *CWMG*, Vol. 87, p. 14.

383 Ibid., p. 15.

384 Ibid.

385 Manu Gandhi, *The Diary of Manu Gandhi (1946–1948)*, (edited and translated) Tridip Suhrud, Oxford University Press (New Delhi, 2024), p. 165.

386 Nirmal Kumar Bose, *My Days with Gandhi*, Calcutta, Orient Longman Limited, 1974, p. 154–55 [Even though Bose is clearly referring to Manu, she is named X in the text, and other women are named A and B. The intentions behind replacing names with abbreviations aren't clear].

387 Ibid., p. 154.
388 *CWMG*, Vol. 87, p. 117.
389 Nirmal Kumar Bose, *My Days with Gandhi*, Calcutta, Orient Longman Limited, 1974, p. 1.
390 Foucault, Michel, 'The Battle for Chastity', *Ethics: Subjectivity and Truth,* (Ed) Paul Rabinow, The New Press (New York, 1994), p. 193.
391 *CWMG*, Volume 32, p. 143.
392 Nirmal Kumar Bose, *My Days with Gandhi*, Calcutta, Orient Longman Limited, 1974, p. 1.
393 Ibid.
394 Janam Mukherjee, *Hungry Bengal: War, Famine, and the End of Empire*, Oxford University Press (New York, 2016), p. 183.
395 Joya Chatterji, *Bengal Divided: Hindu Communalism and Partition 1932–1947*, Cambridge University Press, U.K. 1994, p. 18.
396 Ibid., p. 19.
397 Ibid., p. 182.
398 Ibid., p. 24.
399 Ibid., p. 267.
400 Janam Mukherjee, *Hungry Bengal: War, Famine, and the End of Empire*, Oxford University Press (New York, 2016), p. 218.
401 Ibid., pp. 247–48.
402 Robert Bernasconi and David Wood (eds.), *The Provocation of Levinas: Rethinking the Other*, (London and New York, 1988), p. 163.
403 Gyanendra Pandey, *Remembering Partition: Violence, Nationalism and History in India*, Cambridge University Press (Cambridge, 2001), p. 45.
404 Ibid., p. 45.

405 Ibid.

406 Paul Ricoeur, *Time and Narrative Vol. 3*, (trans.) Kathleen and David Pellauer, The University of Chicago Press (Chicago, 1985), p. 187.

407 Ibid.

408 Ibid., p. 189.

409 Ibid., p. 187.

410 M. K. Gandhi, *An Autobiography or The Story of My Experiments with Truth* (A Critical Edition), (trans.) Mahadev Desai, Yale University Press (New Haven and London, 2018), p. 49.

411 Pandey, Gyanendra, *Remembering Partition: Violence, Nationalism and History in India*, Cambridge University Press (Cambridge, 2001), p. 45.

412 Walter Benjamin, *Illuminations: Essays and Reflections*, (trans.) Harry Zohn, Schocken Books (New York, 1969), p. 255.

413 Gyanendra Pandey, *Remembering Partition: Violence, Nationalism and History in India*, Cambridge University Press (Cambridge, 2001), p. 45.

414 Mahmood Mamdani, *When Victims Become Killers: Colonialism, Nativism, and the Genocide in Rwanda*, Princeton University press, New Jersey, 2002, p. 197.

415 Ibid.

416 Ibid., p. 198.

417 Ibid., p. 8.

418 Bipan Chandra, *Communalism in Modern India*, Vikas Publishing House Pvt. Ltd. (New Delhi, 1984), p. 4.

419 Sugata Bose, *Agrarian Bengal: Economy, Social Structure and Politics, 1919–1947*, Cambridge University Press (London, 2008), p. 182.

420 Partha Chatterjee, *Bengal 1920–1947: Vol. 1 The Land Question*, Centre for Studies in Social Sciences Monograph 4, K.P. Bagchi & Company (Kolkata, 1984), p. 140.

421 Sugata Bose, *Agrarian Bengal: Economy, Social Structure and Politics, 1919-1947*, Cambridge University Press, London, 2008, p. 182.

422 Sugata Bose, *Agrarian Bengal: Economy, Social Structure and Politics, 1919–1947*, Cambridge University Press (London, 2008), p. 183.

423 Ibid., p. 184.

424 Bipan Chandra, *Communalism in Modern India*, Vikas Publishing House Pvt. Ltd. (New Delhi, 1984), pp. 56–57.

425 Ibid., p. 66.

426 Ibid.

427 Ibid.

428 Ibid.

429 Ibid., p. 17.

430 Ibid.

431 Ibid., p. 13.

432 Jawaharlal Nehru, *The Discovery of India*, Oxford University Press (New Delhi, 1964), p. 562.

433 Karl Marx, 'On the Jewish Question', *Marx-Engels Reader Second Edition*, (ed.) Robert C. Tucker, W.W. Norton and Company (New York, London, 1978), p. 46.

434 I am averse to using scientific analogies to explain human life and society, but this is an exception where I want to argue against a rather 'scientific' understanding of society that is averse to considering community.

435 Partha Chatterjee, *Bengal 1920–1947: Vol. 1 The Land Question*, Centre for Studies in Social Sciences

Monograph 4, K.P. Bagchi & Company (Kolkata, 1984), p. lii.

436 Ibid., p. liii.

437 Shabnum Tejani,, *Indian Secularism: A Social and Intellectual History 1890–1950*, Permanent Black (New Delhi, 2007), p. 115.

438 Vanya Vaidehi Bhargav, *Being Hindu, Being Indian: Lala Lajpat Rai's Ideas of Nationhood*, Penguin, Viking (Gurgaon, 2024), p. 340.

439 Dr B. R. Ambedkar, *Writings and Speeches Vol. 13*, Dr Ambedkar Foundation, Ministry of Social Justice & Empowerment, Govt. of India (Mumbai, 2019), p. 62.

440 Ranajit Guha, *Elementary Aspects of Peasant Insurgency in Colonial India*, Duke University Press (Durham and London, 1999), p. 18.

441 Ibid., p. 19.

442 Partha Chatterjee, 'Agrarian Relations and Communalism, 1926–1935', (ed.) Ranajit Guha, *Subaltern Studies Vol. I: Writings on South Asian History and Society*, Oxford University Press (Delhi, 1982), p. 37.

443 Mamdani, Mahmood, *When Victims Become Killers: Colonialism, Nativism, and the Genocide in Rwanda*, Princeton University press, New Jersey, 2002, p. 8.

444 Ibid.

445 Simone Weil, *Formative Writings 1929–1941*, (ed., trans.) Dorothy Tuck McFarland and Wilhelmina Van Ness, The University of Massachusetts Press (Amherst, 1987), p. 239.

Chapter 2: 'Neither a Hindu Nor a Muslim'

1 For instance, Shabnum Tejani takes up the cause of the Muslim minority's grievances and aspirations during the

anti-colonial period without any internal critique, while focusing her critical lens on the colonial administration, the Congress and the Hindu right. Tejani's critique of the secular citizen defined in individualized and universal terms, her concerns for Muslim/minority representation and the necessity for offering protective rights for minority groups in a democracy are pertinent. The problem occurs when she writes: 'Jinnah announced that Direct Action Day would be held on 16 August 1946, reiterating his call for the creation of a separate Muslim state of Pakistan. Direct Action was to be a peaceful mass campaign, but was followed by massacres in Calcutta, marking some of the most brutal communal violence witnessed in this period.' [Shabnum Tejani,, *Indian Secularism: A Social and Intellectual History 1890–1950*, Permanent Black (New Delhi, 2007), p. 240].

That Direct Action Day was a call for 'peaceful mass campaign' sounds straight out of a communal mythology. Jinnah's own statements were, 'Today, we have forged a pistol and are in a position to use it', and 'I am not going to discuss ethics.' There were provocative statements made by other League members like Liaquat Ali and Khwaja Nazimuddin. Tejani is bewilderingly oblivious of facts. Her wishful reading that Jinnah's call to Direct Action was meant to be a 'peaceful mass campaign' is followed by a cryptic 'but was followed by massacres . . .' Tejani seems to avoid any logical connection between her fantasies and historical reality. The 'but' isn't explained, just slipped in as a clause to suggest that a peaceful idea somehow, accidentally, inexplicably, had unintended consequences. Events don't correspond exactly to an act intended towards a certain end. Acts might generate consequences prior to the end in view that would take a life of their own. Such are the unforeseen scenarios of 'unintended consequences' in politics. In Jinnah's case, however, the banality of his words and actions do not warrant any serious scrutiny about consequences. Whether Pakistan lived up to Jinnah's idea or not is less about Jinnah's intentions, and more about the disfigured nature of his idea. In the same way, Jinnah is not responsible for the genocides of partition in a consequentialist way. But that is not the only sort of responsibility. Political leaders who want to establish divisions between people on ethnic, religious or other identitarian lines are not imagining peaceful, non-violent transitions.

2 Mohammad Sajjad, *Muslim Politics in Bihar: Changing Contours*, Routledge (Delhi, 2014), p. 132.

3 Ibid., p. 139.

4 Ibid., p. 140.

5 Ibid.

6 Marzia Casolari, '*Hindutva*'s Foreign Tie-up in the 1930s: Archival Evidence', *Economic and Political Weekly*, Vol. 35, No. 4 (22–28 January 2000), pp. 219–220.

7 Mohammad Sajjad, *Muslim Politics in Bihar: Changing Contours*, Routledge (Delhi, 2014), p. 144.

8 Ibid.

9 Ibid.

10 Bipan Chandra, *Communalism in Modern India*, Vikas Publishing House Pvt. Ltd. (New Delhi, 1984), p. 296.

11 Ibid., p. 297.

12 Ibid.

13 Ibid., p. 298.

14 Ibid., p. 307.

15 Ibid., p. 163.

16 Ibid., pp. 163–164.
17 Ibid., p. 164.
18 Ibid., p. 153.
19 Ibid., p. 154.
20 Ibid.
21 Ibid., p. 37.
22 Nirmal Kumar Bose, *My Days with Gandhi*, Calcutta, Orient Longman Limited, 1974, p. 139.
23 Ibid.
24 *CWMG*, Vol. 87, p. 42.
25 Yevgeny Yevtushenko, *A Precocious Autobiography*, (trans.) Andrew R. MacAndrew, E.P. Dutton & Co. Inc., New York, 1963, pp. 94–95.
26 *CWMG*, Vol. 87, p. 42.
27 Ibid., p. 44.
28 Ibid.
29 Pyarelal, Mahatma Gandhi: *The Last Phase Vol 1*, Navajivan Publishing House, Ahmedabad, 1956, p. 624.
30 Ibid.
31 Ibid., pp. 49–50, 50 *n*.
32 Mohammad Sajjad, *Muslim Politics in Bihar: Changing Contours*, Routledge (Delhi, 2014), p. 167.
33 The Indian Annual Register, Vol. II, July–December 1946, (ed.) Nripendranath Mitra, The Annual Register Office Calcutta, p. 201.
34 Ibid.
35 *CWMG*, Vol. 87, p. 52.
36 Pyarelal, Mahatma Gandhi: *The Last Phase Vol 1*, Navajivan Publishing House, Ahmedabad, 1956, p. 625.
37 Ibid.

38 Ibid., pp. 625-626.

39 Ibid., p. 626.

40 *CWMG*, Vol. 87, p.58.

41 Ibid., pp. 59–60.

42 Mohammad Sajjad, *Muslim Politics in Bihar: Changing Contours*, Routledge (Delhi, 2014), p. 155.

43 Ibid., p. 65.

44 Pyarelal, Mahatma Gandhi: *The Last Phase Vol 1*, Navajivan Publishing House, Ahmedabad, 1956, p. 644.

45 Ibid.

46 *CWMG*, Vol. 87, p. 66.

47 Ibid., p. 69.

48 Manu Gandhi, *The Diary of Manu Gandhi (1946–1948)*, (edited and translated) Tridip Suhrud, Oxford University Press (New Delhi, 2024), p. 186.

49 *CWMG*, Vol. 87, pp. 73–74.

50 *CWMG*, Vol. 87, p. 75.

51 Ibid., p. 79 [The letter is mentioned in Manu's diary: 'Please forgive us for the crime committed by us, we are ashamed that we killed the Muslims that we did and as atonement we make this contribution to the relief fund. We seek your forgiveness and give our word to you that we shall not indulge in such activities henceforth.' Manu Gandhi, *The Diary of Manu Gandhi (1946–1948)*, (edited and translated) Tridip Suhrud, Oxford University Press (New Delhi, 2024), p. 188].

52 Ibid., p. 111 *n*.

53 Ibid., p. 105.

54 Manu Gandhi, *The Diary of Manu Gandhi (1946–1948)*, (edited and translated) Tridip Suhrud, Oxford University Press (New Delhi, 2024), p. 191.

55 Anwesha Roy, *Making Peace, Making Riots Communalism and Communal Violence, Bengal 1940–1947*, Cambridge University Press (New Delhi, 2018), p. 193.
56 Ibid.
57 Suranjan Das, *Communal Riots in Bengal 1905–1947*, Oxford University Press (New Delhi, 1991), p. 197.
58 *CWMG*, Vol. 87, p. 83.
59 Ibid., p. 89.
60 Ibid., p. 119.
61 Manu Gandhi, *The Diary of Manu Gandhi (1946–1948)*, (edited and translated) Tridip Suhrud, Oxford University Press (New Delhi, 2024), p. 185.
62 Pyarelal, *Mahatma Gandhi*: *The Last Phase Vol 1*, Navajivan Publishing House, Ahmedabad, 1956, p. 660.
63 *CWMG*, Volume 16, p. 230.
64 *CWMG*, Vol. 87, p. 115.
65 Ibid.
66 Mohammad Sajjad, *Muslim Politics in Bihar: Changing Contours*, Routledge (Delhi, 2014), p. 165.
67 *CWMG*, Vol. 87, pp. 118–19.
68 Ibid., p. 120.
69 Manu Gandhi, *The Diary of Manu Gandhi (1946–1948)*, (edited and translated) Tridip Suhrud, Oxford University Press (New Delhi, 2024), p. 205.
70 Pyarelal, *Mahatma Gandhi*: *The Last Phase Vol 1*, Navajivan Publishing House, Ahmedabad, 1956, p. 665.
71 Ibid., pp. 206–07.
72 *CWMG*, Vol. 87, p. 125.
73 Ibid., p. 131.
74 Ibid., p. 133.

75 Ibid.

76 Ibid., p. 133.

77 Anwesha Roy gives the details on conversion in Noakhali: 'Conversions particularly distinguished the Noakhali riots. Suhrawardy himself gave the number of converts to Islam as 9895 in Tipperah alone. However, the Simpson Report (an unpublished enquiry report) put the number of conversions in Faridpur, Chandpur and Hajiganj at around 22,550. Ashoka Gupta, an AIWC relief worker who stayed at Noakhali for relief work, also mentions cases of conversions. She cites instances where, after the conversion, Hindus were forced to marry their first and second cousins. In the village of Mirjapur, all Namasudras were also forcibly converted. Conversions had happened earlier in riots, but the scale in 1946 was unprecedented.' [Roy, Anwesha, *Making Peace, Making Riots Communalism and Communal Violence, Bengal 1940–1947*, Cambridge University Press (New Delhi, 2018), p. 198].

78 Eqbal Ahmad, *Confronting Empire: Interviews with David Barsamian*, Haymarket Books (Chicago, Illinois, 2016), p. 99.

79 Ibid.

80 Manu Gandhi, *The Diary of Manu Gandhi (1946–1948)*, (edited and translated) Tridip Suhrud, Oxford University Press (New Delhi, 2024), p. 213.

81 Pyarelal, *Mahatma Gandhi*: *The Last Phase Vol 1*, Navajivan Publishing House, Ahmedabad, 1956, p. 669.

82 Ibid.

83 Ibid.

84 Ibid., p. 670-671.

85 *CWMG*, Vol. 87, p. 168.

86 Ibid.

87 Manu Gandhi, *The Diary of Manu Gandhi (1946–1948)*, (edited and translated) Tridip Suhrud, Oxford University Press (New Delhi, 2024), p. 218.

88 *CWMG*, Vol. 87, p. 174.

89 Ibid., p. 177.

90 Ibid., p. 180.

91 Manu Gandhi, *The Diary of Manu Gandhi (1946–1948)*, (edited and translated) Tridip Suhrud, Oxford University Press (New Delhi, 2024), p. 229.

92 *CWMG*, Vol. 87, p. 183.

93 Manu Gandhi, *The Diary of Manu Gandhi (1946–1948)*, (edited and translated) Tridip Suhrud, Oxford University Press (New Delhi, 2024), p. 229.

94 *CWMG*, Vol. 87, p. 183.

95 Ibid., p. 187.

96 Ibid., p. 202.

97 Ibid., p. 218.

98 Ibid., p. 223.

99 Ibid., p. 228.

100 Ibid., p. 230.

101 Ibid., p. 244.

102 Ibid., p. 258.

103 Ibid.

104 Ibid., p. 261.

105 Ibid., p. 293.

106 Ishtiaq Ahmed, *Jinnah: His Successes, Failures and Role in History*, Penguin Random House India (Gurgaon, 2020), p. 393–94.

107 William L. Shirer, *Gandhi: A Memoir*, Simon and Schuster (New York, 1979), p. 120.

108 Ibid.
109 Jawaharlal Nehru, *An Autobiography*, Oxford University Press (New Delhi, 1980), p. 73.
110 Shirer, William L., *Gandhi: A Memoir*, Simon and Schuster (New York, 1979), p. 120.
111 Ishtiaq Ahmed, *Jinnah: His Successes, Failures and Role in History*, Penguin Random House India (Gurgaon, 2020), p. 420.
112 Ibid.
113 Sharif al Mujahid, (ed.), *In Quest of Jinnah: Diary, Notes, and Correspondence of Hector Bolitho*, Oxford University Press (Karachi, 2007), p. 143.
114 *CWMG*, Vol. 87, p. 280.
115 Ibid.
116 Ibid., p. 288.
117 Ibid., p. 289.
118 Ibid., p. 296.
119 Ibid., p. 297.
120 Ibid., p. 304.
121 Ibid., p. 205.
122 Ibid., p. 338.
123 Ibid.
124 Ibid., p. 374.
125 Ibid., p. 380.
126 Ibid., p. 388.
127 Ibid., p. 194.
128 Mohammad Sajjad, *Muslim Politics in Bihar: Changing Contours*, Routledge (Delhi, 2014), p. 155.
129 Ibid., p. 158.
130 *CWMG*, Vol. 87, p. 424.
131 Ibid.

132 Ibid., p. 435–36.
133 Ibid., p. 440.
134 Ibid., p. 442.
135 Ibid., p. 444.
136 Ibid., p. 452.
137 Ibid.
138 Ibid. p. 452 *n*.
139 Dipesh Chakrabarty, *The Calling of History: Sir Jadunath Sarkar and His Empire of Truth*, The University of Chicago Press (Chicago and London, 2015), p. 30.
140 *CWMG*, Vol. 87, p. 452.
141 Ibid.
142 Ibid., p. 453.
143 Ibid.
144 Nirmal Kumar Bose, *My Days with Gandhi*, Calcutta, Orient Longman Limited, 1974, p. 200.
145 Ibid.
146 *CWMG*, Vol. 87, p. 464.
147 Ibid.
148 Ibid., p. 465.
149 Manu Gandhi, *The Diary of Manu Gandhi (1946–1948)*, (edited and translated) Tridip Suhrud, Oxford University Press (New Delhi, 2024), pp. 253–54.
150 *CWMG*, Vol. 87, p. 474.
151 Ibid., p. 482.
152 Ibid., p. 476.
153 Manu Gandhi, *The Diary of Manu Gandhi (1946–1948)*, (edited and translated) Tridip Suhrud, Oxford University Press (New Delhi, 2024), p. 239.
154 Ibid.,
155 Ibid., p. 254.

156 *CWMG*, Vol. 87, p. 503.
157 Ibid., p. 508.
158 Ibid., p. 511.

Chapter 3: 'The Kohinoor of India's Freedom'

1 *CWMG*, Vol. 88, 1983, p. 4.
2 *CWMG*, Vol. 20, 1966, p. 496.
3 *CWMG*, Vol. 79, 1980, p. 319.
4 *CWMG*, Vol. 88, p. 5.
5 Ibid., p. 7.
6 *CWMG*, Vol. 88, p. 15.
7 Ibid., p. 17 [Gandhi felt repulsed by the 'obscene photographs of actors and actresses [that] are displayed in the newspapers by way of advertisement!'].
8 Ibid.
9 Ibid., p. 30.
10 Manu Gandhi, *The Diary of Manu Gandhi (1946–1948)*, (edited and translated) Tridip Suhrud, Oxford University Press (New Delhi, 2024), p. 261.
11 *CWMG*, Vol. 88, p. 38.
12 Ibid., p. 39.
13 Referring to Hamidullah Khan, the last ruling nawab of the princely state of Bhopal, who reluctantly signed the instrument of accession to India on 1 May 1949.
14 *CWMG*, Vol. 88, p. 46.
15 Ibid., p. 47.
16 Ishtiaq Ahmed, *Jinnah: His Successes, Failures and Role in History*, Penguin Random House India (Gurgaon, 2020), p. 441.
17 Ibid., p. 445.
18 Ibid., p. 103.

19 *CWMG*, Vol. 87, p. 526 *n*.
20 *CWMG*, Vol. 88, p. 113.
21 Jawaharlal Nehru, *The Discovery of India*, Oxford University Press (New Delhi, 1994), p. 382.
22 *CWMG*, Vol. 88, p. 139.
23 Ibid., p. 147.
24 Ibid., p. 148.
25 Faisal Devji, *The Impossible Indian: Gandhi and the Temptation of Violence*, Harvard University Press (Cambridge, Massachusetts, 2012), p. 190.
26 Ibid., p. 191.
27 *CWMG*, Vol. 88, pp. 151–52.
28 Ibid., p. 152.
29 Ibid., pp. 181–82.
30 Ibid., p. 225.
31 Ibid.
32 Ibid., p. 226.
33 Ibid.
34 Ibid.
35 Sudipta Sen, *Distant Sovereignty: National Imperialism and the Origins of British India*, Routledge (New York, 2002), p. XXV.
36 Tagore, Rabindranath, 'Nationalism in the West', *Nationalism*, (intro.) Ramchandra Guha, Penguin Books, New Delhi, 2009, page 37.
37 *CWMG*, Vol. 88, p. 226.
38 Ibid., p. 238.
39 Ibid., p. 303.
40 Ibid., p. 323.
41 Manubahen Gandhi, *The Lonely Pilgrim (Gandhiji's Noakhali Pilgrimage)*, Navajivan Publishing House (Ahmedabad, 1964), p. 41.

42 *CWMG*, Vol. 88, p. 400.

43 Manu Gandhi, *The Diary of Manu Gandhi (1946–1948)*, (edited and translated) Tridip Suhrud, Oxford University Press (New Delhi, 2024), p. 320.

44 Ibid., p. 321.

45 Ibid., p. 322.

46 Ibid., p. 323.

47 *CWMG*, Vol. 89, p. 5.

48 Abdul Wali Khan had participated in the Khudai Khidmatgar Movement and the Quit India Movement, later agitated for Pashtun autonomy after Pakistan's creation and was imprisoned several times by Pakistan's governments. [Manu Gandhi, *The Diary of Manu Gandhi (1946–1948)*, (edited) Tridip Suhrud, Oxford University Press].

49 Manu Gandhi, *The Diary of Manu Gandhi (1946–1948)*, (edited) Tridip Suhrud, Oxford University Press.

50 Ibid.

51 Ibid.

52 Ibid.

53 *CWMG*, Vol. 89, p. 10.

54 Ibid.

55 Ibid., p. 11.

56 Ibid., p. 19.

Chapter 4: 'A Short-Lived Nine-Day Wonder'

1 Manu Gandhi, *The Diary of Manu Gandhi (1946–1948)*, (edited and translated) Tridip Suhrud, Oxford University Press (New Delhi, 2024), p. 330.

2 Ibid.

3 *CWMG*, Vol. 89, 1983, p. 21.
4 Ibid.
5 Ibid., p. 28.
6 Ibid., p. 33.
7 Ibid.
8 Manu Gandhi, *The Diary of Manu Gandhi (1946–1948)*, (edited and translated) Tridip Suhrud, Oxford University Press (New Delhi, 2024), p. 335.
9 Ibid., p. 336.
10 Ibid., p. 337.
11 Ibid.
12 Ibid.
13 Ibid., p. 338.
14 *CWMG*, Vol. 89, p. 50.
15 Manu Gandhi, *The Diary of Manu Gandhi (1946–1948)*, (edited and translated) Tridip Suhrud, Oxford University Press (New Delhi, 2024), p. 341.
16 *CWMG*, Vol. 89, p. 61 n.
17 Manu Gandhi, *The Diary of Manu Gandhi (1946–1948)*, (edited and translated) Tridip Suhrud, Oxford University Press, (New Delhi, 2024), p. 343.
18 Ibid.
19 Ibid., p. 344.
20 *CWMG*, Vol. 89, p. 71.
21 Ibid., p. 72.
22 Ibid., p. 80.
23 Manu Gandhi, *The Diary of Manu Gandhi (1946–1948)*, (edited translated) Tridip Suhrud, Oxford University Press (New Delhi, 2024), p. 349.
24 Ibid.

25 *CWMG*, Vol. 89, pp. 84–85.

26 Nikhil Chakravarty, 'Day One in Calcutta' (*People's Age*, 24 August 1947), (reprinted) *Mainstream*, Vol. XLVIII, No. 45, 30 October 2010. link: http://mainstreamweekly.net/article2420.html.

(Chakravarty, who passed away on 28 June 1998, was the founder of *Mainstream* and a prominent and much regarded journalist in Delhi. My father knew him and asked me to meet him when I visited Delhi as a graduate student in 1992. I have a blurry recollection of that meeting at his residence. I am immensely grateful to Ramnik Mohan, retired associate professor and currently freelancer from Rohtak, Haryana, for sending me the link to Chakravarty's article).

27 Modern ideological gurus—meaning intellectuals and academicians—theorize our sufferings and grievances in a way that puts everything inside a grand design where we find ourselves lost. The cynic philosopher from Romania, E.M. Cioran wrote in *The Short History of Decay*: '[Man] no longer lives in existence, but in the *theory* of existence.' In Cioran's defence, theory does not come close to our problems, but rather turns them into conflicting world-views. Theory keeps us busy in a second-order conflict where consensus is under suspicion. In other words, theorizing has become an unethical practice where even theorists arguing passionately for fraternity are not interested in a fraternal intellectual or academic world, but one where they want to be spokespersons of their ideological version of the truth. [E. M. Cioran, *A Short History of Decay*, (trans.) Richard Howard, Quartet Encounters (New York, 1975), p. 114].

28 Jawaharlal Nehru, *The Discovery of India*, Oxford University Press (New Delhi, 1964), p. 132.
29 *CWMG*, Vol. 89, p. 254.
30 *CWMG*, Vol. 90, 1984, p. 233.
31 *CWMG*, Vol. 89, p. 95.
32 Ibid., p. 104.
33 Ibid., p. 119.
34 Ibid., pp. 119–120 (Gandhi's words are paraphrased.)
35 Ibid., p. 121.
36 Ibid.
37 Ibid. pp. 126–27.
38 Ibid., p. 127.
39 Ibid., p. 124.
40 Ibid., p. 129.
41 Ibid., p. 130.
42 Among the numerous incidents since 2014 that created limited outrage in civil society, some of the most disturbing ones: On 22 September 2015, fifty-two-year-old Akhlaq was dragged from his house and lynched by a mob of two hundred people in the district of Dadri in Uttar Pradesh for allegedly slaughtering a cow. On 9 March 2016, Imtiaz Khan, a twelve-year-old schoolboy, and Majloom Ansari, a thirty-two-year-old cattle trader, were found hanging from a tree in Latehar, Jharkhand, after being beaten with sticks and axes allegedly by cow-protection vigilantes, when they were taking their oxen to sell at the cattle-fair 40 kilometres away from home. On 11 July 2016, cow vigilantes flogged seven Dalit men after tying up their hands for skinning a dead cow in Una district, Gujarat. On 3 April 2017, Pehlu Khan, a native of Haryana, was beaten to death by self-styled cow-vigilantes in Alwar, Rajasthan, on the Jaipur–Delhi National Highway.

On 22 June 2017, Hafiz Junaid, a sixteen-year-old boy from Haryana, was lynched to death in a Mathura-bound train while returning home after shopping for Eid in Delhi.

43 *CWMG*, Vol. 89, p. 131.

44 Pyarelal, Mahatma Gandhi: *The Last Phase Vol II*, Navajivan Publishing House (Ahmedabad, 1958), p. 369.

45 Nirmal Kumar Bose, *My Days with Gandhi*, Calcutta, Orient Longman Limited, 1974, p. 229.

46 *CWMG*, Vol. 89, p. 133.

47 Ibid., p. 134.

48 Manu Gandhi, *The Diary of Manu Gandhi (1946–1948)*, (edited and translated) Tridip Suhrud, Oxford University Press (New Delhi, 2024), p. 356.

49 Pyarelal, Mahatma Gandhi: *The Last Phase Vol II*, Navajivan Publishing House (Ahmedabad, 1958), p. 406.

50 Manu Gandhi, *The Diary of Manu Gandhi (1946–1948)*, (edited and translated) Tridip Suhrud, Oxford University Press (New Delhi, 2024), p. 357.

51 Ibid.

52 Ibid., p. 358.

53 Ibid.

54 Ibid.

55 *CWMG*, Vol. 89, p. 134.

56 Pyarelal, Mahatma Gandhi: *The Last Phase Vol. II*, Navajivan Publishing House (Ahmedabad, 1958), p. 410.

57 Ibid., p. 411.

58 Ibid., p. 412.

59 *CWMG*, Vol. 89, p. 139.

60 Manu Gandhi, *The Diary of Manu Gandhi (1946–1948)*, (edited and translated) Tridip Suhrud, Oxford University Press (New Delhi, 2024), p. 370.

61 Pyarelal, Mahatma Gandhi: *The Last Phase Vol. II*, Navajivan Publishing House (Ahmedabad, 1958), p. 415.
62 Manu Gandhi, *The Diary of Manu Gandhi (1946–1948)*, (edited) Tridip Suhrud, Oxford University Press (New Delhi, 2024), p. 370.
63 *CWMG*, Vol. 89, p. 142.
64 Ibid., p. 142 n.
65 Hannah Arendt, *Crisis of the Republic*, Harcourt Brace & Company (New York, 1972), p. 152.
66 Karl Jaspers, 'Gandhi on his 100th Birthday', in *Mahatma Gandhi 100 Years*, (ed.) S. Radhakrishnan, Gandhi Peace Foundation (New Delhi, 1968), p. 169.
67 *CWMG*, Vol. 23, p. 55.
68 Ibid., p. 442.
69 Ibid., p. 443.
70 Ibid.
71 Étienne Balibar, 'Lenin and Gandhi: A missed encounter?', (trans.) Knox Peden, *Radical Philosophy* 172, Mar/Apr 2012, p. 10.
72 Ibid., p. 11.
73 *CWMG*, Vol. 89, p. 152.
74 Ibid., pp. 152–53.
75 'We the undersigned promise Gandhiji that now that peace and quiet have been restored in Calcutta once again, we shall never again allow communal strife in the city and shall strive unto death to prevent it.' Signatories: Surendra Mohan Ghosh, President, Bengal Pradesh Congress Committee, Sarat Chandra Bose, H.S. Suhrawardy, Niranjan Singh Talib, N.C. Chatterjee, Debendranath Mukerjee, President and Secretary of Provincial Hindu Mahasabha and Radha Kisan Jaidka, Punjab leader. [Reported by *Amrita Bazar Patrika*, 5 September 1947] *CWMG*, Vol. 89, p. 153.

76 Ibid., p. 154.
77 Ibid., p. 154 *n*.
78 Manu Gandhi, *The Diary of Manu Gandhi (1946–1948)*, (edited and translated) Tridip Suhrud, Oxford University Press (New Delhi, 2024), p. 381.
79 *CWMG*, Vol. 89, p. 161.
80 Manu Gandhi, *The Diary of Manu Gandhi (1946–1948)*, (edited and translated) Tridip Suhrud, Oxford University Press (New Delhi, 2024), p. 385.

Chapter 5: 'A Fist Full of Bones'

1 *CWMG*, Vo. 89, p. 166.
2 Manu Gandhi, *The Diary of Manu Gandhi (1946–1948)*, (edited and translated) Tridip Suhrud, Oxford University Press (New Delhi, 2024), p. 386.
3 Ibid.
4 Ibid., p. 388.
5 Ibid., p. 389.
6 Ibid.
7 Ibid., p. 390.
8 *CWMG*, Vol. 89, p. 168.
9 Ibid., p. 169.
10 Manu Gandhi, *The Diary of Manu Gandhi (1946–1948)*, (edited and translated) Tridip Suhrud, Oxford University Press (New Delhi, 2024), p. 391.
11 Ibid., p. 393.
12 Pyarelal writes, when an associate of Gandhi praised the R.S.S. for its work at Wah refugee camp and highlighted its 'discipline, courage and capacity for hard work,' Gandhi replied such qualities were displayed by Hitler's Nazis and Mussolini's fascists and described the R.S.S as 'communal body with a totalitarian outlook.'

Pyarelal, *Mahatma Gandhi: The Last Phase Vol II*, Navajivan Publishing House, Ahmedabad, 1958, p. 140]

13 *CWMG*, Vol. 89, p. 174.

14 Ibid., p. 175.

15 Manu Gandhi, *The Diary of Manu Gandhi (1946–1948)*, (edited and translated) Tridip Suhrud, Oxford University Press (New Delhi, 2024), p. 398.

16 Ibid.

17 Ibid.

18 *CWMG*, Vol. 89, p. 193.

19 Ibid., p. 194.

20 Manu Gandhi, *The Diary of Manu Gandhi (1946–1948)*, (edited and translated) Tridip Suhrud, Oxford University Press (New Delhi, 2024), p. 404.

21 Ibid.

22 Ibid., pp. 404–05.

23 Ibid., p. 405.

24 Ibid.

25 Ibid., p. 410.

26 *CWMG*, Vol. 89, p. 202.

27 Manu Gandhi, *The Diary of Manu Gandhi (1946–1948)*, (edited and translated) Tridip Suhrud, Oxford University Press (New Delhi, 2024), p. 12.

28 Slavoj Žižek, *Violence*, Picador (New York, 2008), pp. 65–66.

29 Manu Gandhi, *The Diary of Manu Gandhi (1946–1948)*, (edited and translated) Tridip Suhrud, Oxford University Press (New Delhi, 2024), p. 411.

30 Ibid., p. 418.

31 Simone Weil, *Waiting for God*, (trans.) Emma Craufurd, Harper & Row New York, 1951 (G.P. Putnam's Sons), p. 114.

32 Simone Weil, *Gravity and Grace*, (trans.) Gustav Thibon, Routledge & Kegan Paul (New York, 1952), p. 119.

33 *CWMG*, Vol. 89, p. 244.
34 Ibid., pp. 199–200.
35 Ibid., p. 244.
36 Manu Gandhi, *The Diary of Manu Gandhi (1946–1948)*, (edited and translated) Tridip Suhrud, Oxford University Press (New Delhi, 2024), p. 433.
37 Ibid., p. 439.
38 Ishtiaq Ahmed, *Jinnah: His Successes, Failures and Role in History*, Penguin Random House India (Gurgaon, 2020), p. 555.
39 Manu Gandhi, *The Diary of Manu Gandhi (1946–1948)*, (edited and translated) Tridip Suhrud, Oxford University Press (New Delhi, 2024), p. 442.
40 *CWMG*, Vol. 89, p. 275.
41 Ibid., p. 299.
42 Ibid., p. 303.
43 Ibid., pp. 303–04.
44 Ibid., p. 304.
45 Manu Gandhi, *The Diary of Manu Gandhi (1946–1948)*, (edited and translated) Tridip Suhrud, Oxford University Press (New Delhi, 2024), p. 455.
46 Ibid., p. 458.
47 *CWMG*, Vol. 89, pp. 357–58.
48 *CWMG*, Vol. 89, p. 379.
49 Ibid., p. 443.
50 Ibid., p. 461.
51 Ibid., p. 480.
52 Ibid., p. 413.
53 Ibid., p. 481.
54 *CWMG*, Vol. 90, p. 15.
55 Ibid., p. 17.
56 Ibid., p. 38.
57 Ibid., pp. 38–39.

58 Ibid., p. 40.

59 Ibid., p. 41.

60 Ibid.

61 Ibid., p. 43.

62 Ibid., p. 126.

63 Ibid., p. 344.

64 Levinas, Emanuel, *Otherwise than Being*, (trans.) Alphonso Lingis, Duquesne University Press (Pittsburgh, Pennsylvania, 1998), p. 55.

65 Ibid., p. 84.

66 Mahatma Gandhi, (ed.) Parel, Anthony, *Hind Swaraj*, Cambridge Text in Modern Politics (Cambridge University Press, 1990), p. 90.

67 Jacques Derrida, *The Politics of Friendship*, (trans.) George Collins, Verso (New York, 2005), p. 65. [Derrida uses the term in connection to Nietzsche's warning that all politics of the new must face the danger of the old attempt to appropriate the neighbour in the name of whose love that politics is fought].

68 Ajay Skaria, "The Strange Violence of Satyagraha: Gandhi, *Itihaas* and History", in (ed.) Manu Bhagvan, *Heterotopias: Nationalism and the Possibility of History in South Asia*, Oxford University Press, New Delhi, 2010, p. 143.

69 Ibid.

70 Ibid., pp. 143-144.

71 Ibid., p. 144.

72 This distinction disqualifies Partha Chatterjee's hasty conclusion that Gandhi's idea of truth "lies outside history" and that this truth "has no history of its own". [Partha Chatterjee, *Nationalist Thought and the Colonial World: A Derivative Discourse?*, Oxford University Press, Delhi, 1986, p. 94].

73 Sigmund Freud, *Civilization and its Discontents*, (trans.) David McLintock, Penguin Books (New York, 2002), p. 47.

74 Emanuel Levinas, *Otherwise than Being*, (trans.) Alphonso Lingis, Duquesne University Press (Pittsburgh, Pennsylvania, 1998), p. 86.

75 Sigmund Freud, *Civilization and its Discontents*, (trans.) David McLintock, Penguin Books (New York, 2002), p. 48.

76 Slavoj Žižek, *Violence*, Picador (New York, 2008), p. 56.

77 Howard Caygill, *Levinas and the Political*, Routledge (London and New York, 2002), p. 183.

78 Ibid., p. 192.

79 Ibid., p. 193.

80 Ibid., p. 87.

81 Sigmund Freud, *Civilization and its Discontents*, (trans.) David McLintock, Penguin Books (New York, 2002), p. 51.

82 Ibid.

83 Ibid., p. 49.

84 Ibid., p. 71.

85 Ibid., p. 78–79.

86 Ibid., p. 79.

87 *CWMG*, Vol. 90, p. 409.

88 Ibid., p. 409 *n*.

89 Ibid., p. 409.

90 Manu Gandhi, *The Diary of Manu Gandhi (1946–1948)*, (edited) Tridip Suhrud, Oxford University Press (New Delhi, 2024), p. 557.

91 *CWMG*, Vol. 90, p. 416.

92 Manu Gandhi, *The Diary of Manu Gandhi (1946–1948)*, (edited) Tridip Suhrud, Oxford University Press (New Delhi, 2024), p. 567.

93 Ibid., p. 585 *n*.

94 Ibid., p. 590.
95 *CWMG*, Vol. 90, p. 465 *n*.
96 Nathuram Godse, *Why I Assassinated Mahatma Gandhi*, (ed.) Gopal Godse, Surya Bharati Prakashan (New Delhi, 2017), p. 18.
97 Ibid., p. 30.
98 Ibid., p. 20.
99 Ibid., p. 41–42.
100 Ibid., p. 104.

Note: In his statement, Godse mentioned that he became a volunteer of the RSS during or after his matriculation, and he also worked for the Hindu Mahasabha without being a member (p. 158). Godse is a symbol of a body of thought that finds its violent solace in history. Godse was bothered by Gandhi's 'eccentricity, whimsicality, metaphysics . . .' (p. 49). For Godse, Gandhi lacked the logical execution of political reason. The more specific political issue for Godse was of course 'Gandhi's pro-Muslim policy'. (p. 54) He lays down the chilling rationale: 'The accumulating provocation of thirty-two years, culminating in his last pro-Muslim fast, at last, goaded me to the conclusion that the existence of Gandhi should be brought to an end immediately.' (p. 49) Gandhi's crime in Godse's eyes was to break away from the logic of historical enmity, and grant the enemy the status of a friend. Godse invoked the epics to establish the law of killing the enemy as a moral action: In the Ramayana, Rama killed Ravana. In the Mahabharata, Krishna killed Kansa 'to end his wickedness' (p. 40), and Arjuna had to 'fight and slay, quite a number of his friends and relations, including the revered Bhishma, because the latter was on the side of the aggressor.' (p. 40) Gandhi, like Bhishma, was on the enemy's side, the wrong side of dharma. Godse shifts from the epic to the historical to register 'the heroic fight put up by the Chhatrapati Shivaji Maharaj that . . . eventually destroyed Muslim tyranny in India.' (p. 40) Ravana and Kansa are figures of evil. Their elimination is morally justified for establishing righteousness in the world. Muslims are the historical equivalents of those figures. The epic and the historical are fused together by a central aspect of naming the enemy. These assumptions are perversely untrue and devoid of political morality. Gandhi did not side with Muslims or Hindus, but put his moral weight behind peace and justice. Gandhi was harsh to both communities whenever he felt they erred in their moral duty and indulged in violence. The Kauravas, with a reluctant Bhishma as their leader, *chose* to go to war with the Pandavas in order to retain their kingdom. Gandhi chose the path of non-violence to establish a sovereign nation. The use of murder as justification for establishing sovereignty has been the bane of military, theocratic, fascist and communist dictatorships. There is no place for it in democracy.

[from Nathuram Godse, *Why I Assassinated Mahatma Gandhi*, (ed.) Gopal Godse, Surya Bharati Prakashan (New Delhi, 2017].

101 Nathuram Godse, *Why I Assassinated Mahatma Gandhi*, (ed.) Gopal Godse, Surya Bharati Prakashan (New Delhi, 2017), p. 19.

102 Ibid.

103 *CWMG*, Volume 9, pp. 498-499.

104 *CWMG*, Volume 32, pp. 101-102 [The fact that Savarkar and others disagreed with his reading of the *Gita* made Gandhi rue Vyasa's narrative strategy of trying to impart 'spiritual knowledge' through the illustration of war.' [p. 102].

105 *CWMG*, Volume 37, p. 136.
106 Janaki Bakhle, *Savarkar and the Making of Hindutva*, Princeton University Press, New Jersey, 2024, p. 121.
107 V. D. Savarkar, *The Gandhian Confusion*, Swatantryaveer Savarkar Rashtriya Smarak Trust, Dadar, Mumbai, Kindle edition.
108 Letter released by Chicago-based researcher, Shridhar Damle, link: https://sangraha.net/s80/NBImages/15001/2019/03/20/2_11_12_01_Consul_1.pdf [Quoted in Sampath, Vikram, *Savarkar: A Contested Legacy 1924-1966*, Gurgaon, Penguin, Viking, 2021].
109 Nathuram Godse, *Why I Assassinated Mahatma Gandhi*, (ed.) Gopal Godse, Surya Bharati Prakashan (New Delhi, 2017), p. 27.
110 Ibid., 21.
111 Ibid., p. 34.
112 Ibid., p. 114.
113 Ibid.
114 Salman Rushdie, *Imaginary Homelands*, Vintage Books (London, 2010), pp. 103–04.
115 *CWMG*, Vol. 90, p. 472.
116 Manu Gandhi, *The Diary of Manu Gandhi (1946–1948)*, (edited and translated) Tridip Suhrud, Oxford University Press (New Delhi, 2024), p. 599.
117 *CWMG*, Vol. 90, pp. 501-502.
118 Manu Gandhi, *The Diary of Manu Gandhi (1946–1948)*, (edited and translated) Tridip Suhrud, Oxford University Press (New Delhi, 2024), p. 606.
119 *CWMG*, Vol. 90, p. 535.
120 Ibid., p. 535.
121 Ibid., p. 535–36.

122 Godse acknowledged that Gandhi had unselfishly undergone 'sufferings for the sake of the nation', and brought about 'an awakening in the minds of the people.' (p. 114) But it pained Godse to believe that Gandhi 'was not honest enough to acknowledge the defeat and failure of his principle of non-violence on all sides.' (p. 114) Godse seems to have not read anything Gandhi said since the Calcutta riots began in August 1946, admitting to the possible failure of his non-violent dream.

It is possible that Godse is lying about Gandhi, going by his double-speak in court that included his efforts to clear the name of Savarkar (to whom he acknowledged his ideological debt) from any complicity in the crime. Godse refuted charges (from Badge's statements in court) of his meeting Savarkar in relation to the plot for Gandhi's murder, and Savarkar blessing him with success for the job. The lack of counter-witnesses helped Godse's account, as he strictly followed the code of circumstantial evidence.

[from Nathuram Godse, *Why I Assassinated Mahatma Gandhi*, (ed.) Gopal Godse, Surya Bharati Prakashan (New Delhi, 2017)].

Select Bibliography

1. Ahmad, Eqbal, *Confronting Empire: Interviews with David Barsamian*, Haymarket Books, Chicago, Illinois, 2016
2. Ahmed, Ishtiaq, *Jinnah: His Successes, Failures and Role in History*, Penguin Random House India, 2020
3. Alam, Javeed, *India Living with Modernity*, Oxford University Press, New Delhi, 1999
4. Ali, Maulana Mohamed, *Presidential Address: Thirty Eighth Annual Session of the Indian Congress Held at Cocanada*, 26 December 1923, Jamia Milia Press, Aligarh, 1923
5. Ambedkar, Dr B.R, *Pakistan or the Partition of India*, Thacker and Company Limited, Bombay, 1945
6. Ambedkar, Dr B.R., *What Congress and Gandhi did to the Untouchables* in *Writings and Speeches, Vol. 9*, (ed.) Vasant Moon, Education Department, Government of Maharashtra, Bombay, 1991
7. Ambedkar, Dr Babasaheb, *Writings and Speeches Volume. 5*, Education Department, Government of Maharashtra, 1989

8. Anderson, Benedict, *Imagined Communities: Reflections on the Origin and Spread of Nationalism*, Verso, London/New York, 2006
9. Aquil, Raziuddin, *In the Name of Allah: Understanding Islam and Indian History*, Penguin Viking, Delhi, 2009
10. Arendt, Hannah, *Crisis of the Republic*, Harcourt Brace & Company, New York, 1972
11. Arendt, Hannah, *Origins of Totalitarianism*, Harvest, Harcourt Brace & Company, 1973, New York
12. Arendt, Hannah, *The Life of the Mind*, Harcourt Inc., Florida, 1978
13. Aristotle, *Rhetoric*, (trans.) C.D.C. Reeve, Hackett Publishing Company, Inc., Indianapolis, Cambridge, 2018
14. Aurobindo, Sri, *Nationalism, Religion, and Beyond: Writings on Politics, Society, and Culture*, (ed.) Peter Heehs, Permanent Black, Delhi, 2005
15. Aurobindo, Sri, *Sri Aurobindo and India's Rebirth*, (ed.) Michel Danino, Rupa Publications, New Delhi, 2018
16. Azad, Abul Kalam, *India Wins Freedom*, Orient Longman, Madras, 1988
17. Bakhle, Janaki, *Savarkar and the Making of Hindutva*, Princeton University Press, New Jersey, 2024
18. Benjamin, Walter, *Illuminations: Essays and Reflections*, (trans.) Harry Zohn, Schocken Books, New York, 1969
19. Berlin, Isiah, *The Proper Study of Mankind: An Anthology of Essays,* (ed.) Henry Hardy and Roger Hausheer, Pimlico, London, 1998
20. Bernasconi, Robert and Wood, David (eds.), *The Provocation of Levinas: Rethinking the Other*, London and New York, 1988

21. Bhargav, Vanya Vaidehi, *Being Hindu, Being Indian: Lala Lajpat Rai's Ideas of Nationhood*, Penguin, Viking, Gurgaon, 2024
22. Bose, Nirmal Kumar, *My Days with Gandhi*, Orient Longman Limited, Calcutta
23. Bose, Sugata, *Agrarian Bengal: Economy, Social Structure and Politics, 1919–1947*, Cambridge University Press, London, 2008
24. Bose, Sugata, *Agrarian Bengal: Economy, Social Structure and Politics, 1919–1947*, Cambridge University Press, London, 2008
25. Buber, Martin, *Pointing the Way*, (trans. and edit.) Maurice Friedman, Harper & Brothers, New York, 1957
26. Caygill, Howard, *Levinas and the Political*, Routledge, London and New York, 2002
27. Chakrabarty, Dipesh, *Provincializing Europe: Postcolonial Thought and Historical Difference*, Princeton University Press, Princeton and Oxford, 2000
28. Chakrabarty, Dipesh, *The Calling of History: Sir Jadunath Sarkar and His Empire of Truth*, The University of Chicago Press, Chicago and London, 2015
29. Chandra, Bipan, *Communalism in Modern India*, Vikas Publishing House Pvt. Ltd., New Delhi, 1984
30. Chatterjee, Partha, *Bengal 1920–1947: Vol. 1 The Land Question*, Centre for Studies in Social Sciences Monograph 4, K P Bagchi & Company, 1984
31. Chatterjee, Partha, *The Politics of the Governed: Reflections on Popular Politics in Most of the World*, Columbia University Press, New York, 2004

32. Chatterji, Joya, *Bengal Divided: Hindu communalism and partition 1932-1947*, Cambridge University Press, U.K. 1994
33. Chaudhuri, Nirad C., *Thy Hand Great Anarch!*, The Hogarth Press, London, 1987
34. Cioran, E.M., *A Short History of Decay*, (trans.) Richard Howard, Quartet Encounters (New York, 1975)
35. *Collected Works of Mahatma Gandhi*, The Director, The Publication Division, New Delhi
36. Derrida, Jacques, *Acts of Religion*, (ed.) Gil Anidjar, Routledge, New York, 2002
37. Derrida, Jacques, *The Politics of Friendship*, (trans.) George Collins, Verso, New York, 2005
38. Devji, Faisal, *Muslim Zion: Pakistan as a Political Idea*, Harvard University Press, Cambridge, Massachusetts, 2013
39. Devji, Faisal, *The Impossible Indian: Gandhi and the Temptation of Violence*, Harvard University Press, Cambridge, Massachusetts, 2012
40. Dhulipala, Venkat, *Creating a New Medina: State Power, Islam, and the Quest for Pakistan in Late Colonial North India*, Cambridge University Press, New Delhi, 2015
41. Foucault, Michel, *Ethics: Subjectivity and Truth*, (Ed) Paul Rabinow, The New Press, New York, 1994
42. Foucault, Michel, *Security, Territory, Population: Lectures at the College De France, 1977 – 78*, (ed.) Michel Senellart, (trans.) Graham Burchell, Picador, New York, 2004
43. Foucault, Michel, *Society Must Be Defended: Lectures at the College De France, 1975-76*, (ed.) Mauro Bertani and Alessandro Fontana, (trans.) David Macey, Picador, New York, 1997

44. Foucault, Michel, *The Politics of Truth*, Semiotext(E), United States of America, 1997
45. Freud, Sigmund, *Civilization and its Discontents*, (trans.) David McLintock, Penguin Books, New York, 2002
46. Gandhi, M.K., *An Autobiography or The Story of My Experiments with Truth* (A Critical Edition), (trans.) Mahadev Desai, Yale University Press, New Haven and London, 2018
47. Gandhi, M.K., Jinnah, Muhammad Ali, (preface) C. Rajagopalachari, *Gandhi–Jinnah Talks: Text of Correspondence and other relevant matter*, The Hindustan Times, New Delhi, July–October, 1944
48. Gandhi, Mahatma, (ed.) Parel, Anthony, *Hind Swaraj*, Cambridge Text in Modern Politics, Cambridge University Press, New York, 1990
49. Gandhi, Mahatma, *Swaraj in One Year*, Ganesh and Co., Madras, 1921
50. Gandhi, Manu, *The Diary of Manu Gandhi (1943–1944)*, (edited and translated) Tridip Suhrud, Oxford University Press, New Delhi, 2019.
51. Gandhi, Manu, *The Diary of Manu Gandhi (1946–1948)*, (edited and translated) Tridip Suhrud, Oxford University Press, New Delhi, 2024.
52. Gandhi, Manubahen, *The Lonely Pilgrim (Gandhiji's Noakhali Pilgrimage)*, Navajivan Publishing House, Ahmedabad, 1964
53. Godse, Nathuram, *Why I Assassinated Mahatma Gandhi*, (ed.) Gopal Godse, Surya Bharati Prakashan, New Delhi, 2017
54. Golwalkar, M.S., *We or Our Nationhood Defined*. Bharat Publications, Nagpur, 1939

55. Guha, Ranajit, *Elementary Aspects of Peasant Insurgency in Colonial India*, Duke University Press, Durham and London, 1999
56. Guha, Ranajit (ed.), *Subaltern Studies Volume I: Writings on South Asian History and Society*, Oxford University Press, Delhi, 1982
57. Haq, Jalalul, *Hindu Tolerance Myth and Truth: A Study in the Thought–Systems of Ramakrishna and Vivekananda*, Institute of Objective Studies, New Delhi, 2014
58. Iqbal, Muhammad, *Stray Reflections: The Private Notebook of Muhammad Iqbal*, (ed.) Dr. Javid Iqbal, Iqbal Academy Pakistan, 2008
59. Jaffrelot, Christophe, *The Hindu Nationalist Movement and Indian Politics 1925 to the 1990s*, Hurst and Company, London, 1996
60. Jalal, Ayesha, *The Sole Spokesman: Jinnah, the Muslim League and the demand for Pakistan*, Cambridge University, New York, 1994
61. Jenkins, Laura Dudley, *Religious Freedom and Mass Conversion in India*, University of Pennsylvania Press, Philadelphia, 2019
62. Jinnah, Mohammad Ali, *Jinnah: Speeches and Statements 1947–1948*, Oxford University Press, Oxford, 2000
63. Jinnah, Muhammad Ali, *Quaid-I-Azam Muhammad Ali Jinnah (Speeches, Statements, Writings, Letters, etc.)*, (edit.) Muhammad Hanif Shahid, Sang-e-Meel Publications, Urdu Bazar, Lahore, 1976
64. Krishnan V., Govind, *Vivekananda: The Philosopher of Freedom*, Aleph, New Delhi, 2023

65. Levinas, Emanuel, *Otherwise than Being or Beyond Essence*, (trans.) Alphonso Lingis, Duquesne University Press, Pittsburg, Pennsylvaia,1998
66. Levinas, Emanuel, *Totality and Infinity: An Essay on Interiority*, (trans.) Alphonso Lingis, Duquesne University Press, Pittsburg, Pennsylvania, 1969
67. Maksud, Syed Abul, *Gandhi, Nehru and Noakhali*, Mahatma Gandhi Smarak Sadan, Dhaka, 2008
68. Mamdani, Mahmood, *When Victims Become Killers: Colonialism, Nativism, and the Genocide in Rwanda*, Princeton University press, New Jersey, 2002
69. Manto, Sadat Hasan, *Stars from Another Sky: The Bombay Film World in the 1940s*, (trans.) Khalid Hasan, Penguin Books, New Delhi, 1998
70. Marx, Karl, 'On the Jewish Question', *Marx–Engels reader Second Edition*, (ed.) Robert C. Tucker, W.W. Norton and Company, New York, London, 1978
71. Mujahid, Sharif al (ed.), *In Quest of Jinnah: Diary, Notes, and Correspondence of Hector Bolitho*, Oxford University Press, Karachi, 2007
72. Mukherjee, Janam, *Hungry Bengal: War, Famine, and the End of Empire*, Oxford University Press, New York, 2016
73. Naipaul, V.S., *India: A Wounded Civilization*, Picador, 2002, London
74. Nehru, Jawaharlal, *An Autobiography*, Allied Publishers Private Limited, Delhi, 1962
75. Nehru, Jawaharlal, *Selected Works of Jawaharlal Nehru Volume 15*, Orient Longman, New Delhi, 1982
76. Nehru, Jawaharlal, *The Discovery of India*, Oxford University Press, New Delhi, 1964

77. Pandey, Gyanendra, *Remembering Partition: Violence, Nationalism and History in India*, Cambridge University Press, Cambridge, 2001
78. Paz, Octavio, *In Light of India*, (trans.) Eliot Weinberger, Harcourt Inc., New York, 1997
79. Paz, Octavio, *The Collected Poems 1957–1987*, (trans.) Eliot Weinberger, Indus (Harper Collins), New Delhi, 1992
80. Pyarelal, Mahatma Gandhi: *The Last Phase Vol I*, Navajivan Publishing House, Ahmedabad, 1956
81. Pyarelal, Mahatma Gandhi: *The Last Phase Vol II*, Navajivan Publishing House, Ahmedabad, 1958
82. Ricoer, Paul, *Time and Narrative Volume 3*, (trans.) Kathleen and David Pellauer, The University of Chicago Press, Chicago, 1985
83. Rimbaud, Arthur, *Collected Poems*, (trans.) Martin Sorell, Oxford University Press, New York, 2001
84. Ritsos, Yannis, *Repetitions Testimonies Parenthesis*, (trans.) Edmund Keeley, Princeton University Press, Princeton, New Jersey, 1991
85. Rousseau, Jean-Jacques, *Emile or On Education*, (trans.) Allan Bloom, Basic Books, USA, 1979
86. Roy, Anwesha, *Making Peace, Making Riots Communalism and Communal Violence, Bengal 1940–1947*, Cambridge University Press, New Delhi, 2018
87. Rushdie, Salman, *Imaginary Homelands*, Vintage Books, London, 2010
88. Rushdie, Salman, *Shame*, Vintage, London, 1995
89. Sajjad, Mohammad, *Muslim Politics in Bihar: Changing Contours*, Routledge, Delhi, 2014
90. Samaddar, Ranabir (ed.), *Reflections on Partition in the East*, Calcutta Research Group, Calcutta, 1997

91. Sampath, Vikram, *Savarkar*: *A Contested Legacy 1924-1966*, Penguin, Viking, Gurgaon, 2021
92. Saraswati, Dayanand, *The Light of Truth*: *Satyarth Prakash in English*, Vijaykumar Govindram Hasanand, Delhi, 2018
93. Sarkar, Sumit, *Modern India 1885–1947*, Palgrave Macmillan, New York, 1989
94. Savarkar, V.D., *Hindutva*, Veer Savarkar Prakashan, Savarkar Sadan, Bombay, 1969
95. Sen, Sudipta, *Distant Sovereignty*: *National Imperialism and the Origins of British India*, Routledge, New York, 2002
96. Sharma, Jyotirmaya, *Elusive Non-violence: The Making and Unmaking of Gandhi's Religion of Ahimsa*, Context (Westland Publications Private Ltd.), Chennai, 2021
97. Sharma, Jyotirmaya, *Hindutva: Exploring the Idea of Hindu Nationalism*, Harper Collins (New Delhi, 2015).
98. Sharma, Jyotirmaya, *A Restatement of Religion: Swami Vivekananda and the Making of Hindu Nationalism*, Yale University Press (New Haven & London, 2013).
99. Shirer, William L., *Gandhi: A Memoir*, Simon and Schuster, New York, 1979
100. Sinha, Braja Kishore, *The Pilgrim of Noakhali*, The Photographer, Calcutta, 1948
101. Skaria, Ajay, *Unconditional Equality: Gandhi's Religion of Resistance*, University of Minnesota Press, Minneapolis/London, 2016
102. Tejani, Shabnum, *Indian Secularism: A Social and Intellectual History 1890–1950*, Permanent Black, New Delhi, 2007

103. Tagore, Rabindranath *Letters from Russia*, (trans.) Dr Sasadhar Sinha, Vishva-Bharati, Calcutta, 1960
104. Tagore, Rabindranath, *Nationalism*, (intro.) Ramchandra Guha, Penguin Books, New Delhi, 2009,
105. Veer, Peter van der (ed.), *Conversion to Modernities: The Globalization of Christianity*, Routledge, London, 1996
106. Veer, Peter van der, *Religious Nationalism: Hindus and Muslims in India*, University of California Press, Berkeley and Los Angeles, 1994
107. Veer, Peter van der, *The Modern Spirit of Asia: The Spiritual and the Secular in China and India*, Princeton University Press, Princeton, 2014
108. Viswanathan, Gauri, 'Colonialism and the Construction of Hinduism', in (ed.) Gavin Flood, *The Wiley Blackwell Companion to Hinduism: Second Edition*, Blackwell Publishing Ltd, Oxford/UK, 2023
109. Vivekananda, Swami, *The Complete Works of Swami Vivekananda Vol IV*, Advaita Ashram, Calcutta, 1958
110. Wavell, *The Viceroy's Journal*, (ed.) Penderel Moon, Oxford University Press, Delhi, 1973
111. Weber, Max, *The Protestant Ethic and the Spirit of Capitalism*, (trans.) Talcott Parsons, Scribner, New York, 1958
112. Weil, Simone, *Formative Writings 1929-1941*, (ed., trans.) Dorothy Tuck McFarland and Wilhelmina Van Ness, The University of Massachusetts Press, Amherst, 1987
113. Weil, Simone, *Gravity and Grace*, (trans.) Gustav Thibon, Routledge & Kegan Paul, New York, 1952
114. Weil, Simone, *Waiting For God*, (trans.) Emma Craufurd, Harper & Row, New York, 1951 (G.P. Putnam's Sons)

115. Yevtushenko, Yevgeny, *A Precocious Autobiography*, (trans.) Andrew R. MacAndrew, E.P. Dutton & Co. Inc., New York, 1963

116. Žižek, Slavoj, *Violence*, Picador, New York, 2008

Index

Scan QR code to access the
Penguin Random House India website